THE BURNING STAKES

A NOVEL OF THE LATE ROMAN EMPIRE

EMBERS OF EMPIRE VOL. VI

Q. V. HUNTER

Eyes and Ears Editions
130 E. 63rd St., Suite 6F
New York, New York,
USA 10065-7334

Copyright © 2016 Q. V. Hunter

☧

All rights reserved
No part of this publication may be reproduced, stored in a retrieval system, or transmitted in any form, or by any means, electronic, mechanical, photocopying, recording or otherwise, without the prior permission of the Publishers.

ISBN 978-2-9701084-0-5

This novel is entirely a work of fiction. The names, characters and incidents portrayed in it, while at times based on historical figures, are the work of the author's imagination.

Q. V. Hunter has asserted the right under the Copyright, Design and Patents Act, 1988, to be identified as the author of this work.

eyesandears.editions@gmail.com

ALSO BY Q. V. HUNTER

The Veiled Assassin, Embers of Empire, Vol. I
Usurpers, Embers of Empire, Vol. II
The Back Gate to Hell, Embers of Empire, Vol. III
The Wolves of Ambition, Embers of Empire, Vol. IV
The Deadly Caesar, Embers of Empire, Vol. V

TO P, 'OUR ROCK'

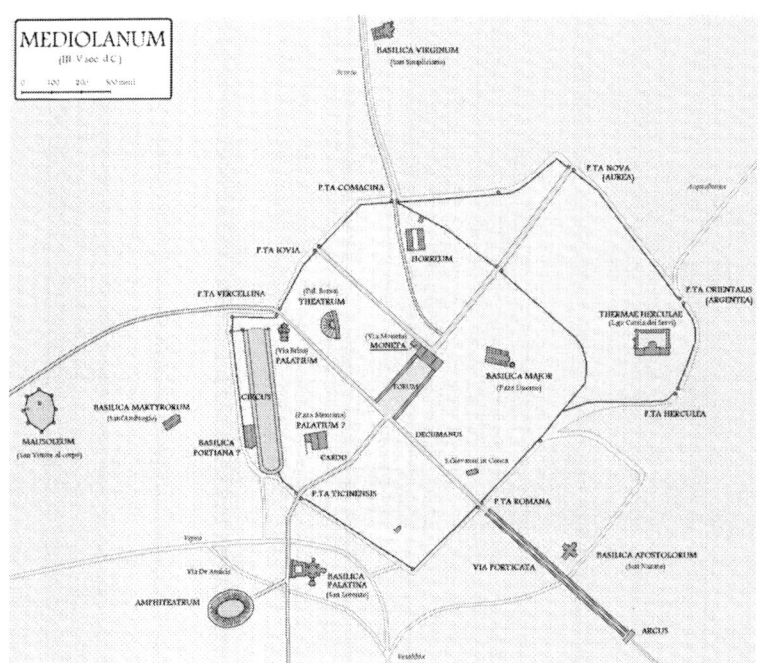

MEDIOLANUM, IMPERIAL CAPITAL

SIRMIUM, IMPERIAL CAPITAL

THE ROMAN EMPIRE OF THE EAST, 4TH CENTURY

TABLE OF CONTENTS

Chapter 1, Barbatio's Curse 1
Chapter 2, An Omen All Our Own 17
Chapter 3, A Question of Purple Ink 33
Chapter 4, Volumes of Suspicion 49
Chapter 5, Gentlemen of the Jury 63
Chapter 6, The Empty Cage 79
Chapter 7, A *Schola* of Virgins 95
Chapter 8, The Scent of a Greek 109
Chapter 9, Smashing Links 125
Chapter 10, The Sword of Honos 139
Chapter 11, Restitution 155
Chapter 12, A Roll Call of Revenge 169
Chapter 13, The Veiled Vestal 183
Chapter 14, Office Routine 199
Chapter 15, A Social Visit 213
Chapter 16, A Family Brothel 227
Chapter 17, A New Management Plan 241
Chapter 18, 'Argentoratum' 257
Chapter 19, City of the Blind 273
Chapter 20, The Imperial Scapegoat 289
Chapter 21, The Burning Stakes 301
Chapter 22, Verus' Testament 313
Chapter 23, Apodemius' Legacy 325
Chapter 24, Apollonia's Fire 339
Historical Notes 351
Places and Glossary 357
Acknowledgments 371
About the Author 375

Chapter 1, Barbatio's Curse

—Nearing Mount Taurus, November 1, 361—

I laid a warning hand on his chest and hissed, 'Stay here. Don't talk to *anyone*—or be run through for a deserter.'

Skulking under a muddied hood, the fugitive Consul Florentius nodded. He bristled at taking brusque orders from a mere freedman, a Numidian-born *agens* smuggling him to safety. But somewhere on the state road between Sirmium and Singidunum, the Roman politician had swallowed his last morsel of pride.

I ignored his truculence and treated him like any other patrician refugee in ignominious flight. He'd become just another troublesome politician using my *schola*'s escort services to cross enemy lines in the midst of a vicious civil war.

'I'll stand with those centurions over there—'

'No! Nobody in this camp learns you're here before Emperor Constantius. That's my training. You stick to it.'

Back in 357, Florentius had shown me all the arrogance of a Praetorian Prefect for Gallia who despised his inexperienced caesar and resented the meddling of an *agens in rebus* like myself.

But that was before he urged the upstart Caesar Julian into the fray of the Battle of Argentoratum only to see the imperial family's bookworm emerge with an almost mythical victory against the Alemannic horde. After too many bitter power struggles with Julian, Florentius had retreated back to the protection of the senior sovereign. He'd risen to an imperial consulship, only to see the despised Flavius Claudius Julianus Augustus lifted up on a shield and acclaimed Emperor of the West by his adoring auxiliary forces.

Racing full pelt for sanctuary with Constantius' army on the Eastern front, the stiff-necked Florentius had finally digested his tumble from imperial heights. Tonight he owned nothing, not even the ragged *birrus* disguising his towering shoulders.

But at least he was alive.

This was more than any *agentes* could confirm so far of the Empire's other consul-on-the-run, Taurus. These two were only the most senior of Constantius' courtiers fleeing Julian's army on its westward march to vanquish his cousin.

I continued alone up the camp's Via Praetoria. Tall torches sent shadows dancing on row after row of tent roofs. The night air sang with the comforting hum of an army at rest—the tremolo of an insomniac's flute, the giggle of a camp follower with too much wine in her, and the animal rumble of thousands of soldiers snoring eight to a tent.

The troops slept deeply. In civil showdowns, Constantius always won. But tomorrow meant another day's long march toward the battlefront facing Julian. Yes, these men knew they would prevail, but first they had to fight.

I reached the perimeter of the imperial tents and showed my *insignia* to the senior man on duty. He was a *candidatus* wearing an impeccable white tunic from the *scholares* guarding the emperor.

He peered through the torchlight at my stubbled chin, the half-moons of sweat under my tunic sleeves, and the dust covering my high-cuffed boots.

He paused, unsure.

The red-eyed charcoal chunks of a cooking fire collapsed into smoking embers a few yards away. Behind the imperial tents, eunuchs supervised slaves cleaning up after the Emperor's meal and toilet.

'His Divinity is fatigued. Come back at daybreak.'

'Urgent correspondence.'

He glanced at my riding helmet. 'Can't be that urgent.'

I wasn't wearing the *agentes*' telltale white feather on my *petanus*. The feather signaled to layover stations and gatekeepers across the Empire that a rider mustn't be delayed. So I couldn't be announcing an imperial birth or death, or the loss of a major battle.

—THE BURNING STAKES—

I shook my head, refusing his bait. The defection of an imperial consul was important business, but I could hardly confide it to this self-important lout.

'The Emperor will be angered at any delay.'

'Then he'd be angry at your stupidity, wouldn't he?' Bright moonlight reflected off his crooked teeth.

I paid the bastard for access. After all, what was my expense allowance for? Every man had his fee and every guard his tip. The whole Empire ran on petty bribes, favors, and letters of reference.

Fatigued or fresh, even after midnight on a march across the sparse wastes of Cilicia, His Divinity wasn't alone tonight. A gaggle of eunuchs, cooks, barbers, slaves, scribes, and officers inflated the leather limits of his tents into a mobile *consistorium*.

Through the ministrations of a hairless attendant wiping off the lip of a silver water pitcher with a gold-threaded towel, Constantius' heavy cow-eyes spotted me entering the tent.

'*Agens* Numidianus!'

I prostrated myself onto the pounded earth and 'venerated the purple.'

'*Imperator*, I deliver a copy of the Caesar's latest letter to the people of Athina, Sparta, Korinthos, and Roma.'

'What could Julian's defense possibly be, we wonder?' Decades of posing like a marble statue rendered Constantius too stiff to shrug his heavy shoulders, even with rhetorical resignation.

I handed my packet to an *adiutor* and prostrated myself again at a respectful distance from the portable *cathedra* draped in purple damask. The *adiutor* passed the packet of folded *vitulinum* to a chamberlain washing the sovereign's feet.

Only the Lord Chamberlain *Praepositus Sacri Cubiculi* Eusebius and his sexless minions of the bedchamber touched the Emperor. I correct myself—Constantius' third wife Faustina must have come into some kind of bodily contact eight months ago, because the Emperor had finally achieved the seemingly impossible. While Julian's troops advanced toward the Eastern Army, Constantius' longed-for heir was also on its way. The birth of a new Constantine made Julian's inevitable defeat easier to contemplate.

'You're based in Sirmium, correct?' Constantius untied the tasseled ribbon and broke our *schola*'s seal.

'Yes, *Imperator*, four years now.'

'What news from the front line?'

'Commander Jovinus continues along the Danuvius for his rendezvous with Julian's army in Sirmium and with the third contingent under Commander Nevitta. I left Sirmium only minutes ahead of Julian's arrival.'

'Then the rumors in Antiochia that the Caesar has reached our Pannonian capital are true.'

'Yes, *Imperator*.' I enjoyed an excellent view of the Divine Feet being dried and dressed in fresh socks.

'We're sorry to hear you confirm it. Was there strong resistance?'

Did I dare to describe the rapturous reception Sirmium offered Julian?

'Sirmium's loyal defense was . . . insufficient, *Imperator*.'

'Obviously.' He gazed down at my groveling back. 'Surely, Numidianus, your dossier on us includes the note, *His Divinity has no sense of humor*.'

I pushed my nose deeper into the grit. It would take some minutes for the Emperor to scan my copy of Julian's appeal to the Athenians. I knew every word, of course. Against formal instruction and following common *agentes*' practice, I'd memorized Julian's excuses for rebellion as I copied the original.

Such snooping was routine. It was an *agens*' job to know as much as he could for the service of the Empire. It was the main reason bureaucrats, churchmen, highly placed courtesans, and your average tax-cheat spat out the expletive, *curiosi*, behind our backs.

Constantius blinked. 'The Caesar calls us a murderer.'

Julian's denunciation was treasonous, but true. Constantius had murdered every male in his family except for two cousins, the young half-brothers Gallus and Julian himself. But to point this out was hardly gratitude from Julian—promoted to caesar by the murderer himself.

After another few minutes of reading, Constantius muttered, 'Julian nominates that crude, vulgar Frankish cavalryman, Nevitta, as one of his consuls-elect. Oh, the Roman patricians won't like that. They forgive anything and everything except bad manners.'

The Emperor tossed my painstaking copy of Julian's invective on the ground next to my shoulder.

'Thank you, *Agens*.' He took a long drink of wine diluted to a pale pink. 'We have not seen you in some years, have we?'

'Please allow a humble freedman to express condolences to His Divinity on the passing of the beloved Empress Eusebia and to express congratulations on the Empire's happy expectation from the Empress Faustina.'

'Thank you. How much has happened since you first knelt at our feet at Mursa.'

One could see his dogged mind plod and sift through rafts of soldiers, advisers, and attendants who reported before his *cathedra*. I was a familiar face, but hardly a privileged *proximus*.

'Yes, how much has happened and how many have come and gone. Magnentius, Vetranio, Nepotianus, Silvanus... Gallus... Interesting... We note that among all our *agentes*, Numidianus, you have dealt in person with all these criminal usurpers.'

Coming from his unsmiling lips, this sounded like an accusation of lousy political judgment on my part. His dull eyes gazed past me at the heavy flap of his tent, as if these ghostly traitors had followed me through the moonlight for an audience tonight.

'I never met Nepotianus,' I said. 'Though I would have gladly cut his throat myself. His felons slew the blind patriarch of my household, Senator Manlius, in the bosom of our library during the 350 riots.'

Constantius pointed at the vellum still lying open in the dirt. 'So much disloyalty to our throne! Yet we could not have imagined our cousin's audacity—but then your dossier on us no doubt also adds, *His Divinity has no imagination*. We are thirsty. More wine.'

I lay there, nostrils full of dirt, fighting off my own parched cough.

'Do you have anything more for us, Numidianus, anything but grievous news?'

I'd seen Constantius implacable, immovable, and emotionless. But I'd never before seen him so listless.

'Yes, *Imperator*. I've escorted Consul Florentius, Praetorian Prefect for Illyricum, to safety here. Both consuls fled their posts as Julian's army approached Roma. I regret to report that Consul Taurus is still unaccounted for. Florentius is waiting for an audience now.'

'We are too tired. Leave Florentius for tomorrow. You may rise. But ride with our scouts, Numidianus. Perhaps tomorrow we will be in a better frame of mind to hear *exactly* how the traitor Julian was welcomed by the people of our beloved birthplace.'

※ ※ ※

I wasted many sleepless hours tossing on a borrowed army cot and composing evasive euphemisms for Julian's lightning takeover of Sirmium where he was greeted with flowers, chariot races, and cries of 'Augustus!' and 'Lord!'

My night's worries were a waste of energy. I carried no further responsibility for the petulant consul and waited in vain for an imperial summons. After a shave and a breakfast of bread, dates, chickpeas, I mustered a fresh horse. At the trumpet's call, I saddled up with the vanguard hundreds. Perhaps Florentius' desperate dawn plea for honorable reinstatement had killed the Emperor's appetite for details of his Sirmium humiliation.

I could relax among the *exploratores*. Specialist *immunes*, they were called on to serve but not fight. Like any men who revel in information gathering, they were a garrulous bunch. In the first hour, I heard many tales of the 'enemy' Julian—particularly from Nicandro, a one-eyed, whip-thin spotter from the southern tip of Italia. He confided rumors the scouts thought better kept from the dispirited Constantius, so visibly worn down by years of Persian attrition.

'. . . and you've heard the one about the liver divination, I suppose?'

'There are so many variations,' I bluffed.

—THE BURNING STAKES—

'Well, this is the true version, see, told to me by a bargirl whose aunt runs a *caupona* in Dacia. Julianus Augustus was passing through. He orders the locals to send some soothsayers into camp. He's nervous, see? And why not? Our side has his side out-trained and out-numbered. And so there he is, getting the *haruspices* to root around the bellies and bowels of poor butchered creatures and telling the *augures* to keep watching for birds overhead—hours on end. But nobody spots anything that's going to help Julian beat us—that's for certain.'

''Course not.'

'Anyway, some Gaul named Aprunculus decides it's high time to bring the whole show to a halt—like you do when the play drags on longer than your bum can bear? He tells Julian that they've found an animal liver covered with a double lobe.'

'Indeed. Did they really find such a bird?'

'Oh, sure. And that poor fool Julian is thrilled, *thrilled*, poor bugger!'

Nicandro loosed a belly laugh over the thunder of hooves and rolling wheels.

'Would you believe it, *Agens*? Some dead bird has a double liver and all the Caesar's problems are solved! How in Hades is a double liver going help him when he meets up with us?'

'Perhaps Julian's been reading too much Suetonius,' I muttered.

'What's that, *Agens*? Sooey-who?'

'Suetonius,' I shouted at Nicandro over our rumbling progress. 'C. Suetonius Tranquillus! The author of *The Lives of the Twelve Caesars*.'

'Haven't got to that one yet!'

'When the great Augustus was taking auspices in his first consulship, twelve vultures appeared to him. When Octavian slew the birds, they all had livers doubled inward at the lower end.'

'Neptune's' Balls! A bit weird, that.'

'Our ancient soothsayers told Octavian it was a good omen.'

Nicandro chortled. 'Who believes in *haruspices*' rubbish these days?' He wagged a meaty finger at me. 'So that only tells me that Julian's Gallic fraud knew his Suetonius as well as you do, *Agens*! He made it up so that they could all stop scanning the clouds for Julian and get some sleep.'

I had no intention of arguing with Nicandro. But I didn't dismiss omens so readily. Any man who ignores the Fates' messages is a man inviting his own comeuppance.

We were only three miles from the town of Tarsus and passing through a suburban estate marked as Hippocephalus on my *schola* road guide. Nicandro's unit leader halted our line with his raised palm.

A man's corpse sprawled just off the right verge of the *Cursus*. We assumed from its bloodied tunic and coarse footwear that it was male—for the head had been torn, not sliced, off with unthinkable brutality and the unlucky victim left to rot in the dry desert's winter sun.

'He must have died over there. See the stains on the ground? But he's stretched out now pointing toward the west,' Nicandro whispered. '*Occidum* symbolizes death, doesn't it?'

'So they tell us.'

He shouted to his fellow scouts. 'This *centenarius* here knows all about old superstitions. This means one of us is "headed west", doesn't it? One of us is going to die.'

'Stop yakking. Don't let the Emperor see it!' the *exploratores*' commander ordered. A dozen scouts dismounted and dragged away the gruesome mess. But they found no hiding place—not a ditch or boulder—on this sterile stretch. They were struggling to improvise a rocky cairn over the neck stump when Constantius and his guard reached us. Expressionless as always, the Emperor gave no reaction to the bad omen.

By nightfall, the *mensores* had marked out camp south of Tarsus and victualers had gone to purchase provisions. Constantius inquired hourly for any other omens, 'for the sake of general morale,' he said. He'd suffered a long summer of fighting off King Shapur II's Persian advances. Now it was winter and campaigning should have ended. The rank and file were impatient to get this conquest of Julian done with.

Yet the only event was Nicandro's sudden collapse with a high temperature. Through his open tent flat, I heard his delirious chuckle as *contubernales* plied him with medicinal wine.

From the imperial dining tent came sounds of jesting as slaves ran in and out, bearing platters of fresh roasts and embossed silver pitchers of *conditum*. Florentius could be overheard ridiculing the 'omen' of a headless corpse pointed west.

After all, what were the odds of our 'old gods' being so angry with the Emperor as to strew a random body in his path?

I went to check on Nicandro at dawn. His corpse was laid out, ready for cremation, at the rear of his tent.

⚰⚰⚰

A *tribunus* tumbled out of his saddle next. Fever raging, he continued our journey on his back under blankets in the baggage train. We resumed our march into the pink-gray shadows of dawn.

Now, when I least expected it, I was summoned to the Emperor's side. I cantered toward him under the scrutiny of his protective guard circle. I was fully expecting the sovereign wanted more painful details of Julian's triumph in Sirmium.

I was wrong.

'Numidianus, while we were fighting the Persians, were you among those escorting General Barbatio to his execution?'

I nodded. Barbatio's death was a painful memory I'd tried to chase from my nightmares for the last two years.

'How did our *Magister Peditum* die? Honorably?'

Convicted of treason, the lumbering Dacian, General Barbatio, had died whining like a craven cur. He'd begged forgiveness for his foolish wife's crazed fantasy that her husband might inherit or seize Constantius' throne and dump her to marry the beautiful Empress Eusebia.

The whole affair bordered on the tragi-comic. Only a besotted idiot like Assyria could have imagined the exquisite Macedonian empress would have looked at the coarse Barbatio as a possible replacement for the upright Constantius.

Barbatio's disgrace had marked a pathetic end to a soaring, if sordid career. Still, no sovereign likes to picture a once-trusted general whimpering away his final moments.

'General Barbatio died—perhaps not as nobly as some—but... but... perhaps his crime was only blind loyalty to an ambitious, jealous harridan of a wife, *Imperator*.'

I wasn't sure Constantius had heard me over the rumble and clatter of the march until he said at last:

'We do not like your observation, Numidianus. You imply injustice. Our State cannot be called unjust.'

'I did not say Barbatio was innocent, My Divinity.'

While Barbatio beat back the Juthungi Alemanni on the Rhaetian border with Italia, his illiterate Assyria had succumbed to a fit of hysteria and employed a slave girl from Agrippina trained in code to be her scribe.

Unfortunately for Barbatio and spouse, their resentful slave still harbored futile loyalties to her previous owners, the Franco-Roman family of Barbatio's predecessor, the doomed usurper General Silvanus.

Taking her revenge, the slave girl smuggled a copy of Assyria's inane ravings to Barbatio's rival, the vicious, scheming imperial councilor, General Arbitio. Once that letter fell into the hands of the imperial *quaestores*, Barbatio's conviction was sure.

General Barbatio and his over-imaginative Assyria faced trial for treason. I was assigned to arrest and escort him to his hearing.

'You know, this was all fated, Numidianus,' Barbatio told me. 'Last year a swarm of bees flooded our country estate. The soothsayers said that the swarm portended danger. Assyria tried to smoke them out until our villa was black with her fires. But I was stupid and ignored the omen.'

He rubbed his sagging jowls grizzled with black stubble. 'Will they burn us at the stake?'

'Make a full confession and they might behead you.'

'You could help us escape,' the Dacian veteran growled when the rest of our escort trotted ahead out of earshot.

'Go with honor, General. For once.'

'Honor! You think that's how I made *magister peditum*? Just my luck to draw Numidianus from the pack—the one *agens* I can't bribe.'

'Then disown Assyria in public. Divorce her for her folly. Bluster it out like your beloved mentor General Ursicinus.'

'I will never betray my wife. She loves me. For old times' sake, Numidianus, take pity. Turn a blind eye.'

'For old times' sake, I must refuse.'

—THE BURNING STAKES—

You might say I betrayed my old acquaintance. He'd been a roughneck lieutenant to my commander while I slaved as a *volo* in a Numidian army camp twelve years ago. Since then, I'd witnessed Barbatio betray half the Western Army by retreating with his other half to safety from Alemannic invaders. Worse, I'd known Barbatio was a slaver trading in Roman citizens. He'd trafficked in civil war captives and let the mother of my son be shackled and enslaved in a vast Hispanic *latifundium*. Only by blackmailing Barbatio had I retrieved Kahina from death. But it was too late to restore her blithe and beautiful former self.

I'd long wondered whether Barbatio was guilty of the highest treason as well—of conspiracy in league with the proud Commander of the East, Ursicinus, to overthrow Constantius. Assyria's letter was indiscreet and idiotic, but it merely confirmed my suspicions of his long-simmering ambition.

I felt no misplaced sentiment for his final troubles and within a week had delivered Barbatio to the waiting guards at the inner gates of the Mediolanum Palace compound.

Constantius noticed my silence.

'We just asked you how General Barbatio died, *Agens* Numidianus.'

'Barbatio died threatening me personally, *Imperator*. He laid a curse on my head.'

'*Christos*! Why?'

'He shouted to the court that I'd be blamed for the execution of Caesar Gallus, that we would all pay one day—our service's *magister*, Apodemius, the witnesses you sent with your Lord Chamberlain to that dungeon cell in Pula, and even myself who only escorted Caesar Gallus from Antiochia.'

Constantius fixed his gaze on Mount Taurus on the western horizon. Anyone riding ten feet behind us would hardly know we conversed.

'Continue, Numidianus.'

'Barbatio was the man who brought his sword down on your cousin's neck, but his dying words were a prediction that there would be retribution someday. It was a curse, *Imperator*, but it is a curse you might still lift from our heads.'

Constantius' face reddened. I'd seized this rare chance to clear the air. The morning Apodemius and I had pitched Gallus' bloodied red slippers at the imperial dais, Constantius had claimed to his listening councilors that he'd rescinded his order to kill his cousin.

Seven years had passed. But I cannot forget *Magister* Apodemius' stunned reaction to the Emperor's public disavowal of our mission. Had we just executed one of the very last Constantines—a caesar and imperial heir apparent—by mistake?

Even on this promising winter morning with Constantius primed to teach a fierce lesson to another upstart caesar, my *schola*—for all its tools and avenues of intelligence gathering—still did not know if such a letter of rescindment had left Constantius' court.

Heavy blame cloaked our *schola*'s reputation still, though Emperor Constantius ignored the mystery and Apodemius never raised it. Only Caesar Julian still flaunted open anger over his half-brother's decapitation.

We rode another half a mile before the Emperor turned to me again.

'We did dispatch a rescindment, Numidianus.'

'Addressed to whom, *Imperator*?'

'To the Lord Chamberlain Eusebius, of course. Whom else do we hold most in our trust?'

Roman pundits quipped that even Constantius enjoyed only 'some influence' over the powerful eunuch Eusebius, imperial councilor *cum* bath attendant supreme. At this moment, the Lord Chamberlain followed our column in a stately gold-figured carriage with other members of his brotherhood assigned to the intimate care of the emperor.

Eusebius was a foul and slippery powerbroker, jealous of any rival for Constantius' attention and therefore enemy to any caesar, general, or *schola* whose honesty threatened his greasy reign.

Knowing Constantius' blind reliance on this fat and greedy spider of a 'man,' I measured my words: 'I can't say whether I am relieved or dismayed to hear it from your Christian lips, *Imperator*. But I swear by both the old gods and your New, that your rescindment of the execution order was not received.'

'So we were told.'

Had Constantius resigned himself to believing no one?

—THE BURNING STAKES—

'Apodemius never lied to you, *Imperator*.'

Constantius closed his eyes and twitched the jewel-studded reins of his mount. A red flush darkened his brow and deepened to a lurid purple. Barley grains of sweat popped out underneath his bowl-like fringe of dark hair.

Could my insubordination anger him so much? No—my reaction was unthinking as I cried out, 'A medic, quick!'

Three guards galloped away down the column to fetch Constantius' personal physician.

He swayed with a slight lift of a hand. 'No, no, Numidianus. Please, calm yourselves, *tribuni*. The rocking of our horse will remedy any lightheadedness. Is that not what our surgeons so often recommend? The Rocking Therapy?'

Our serpentine march resumed its brisk pace. Within five minutes, a senior *medicus* and a court physician appeared in tandem, their horses falling in behind His Divinity's by a discreet few yards. I was sure that the Lord Chamberlain's carriage was already racing up the line to join the head of the march.

'*Imperator*, please forgive my provoking old grievances.'

Constantius stared ahead, his complexion vivid with sunset hues of orange and red. 'No, no, forgive us our vacillation, *Agens* Numidianus. Any man may be guilty of willful misdeed—even an emperor serving Christ on earth—but our priests also preach there is the Sin of Omission. If your *magister* did not receive our rescindment, then our trusted notaries of the *sacra scrinia* in Mediolanum should be questioned again. Our document should be traced. This sad mystery should be solved.'

'An inquiry would be most welcome. It would absolve innocent imperial servants who never cease to love Your Divinity as well as serve your Empire, *Imperator*.'

An imperial eunuch galloped forward to mop sweat off the Emperor's brow and hand him a silver flask of cooled *posca*.

'We have always loved Truth, yet so rarely recognized it in time,' Constantius said to himself before Prefect Florentius shooed me away from His Presence.

But I was happy to let my horse fall back. I'd seized my moment. There would be an inquiry. The *schola* would be cleared at last.

Next morning our march was slowed by broken paving and deep ruts in the *Cursus* outside Mopsucrenae, twelve miles beyond Tarsus and the last relay station before the route's ascent through the Cilician Gates and across the snowy passes of the Taurus mountains to Cappadocia. Using the damaged paving as an excuse, the *Magistri Militum* halted our progress and commanded their engineers to ride ahead with the scouts to survey the next leg.

I lingered with the main army, watching some men refresh their horses and others relieve themselves in the passing waters of the River Cydnus. Centuries ago this current had wafted Cleopatra's perfumed and flowered barge to an overawed Marcus Antonius but no one around me cared for the ancient stories I'd devoured as a slave child.

After a wait of three hours, I ferreted out Florentius standing with senior commanders outside the imperial tents.

'*Praefecte*, these troops have crossed rough desert paths all summer. The road ahead must be more than adequate.'

In the distance, the obese Eusebius' face dripped with nervous sweat, even in a chafing wind that whipped his maroon damask robes around his chubby legs. Half a dozen of his obsequious brethren cowered under flapping pennants behind the rear wall of Constantius' private tent.

Florentius lifted his ornate praetorian prefect's cloak to shield them from my view. He hustled me away from a cluster of murmuring tribunes.

I shook his hands off my shoulders. 'What's wrong, Florentius?'

Near the entrance to Constantius' leather-walled sanctuary, *Magister Equitum in Praesenti* General Arbitio was debating with the Alemannic *Magister Peditum*. Agilo was a *scutarius* who'd shot to power after Arbitio framed the aged General Ursicinus for the loss of the border fortress of Amida to King Shapur.

Both Arbitio and Agilo had his own personal adjutant hovering behind him, as if their shoulder blades needed protection at all times from a collegial blade. Arbitio pressed some point home with his index finger into Agilo's chest with presumptuous disrespect. Agilo's hawkish, high-cheeked face lost all its roughened color. Behind Prefect Florentius' attempt to block my observation, some two dozen other officers tossed odd, panicked glances over their armored shoulders, as if Persian archers were on the horizon.

What was wrong?

This ragged colloquium gave the impression of a frieze carved into Trajan's column mid-action—some men frightened, others resolute. Something had stripped away their markers of hierarchy, procedure, military conduct, and authorial bearing. The most powerful men of the Roman Empire stood in the dust of Cilician highway arguing like a band of leaderless *tirones*.

General Arbitio inhaled with displeasure at the sight of me. None of these men had reason to favor my presence—far from it—but I ignored Florentius' attempts to dismiss me. Florentius could hardly shun a man who'd saved his life only weeks before—no matter how inferior a *centenarius* ranked to him now.

'Why have we stopped? You're hiding something. You all are.'

'Don't raise your voice, Numidianus. Don't trigger the horns' *alarum*. Before dawn, His Divinity's fever worsened. No drink would pass his gullet. He burned to the touch. I've never seen the like.'

'Can the physicians do nothing?'

Agilo stormed past me with his staffer racing on his heels. Florentius glanced over his shoulder at Arbitio. 'Constantius asked for water—and a towel.'

'Water? Nothing more? Get him medicine, quick!'

'And a priest to baptize him. That old priest over there.'

'That "old priest" was none other than the great theologian Arius' former deacon, Euzious of Antiochia. He knelt in prayer on the far side of the road and looked sorely tested by months of marching on campaign to serve Constantius' daily religious needs. The winter breeze carried his muttered prayers to our ears, but no one took any notice.

'Why are you all standing—?'

Florentius nodded.

Constantius II had died.

The faces around me were creased with revulsion, fear of contagion, and political panic but not one man let out a single tear or wail of grief. Not even Euzious broke his recitation for a sincere moan.

At this minute, the body of our emperor lay abandoned inside his grit-blown tent, far from his pregnant empress and familiar palace walls. It felt like no more than a *consistorium* meeting that had gone terribly wrong. Constantius had served as best he knew how. Whatever his failures, this seemed no way, no place, no manner for such a Constantine to die.

Florentius said, 'Eusebius and Arbitio have ordained that *Comites* Theolaif and Aligildus leave for Naissus immediately. Given your expertise with the route and layovers, perhaps you should go back with them to guarantee nothing slows them down.'

'Back to—?'

'We give you two weeks' head start to inform Flavius Julianus that he's emperor. You must outpace Mercury himself to ensure rumor doesn't prompt the ears of usurping troublemakers across the Empire. We can't risk Flavia's baby coming early and throwing everything into chaos. Leave within the hour.'

We left faster than that. Only as we rode off did wailing from the imperial tent—dutiful and politic—follow us on the wind. We rode for miles past mystified soldiers still stretched out along the *Cursus*.

This time I wore the white feather of urgency.

Chapter 2, An Omen All Our Own

—TO NAISSUS—

Florentius' smirk confirmed my suspicion: assigning me as escort to Counts Theolaif and Aligildus rid Mopsucrenae of an inconvenient witness. We *agentes in rebus* were the throne's independent 'eyes', beholden to no other department of the civil service or the military. We answered through the *magister officiorum* directly to the Emperor himself.

And the Emperor had just changed.

These commanders conferring in the desolate dust had no idea of their future. If they had to position themselves to face an unpredictable young sovereign, they didn't want their haggling to be reported to Julian by an imperial spy.

We galloped off. Caesarea, Ancyra, Claudiopolis—cheerless relay stations—flew past us in a blur. I negotiated the swiftest horses, quickest meals, and the greatest discretion from curious *mancipes*— the *mansiones*' managers—and their grooms on the *Cursus*.

The closer we got to Constantine's New Roma, the riskier the questions prompted by my white feather and by the nervous agitation my two companions and their subordinates could not conceal. We would never again bear a message so grave for the security of state. As we thundered in and out of one *mutatio* after another, swapping mounts at record speed, more than a thousand courtiers idled in their palace, waiting for Constantius to return victorious over Julian's legions.

I argued the envoys and their unit into a sea crossing to Constantinopolis from Heraclean Pontica instead of continuing on the main road leading through busy Nicomedia. And despite their violent seasickness after braving rough winter currents, I allowed them a scant hour by the sundial to recover and bathe—only as much time as I needed to pry the best horses from the *tribunus stabili* in charge of the imperial teams.

We'd avoided the press of curious imperial officials and attendants in the Great Palace and now we tackled the last sprint of our marathon. As a slave boy in the cobwebbed study of the blind old Senator Manlius, I'd read book after book out loud. But which author wrote of geese fleeing the heat of the East? No sooner do they begin to traverse Mount Taurus, which abounds in dangerous eagles, than the geese hold pebbles in their beaks. Even extreme necessity calls forth no suicidal honking from them. Only after these wise fowl have escaped Mount Taurus' eagles do they spit out their pebbles and fly on.

I clamped down on my imagined pebbles of silence. We raced westward, Constantinopolis behind us, Mount Taurus crossed.

At last we crossed into my own zone of responsibility for all state roads and postal services. We rested in Philippopolis while I dispatched two of my most discreet *circitores* to prepare a highly secret stopover in Serdica. We still had to make the last and most sensitive crossing across territory disputed by the two armies and monitored by Julian's scouts before Naissus.

This was the supreme mission of my career so far, a career that had seen dangerous setbacks. As a young *agens*, I'd run my sword through the dissolute Emperor Constans while defending my commander's back. As *biarchus*, I'd escorted Constantius' cousin Caesar Gallus to his execution in a dank Istrian cell. And my career had suffered further when I'd failed to prevent the underhanded assassination of General Silvanus, a loyal Franco-Roman cornered into treason by imperial intrigants back at court.

Other *agentes* had risen faster up the ranks than myself. But under the patient correction of our *magister agentium in rebus*, I'd made *centenarius*, upper class.

But the ageless Apodemius was inching toward retirement. As for myself, I must have reached some invisible watershed as well. Who would have predicted that a Numidian freedman would carry in his calloused hands the responsibility of hiding a political cataclysm secret from the entire civilized world until the transition of power was secure and the Empire at peace?

I'd never before supervised so sensitive an operation as concealing for weeks on end a Roman emperor's sudden death.

Nothing must go wrong.

Nothing did go wrong.

'There they are!' Aligildus shouted. He pointed to Julian's eagle standards waving over the palisades of a vast army camp staked west of Naissus. The envoys and I bathed and changed. We continued the final mile with less haste but more apprehension. The counts and their men now rode flanked by half a dozen of my *agentes* collected en route.

Such excessive precautions were probably unnecessary. Though we arrived from the enemy camp, we were protected by an institution even Julian wouldn't dare disregard in his ambitious haste to turn the Empire on its head—the timeless custom of Roman law.

※※※

For a covert mission that had gone so smoothly over so many miles of terrain, we made an inauspicious start with Julian himself. We were no more than twenty feet from the central parade ground surrounding his imperial tent when we rode within sight of him seconds from mounting his own magnificent charger.

Perhaps our unexpected arrival was to blame for what happened next. Galloping up the camp's Via Principalis, we distracted the soldier hoisting Julian up to his saddle. The boy lost hold of Julian's boot and fell thudding sideways into the pounded dirt. Julian vaulted into empty air and tumbled down after him. Righting himself with damaged dignity, our new sovereign looked up just as Theolaif and Aligildus prostrated themselves in fresh uniform and full armor.

The counts' theatrical gesture proved more eloquent than any words I could have mustered. I remained standing, holding the reins of our horses steady. I could observe for myself how

Julian's dismay at his *adiutor*'s stumble—another bad omen?—gave way to complete elation.

His heavy Constantine eyes lit up at the sight of my white feather. His stocky body trembled. He lifted his right hand to the skies he'd examined so anxiously for weeks.

'An omen all our own! See how the man has fallen who raises me to my high estate!'

One marveled at Julian's swift wit: the true 'fallen man' who'd just vaulted him to power was rolling in state toward his interment in the eastern capital.

Within seconds, an explosion of acclaim rolled in waves over the camp. Julian's thousands of weary officers and men celebrated an extraordinary reprieve from civil war tossed into their laps by the gods. Birds' entrails, double-lobed livers, soothsayers' over-eager reassurances—what were promising omens compared to peace itself?

The acclaim grew deafening. The two counts rose to their feet and stood with me drowning in the engulfing clamor. Julian circled the parade ground, his hands aloft in praise of Fortuna.

Did Julian's appearance surprise me? It was obvious how ambition had swelled his confidence from his days as a stammering, unwashed Athenian scholar. Over his six years' transition from aspiring military subordinate to Constantius challenger in the field, he'd broadened in stature and shaved off his philosopher's beard, playing the imperial Christian cousin to the very hilt of his busy *spatha*.

What a useful charade it had been! Already the philosopher's fuzz was sprouting back. His eyes radiated a canny gleam of satisfaction that his prayers, sacrifices, and chaste devotion to the true gods had not been wasted. From now on, the Empire would be his to reform, educate, and convert. There would be no more inscrutability, no stiff-necked facade—not from this young ruler already dodging into his tent to prepare for his triumphant march.

My mission was complete. Ignored by hundreds of excited soldiers dispersing around me, I watched the dust swirl and settled back to the ground. Theolaif and Aligildus would join fellow officers while I would tent without complaint with any *contubernales* short an eighth man. Exhausted by the tumult of the day, I wanted to get back to Sirmium to enjoy the certainty that the Empire was in the hands of a man who certainly didn't need me.

Within a single hour, it seemed I was wrong.

₽₽₽

'Argentoratum, correct? We haven't met since the morning after my victory at Argentoratum. I sent you packing off to Roma with that beast, Chnodomarius *Rex*. And since then?' He was half-naked and leaning over an iron basin on a tripod, sluicing water over his rounded shoulders with a tin cup.

'Promotion to *centenarius* and chief of Sirmium hub, *Imperator*.'

'*Augustus* will do. Sirmium is an Arian stronghold. You haven't turned Galilean on me?'

'No, *Auguste*.'

'Oh, stand up, stand up, Numidianus! You hardly knelt to me that night I came to your room begging for a quickie road warrant out of Mediolanum.'

'As I recall, I was already dragging on my knees, thanks to a mugging from Paulus Catena that you fortuitously interrupted.'

Julian gave a high-pitched laugh at our changes in fortune. I suppressed even a smile. It wouldn't do to forget his ascent to supreme authority. I'd long determined to correct his distaste for our *schola* and for its demonstrated loyalty to his enemy cousin.

For the service's sake, I must take great care to make a fresh beginning here and now.

'You know, Numidianus, the first thing I did on setting up winter base in Lutetia was to toss your thuggish *Ducenarius* Gaudentius back to the Castra on his ass.'

'Hardly mine—'

Julian took a deep draught of cold *posca*. 'That Neapolitan was a spy and not even a clever one. He's a gangster—no letters, no culture, not a crumb of spiritual understanding, no loyalty to anything higher than—where did the shaven-skulled brute go after Lutetia?'

'Constantius promoted him out of our *schola* to *notarius* and dispatched him to North Africa to cut off all your oil and corn supplies.'

'Was that Gaudentius? By the gods!' Julian wrapped a moth-eaten *susurna* around his bare shoulders. 'He certainly took his revenge on me. Some territories faced famine because of him, but what damage can he do me now?' He crowed, plucking at his uncombed cheek bristles. 'Now that I'm in charge, grain will fill the streets of Roma once again. I intend to cleanse Constantius' Augean stables—rid his courts of hangers-on, parasites, eunuchs, hairdressers, cooks, priests, whores,' he pulled up his stocky frame to look me straight in the eyes, 'and . . . spies.'

'We all serve the Empire.'

'I'm certain you do, Numidianus. Perhaps that's why no man trusts you. After all, who or what means empire to you, hmm?'

I nodded but said nothing. This evening Julian had all the answers.

'Now empire means me.'

He inhaled deeply, as if the fug of his ill-kempt tent had just turned richer and cleaner. He took no notice of a eunuch packing up his few and ostentatiously coarse tunics. Nor of an *adiutor* leaning in through the tent door to signal the camp's swift progress in pulling up stakes.

'I have another quarter of an hour before addressing my staff, Numidianus. Amuse me. Detail for me my last correspondence. Let me delight in hearing how you tracked and trailed my alliances using your clumsy surveillance.'

So with embarrassment buttressed only by professional dignity, I detailed his letters defending his usurpation against his murderous cousin.

Julian's ironic clapping at my recitation unnerved me.

'Before I leave here I'll write more letters. You'll carry them. I must write Uncle Julian first. I'll order *flamines* to offer thanks to the gods on our behalf . . . and of course, a letter to Aetius, the Christian who was so good to my poor brother but exiled because he would not bow to that Arian cult . . . and to my old schoolmate from Athina, the Cappadocian Basil. He must come to help me in Constantinopolis.'

'Surely you need someone to start your biography. Such a meteoric rise must not go undocumented.'

A thick imperial eyebrow shot up. 'That is impudent sarcasm, Numidianus, but I don't mind, I don't mind. You're right. If there's any time left before break of camp, I'll write the Armenian sophist Prohaeresius to offer him any records he might need. You see, great men must all race to my new court, using the state roads as their own. Neo-Platonists and Christian dissidents will mingle and argue freely among themselves.'

He gave a strange giggle, then struggled to collect himself.

'You saw Constantius read my defense to the Athenians?' He shifted his hairy torso from side to side in a moment's discomfort, as if remembering his late cousin's claimed divinity.

'I delivered a copy myself.'

'And did he flinch at my blaming Eusebius, "that execrable eunuch," for Gallus' murder?'

I lowered my gaze in answer.

'I see. All the time you were reading over the Emperor's shoulder, our *agens* was thinking, "How presumptuous this chattering goat of a little Constantine is".'

Julian laughed inches from my face. 'How shocked you must have been to hear me suddenly declared the heir by Constantius on his deathbed.'

My head shot up. He caught my startled stare.

'He named me as his heir, Numidianus. You heard him.'

'I didn't witness the death in person. I know he asked for water and a towel. Florentius and the *consistoriani* announced their decision outside the imperial tent.'

'But it was not *their* decision, African. It was my cousin's last testament.'

Julian's heavy, knowing eyes examined me, waiting. He hadn't slept well for days on end, no doubt studying the sky for bird omens and readying his war game according to ancient tomes of Julius Caesar.

Did I dare contradict him? Had he summoned me to his tent to lay his fears of a challenge to rest? I was sure the envoys had reported no deathbed declaration. Had some faster account of that confused debate in the wilds of Cilicia flown over our heads leaning over our saddles into the winds between Tarsus and

Naissus? Had some heavenly *ballista* wielded by Mercury delivered Julian's nomination from Constantius' dying lips?

Julian laughed again. 'Have no fear, Numidianus. Our late emperor's undoubted gift to me was all to the good of the gods. I shall carry his body to its final resting place on my own shoulders. My public display of humility will secure the love of Constantius' troops. I shall free the Christian factions to devour each other—such is the Galileans' happy wont. You see, I mean to be the greatest ruler of our age.'

'Let our *schola* help serve your purpose.'

'Starting how?'

'I trust in your divine sense guided by the gods, but surely don't start with sacking bath attendants or legions of pastry chefs. Signal the beginning of a reign of Justice. Signal an end to whispering campaigns and terror. Arrest Paulus Catena who filled the sewer gutters of every palace with entrails, bones, and blood of innocent men tortured on a whim.'

'Clever, Numidianus. You know that too much love of virtue and justice is my Achilles Heel. But why Catena first?'

'Because that is how we first met, *Auguste*, only minutes before you were to be thrown to Catena's instruments on an accusation of conspiracy with your half-brother, the Caesar.'

'I haven't forgotten your helpful testimony. But neither of us is a sentimental man. You make an astute political suggestion. You know that many of my troops were once supporters of the usurper "Emperor" Magnentius. They nurture a deep hatred for Catena's vicious purge of Magnentius' followers. As do you, Marcus *Gregorianus* Numidianus.'

He threw off the threadbare *susurna* and reached for his longer, formal cloak. 'I grant you Catena. You'll carry a sealed warrant for his arrest.'

'All who suffered under his cruel whips and hooks will love you.'

I stretched out full length at his scruffy boots. For once, prostration felt sincere. I knew Julian to be ambitious, headstrong, violent, impetuous, and fueled by a mystical vision of the gods at his back. But perhaps the Scales of Justice would become more than myth.

—THE BURNING STAKES—

'Oh, get up. I only do the right thing out of gratitude for your service at Argentoratum.'

As I hurried away, my new sovereign yelled at my retreating back like a ten-year-old schoolmate, 'Let that be our watchword, Numidianus. Ar-gen-tor-a-tum.'

※ ※ ※

Cheered by his troops at dawn, Julian presided over the lavish and gory sacrifice of a hecatomb of oxen to the gods who so favored him. His excited departure for Constantinopolis promised a whirlwind march rivaling a second Triptolemus who circled the earth in a chariot drawn by winged serpents. Moving his men at the army's fast-pace, I estimated the Western Army might reach New Roma as early as the second week of December.

I was too tired to trust myself to make the last essential leg from Naissus to Mediolanum Palace announcing Julian's ascension. I dispatched the first of a relay chain of our best riders to carry the news by twenty-hour relay to key points west. I enjoyed two good nights' sleep en route and continuing alone from Naissus to my beloved old Roma, I left the imperial warrant for Catena unexamined. But being well trained, I scoured Julian's private letters for more clues to new policy. Julian was just turning thirty years old. He might rule another thirty. How did the Emperor think?

To Maximus, the philosopher friend in Ephesus he so admired and missed, he wrote:

Everything crowds into my mind at once and chokes my utterance, whether you please to class such symptoms among psychic troubles, or to give them some other name . . .

I worship the gods openly, and the whole mass of the troops who are returning with me worship the gods. I have offered many hecatombs as thank-offerings in public. The gods command me to restore their worship in its utmost purity, and I obey them, yes, and with a good will. For they promise me great rewards for my labors, if only I am not remiss . . .

What a gushing schoolboy still strutted inside that new purple cloak! So Julian's pagan worship was in the open after years of semi-secrecy. What did this portend for the Christian theological rivalries that had preoccupied Constantius, Christ's uneasy 'Divinity' on earth?

Hours before dawn, I reached the old capital and hurried through the registration preliminaries at the Collina Porta. Soon I'd crossed the busy city, mounted the Caelian Hill, and was through the Castra Peregrina's gates. I skirted past our ancient Temple of Jupiter Redux. For centuries this modest site had received the sacrifice and prayers of successful agents leaving or returning from mission. This morning it stood neglected, long bolted shut on Constantius' order.

Could those carved, narrow twin door be unbolted now and the old altar re-sanctified to receive our prayers? I would be the first to thank the gods we'd been spared another civil war. The Manlius family had suffered too grievously in the last one.

In the gray light, the Castra courtyard bustled with *agentes*, cadets, trainers, and slaves, all moving in silence with an air of purpose. Two years ago, Constantius had laid down strict new regulations for recruitment; the *magister officiorum* was to weed out any *agentes* 'of unworthy birth or bad character and to see that promotions came only from merit and seniority—not money or connections.'

Unworthy birth . . . *Magister* Apodemius knew full well my pedigree on my father's side as the bastard of the Manlius *gens* so long prominent on the Senate floor was impeccable. If my mother was a discarded Numidian seamstress, it wasn't her fault—or mine.

However, it was too broadly known that I'd started life as a slave. Apodemius transferred me to manage Sirmium, safe from the reformist scrutiny of his incoming successor. The *magister agentium in rebus*-elect Servius Atia Otho, might use my low birth and ambiguous service record as an excuse to install his own man in Sirmium, the pivot point between Eastern and Western empires.

'You're late.' Ahenobarbus smiled his welcome, grabbed my upper arm, and hurried me toward the rundown room that housed our canteen.

'I'd say I'm twelve hours early to share a briefing with the *Magister*.' Apodemius only worked by night.

—THE BURNING STAKES—

Ahenobarbus shook his dark red thatch of close-cropped hair. 'Each morning Otho holds a First Meeting to sort all the important business in one big assembly. Then we break into groups and coordinate the day's labor to ensure that there's no overlap.'

Ahenobarbus sounded resigned. His one-year attachment as *principatus* to a praetorian prefect was to have been the lucrative culmination of a long career. Not incidentally, it had been the late Constantius II's trick to install a senior *agens* as watchdog in the office of every top official in the Empire. But my respected colleague's reward had been delayed by this change of *schola* leadership, in turn postponing his hard-earned, if comfortable retirement basking on some Sicilian shore.

We bumped into the Poisons Master wiping his hands on his tunic in his haste to make the assembly in time.

'I don't have to attend, Ahenobarbus. That has nothing to do with my day—'

'Don't argue or your absence will be marked against you.'

The broad courtyard surrounding the main office building and the paved alleyways between our barrack cells and the dilapidated detention house had been swept clear of old statues and *memoria*. New window glass reflected the low rise of the winter sun from the ground floor. New shutters covered the windows running along the two upper floors and fresh paint brought the old Castra compound to life, though I can't say the morning rays were flattering to the quick refurbishment.

'I have a warrant for the arrest of Catena. I'll hand it to Otho myself and tell him I'm skipping his meeting.'

We waited behind a crush of agents pressing into the crowded room. Ahenobarbus lowered his voice. 'Otho won't see you just like that, not without an appointment. He publishes his agenda at the beginning of each week according to written requests.'

I burst out laughing. 'What if something comes up on a Wednesday? Oh, all right, I'll go straight to Apodemius. The sun's not up yet. He might still be in his office.'

Ahenobarbus' grip tightened on my arm. I winced.

'Not allowed, Marcus. No one sees the old man these days. It's seen as disrespectful to Otho's new authority.'

I extracted myself from his grip and held back from the men thronging into the large room. I missed the chaotic hubbub of *agentes* mingling willy-nilly over their light breakfasts to compare notes however they chose. But modern times meant keeping up with administrative innovation. Slaves passed neat trays of fresh pastries—horn-shaped buns, egg breads, and fruit tarts—down the rows of seated *agentes*.

'Do I know you, *Agens*?'

It was the baritone greeting of Otho himself, the last to arrive in the company of two clerks shuffling notes. I squinted against the first streak of sunlight glinting off a polished water pipe behind him.

'Numidianus, *Magister*. *Centenarius*, Sirmium base.'

'You chose your riders well, Numidianus. They delivered the news of Julian's ascent in record time.'

'Thank you, *Magister*. Now I deliver an imperial warrant for the arrest of Notary Paulus Catena.'

I thrust Julian's sealed document into his unprepared palm and laid mine over it to secure his attention. 'I apologize, *Magister*, but you understand, this couldn't wait. To my knowledge it is your first written instruction from our new sovereign.'

Otho gave a slight smile. You'd think he'd already received a fistful of Julian's overheated memos. I admired his aplomb and gave him a belated salute, removing my *petanus* out of respect for his new position.

'Anything else?'

'Some of Julian's letters, mostly to philosopher friends, to be redistributed to various stations. En route I copied each and every one for your perusal and archiving.'

'Excellent work. After the First Meeting, attend my Small Group where we will attack the Catena assignment without delay.'

※※※

I'd started well with Emperor Julian. Now my powerful new superior had termed my judgment in subordinates 'excellent.' *O, tempora*, how times had indeed changed.

—THE BURNING STAKES—

I waited outside the main building for this Small Group Meeting, where Ahenobarbus found me after a solitary hour.

'Otho doesn't work here, you ass. He set up in an open office above the gymnasium.'

'The old warders' dormitory?'

'Refurbished. There's a fresh breeze off the hill. Feel it? A new wind in our sails, my African friend. No more small, cramped offices from now on.'

Otho wasted no time opening the Catena warrant. He cocked an eyebrow as he scanned its lines. As he jotted notes on a wax tablet, he asked me to tell them everything I'd seen—officer for officer, gesture for gesture, word for word. I did my best.

'Now we want your analysis of the balance of power, Numidianus. Your conclusions.'

'Here?'

I'd never before given a public briefing to so many agents in one room. Otho's 'Small Group' was over two dozen men. In the old days, Apodemius had half-listened, usually alone or with one or two trusted fellows, to my misguided attempts at political assessment before dismissing me with a gnarled hand stinking of joint liniment.

'Don't be shy, Numidianus,' said Otho. 'This is the new routine. Each man owes us his valued views, whatever his rank. You're all trained observers.'

They listened to me almost too raptly. I described Constantius' last days in Mospucrenae and the acclamation of Julian in Naissus.

Cassius, a rider I'd known in Mediolanum, spoke up: 'But Julian's a pagan. He can't be Lord Chamberlain Eusebius' nominee. Our empire's official cult is Christian and Eusebius has spent years worming his way into Church circles. He's masterminded synod after synod to expand his property holdings—'

'And through the Church, built an intelligence network independent of our own,' another man interjected.

I agreed that the Lord Chamberlain Eusebius would have preferred to stall—to wait to anoint the widowed Empress Flavia's newborn, a Constantine innocent he might easily control as unofficial regent. But within the hour of Constantius' death,

Eusebius' beady eyes had missed nothing on that windy stretch of Cilicia where General Arbitio and Commander Agilo argued by the roadside. Arbitio had won that spat and sent Agilo packing. Eusebius had tossed his final dice in Julian's direction because Julian was the only compromise that kept the ambitious Arbitio from supreme power and saved the lesser generals from a challenge too overwhelming.

I answered: 'Eusebius is taking a chance, Cassius. Perhaps Julian's obvious contempt for Christian infighting might leave the Lord Chamberlain the vacuum in which to spin his usual webs without interference.'

'Well said, Numidianus.' Otho turned to the others. 'Do we have any up-to-date information on Paulus Catena?'

Rumored sightings of 'The Chain' were tossed up—none convincing to me. Among these men, only Ahenobarbus equaled my unhappy familiarity with Constantius' state torturer.

I reclaimed the floor: 'Catena's features are mismatched and ill suited to both face and figure. I ruined his voice box with one of the bootlace garrotes issued here at the *schola* in a fair fight during the civil war. He's hated from Britannia to Egypt for his indiscriminate inquisitions under Constantius' banner. Many an honorable man can make a fatal mistake during troubled times. He might obey a misguided commander with a loyal heart or be swept off-kilter, prey to temptations strewn in his path by political currents.'

Otho looked into my eyes. He'd read my dossier closely. He knew I was the son of the rebel commander following the barbarian usurper Magnentius. I kept talking through a sudden frisson of exposure:

'But Catena is different from any ordinary citizen—or any ordinary traitor, for that matter. For those of you who missed Constantius' treason trials, Paulus Catena is far from a misguided rebel or foolish gossip who offended the Purple. He'd never doom himself with treasonous jokes in his cups at a governor's provincial banquet. Catena is the only man I've ever met drawn to pure evil. He feeds on the agony and blood of others in the way men of weak character gorge themselves on easy gold or false praise. Catena was never misled by an idealistic reformer. He was never seduced by loyalty to the wrong Constantine weakling.

—THE BURNING STAKES—

Notary Catena is an inhuman wellspring of dark, foul sewage that contaminates the cellars of every imperial palace from Treverorum to Antiochia.'

'We will get him, *Centenarie*,' cried a tenor from the back of the room. I recognized my young Franco-Roman recruit, Junius Silvanus, known to the *schola* as Merovianus for his own safety. 'The Chain is too hated to enjoy sanctuary for long.'

I shook my head at Junius. 'He'll be hard to corner. Like a snake in the reeds he may slip through our fingers for months to come.'

Otho sounded a note of confidence. 'We control the roads. We monitor all communications. But Numidianus, I read that Catena is only part of this affair.'

I hadn't opened the warrant Otho held in his hand, so his next words stunned me along with the others: 'All of us look forward to hauling Catena in chains to meet his just desserts. But Julian also calls here for the arrest of both our imperial consuls, Taurus and Florentius.'

General outrage burst out across the room. 'Our *consuls*? The highest in the Empire? On what criminal charges? Why?'

The hubbub subsided before Otho could ask, 'Numidianus, you accompanied Consul Florentius to the safety of Constantius' camp. Was he reinstated?'

'Yes, *Magister*. As Praetorian Prefect.'

'Where was Consul Taurus when you last saw him?'

'Taurus never sought my help in Sirmium.'

I described the speed with which Julian had halted his winged progress only in Bononea, nineteen miles from Sirmium. As the moon was waning he sent his Commander of the Household Guard, the German Dagalaifus, with a light-armed force to surprise the capital's defending commander, Lucillianus, sound asleep in his bed.

'Florentius panicked. He said both consuls had somehow scrambled without guard or guide over the Julian Alps together. But Prefect Taurus feared for his family and returned to hide in Italia. Florentius preferred to trust his chances to a previous acquaintance with me in Gallia—not to mention the power of my road licenses. I slipped him out of Sirmium just in time.'

'If our imperial consuls find themselves in chains, no one of the old regime is safe,' Ahenobarbus said.

I added, 'These are hardly the men I would have rounded up first—Eusebius or Arbitio. We could prove that Arbitio's plotting brought down General Silvanus, one of our ablest commanders.'

Junius tossed me a grateful smile for praising his betrayed father.

'We must inform the Old Man about the consuls,' Ahenobarbus said after a heavy pause.

Otho shook his head. 'On no account, *Princeps*. Apodemius is writing his memoirs. My orders are in keeping with his advanced age and precarious energies. No one disturbs Apodemius' serenity.'

'He'll be angry if we do not,' Ahenobarbus insisted. His green eyes lowered, giving Otho the chance to reconsider. 'A courtesy conference, if you will, *Magister*.'

Otho relented. 'A courtesy call, then, no more.'

A frosty dawn greeted us outside the meeting room. A weak winter sun struggled over the Castra's ancient walls. Its rays were useless had I tried to tell time by any shadow on our ancient, weathered sundial. But I found myself staring at a modern water clock, a *clepsydra*, protected from the weather by a pristine marble shrine—like some cult statue or Christian saint.

'Imported from Constantinopolis and just installed,' Cassius explained, 'with gears and calibrations to account for the change of seasons and temperature of the water. It's about time we modernized this compound. Mediolanum has had one like it for decades but not this efficient. See? There's a dial face showing us the time. No more guessing in murky weather.'

I didn't need some new timekeeping apparatus to tell me we'd have to hurry to catch the nocturnal Apodemius. And for reasons I could not articulate to myself since arriving at the Castra, I needed to see him now even more than he needed to see me.

Chapter 3, A Question of Purple Ink

—THE CASTRA PEREGRINA, ROMA—

My unexpected appearance at Otho's meeting prompted the younger *agentes* Junius and Cassius to linger outside the meeting room and welcome me back to Roma with hearty embraces. Ignoring rank and protocol, they trailed Otho, Ahenobarbus, and myself toward Apodemius' old rooms, making no attempt to hide their curiosity. Neither of the senior men rebuffed them.

The four of us followed Otho in his smart bleached tunic with its embroidered *orbiculi* across the torch-lit courtyard's wet stones. Junius chattered to me about his progress at the Castra. He still saw me as his mentor and champion. I'd rescued him from near-certain punishment for his father's political suicide by recruiting him into our service school. But as we walked, the young Franco-Roman prince's happy news—that he'd graduated from *eques* to *circitor* and was now riding the postal loop between Roma and points south—couldn't hold my entire attention. I picked up signs of *Magister* Otho's new management of the Castra everywhere I glanced. Repairs to our sagging gutters kept the winter drizzle under better control. Workmen had repointed the aging brickwork and replaced broken marble flagstones. Fewer *agentes* stood idly conversing in doorways or the alleys flanking our sleeping quarters. Even without a head count, it was obvious that Otho had beefed up the army of slaves doing our laundry, gymnasium, and bathhouse chores.

So far I was impressed by our incoming *magister*. Otho seemed the kind of administrator smart enough to listen to any *agens* offering sound suggestions. He even allowed the Franco-Roman kid bouncing along on my heels and Cassius—known for his dubious dice games—to join on our visit to the retiring recluse Apodemius.

But I withheld my final judgment. Letting Junius and Cassius tag along was a bad sign. It hinted that Otho regarded any meeting with the old man as unimportant. Did Otho ever do more than pay courtesy calls on his cantankerous predecessor? Did he value the outgoing *magister*'s bottomless store of experience? Did he sufficiently reckon with the old enmities that still dogged our work?

Or was our new boss of a mind to simply plaster over political rivalries, hoping they'd die with Apodemius?

Otho led us up the creaking wooden steps to Apodemius' two rooms. He gave a polite knock with his toe on the door to the outer office and we entered.

I didn't recognize the young clerk manning the desk guarding the inner study. He was preparing the incoming memoranda for Apodemius, but even here things were different. Instead of original notes and messages, he was merely sorting standard copies of *schola* traffic on the cheap *taeneotic* papyrus used throughout the Castra for internal communications.

Where was Apodemius' usual mess of 'real mail?' Normally his desk was covered with every possible variety of letter. Where was the tumble of ragged, randomly sized, occasionally even exotic notes, on cloth, vellum, papyrus or even wood that Apodemius used to receive from all corners of his extraordinary network of informants? Usually his clerk would look inundated with original information from *agentes* posted in every imperial mail hub and provincial prefect's office—not to mention intelligence from hundreds of secret watchers Apodemius employed across the Empire. It looked like Otho kept his predecessor informed with daily updates, neat reports regurgitated and copied for Castra records.

Fresh information was no longer going to the old man first.

Nor did I detect any signs—bottles, towels, or stinks—of the deaf masseur who used to treat the old spy's arthritic joints with exotic lotions and liniments on a long, high couch in the inner office.

So it must be true: the nightly hours Apodemius put in were his own to fritter away, perusing internal communications without responsibility or writing his memoirs. But if he wanted medical attention or a massage, he was now idle enough to take his creaking bones to a more appropriate and private setting.

At the sound of our voices, Apodemius opened his inner door. That in itself was unusual. I'd spent many a nervous hour fidgeting away on a bench in the outer room, waiting my turn to report my latest failings to Apodemius. He'd always received me from behind a desk smothered with work underway or lying prone on his massage couch, unwilling to waste a minute of his long night debriefing *agentes*.

His changed appearance was even more distressing. His hair was as ever—snow-white wisps floating around his high scalp as if each tuft had a mind of its own. But he'd lost weight he couldn't afford. His bleached ivory wool robe hung formless over his skeletal torso. What had been minor jowls drooped on either side of his strong jaw like dog-like wattles.

His complexion was no better. Always so pale from nocturnal habits that one of his favorite disguises had been to cover himself in cork black or any home-brewed stain, his skin was mottled by large brown coins across his forehead. A painful-looking red growth studded a chin covered with unappealing white bristles.

Why had no one sent our Castra surgeon to burn away that mean tumor with his heated *cauterium*?

Apodemius rubbed his twisted arthritic hands together with pleasure at our consultation. '*Io, Saturnalia*! Such a delegation! What's the occasion, *Magister* Otho?'

'Our Numidian is just in from Sirmium carrying a warrant for Notary Paulus Catena,' Otho announced.

The five of us arranged ourselves in the cramped space as best we could. I pulled out the old 'interrogation' stool for Otho. The rest of us leaned against the massage couch or a nearby sideboard holding dented vessels and battered wine-heating kit utensils.

Apodemius sipped a steaming tonic from a simple silver cup. 'Catena! Hah! So the mastermind of linking false evidence into chains of death will finally see his evil links smashed once and for all. No one of any faction or faith will mourn that hound.'

Apodemius' offices were so cold, none of us shed his winter cloak. Was the hypocaust piping leading to these rooms the only part of the Castra not yet repaired?

The old man glanced at his successor over the lip of his cup. 'Surely, Otho, Catena's warrant can't be the only juicy bone you toss an eager old dog?'

'No.' Otho shifted on his stool. 'Emperor Julian's first move has been to attack Constantius' court at the highest level. Numidianus delivers Julian's orders to arrest both imperial consuls.'

'Both? Florentius? I'm not surprised,' Apodemius mused. 'You can imagine Julian's pent-up anger at Florentius. He still blames Florentius for Constantius' order that Julian lose his crack auxiliary units to fight on the Persian front.'

I commented: 'And more—Julian and Florentius were already at loggerheads over taxation when I served in Gallia in 357. I wasn't surprised when Florentius fled Julian's camp to Vienna on the Rhodanus—pretty much as soon as Julian declared himself emperor. And as Julian marched south, Florentius fled Roma. Now he's on the run a third time.'

'Florentius makes a bad habit of flight, it seems.' Otho cocked a skeptical eyebrow.

'Yes, but not our other consul, Flavius Taurus,' said Apodemius with a thoughtful exhalation. He fixed his eyes with absent reflection on his strongbox sitting in the corner of his office. It contained his tightest-held intelligence on persons across the breadth of the Empire. 'Taurus is a respected servant of the Empire, a superb praetorian prefect of Italia who deserved his consulship. *Taurus* to face trial? In the gods' names, for what?'

'In any case, we must obey Emperor Julian's warrants,' Otho said, 'without equivocation or delay.'

'Oh, definitely, *Magister* Otho. Our new Constantine may be testing the loyalty of our service.' Apodemius smiled up at the line of us standing. 'Now, *Magister* Otho, I surmise you included Cassius in this meeting because you already plan that our energetic *biarchus* will supervise the order to block all roads, gates, layover stations on the *Cursus*, and ports in our hunt for Paulus Catena?'

—THE BURNING STAKES—

This was outright mischief on Apodemius' part. We all knew Cassius' presence in the room was unplanned, but Otho dared not admit it. The startled Cassius gasped at being entrusted with the biggest manhunt of the season.

Arthritis had turned Apodemius' hands to lobster claws. He wagged a crippled finger in Cassius' direction. 'And if you also happen to catch a consul or two in your net, ask for instructions before moving eastward with your prisoners. You understand?'

Otho didn't like the way Apodemius had started giving Cassius instructions. He rose from the stool and straightened his tunic.

'We have intruded too long. We must leave you to continue work on your reminiscences.' Perhaps he feared that young Junius was about to be assigned the interrogation of a consul or two?

'Before you go, fellows, you might consider looking for Florentius in Africa. Ask Numidianus later for tips on geography there.'

This set Otho back on his heels. He scanned Apodemius' desk for telltale intelligence papers that hadn't first passed through his own manicured fingers. With tightlipped asperity he asked, 'Why Africa, *Magister*?'

'Only an educated guess, *Magister*. I suspect that Florentius and his family sought the protection of our former colleague *Notarius* Gaudentius in North Africa even before Constantius' corpse reached its cold bier. Remember, both Gaudentius and Florentius were notable failures in Julian's coterie. The passage from Cilicia to Egypt or Numidia would be difficult at this time of year, but not impossible for a praetorian prefect of Florentius' authority and means.'

I didn't trust Gaudentius now any more than when I'd suspected him of poisoning Apodemius to succeed him as chief of the *schola*. I'd been wrong about the poisoning, but not about the man's ambition. I seized my chance to say so now:

'Then Florentius is a fool. What could Gaudentius do, now that his sponsor Constantius is dead? In fact, Gaudentius is very likely to *betray* Florentius to please Emperor Julian, just as he jumped rank over you, *Magister*, to curry favor with Constantius.'

Apodemius chuckled. 'You see, *Magister*? You see how old rivalries die hard among our men? Our Marcus Gregorianus Numidianus, a freedman with a superior education and decent Roman table manners, dislikes the coarse, street-fighting Neapolitan. Even a conscientious administrator like you, Otho, can't heal old sores overnight.'

Apodemius chided me: 'Don't fault Gaudentius for past sins, Numidianus. We didn't train you men to be ambitious, duplicitous informers only to ask you to drop your skills at my door. Promoting Gaudentius to *notarius* shifted him closer to Constantius who was always his true love. And it kept the ambitious thug out of my poor thinning hair.'

He was patronizing all of us. Otho was right. It was time to leave Apodemius to his scribbling.

Apodemius wave his gnarled hand. 'You'd better get back to your paperwork, *agentes*, in duplicate! And Otho, surely you have many Saturnalia obligations to the *clarissimi* and *spectabili* houses of Roma. Astute politicking is so important for a rising man.'

Apodemius recommended socializing to Otho? Never once to my knowledge had Apodemius ever graced a banquet given by the Eternal City's chattering socialites.

'Why not leave Numidianus with me, Otho? His work is in Sirmium. He has nothing further to do here in Roma. Nothing at all.'

Apodemius sounded disappointed—with my prosaic performance during four years in Sirmium? It was true I'd had recruited no one, sent in only routine reports, and copied correspondence that merely confirmed existing impressions of the two competing courts of Julian and Constantius.

The floor under Apodemius' disheveled desktop was scattered with bent pins he was probably too pain-wracked to scoop up. While I waited for the others to take their leave, I gathered them up and gazed over the hand-inked map of the Empire pinned to a thick cork mat on the wall behind his desk.

The old man had punctured its vellum so many times, leather shreds of the Rhenus dangled down in strings. Clustered painted pins and tiny flags cut from colored ribbons marked the stream of our two Roman armies merging toward a big gold tack marking Constantinopolis. Forests of tin buttons showed where Julian had stationed units to guard Gallia.

The map told a stark story. Gallia was secured along the very same borders it enjoyed when Julian arrived there in late 355. Meanwhile, the forts and castles of Drusus and the lines set by Hadrian, the Antonines, and Probus sat abandoned and the triangle of the Agri Decumates had been lost entirely. Every trace of Roman influence, once so powerful among the Trans-Rhenan tribes, stood obliterated.

There was a gaping hole leaking bits of crumbling bark from the center of 'Med . . .num,' for Mediolanum. The biggest shock was the garish Persian pin stabbed into our great eastern city, Amida, just lost to Shapur's bloody onslaught.

I shivered under my *sagum*, thinking of the Persians dragging away Roman prisoners for enslavement on the Euphrates.

Apodemius took a small glass vial sitting on his sideboard and added one meticulous drop into his concoction. He emptied the cup and sighed as the drink took effect. He hobbled back to his goatskin chair with the cushion stuffing leaking from its popping seams.

'Well, here we are! Two idle men, right? You find me decrepit. Don't deny it! I can see it on your face. Well, you're hardly the same fresh-faced *volo* whom Leontus Flavius sent flayed raw to spy on a nest of Circumcellions in 347. Do I detect a little thinning around the edges of that curly bronze hair?'

I wriggled a rueful eyebrow.

'Perhaps, *Magister*. But when it's half gone in ten years, I promise not to comb it over my sweating scalp like the *consistoriani* Arbitio or Lampadius.'

'You've lost much innocence, Numidianus, but you won't lose your looks. I wonder that no Sirmium heiress has snapped you up during your posting in Pannonia.'

'None so far, though the local ladies don't complain of my neglect. You've never cared about any passing flirtations before now.'

'No gold-digging dancer yearns to share your responsibilities for the Manlius revenues?'

'The Castra trained me to be discreet at all times.'

'Yes. You've sometimes been too trusting, but never indiscreet—in all your years of service. It's the child slave in you, always observing in silence.'

'I notice you have only two mice left.'

His *apodemi*—furry, scratching namesakes that must have changed generations many times but always looked the same to me—lay sleeping on straw in a cage underneath the map.

He stuck a knobby knuckle between their bars and gave one pet a gentle tickle. 'Well-spotted. Last year I used two as tasters— a gift box of dried fruit from Alexandria—and our family got a rude shock, didn't we, little survivors?'

He stared vacantly, fingers fiddling with a wisp of his cloudy aureole. I knew better than to interrupt such deliberations. I'd soon find out why he'd really detained me.

'Did you obtain any audience with the sovereign?'

I knew which sovereign he meant. I described my ride in Constantius' company, his swaying with fever in his saddle, and his inquiry about Barbatio's death. I repeated to Apodemius the condemned general's vindictive curse that we'd all pay someday for Caesar Gallus' execution. I repeated the emperor's claim he'd sent a rescindment of the death order to the eunuch Eusebius. And I conveyed his promise to reopen an investigation.

'Constantius' temperature was probably soaring even then. I think he was just expressing regret. It was wishful thinking. He hoped that posterity would judge him more clement toward his own flesh and blood than he was.'

Apodemius lifted two bleary eyes to mine. 'It was more than wishful thinking. He called you to his side for a reason. He had a change of heart, Numidianus. His Christian conscience was troubled. The rescindment was real. His order to spare Gallus was drafted and sealed.'

'You know there was no such thing. I was always at your side as we escorted Gallus, from Constantinopolis to Pula.'

'Constantius suffered regrets, even remorse.' He shifted with a grimace in his seat. His hip joints gave him pain.

'Well, I saw that. But he was confused by fever. After all, he reigned as caesar and then emperor for decades. How many thousands of orders and rescripts did he sign with that ludicrous flourish of his—*Master of the World, Our Eternity*? Had an imperial stay of execution got mislaid in transit, surely it would have re-surfaced by now.'

'And what if it resurfaces?' He leaned toward me across his desk, his eyes blinking wide.

'We swear we never received it and not for the first time.'

'Who will believe us? Not my enemies.'

'You have too much time on your hands, *Magister*. Don't brood on Caesar Gallus' execution. It's been seven years. It's an old story.'

He frowned and rose on those bony sticks he called legs and limped over to the strongbox in the corner. Taking a key from a pouch hanging off his unfashionably thin belt, he unlocked the lid and lifted a folded document from the bottom of a jumbled stash of sensitive treasures. I read its few words, fewer than the signature itself.

'This looks like a hasty retraction—' I gulped.

He grinned, finally pleased with me. 'Exactly. What's wrong with it?'

'It's not Constantius' handwriting. The original signature would have been in the purple ink made exclusively for his use. But is this a faithful copy? Where did you get it?'

'Young Benedictus got it for me—oh, you don't know the lad. He's a great winkler when it comes to archives.'

He rambled as he returned to his chair, '... one of my best potential Christian recruits before... resembles a painting of Diocletian's martyrs... white-skinned with freckles, huge eyes of devotion rolling heavenward from the burning stake—oh, never mind.'

He plucked at the parchment skin covering his own tortured-looking elbows. 'Don't you realize what this might mean, Numidianus?'

'It means you have a copy of something. You have no proof there was an original with this same wording. And you have no proof anything was sent.'

'And no proof it was NOT sent.' His hands trembled. With age? With fear? 'You say, Constantius told you he addressed it to Eusebius?'

'Yes, *Magister*.'

'In the wrong hands, the original of this with the imperial signature in purple ink could be my death sentence. An enemy could claim they knew or saw me receive it before lopping off that mad Constantine cousin's pretty head.'

'You're convinced there was foul play somewhere along the way, *Magister*? The imperial postal service is our own *schola*'s responsibility.'

'I've always suspected it—from the minute I tossed Gallus' bloodied slippers on the dais steps in triumph and looked up to see the Emperor's frozen expression instead.'

'You're imagining it, *Magister*. I was there, worshipping the purple, prostrated alongside you. Of course Constantius looked frozen. His Divinity's face never betrayed any emotion—ever. He thought it *undivine* to look human.'

'The question is, did the original of this reach the Lord Chamberlain Eusebius? Was he sitting there in that cell in Pula, watching Barbatio lop off Gallus' head under my own supervision, with a rescindment hidden in the folds of his robes?'

'Surely there would be a record of the letter's dispatch? What are all those scribes and archivists in Mediolanum for?'

'Why do you think I'm still rotting in this moldy old office?'

'Writing your memoirs.'

'Don't mock me, Numidianus! I've been trying to contact every possible rider, retired or still in service, from Mediolanum court to Istria for the year 354. So far no one, official or unofficial, courtier, *agens*, or slave, admits to delivering such an order to Eusebius. I dare not question his eunuchs.'

'Your rider might be dead by now. Anyway, why would Eusebius keep such a document secret for so long?'

'Because just as it might prove my death sentence, it could serve as his stay of execution, if produced at the right moment.'

'You're safe, *Magister*. You've retired. No one cares about Caesar Gallus now.'

'Oh, you're wrong, Numidianus. Our Julian still cares very much. I'm not thinking of myself, Numidianus. I'll die soon enough. But the *schola* may be destroyed with me. I cannot retire until I get my hands on the original rescindment and burn it to ashes.'

—THE BURNING STAKES—

※※※

I borrowed a desk and stool in the Castra secretariat and collected my reports sent from Sirmium so I could compose the 'annual review' Otho requested of all main stations. There were other *agentes* in from the field stuck toiling on the same task at desks nearby. I recognized one or two, but no one seemed in the mood for holiday conviviality. A shared distaste for bureaucracy kept our heads bent low to finish before it was time for baths and supper.

As soon as I finished a few more lines, I could head up the Esquiline Hill to share the evening *cena* with my son, his mother, and our familiar household.

'That beastly fog's thick outside,' said Junius, leaning over my shoulder. I had nothing to hide from him, but he was a nosy lad—in other words, well trained since I first entrusted the runaway imperial hostage to the security of the Castra under his assumed name. He would always be 'Junius Silvanus' to me, whatever undercover disguise he needed.

'At least we have no Frankish snow during a Roman solstice,' I said.

'Better an honest snow under a clear sky than this morbid Roman *bruma*.'

I filed my report with the clerk, and flinging a brotherly arm over Junius' shoulders, led him out into the courtyard before he could provoke my fellow scribblers with his overeager peeking.

With each year, he resembled his dashing father, General Silvanus, all the more. Only a change of name and the protection of our training school had kept the hostage boy safe from reprisals at Constantius' court in Mediolanum during his father's usurpation in Agrippina. It was no coincidence that his first field assignment kept him riding southwards, never northwards.

'You remember spending Saturnalia with us that first winter?'

'It was more than a holiday for me, Numidianus. Your family offered me a safe and private home, with no suspicious eunuchs and spying guards around each palace corner.'

'You were very brave. It was bad enough losing your father, but you suffered even more that your mother had to believe you dead as well. You wept alone in your room while the others were exchanging Saturnalia presents.'

'You weren't there. How do you know?'

'Verus spied on you.'

'Then he's as bad as a eunuch. I was just a child.' Junius pulled himself taller underneath his long *paenula* against the swirling mist as we headed down the Caelian Hill. 'Nothing escapes Verus, that old fart.'

'Shush, Junius. The Manlius *dispensator* is not an old fart. Or a sot. Or a fussbudget.'

We loped, our long-legged strides in rhythm.

He laughed. 'Or a nag. Or a walking wine bladder.'

'Or a bow-legged old woman with a good heart!' I slapped his back. 'Come home with me, now! Verus would be happy to see you after so many years.'

'No, thanks. I was headed to a *popina* I know.'

'I won't hear of it. You're too young for hags and whores.'

We reached a fork at the base of the Esquiline Hill where I steered him by the shoulders toward the Manlius house. Dozens of people scurried past us in the cold, followed by their slaves carrying packages and food. The mood was festive and friendly—if nearly frozen.

'Wait, you're right.' I halted. 'I almost forgot the season. The servants will have quit the kitchen. They're expecting us to cook and wait on them as of tonight.'

'Not a December custom we followed up north.' He sniffed Germanic disdain for ancient Roman revels. He might look like his dashing father, but he had a touch of his hostage mother's suspicious, judgmental nature.

'Saturnalia's not all feast and fornication, boy. Soon the sun begins to mount in the sky again. The earth turns on its axis. Show some respect for the traditional Romans' marking the seasons' reversal. I don't care what you Christians make of it—the slaves and servants will have their holidays getting us to serve them hand and foot.'

—THE BURNING STAKES—

He popped a street vendor's candied date into his mouth. The boy hadn't yet found a reliable barber on his rider's budget. His upper lip was nicked in two places.

'As I recall,' he said, chewing with a full mouth, 'your household's "day off" lasted nearly two weeks. We suffered unmade beds, overflowing chamber pots, and Lady Kahina's Numidian eggs with anchovies and olives—until your slaves rebelled. After too many sloppy omelets and cheap catering from the street, they tossed off their holiday "hats of freedom" and reclaimed their pots and kitchen rags with obvious relief.'

'Hats of freedom . . .' I glanced at him, recalling a fevered night six years ago when our castrated Toxandrian *agens* Meroveus demanded that this hostage Franco-Roman boy proclaim him free and place the brimless felt *pileus* symbolizing manumission on the older man's shaven scalp.

Junius shrugged. 'I prefer one day of Christmas, thank you. At least in Agrippina, the gutters aren't clogged with drunks and *sigillaria* trash.'

We dodged into The Poor Man's Minerva, a reliable *taberna* a few steps from our neighborhood temple.

The dining room was, unsurprisingly, jammed with my well-heeled neighbors suffering the same slave-less Saturnalia state. They were filling their stomachs with decent fare before facing their wives' amateurish holiday cuisine.

We waited behind a press of noisy customers to place our orders at the grill buffet.

We had to share a table with two fat wig wholesalers haggling the wholesale price of *capilli Indici*. They argued at the top of their voices and waved sample hanks of black hair imported by the ton in each other's faces.

Junius extracted a curl of flying human hair from his collar. 'What a crush! All this shopping! All these games of changing places! I prefer Christmas, a time of renewal and rebirth, not reversal.'

'With the girls down at your *popina*? I suppose.'

He blushed.

'There are other reversals this Saturnalia, Junius.' I lowered my voice.

'You mean Julian ordering everyone to restore the temples with the old altars and shrines?'

'Perhaps. He's a devotee of our old cult and even more of odd, new magical beliefs. But I was referring to reversals of a different nature. Political—not spiritual.'

We dug into our cabbage rolls and steamed cauliflower casserole. I poured him a full glass of good *conditum*.

'Junius, how do you reckon you stand under our new leadership?'

'*Magister* Otho? I like him.'

'Why?'

'He's fair and open. We trainees never laid eyes on the old man from month to month. Now that I'm a rider, I see even less of the Castra. But Otho makes sure we're kept abreast of everything. He imposes strict routines on morning assemblies, weekly reports, and regular evaluations. He's reforming the service from the bottom up.'

'And you like these new routines?'

'Well, I never really knew the old. But least Otho is accessible to all the ranks by daylight.' He paused. 'Speaking of hiding, Numidianus, I get it that Notary Gaudentius might want to lay low for a while. But why Consul Florentius?'

'You heard us. Florentius' mistake was to advise the Emperor to claim Julian's best units for the Persian front.'

'So that's why Julian revolted.'

'Partly.'

'Who would have won if Constantius hadn't dropped dead like that?'

'Well, he did drop dead.'

I mopped up the last of the cumin sauce with a piece of bread.

'Junius, if you had to decide between the *schola* and the Empire, which would you choose?'

He frowned. 'The *schola* serves the Empire.'

'If you had to choose between obedience to the Empire or to, say, Otho, what then?'

'But *Magister* Otho serves the *schola* that serves the Empire. What are you driving at, Numidianus?'

—THE BURNING STAKES—

'Apodemius always insisted that we serve nothing and no one but the Empire in the end. But how do we know...? Who decides? If I asked you to obey me and no one else, could I rely on you?'

Junius looked unsettled. 'I think your wine is too strong, Numidianus.'

'I'm sorry, boy. I don't know what I'm asking.' I paid our bill.

We dragged our groaning bellies past a group of holiday makers heading for the Temple of Minerva Medica and continued up the street to the Manlius house. No doorway lamplight could pierce the dense cloud obscuring our progress, but the quarter's *aediles* had mounted massive torches so that pedestrians might avoid stumbling into the wet filth of the gutters.

Finally our great fig tree loomed up through swirling mist. It stood in front of the entrance gate bolted by Verus' minions. Someone had chopped off the limbs that brushed over the wall itself. The lopsided tree reminded me of a war veteran begging down in the Subura, with amputations on one side only.

As Junius and I waited for someone to admit us, the young prince suddenly turned to me with an earnest expression in those handsome brown eyes so like his doomed father's.

'Numidianus, perhaps it's not the politic answer to your "test" down there but here's my reply. I'd obey you, first and last, over anyone else at the Castra. When my father claimed the purple, your quick thinking saved my hostage throat from being cut by those politician vipers in Mediolanum. But please, Numidianus, never ask me to choose between you and my new duties. And never ask me to choose between the Castra and the Franco-Romans who rallied behind our family up north.'

Why did I need to know who was loyal to *me*? Why should such a choice ever arise? I couldn't even explain to myself what had prompted that question.

The Fates then whispered something in my ear. I heard warnings but nothing distinct through the happy clamor that greeted our arrival through the gates. I couldn't make out their message—not through this vaporous night—at least not yet.

Chapter 4, Volumes of Suspicion

—THE MANLIUS TOWNHOUSE—

A slave took our wet cloaks and ushered us through the *fauces* into the reception hall. I hesitated, braced for Leo's usual rush into my arms in welcome. But the boy didn't appear, so I led Junius into the general mayhem of slaves decorating the winter dining room with winter boughs and imported flowers. Once again, Kahina and Verus had lost control of the *Saturnalia* preparations and I would find some questionable expenses tucked into our family accounts for the coming months.

Leo sprawled on the floor of the family's private salon with a friend his own age. He was scribbling with a *stilus* on a wax tablet.

'This is where you should tackle him. He's the quickest. If I get the ball, I can run past the scrum of all of the others and make a wide throw to Festus.'

'Why am I always the one who has to wrestle the fat asses into the dirt?'

'Because I'm taller. I have a better chance of catching a high throw above their heads. That's why it didn't work last week. You kept throwing to Priscus. He's too short.'

'Hello, Leo.' I stood over the two youths absorbed in their wax etching of a *harpastum* playing field. Leo had made arcs and gouges marking out strategic plays.

'Oh, this is our freedman, Numidianus,' Leo told his friend. 'This is Sextus.'

'Aren't you going to introduce Junius? You haven't seen him in years.'

The two boys rose up off their stomachs with unattractive reluctance to greet us properly.

'I never would have known you,' Junius told Leo.

Indeed, I might have said the same thing. My son, though unacknowledged for so many entangled legal reasons protecting his enormous estate, had shot up to an astonishing height during my last absence. Turning fourteen, he was no longer a child. Sinewy new muscles fought lingering traces of baby fat. His lower face was covered in a blanket of dark down. It was another year before he'd deposit his first whiskers in the ritual *barbitio depositio*, but his cracking voice and truculent tone were unavoidable reminders he was growing up.

Poor Leo was entering that age when he was a lovable embarrassment to himself, though his mother insisted otherwise. Apparently our gangly Leo was a heartbreaker in the eyes of the twelve year-old girls of his elevated social set. He would soon find himself a sought after as a fiancé by both respected old Roman *gentes* and nouveau-riche clans.

But none of this bothered me as much as his indifferent greeting in front of Junius and Sextus and his offhand 'our freedman.' I was tempted to upbraid him and announce myself as his sire, then and there—his rights and assumptions about the Commander being his father be damned.

As his 'freedman' would I soon have to bend my head to this lad? Where was my bookish boy who once poured over Catullus' erotic poetry with prurient curiosity or soaked his innocent head in histories and essays in the old Senator's priceless library? This was the sole Manlius heir? A sullen, slope-shouldered fuzz-wit obsessed with mindless bouts of ball-tossing?

No one noticed my distress. Junius was already locked in avid conversation about boot soles and team rankings.

I looked for Kahina, through the public rooms, in and out of her private chambers and past the mist-filled gardens. I found her at last in the kitchen next to the servants' quarters. She was stirring eggs in a great red pottery bowl with a wooden spoon. A few of the slaves' children—too young to care which dining room they sat in—were cracking more eggs to feed the dozens of mouths busy trying on their costume 'finery' in our public rooms.

—THE BURNING STAKES—

She sighed with relief to see me returned to Roma safe—or perhaps gratitude that in the Saturnalia game of 'reverse the household,' I'd turned up to help out.

'You've started all this a bit early this year, haven't you?'

'Oh, my dear Marcus. I'm already so tired. I thought I'd give them omelets with zucchini and peppers. What do you think?'

'I think they expect anchovies and olives. And I think they all love you for it. Listen to them laughing out there, with their jokes and mockery. Where's Verus? Why isn't he rehearsing his role as the Senator of Chaos?'

Just then one of our estate slaves appeared at the back door leading onto an alleyway shared by the substantial residences along our street. He rolled two great point-bottomed *amphorae* of wine across the kitchen floor and into a storage alcove.

Kahina looked on helpless as the good-natured ruffian returned—still wearing a wet *sagum* from his commute from our nearest vineyards—leaned over Kahina and ripped off a piece of flatbread, as if he'd greeted us all far too many times for one week.

Kahina threw her spoon down on the table. She was truly on edge, though too simple and gentle a soul to lose her temper outright. Tears welled up in her large brown eyes. I noticed some first gray strands protruding from the chestnut braids circling her head.

'Verus ordered that wine?' I asked.

'Verus ordered the wine for all of them, just as I asked last week,' she said. 'Then he placed the same order, again.'

'This is the same order for a second time?'

'The *fourth* time, Marcus. He doesn't remember that he already told the man to drive in with it days ago. We now have enough wine in the house to last us until Saturnalia 365.'

I put a comforting arm over her slumped shoulders. 'We've talked before about reorganizing everything to shift the load off him.'

'I can't manage the estates and household without him, Marcus.'

'Where's Verus now?'

'In bed, resting up to play "The Master".'

'I'm sorry. I didn't expect things would change so fast.'

'Did you see Leo? Did you talk to him about going away?'

'I took months for Libanius to answered my application letter. And I admit, I've dragged my feet. In the meantime, things have shifted in the East. Maybe there's too much upheaval and change in the East for a sheltered Roman boy like Leo.'

Her shoulders stiffened at my touch.

'Just as well you did! I told you, Marcus, I cannot agree! I will not agree! My friends say that your Libanius the Philosopher is a notorious pagan!' Her voice snapped hard as a centurion's whip with righteous Christian resolution.

I left her to the eggs and returned the public rooms to check on the preparations. Leo's teacher, the *rhetor* Antonius Drusus, was helping one of our prettiest servants, a freedwoman elected to help the cook play "The Mistress," light lamps around the edge of our *lararium*, the house shrine to the old gods. Our festivities were a hodgepodge of Christian thanksgiving and piety for some of our household leavened with lighthearted pagan bawdiness for the less religious-minded. These December frolics resembled many a modern Roman family's celebration and our merrymakers tolerated each other's cults better than they tolerated mishaps with the laundry.

Among the Christians in our household, only Kahina was so upright and passionate, so unbending, in her devotion.

'*Io, Saturnalia*, Numidianus!' Antoninus Drusus looked more prosperous than ever. This evening he'd left his own comfortable apartment north of the river to help us get ready.

From the neglected gray ashes of previous offerings, Drusus rescued a rather pathetic and twisted little relic of the Old Senator's era.

'You come in time to register the damage. Your Vesta of the Hearth has rusted green, look here, and something has crumpled her little *palla*.'

'I'm afraid *Domina* Kahina would rather burnish her soul's grace for the hereafter in heaven than do pagan chores on my behalf, Drusus, especially when I'm not here most of the year.'

'Should we all buy a set of new *lares* now that Julian is emperor?' he asked. Antonius Drusus was an enlightened Christian teacher around Roma, respected for both his classical training and a political familiarity with the Christian powers-that-be. He kept his ears attuned to shifting political winds.

'Julianus Augustus predicts that a tolerant policy will set the Christian factions at each other's throats. He may be right. We'll have to wait and see.'

'But the boy's education can't wait. Will you still send Leo to Antiochia?'

I drew Drusus away from the shrine and into an alcove, safe from curious ears.

'I hesitate. It's not Libanius *per se* that bothers me, Drusus. It's the East, too unstable, even with me watching from Sirmium. Just too far.'

'May I suggest a compromise, Marcus Numidianus? During the last summer months, when the probability of civil war between the Constantines loomed over us all, I took the liberty of writing about Leo—his quick wits, his future responsibilities, his noble heritage—to Decius Magnus Ausonius.'

'Ausonius? The Christian poet in Burdigala? I want only the finest for my . . . ward. Libanius is the finest.'

'Ausonius is more than a poet. He trained as an advocate, but he prefers teaching. He's been *grammaticus* and then *rhetor* at Burdigala's school for decades. His uncle Aemilius Magnus Arborius tutored one of the Constantine boys—'

'—hardly a recommendation. Which son? Constans was a dissolute pig and Constantius a ruthless murderer of his own kin. Some education for Leo! Not one of the Constantines ever cracked the spine of a *codex* except Julian and he was tutored by Mardonius the Eunuch.'

My outburst drew sly glances from the household members rehearsing a song around the fountain in the atrium.

'Please consider Ausonius. He's the son of a physician, Julius Ausonius, of Greek ancestry. His mother was the daughter of Caecilius Argicius Arborius, descended on both sides from great Gallo-Roman families of that region.'

I lifted a cynical eyebrow in wry appreciation of Drusus' social acumen fed by his own ambition for good appointments.

'You have such a useful grasp of the great and good, Drusus Antoninus.'

'Ausonius will steep Leo in all that's required for a career as a Roman litigator. And Western Gallia is quiet, green, clean-living, and *peaceful*. It is not Antiochia.'

I relented a jot. Libanius was the most accomplished teacher I'd courted on Leo's behalf, but I'd also seen Antiochia—its shallow morals and stifling Eastern climate. I'd even survived a killer earthquake in its streets. I was hardly a dedicated fan of Libanius' hometown.

'Old Senator's Manlius' second wife, the Commander's mother, was from old Gallic nobility. It's not entirely inappropriate.'

'You'll lose nothing by choosing 'Ausonius over Libanius, I assure you. Kahina should be happy with a Christian teacher of such renown. And in case of any outbreak of trouble, Leo won't be too far from your cattle-breeding holdings just to the south.'

I'd forgotten how Drusus had used our Manlius account books to set Leo arithmetic problems.

'Have you spoken to the boy yet?'

'Of course not, Numidianus. You hold the *tutela testamentaria*. It's your decision.'

'I've decided. Send a message to my friend Cornelius to take his *spatha* out of retirement. You'll need protection on the road.'

'If Cornelius agrees, we three can leave right after Saturnalia.'

'That's going to be very hard for Kahina.'

'But I assure you, Numidianus, Leo will need little persuading. Ausonius' staff is very keen on Juvenal's *mens sana in corpore sano*.'

'And they build these healthy minds in healthy bodies exactly how?'

'They play a lot of *harpastum*.'

⚜⚜⚜

I caught Junius just as he was paying his polite farewells to the household and saw Drusus had gone to help Kahina plan the coming orders of platters of fruit, pastries, and roasted delicacies from the ovens of *tabernae* in our neighborhood.

'Verus?' I called, heading down the short corridor leading from the kitchen to the familiar rooms in which I'd grown up. I passed my own former room, where I'd once slept on a pallet next to my seamstress mother. A pair of laundry slaves used it now. As *dispensator*, Verus commanded the best room farther down, with a window that allowed breezes coming up the alley along the back wall to waft away cooking smells.

I nearly tripped over a carved wooden trunk in which he stored his best clothes, his toilet box for trips to the baths, and whatever souvenirs he kept from our trips together to supervise the Manlius estates. These business excursions had constituted his only chance for a bit of tourism. His collection of provincial knickknacks was second to none.

'Marcus!' Verus started from his pillow and pulled himself up from a mountain of quilted covers.

'What are you doing lying in the gloom, Verus?'

I borrowed a small flame from the kitchen to set his bedside lamp aglow. I nearly overturned a forest of glass vials, tiny spoons, cups, and ointments—the medical regime that kept him going. He hadn't had a shave in a week.

'You find me on my deathbed, boy.'

'Nonsense, you faker. That's quite a household you've built up out there while I've been gone. I can't wait to see the bills for this month of partying.'

'We needs them new slaves, Marcus. The boy's got friends who come over all the time and those rascals are always so hungry! I don't know where they put all that food. And every week the *Domina* hosts her prayer society—'

'Sh, sh, I'm not scolding you, Verus. To the contrary. Now, where's that wall-eyed slave boy, the one who helps you dress?'

'Well, out in the *triclinium* in a borrowed tunic, of course, pretending he's the ham wholesaler just so's he can scarf up all the sliced meats before anyone else.'

I could hardly make out the old man's hoarse whisper over the girlish shrieks of some scrubber getting tickled in the echoing rooms beyond the atrium.

'Listen to that, Verus. Remember just after the civil war? We had a few laundry boys and only Leo's nurse Lavinia to tend Kahina's wounds. That's a mob out there! I spotted a few new faces. You've rebuilt the Manlius household into a happy family. I thank you from the bottom of my heart, you old drunk.'

'Won't be the same with Leo and Kahina gone,' he muttered.

Kahina gone? I didn't correct him. Kahina was right to warn me Verus was getting things muddled.

'Leo's a big boy now. Let's get you out there, now. It'll be Leo's job to pretend to be you and it's your job as the Senator to give him orders for everyone's entertainment.'

'No, no, I'm not up to rehearsing now,' Verus muttered. When I got him to his feet, I realized his bowed back was no good at all anymore.

He held out my grandfather's precious walking stick. 'I've borrowed this from the Senator's study,' he said.

Unseen in the dim lamplight, I bit my lip. The shaft was made of carved oak with a gold and ivory top that had glinted in the Roman sun as he strode through the Forum to the Senate. It had been the slave-child Marcus' job to carry his wax tablet or scroll of notes while he could still make out his letters. Later, I'd helped the blind politician dismount from his litter and led him by the end of this very stick through the press of petitioners and market-goers.

When did the Senator guess that I was his bastard grandson? When I first arrived from Numidia with my mother to be bought off the platform of Roma's main slave market by my own father? I could never be the legal heir the Senator and his soldier son Atticus held out for all those years. The Senator had amended his will as soon as Leo was born to Kahina and raised into the air by the Commander seven days later, in Romans' ancient ritual of legitimacy.

But the Senator had provided for the displaced Numidian bastard. He made me the estates' chief administrator and the guardian of his legal heir. I watched over Leo in silence. I knew the infant was the Senator's great-grandson, not his grandson, by an accident of innocent love one night in a Numidian desert.

In the end, we were all of Manlius blood.

Verus misread my silence.

'You don't think the Senator would mind, do you, boy? I should have asked you first but after all these—'

'No, no, of course not, Verus, of course not. Keep the stick. A famous drinker like our Verus must always stagger home in style!'

—THE BURNING STAKES—

The decorating party went on and on, enlivened by our cook's bold complaints about the omelets being cold and the foodstuffs not what she, the 'Lady of the House,' expected. I tried to keep my sense of humor, even when I overheard too much arguing over who had to play myself.

A grinning litter bearer who served Kahina for her endless commutes to church lurched up to me. He wore a battered riding helmet with a bird feather stuck in its band that I'd bequeathed to Leo years ago. I flinched to think how carelessly the boy handed it over without a sentimental pause. I hinted that Drusus should play me instead.

But in truth, it was Verus' slip of the tongue about Kahina that had darkened my homecoming. I returned to the kitchen. Kahina was waving off platters of food and wiping her brow with a towel.

'Kahina. Verus just said something odd, about your leaving with Leo.'

'I told you, he's muddled these days. Leo doesn't need his mother trailing off to Antiochia with him.'

'Look me in the face.'

She lifted a face full of fear and sadness to me. Faint traces of my beautiful lover of one night—only one night!—were still there. But dutiful marriage to the Commander, my father, the long years of raising Leo during my rise to *centenarius* from posting to posting, not to mention enslavement, marked her face.

'What's the matter, Kahina? Verus is not *that* muddled.'

She threw up her hands in frustration. 'There are rumors, Marcus, rumors about Emperor Julian. No one knows what a pagan emperor might do to us. Some priests are predicting persecution and martyrdom.'

'Don't listen to such priests, or for that matter all those socialites who make such a public show of their faith, Kahina. I'll protect you if it comes to it.'

'Protect me? Like before?' She sounded bitter as well as scared. She reached back and pulled down her wide neckline. Hispanic slave drivers' whips had left her back rutted with thick, uneven scars.

I took her hand and ran my finger along the scar around the wrist where cruel shackles had nearly crippled her. Months of nursing and quiet had restored her ability to talk to us, to care for Leo, and to mix with understanding friends. But something had been lost forever—the lively light in her eyes when she first met me and a native intelligence that helped me overlook her naive determination to join the ranks of Donatist martyrs in our native province.

And now, I noticed, she was reverting to Numidian dialect, slurring her 's' into 'sh'—in a mix of Punic and Latin that marked her as a former servant from a colonial estate.

'Marcus, come with us back to Numidia—'

'So Verus was right. Who's *us*?'

'I can't live here, not once Leo's gone. Even now, he all but hides me in my bedroom these days from shame—what with his spouting all that reading to lord it over his *harpastum* teammates.'

'All boys his age push away their mothers—who's *us*?'

'Leo's not the only one with friends. I have friends, too, Marcus!'

'Socialites—!'

'—no! Humble Christian women. Some are planning a pilgrimage to North Africa as soon as the seaports open up in the spring. They asked me to retreat with them into the desert where God protects the truly faithful—before Julian's persecutions begin. It might be bad, like Domitian all over again. Like nothing our times have seen . . .' Her brown eyes widened.

Domitian's frightful persecutions of old had nothing on the gruesome Numidian martyr lore that had once inspired the girl Kahina. Underneath the worn out Roman house mistress, I caught a glimpse of the would-be saint, the runaway I embraced on the eve before her sacrificial leap with other Circumcellions to a death on the rocks below. Martyrdom seemed to be one of the few prospects that brightened her matronly face.

'The danger of civil war is over. Finally, the Empire has only one emperor from Britannia down to Jerusalem.'

'But the pagans' retribution—?' She withdrew her hand from mine and thrust both stubborn fists into her lap.

'Retribution for what? Constantius bolted our temples, no more. No one's going to hurt you again, Kahina. Forget the old nightmares.'

—THE BURNING STAKES—

Her voice came out strangled with resentment. 'You only want me here, guarding your precious Manlius household and treasure until the day you can retire to ... sit in the atrium on rainy days or in the garden in good weather ... or receive clients in the hall? You have that to look forward to, the great freedman Marcus Gregorianus Numidianus, a powerful *princeps* or some other empty title.'

I left her sitting there on the kitchen stool, brooding and angry, nursing her vague dreams of escaping Roma's depressing wet winter fogs and humid, feverish summers. She dreamt of Numidia's dry sun and clear plateau breezes.

⚜⚜⚜

'May I catch a last word before you go back to headquarters, Numidianus?'

It was Drusus, again, his hands washed clean of kitchen grease and his borrowed apron cast off for departure for home. He had at least one baby by his wife already and if I recalled right, another on the way.

'Forget my earlier hesitations, Drusus. Finish the arrangements with Ausonius. I'll inform Leo and Kahina as soon as Ausonius confirms his place. I'll be happier in Sirmium to know Leo is safe in Burdigala.'

'That's not it.'

He walked with me into the foyer. No servant was on hand to unbolt the gate. Our conversation would be truly private.

'One of Senator Manlius' most valuable scrolls is missing.'

'Which one?'

'I'm sorry to tell you, the early edition of *Speeches of Cicero*, annotated in the Senator's own hand.'

'Doubly valuable. When did you discover this?'

'First, Leo and I came upon Verus alone in the study a few weeks ago. He was acting furtively but I didn't say anything untoward in front of Leo. I didn't want to diminish Verus' authority over the boy any further.'

'Leo's acting disrespectful to others as well?'

Drusus shrugged it off. 'The boy's preparing to leave his home. I've seen it before with other students his age. Deep down they're very nervous, so they reject their parents and teachers ahead of time.'

'Practicing standing on their own.'

'Exactly. Anyway, Verus explained to me later that he'd found the study padlock broken open. The paint on the doorjamb was scraped, as if someone tried loosening the padlock ring screws with a knife.'

'I'm glad Verus cleared things up with you.'

Drusus whispered. 'After Verus alerted me about the lock, I went back and checked the study shelves. Only then I saw the scroll was gone. Verus acted very upset when I informed him.'

'I'm sure he was. Perhaps he forgot to lock the study door himself after doing his rounds?'

'And faked a break-in when he suspected there'd been an intruder? Or even committed the theft?'

'Don't be mad, Drusus! Steal a *Cicero*? Not Verus.'

'He's spending a fortune on medicines.'

'I noticed that when I looked in on him. Do you think he suspected one of Leo's rougher friends was after quick pocket money?'

'He certainly didn't want Leo to overhear.'

'Whew! That's quite a lot of pocket money if the thief finds the right buyer. Soren the Bookseller, for one, would love to get his hands on that *Cicero* marked up by one of the greatest orators of modern times.' I had a sudden thought. 'Drusus, who gave the orders to trim back our fig tree?'

Drusus smiled. 'I did. I said the tree needed pruning. I also want to believe a stranger broke in—a sneak thief climbing the tree to drop over the wall. I chopped off his route.'

'It's a clever thief who knows which scroll box holds one of our most priceless works.'

'I've secured the rest of your valuable volumes myself in the old treasure box that held the Senator's will. I shoved the box in with the wine and grain sacks.' He gestured to our storage room off the foyer.

'I'm lucky to have someone so alert on the spot, Antonius Drusus. I have to finish up at the Castra and return soon to my post in Sirmium. You'll have to keep a eye out.'

THE BURNING STAKES

'Don't worry too much. You can count on me. We'll find the scroll sooner or later, Numidianus. Something that precious can only realize its worth by moving through knowledgeable hands.'

The house rang tonight with cheerful jests and bustling activity. But underneath the holiday atmosphere, I sensed the end of a period in our lives. I couldn't leave everything to Drusus. What might we lose next?

Chapter 5, Gentlemen of the Jury

—THE TRAJAN BATHS—

The next afternoon, Junius found me scribbling hard to finish my report for Otho. He suggested we break for a session in the modest Castra gymnasium and baths. I wanted and needed the refreshment of hot steam purging my skin of the Roman winter fug of crowds and holiday excess but I excused myself from his companionship.

When a German or Gaul wants to mull over his thoughts, he retreats down some leafy forest path away from the smoke of village fires or heat of petty curial debates. But when a Roman *agens* wants to be alone, he shuns the Castra facilities and plunges into the hubbub of hundreds of bathers rubbing oiled shoulders at the Trajan Baths.

I strode down the chilly slope of the Caelian Hill and, reaching the Oppian plateau of Trajan's great recreational complex, crossed the grassy park and soon dropped my clothes into the hands of a changing room slave.

What could be more anonymous than this? There was a vast crowd. These were the best baths in the Empire—great chambers of health and hygiene echoing with holiday greetings and cheerful chatter. The underground heating almost burned the soles of my feet. A gust of dry heat billowed out of a sauna room as two potbellied strangers returned to the *caldarium*'s hot pool.

Such bliss; no one recognized me, basking my weary frame along a marble bench among the merchants, politicians, wholesalers, soldiers or whomever who could afford the entrance fee. And the citizens were outnumbered five to one by their personal retinues of slaves and scores of attendants armed with *strigiles*, towels, brushes, tweezers, and scissors—yes, yes, here was a forest a true Roman could get lost in to find peace.

I closed my eyes and luxuriated in anonymity.

'Why, Numidianus! That is *Centenarius* Numidianus under that towel, isn't it?'

My steamy cloud parted. I stared into the freshly scraped jaw of Otho. He was staring down at the grid of rigid white scars left by a Numidian whip across my shoulder blades.

'*Magister*—'

'No, man, don't get up. Rank means nothing when we stretch out here, butts to the breeze. Anyway, I had every intention of catching you before you returned to Sirmium. I had a letter from an old friend in Antiochia—one more influential than ever now—your ward's prospective teacher, the philosopher Libanius.'

'Ah. He wrote to you about our application to his school?'

'Are you surprised? Roma runs on references, for better or worse, though our new emperor may elevate merit to its proper place.'

'We can only hope so, *Magister*.'

Otho had taken me by the upper arm and was ushering me off to the toilets. It seemed we were to confer not only butts-to-the-breeze, but butts-to-the-marble as well.

'We hope to entrust the Consul Taurus to your personal escort as far as Sirmium for the coming tribunal, Numidianus. Let's give your stay at headquarters a few more days to wait for news of his arrest?'

'Conducting Taurus to the East would be a sad privilege, *Magister*. Apodemius is not the only one to think Taurus innocent of any possible crime. I shall assign my best men to continue with him toward Constantinopolis.'

'Farther than that, I'm afraid. We've learned that his hearing will be held in Chalcedon.'

'Chalcedon?' I'd escorted Caesar Gallus through this suburb in 354. 'That's a mean, shabby location. Why the gods in Chalcedon?'

Otho finished his shit with his trademark efficiency. He rinsed out the *spongia*-on-a-stick in the gutter of fresh water rushing past our bare feet. The sea sponge hardly seemed soiled, as if Otho's efficient administrative reforms included some improved technique for defecation.

'Let's take a cool swim,' he said, 'and I'll explain what your poor client Taurus will be facing.'

First we did a couple of laps up and down the *frigidarium* waters. I was careful to lag half a length behind Otho's powerful stroke. It wasn't hard. I would always be, athletically speaking, a son of the Numidian desert plateau, more comfortable in a saddle than a swimming pool.

Otho seemed determined to tire himself out within some fixed time limit. He was soon panting. He flung both arms over the marble edge of the basin and turned a flushed face to mine.

'You see, *Agens*, Taurus' trial is to be held behind closed doors under heavy guard and the watchful eyes of Constantius' Ioviani and Herculiani commanders.'

'How judicious of Julian to include the crack troops of his defeated enemy. But still, why Chalcedon?'

'So Julian can hold himself aloof, keep his hands clean of any factional ugliness to come. Holding the trial across the Strait of Bosporus from Constantinopolis avoids the appearance of interference—'

'And any hope of imperial rescue. Has anyone else been named for trial?'

Otho lifted himself out of the water by his powerful forearms. I tried to match his sleek grace. He was not as tall as I but constructed along the lines of the Greek ideal. A single loose towel tied around his hips did nothing to reduce his animal authority. How different from our goat-like emperor, covered in uncombed beard and ungainly body hair, shoulders stooping like a student's under his over-polished armor, and his thick lower lip stammering on and on.

Even Julian's most loyal adjutants called him 'the chattering mole.'

Otho scanned the passing bathers and lowered his voice for fear of being overheard:

'This affair will not end with Constantius' consuls or that bastard Catena.'

I leaned closer, unclear why he'd single me out for confidence.

He chuckled, 'Since Julian reached Constantinopolis, official traffic from the East has doubled. I'm receiving fresh updates each day. But the information is incomplete. Still, if we can't yet predict whom else will be charged or with what, then let's examine Julian's jury selection for clues to our *schola*'s future. I'd be grateful for your comments.'

'Of course. Who chairs the jury?'

'Praetorian Prefect of the East, Saturninus Secundus Salutius. You nod, Numidianus. Do you know him?'

'I met Salutius in Julian's Gallic camp years ago. Salutius is a Gaul, an esteemed and well-educated pagan. He won't preside over injustice. Consul Taurus is sure to survive unscathed.'

'Perhaps. Wait until I name the other judges.'

Otho grabbed a nearby cup of *strigiles* and lined them up in ranks down the marble curb in front of our bare toes.

'This wooden one is Jovinus, soon to be *Magister Equitum* for Illyria.'

'Wooden indeed. A Constantius loyalist, Jovinus made no strong impression on me in Mopsucrenae, but he can do little harm.'

'Three, ex-consul General Arbitio, another Constantius man.'

I hunched over my feet, staring down at the pointed steel bath tool standing in for that foul enemy of truth.

'*Magister*, you must know General Arbitio is the worst kind of ambitious intriguer. Arbitio was a fickle flatterer of Constantius. He was a coward who hung back from Alemanni attacks to let brave tribunes die for him on the front lines. When it served his purpose, he was an ally of that slimy eunuch Eusebius on the *consistorium*. Both were determined to bring down any rival general who stood in the late emperor's favor—first General Silvanus, then General Ursicinus, and finally dull-witted General Barbatio.'

I leaned back on the bench and pulled my towel tighter around my shoulders. What game could Julian be playing by befriending his enemy, Arbitio?

Otho laid down a fourth *strigil*, of bronze, 'the Alemannic officer Agilo,' a fifth in rusting lead for 'Commander Nevitta,' and another in green stone, 'Mamertinus.'

—THE BURNING STAKES—

Otho added, 'By the way, Nevitta and Mamertinus are to be Julian's consuls for 362.'

I detected a pattern but hesitated to speculate out loud.

'Go ahead, Numidianus. I've read your reports. You're capable of a useful interpretation.'

'As a fellow pagan, Salutius will be Julian's key front man. But apart from Salutius and Mamertinus, all the others are powerful military veterans—two loyal to Constantius and two to Julian. So far, there's balance, but you say the only observers will be officers of Constantius' crack legions, the Ioviani and Herculiani? Then I anticipate that General Arbitio will dominate the proceedings.'

'Why? The others are just placeholders and stooges?'

'Far from it. But Julian needs our divided army to re-unite and only Arbitio can cajole reluctant commanders into supporting Julian. Julian must appease Arbitio above all. He will give him a free hand and Arbitio has no loyalties to anything but his own ambition.'

'Your conclusion?'

'Julian knows the imperial diadem fell into his lap too easily. He's staging a military show trial against certain vulnerable courtiers to placate Constantius' army. Any coming arrests may be men of integrity who threatened Arbitio or offended the military elite.'

'Thank you, Numidianus. That was my own hunch but unless more men are accused, we can't test our theory. Consul Taurus did nothing wrong in fleeing to the shelter of his emperor, even if he didn't make it in time. Consul Florentius believed in the policies he recommended—the extra Gallic taxes, the troops for Persia. They aren't criminals.'

I gazed at a wall mosaic of grape harvesters. In the end we all reap what we sow.

'*Magister* Otho, the worst part is that our own *schola* must execute the warrants and deliver innocent men to such "justice." I wish we could keep our hands clean of political games we don't understand.'

'Julian knows our *schola* was a favorite tool of Constantius' reign. He must test our loyalty,' Otho said.

One or two famous faces had recognized or greeted Otho during our quiet exchange. Now his manicured hand swooped down and tossed the clutch of scrapers back into their holder. For a minute, I had the impression he was afraid these passersby might divine our sensitive deliberations from that innocent row of sticks.

⚔⚔⚔

Freshened in body but unsettled in mind, I tipped the slave for my garments, wrapped up warm, and sauntered out of the complex across Trajan's cold and empty gardens. There was no hurry now—not if I had to wait to add a terrified Taurus to my baggage.

A low rumble of human excitement in the distance floated on the breeze rising up the Oppian's slope from the direction of the old Forum. Anxious for any kind of distraction, I turned away from the Caelian Hill and headed down the familiar streets and alleys toward the river. Within half an hour, I found myself pushing and shoving my way into a mushrooming mass of Romans thronging the public space.

All eyes were strained to make out the entrance to the Senate House.

'What's happening? Did Brutus stab Julius Caesar again?' I asked a chubby butcher in a blood-streaked apron. His thick fist was still clutched a gristly meat cleaver. Whatever drew this emotional audience, it would have to be something dramatic to lure a sharp-eyed meat vendor away from his hooks and slabs. Any street urchin might snitch a nice side of lamb while our butcher wasn't looking.

He turned a tear-streaked face to me, his ruddy cheeks gleaming in the late afternoon's fading sunlight.

'The gods will bless us with peace from now on,' gulping a happy sob.

'How so?'

'You haven't heard? Julian is restoring the Altar of Victory to us. They're bringing the statue into the city now on an oxcart by special dispensation of the curfew against heavy vehicles. Julian wants to put her back into the Senate while there's still daylight for us all to witness her arrival.'

'May the gods bless our new emperor,' I murmured, moved to the quick. How well I recalled that black night in 357 when Verus and I had huddled behind the Forum's lonely pillars watching Constantius' furtive legion steal our protectoress away under cover of military blankets and folded pennants.

I watched there for more than an hour, soaking up the Roman citizenry' relief and gratitude. What a pity that Verus was too lame and befuddled to get down here in time to cheer on the soldiers as they mortared the goddess back into position.

But it would cheer him up to hear that our great city enjoyed her protection once again. I resolved that, once our old *dispensator* was feeling better, I'd bring him down by litter and make sure he saw the Altar standing with orb and wings aloft returned to her marble podium.

I worked myself free of the crush in the direction of the Esquiline and maneuvered through hordes of shoppers still perusing the *macellum* food stalls for *garum*, leeks, onions, olives, honey, preserved fruits, fish, sausages—the common stuff of our evening repasts.

Incense sellers wafted their jasmine sticks in my face and sandal makers dangled fresh wares still stinking of the tanners from tall sticks they propped into cracks in the paving.

In Roma, anything was for sale—from the cheapest penis amulets or pottery god statuettes with flaking paint to diaphanous silk and gold-threaded brocade that cost more per bolt than those naked Armenian slaves chained to a nearby platform overhead.

A sinkhole of sadness opened up in my soul. I loved it all but would soon have to leave again. These were the smells and clamor of my years as a scampering slave running errands or leading the blind Senator with a solemn on my childish features set in a comical scowl I thought worthy of the great rhetorician's reputation.

This afternoon distant Sirmium seemed only a paltry Pannonian capital offering miniature imitations of everything that was great about my boyhood home.

Perhaps it was the ordinariness of this particular market that made me most nostalgic. The true luxury shops sat north of the river on the old Campus Martius. Right now, during the days of Saturnalia, thousands of wax or pottery *sigillaria* figurines dangled over those streets for gift-givers doing last-minute rush shopping. Old voting cells from ancient Republican days were now shop stalls displaying younger slaves, far more beautiful than these Armenians. Hawkers would be praising the allure of the finest pearls and gems, precious goblets of Frankish glass, Corinthian bronzes and . . . valuable books. Soren the Bookseller kept a modern shop up on the Campus Martius jostling in a row with other antiquarians of widespread fame.

But I knew that was only where Soren fleeced eager collectors from out of town. His knowledgeable daughter tended that showcase for him and when a visitor didn't know the value of a fine *codex* or scroll on offer, her black-lined lashes batted at him until he did.

My boots had reached what was left of the old Argiletum, the northeast road that led away from the *fora* into the seedy depths of the Subura.

No, Soren's real base was around the corner—a mean ground floor office among the brothels and run-down *tabernae* in the heart of these slums. Here he waited, crouched like a cat outside a mouse hole, close and convenient to the aristocrats' houses on the Esquiline and Caelian hills. Scions of Roma's old families, on discovering that centuries of living above their means had left them down-at-heels, could slip downhill, hoping Soren would convert their ancestors' first-century vellum, parchment, and papyrus into fourth-century gold.

'I know you, stranger,' the Greek said, as I thrust my boot under his grille just before he padlocked it tight for the day.

'Soren, it has been too many years for you to know me.'

He smiled with what teeth he had left. 'I never forget a bookworm with a North African accent,' he said. 'Years go by. You go by—passing my shop front. You are not the only man who sees things. I see things. I see people coming, going, coming, going.'

'Roma is a big city.'

—THE BURNING STAKES—

'No, Roma is a small village for a man with two good eyes who knows how to watch. Little African bastards grow big, too important to stop and talk to old Soren the Bookseller.'

'You still talk like a Greek fresh off the boat. Who would believe you deal in the Greats?'

'And you wear insignia of an *agens centenarius*, little Marcus. Slave boy that once came to buy fine books with old Senator now stands head taller than me.'

'I'm looking for the Senator's *Cicero* speeches, Soren, the scroll you sold him decades ago.'

Soren pretended surprise. 'It's on the market?'

'If not, it may soon be. Are you handling it? Who took it? Does the Manlius House have to buy it back a second time?'

The old Greek brushed some flakes of papyrus off his much-mended, overbleached tunic. 'At 361 prices, dear Marcus. No! Soon 362 prices! But . . . I don't have it.'

'Who does?'

He shrugged. 'I don't know.'

He knew something. He avoided my gaze, fussed with his rattling padlock, and tightened an old-fashioned thin belt. He seemed to have aged a hundred years or none at all—Soren had seemed as antique as his wares from the very first day I looked up to watch him haggle with the Senator over a rare volume by Plinius the Elder.

I embraced his hunched shoulders with a more than 'friendly' squeeze.

'You never had the reputation of handling stolen goods, Soren. Why start now?'

He shifted out from under my arm. 'If I hear of Chickpea's Speeches, how do I reach you?'

'A message to the Castra will find me.'

He nodded, keeping his eyes on the passersby. 'Sure.'

'You know I'll pay top price to get the Senator's marginalia back in his study where it belongs.'

The old man's face clouded over with something he didn't want to say. If the Cicero scroll had been in his possession, he would have offered me some thick retsina and started our bargaining with the steepest price possible, right then and there.

Instead, he muttered, 'Sometimes, little Marcus, a *curiosus* can be too curious for his own good. In my long experience, some mysteries about missing treasures are best left unsolved.'

※※※

Light drizzle of the early evening fell like mule's piddle as I reached the Castra front gate. I had to wait far too long for one of our sentries to rush out from shelter to admit me, but I tipped him nonetheless. I was feeling light-hearted again.

My political exchange with Otho at the Baths had left me hoping my place in the new *schola* hierarchy might be stronger than before my arrival from Sirmium. I'd also put Soren and his network on notice that our Cicero had been burgled. And my exhilaration at seeing Julian liberating us pagans from Constantius' tiresome Christian constrictions on the Altar of Victory buoyed my spirits. Had our Temple of Jupiter Redux not been bolted shut for years, I would have dodged straight in to offer the gods my grateful prayers.

The Temple stood in deep shadow tonight, overwhelmed by a classroom building erected between the outer wall and the Temple entrance a century ago. Modern times had left a walkway scarcely the width of one man to get to the old temple's double doors.

Something caught my eye. I peered through the drizzle. Was the temple's left door fixed tight?

I squeezed my way under the eaves. The door was no longer bolted. Though it stood closed, it hung uneven with its twin. Whether someone had unlocked or forced the rusty padlock was hard to tell without a lamp.

I eased the heavy oak wide open and thrust my head inside. 'Anyone here?'

My voice echoed off ancient granite. My nostrils filled with the scents of dirty marble, mucky residue from centuries of incense and offerings, and the rot of old wood and unwashed altar hangings.

And human sweat. Fresh and nervous perspiration, as distinct as the smell of your friend in full armor moments before a battle charge. Pungent, acrid, fearful.

I unsheathed my *pugio* and inched into the Temple, shutting the door softly behind me.

'Who's there?'

I wasn't worried I wouldn't see a stranger attack. I was sure to smell this one coming. The hideaway hadn't bathed for days.

He rose from his hiding place. I could make out the very tall outline of a cloaked man, his face hidden deep under his hood. I heard the slide of metal against belt ring. He, too, had drawn a weapon.

'I'm *Centenarius* Numidianus. Declare yourself.'

The man stood for a long time in silence. Neither of us moved.

I waited with a sense of protection from the invisible gods around us. The worst thing that could happen to me would be to trip as I closed and padlocked the door behind me.

After many tense minutes of determined stillness, he shifted in his boots and asked low and clear: 'Numidianus? The North African freedman of the late Commander Gregorius?'

'Do I know you?'

'No, you do not. Though too many know me by sight alone. Are you the same Numidianus who testified on Emperor Julian's behalf during the Gallus treason trials?'

'Who are you? Show your face.'

'The same Numidianus whose *spatha* defended General Silvanus against Ursicinus' assassins?'

'Yet failed to save his life or clear his name. Step forward. Drop your weapons.'

'You're the *agens* Numidianus who carried Silvanus' adjutant Proculus in your own arms to safety from Catena's claws and whips?'

'Yet good and honest Proculus died of his tortures in bed some months later.'

'You call yourself *centenarius*. I heard it was a *biarchus* Numidianus who escorted the Alemannic *rex* Chnodomarius to sanctuary here in the Castra?'

'Chnodomarius died within these walls of congested lungs and a broken heart. I often fail. Your praise makes me suspicious.'

'Oh, there are darker stories about you, Numidianus, but I don't listen to slander.'

He sheathed his sword. With his striker and flint, he set a lamp going. The dank temple danced with the shadows of painted statues, memorial busts, and ritual basins. But the most startling shadow of all was the stranger's: his looming figure poised behind the temple's long altar cast a silhouette up one wall and halfway across the ceiling.

'If you are indeed that Numidianus, then look upon the face of your fugitive consul, Flavius Taurus.'

Even had he been of normal height, he could never have stayed fugitive much longer with that distinctive face—a telltale black birthmark the width of a *solidus* spanned his unshaven, haggard right cheek. This signature was sure to be part of the description sent out to all city gates and layover stations between Roma and adjacent provinces.

'You come here to give yourself up to our escort? Why hide in an abandoned temple?'

'Not to surrender! Never! I was promised I would be safe here from arrest.'

'By whom? Who let you in? When?'

'I cannot name him.'

'Whatever his name, he was a disloyal friend to both you and the Castra. I'm the agent assigned to escort you as far as Sirmium to your hearing in Chalcedon.'

'Chalcedon? No! No! Tell no one you found me here. Let me slip away.'

'You won't get far, Consul. The roads are watched. The *mansiones*, even the meanest *mutatio*, has your description.'

He touched his cheek in an instinctive gesture. He'd spent a long childhood hiding that disfigurement from bullies.

'The street says Constantius loyalists hold out in Aquileia. I can make a run for it.'

'Aquileia won't hold out for much longer, Julian will see to that. But you have nothing to fear from a fair tribunal. The warrant for your arrest dismayed every good citizen who heard it.

Your reputation is impeccable. The *magister* of this *schola* vouches for it himself.'

'Yes, yes.' Taurus nodded as if he'd heard Apodemius himself. 'Numidianus, you must ride the whole distance with me. You must vouch for me before the jury, as you did for others.'

'How could I testify on your behalf when we never crossed paths?'

'That doesn't matter! What matters is that they believe you. There have long been rumors that once, on the Emperor's birthday in Arelate, you even defied Catena to his face. You defended the wretched rebel followers of Magnentius. Surely you can do as well for me, an honest consul, a hundred times more loyal to the Empire than any rebel! Or do this for my innocent sons—Armonius, Eutychianus, and Aurelianus—'

He suddenly dropped across the cold flagstones and extended his hands toward my boots in prostration.

'I am innocent of treason, *Agens*. All men who know me regard me as a loyal servant of the Empire. When I was up in Gallia, it was I—'

'Who told you to hide here?'

'One I trust.'

I hesitated, silenced by Taurus' abject humiliation. A Roman consul lay stretched in supplication at the feet of a lowly freedman. But he was a Christian Easterner of modest origins, a former notary who had followed Constantius to the West. And I was raised a Roman in whom aristocratic Manlius blood flowed. That ancient line called me to my imperial obligation. Yet that same sense of honor held me back from handing over an innocent Christian politician to an uncertain army court presided over by a pagan Gallic *literatus* Salutius and an amoral general like Arbitio.

'I must do my duty, Consul Flavius Taurus,' I said. 'I'm leaving now to collect the Castra guards who will place you in detention until our departure for Sirmium. I can't accompany you beyond my posting, but I will treat you well according to *schola* protocol at all times, in accordance with my training out of respect for your station.'

He could have attacked me or sobbed in despair. He rose to his full height. He had detected the odd, slow precision of my statement. He had picked up my hint. He understood me. I was leaving him to choose between his sense of honor and his instinct for self-preservation.

I continued: 'This will take me five minutes. Five minutes before I return with the warrant. Do you understand me, Consul?'

'I do understand you, Numidianus. You will return in five minutes.'

'Five minutes by that water clock outside the main building.'

He'd already seized an embossed leather sack of his personal belonging from behind the altar to make his getaway as soon as I turned my back.

'Your wife will miss you greatly, Consul.'

'She and my sons are waiting not far away.'

So he had been hiding here, with his wife and sons positioned somewhere in the city, all of them promised assistance—but from whom?

'I repeat. I return in five minutes.'

'Thank you, Numidianus.'

I went outside, closed the oak door behind me and breathed in the fresh, wet breezes brushing the Esquiline. There was no need to monitor any water clock. I pulled my cloak tighter and considered where I might find Ahenobarbus.

I'd got only twenty feet across the compound when a dozen guards rounded the main building in the drizzle and trotted straight at me. Something had gone wrong.

There would be no five minutes' margin for the Consul's escape. Taurus would not see his family again.

The guards brushed past me and squeezed themselves in a column like a determined snake down the narrow passage to the narrow Temple doors. They dragged Taurus from his sanctuary, four men on each side, so that he had no hope of wresting himself free, though he stood easily a head taller than the Castra guard commander.

He spotted me backing off in confusion into the thickening rain. He glared at me, eyes bulging with fury at my assumed betrayal.

'Damn you, Numidianus, *Curiosus* Scum!' he spat out. 'Your enemies were right to call you a killer—killer of Constans, of

Magnentius, of Gallus. You, upright? Now I know which stories to believe!'

Dozens of *agentes* were ending their day and crossing the wet courtyard in their woolen *paenulae* for a meal or a workout in our gymnasium. Heads turned and stared at our guards strong-arming Taurus past the main building. With that birthmark, many realized who he was.

Taurus was still damning me as they dragged him to the detention cells in the far corner of our compound underneath the shadow of the Aqua Claudia, the cells where the defeated Chnodomarius had died.

I looked at the anxious, embarrassed expressions turning away from me as my fellow *agentes* hurried away on their business. It was bad enough to be publicly cursed by one of the two most senior civil servants of our empire. But worse was what they did not know.

Who was his 'friend' with knowledge of our gates, our guards, and our neglected temple? That 'friend' had promised Taurus sanctuary inside our Castra—and then betrayed him.

Now I caught the blame.

Chapter 6, The Empty Cage

—THE CASTRA PEREGRINA—

I retreated to our now desolate canteen undergoing yet more upgrading into Otho's main meeting hall. Half the room was curtained off to keep dust from flying into the food. Plasterers were covering old graffiti and ribald 'murals' sketched on the walls by generations of *agentes* in from the field.

They were working fast, despite the damp weather. Foot by foot, our unofficial service history was disappearing under the scrapers' iron trowels and hawks. I'm not an overly sentimental man, but my favorite joke was a charcoal cartoon of a muscular, shaven-headed Gaudentius in a woman's tunic and dainty slippers batting his long lashes at Constantius II lounging lopsided on his dais.

I winced as one wide swipe of wet plaster eclipsed half of what I would forever after mourn as a loss to great art.

The other half of the room remained open for supper service but smelt of lime and whitewash. There were just enough tables for a dozen men to eat and move on—the ramshackle space no longer echoed with late night conviviality.

This evening half a dozen riders sat in a cluster murmuring over two square tables shoved together. Heads bent over their dirty pottery dishes, they dropped their voices when I settled down at as discreet a distance as possible in that truncated space. One young man sitting with his back to me still wore boots splattered with mud. His waterproof *sagum* dripped rainwater over a bench between us.

These youngsters needn't have worried about a *centenarius* eavesdropping on their novice road adventures. I'd heard all possible tales and hot tips during my long stint riding the postal circuits a decade ago. Was there still that balding whore offering her contorted 'rare Indian specialty' along the road between Lissus and Dyrrhachium? Or the lonely crossing over the

Rhodanus where the ferryman made you pay *before* embarking and then *again* before getting off? Or the gambling den in Cularo where the dice were as crooked as a dog's hind leg? . . . Well, there must be lots of those all over.

If there were few diners tonight, there were more than enough slaves—washing up dishes, scrubbing the floor, and making all the impatient signs of a kitchen crew keen for sleep.

'Get me a bowl of *puls*, very hot and very thick,' I told a server who'd avoided my eye for a good two or three minutes while he polished the tarnish off a dented silver pitcher. My socks and boots were wet. My stomach rumbled, cold and empty, with nothing but Taurus' curses to churn over. I must be the only *agens* in the entire headquarters who still heard the consul's angry voice reverberating off our stone enclosures.

The lentils came with a crust congealed on top and a hard, single flatbread for scooping out the bottom of the bowl.

As I wrenched the bread in two, I overheard someone drop the name, 'Evagrius.'

Another rider corrected the first: 'No, you're confusing him with Evagrius, a friend of Emperor Julian. The one on your list is . . .'

They noticed me prick up my ears and huddled closer. I listened harder, fixing my gaze on the notice board in hope of a *mensa secunda* that was still edible.

The young men rose to their feet and, ignoring my nod of acknowledgement, shuffled past my stool and pulled their heavy hoods forward over their brows against the rain now drumming on the courtyard paving.

I recognized one rider. I reached out without warning and stopped him hard in his tracks as the other five filed out the door.

'Decebalus. Thracian, right? Salona station?'

'Yes, Centenarius Numidianus. I arrived this afternoon with state mail for the *Magister*.'

'Business about the mint?'

'No . . .'

I tightened my grip on his forearm for not acknowledging me earlier. I pulled him down on the stool next to mine. He gave me a sheepish smile. It was more fun to gossip with fellow *equites* than keep a weary superior company on a wet, winter's evening far from the Saturnalia feast back home.

'More urgent mail?'

'Urgent enough to keep me riding relay pace in from the coast after a miserable winter crossing. I'll be glad of a dry mattress. That meal was lousy. Have all the decent cooks taken off?'

'What did it say?' I tapped a tin spoon on my empty glass.

'What did what say, *Centenarie*?'

'Your mail. What was it?'

'A letter via your Sirmium office from the Naissus station, sealed fast, tied with thick embossed ribbons, addressed to the *Magister*.'

'I won't ask you a third time, *Eques*. What did it say?'

He swallowed and examined his muddy boots. In the hierarchy of the *schola*, we all served the Empire. We also sought to please the incoming management. But down on the level of the *Cursus Publicus* where pay was thin and favors flourished, our nervous Thracian answered to me first. If he didn't satisfy my curiosity, he might spend many more blistered years short of sleep and riding a squeaking wet saddle.

He glanced behind him. The fading laughter of his pals told us they'd rushed across the courtyard to dodge under the eaves of the long dormitory barrack. We sat, left to our privacy by indifferent slaves busy eating their very hot, fresh *puls* and soft, steaming bread in a back room behind the ovens and grills.

'More warrants for arrests, *Centenarie*.'

'I see. Call me Marcus Numidianus. Warrants for whom?'

He relaxed a jot. 'I didn't recognize all of the names. Top Constantius officials, according to one of my mates there.' He glanced at the vacated stools next to us.

'But you remember the names?' Here was a better test of his Castra training than the endurance of sore buttocks.

He cleared his throat. 'Saturninus, a former steward of the palace?'

'Yes, and—?'

'Cyrinus, a notary. And a certain Evagrius, but I wasn't sure of the title from the handwriting.'

'Most likely Evagrius, Constantius' Count of the Privy Purse. The other Evagrius is a pal of our new emperor. That's it?'

'As far as I can recall . . . Marcus Numidianus.'

'Thank you, Decebalus. Go join your friends.'

'I'm keen to do my best.' He hesitated before rising. 'You won't tell *Magister* Otho I read his mail, will you?'

I patted his shoulder. 'No need. He assumes it, Decebalus.'

※※※

Was that still true? Or did I speak out of turn? Apodemius had encouraged his couriers to read everything to learn as much as they could. We were trained to re-secure communications with seals copied from official instruments swiped off desks across the wide Empire.

But had this changed? Perhaps it wasn't just the canteen walls that were being whitewashed. Did Otho's tighter administration mean more deference, discretion, and obedience than under Apodemius?

Already the change of regime was dramatic. Decebalus' mailbag warrants for respected officials rolling off the tablets of Chalcedon's scribes unnerved me anew. Emperor Julian was ambitious—even ruthless—keen to add his name to the history books. But I thought I knew the man by now. Wasn't justice one of his much-vaunted principles? Surely he didn't want to start off with a reputation as an unjust tyrant.

Yet it seemed that the names of loyal imperial servants were tumbling fast.

A gutter's worth of rainwater hit my face as I exited the canteen. A relieved kitchen slave slammed the door on my heels.

My next move was to await Otho's disposition of the prisoner Consul Taurus. I would spend the night on a borrowed cot in one of the officers' rooms a corridor away from Decebalus and his friends.

I lit a lamp, checked that the bedding was clean and dry, and lay down in my tunic and trousers. I left the tiny oil flame burning.

I must have dropped off fast and deep. It took me many seconds to resurface from groggy sleep and reach for my *pugio*, only to find my intruder was only Ahenobarbus dragging a wooden stool to my bedside.

'Something wrong? Why did you sneak up on me like that?'

He laid his head in his hands. Even after all these years, the *princeps*' coarse auburn hair was thick as ever, but trimmed closer than usual to his scalp. 'Oh, Marcus, you shouldn't have. You really shouldn't have.'

'Shouldn't have what?'

'Cornered that Thracian kid who delivered the last packet from Salona.'

'What do you know about that?'

'You were overheard.'

'No one was there!'

'You, of all people, Marcus, should never discount the long ears of slaves.'

'The kitchen staff? Spying on their own *agentes*? Why would I guess that? Spying for whom?'

He shook his head, as if saving his breath. 'Another message just came in, an hour ago.'

Many hours must have elapsed since I sank into exhausted oblivion.

'Two more names,' he whispered. 'Florentius Nigrinianus—'

'No!' I bolted upright. 'Florentius Nigrinianus is the most honest and reliable of officials. He was Acting *Magister Officiorum* during our investigation of the Silvanus affair. Without his summoning the expert scribes and *quaestores*, the forgeries in Silvanus' name would never have been exposed.'

'The same man. No crime could be found against him but he inquired into the loss of Amida to the Persians—'

'And that's the army's sorest molar.'

Ahenobarbus nodded. 'His sentence has already been handed down. Imprisonment on the island of Bua off the Dalmatian coast.'

'How can that be? So fast? He'll appeal—'

'Julian has given the tribunal exceptional powers to judge and execute without delay or appeal.'

By now I was wide awake. I splashed chill water on my face from a basin in the corner.

'The other name?'

'Palladius, a former bigwig in the East.'

'It can't be, Ahenobarbus. That Palladius has been a *homo privatus* for years now. He only came out of retirement to make the official offering to Zeus during the '56 Olympic Games. Besides, he's a diehard pagan. What could Julian have against an old-timer like Palladius?'

Ahenobarbus sat, hands clasped, head bowed, weighing his thoughts. Long years as our chief *ducenarius agens* in Constantius' court had made him a very circumspect man.

'Marcus, do you recall I escorted Apodemius and you into the *consistorium* the morning you arrived in Mediolanum from Pula? Apodemius threw Caesar Gallus' red slippers to the foot of the dais as proof he'd carried out Constantius' execution order?'

'Of course.'

'Do you recall the expression on the Emperor's face?'

I tried to shrug it off. 'Ahenobarbus, no one could read that man's wooden features for four decades.'

'Constantius told the *consistoriani* present that he'd sent a second order to spare his cousin's life.'

Ahenobarbus waited for my reaction. I picked up my wet *paenula* lying in a puddle on the floor where I'd dropped it. I folded it with care.

The lamp flame flickered shadows across my visitor's creased brow. 'I can read your thoughts, Numidianus.'

'You can't. I don't know them myself. Are you warning me of something?'

'Palladius became *Magister Officiorum* in Constantius' court in late 355.'

'Which must be why I was left with only an acting MO during the Silvanus business that autumn. So?'

'—until suddenly he retired for good. Do you know *why* Palladius retired faster than a *ballista* bolt?'

'Should I? It's late. I'm wearying of these riddles, old friend. Surely even a *princeps* needs his sleep.'

'Because Palladius' previous post was *Magister Officiorum* to Caesar Gallus. Palladius was an Antiochene *notarius*, assigned to the Caesar's *comitatus*. Rumors spread that Palladius poisoned Constantius' mind with damning stories about little cousin Gallus that were leaked to the *consistoriani* in Mediolanum.'

'You mean reports that reached Arbitio, Eusebius, and the others?'

'Exactly, prompting Emperor Constantius to send you, Marcus, to investigate specific accusations against Gallus and his demon wife.'

'But Palladius was hardly alone in that. There were others tattling on Gallus—Thalassius, Barbatio—lots of officials were disgruntled or disgusted by the Constantines' blood thirst. Neptune's Balls, Constantia decorated her private suite with jeweled whips and golden handcuffs.'

My cell felt dank and cold. I lit my brazier and digested Ahenobarbus' warning. Barbatio had gone to his death predicting that the Gallus affair would be my downfall but I said nothing of Barbatio's curse to my fellow *agens* tonight. Ahenobarbus should not think I gave any weight to the dimwitted general's hysteria.

'You don't admit any link between Chalcedon and the Gallus execution could be worrying, Numidianus?'

'No, I don't. And I'm not letting the strange new ways around here muddy my thinking,' I told him. 'Maybe I feel a changed atmosphere because I've been away in Sirmium for so long. I come back to headquarters and what do I find? Canteen slaves reporting on us *agentes* inside our own walls? Daily reports to be hand-copied in triplicate? Obligatory meetings every single morning? Small Group deliberations?'

'It's Otho's improvement, efficiency, modernization—'

'It's excessive, my senior friend. It leads to overthinking everything. Let's keep this simple. Otho and I agreed in the Baths of Trajan only this afternoon that this Chalcedon tribunal is about Julian winning over the Eastern Army—Constantius' Herculiani and Ioviani commanders will be the privileged observers. More to the point, it's about Julian appeasing the one powerful enemy most likely to challenge his reign—General Arbitio. So Palladius got up Arbitio's nose somehow.'

Ahenobarbus rose, shaking his head. 'It may not be just about the army, Marcus.'

'Then it's about officials who offended Julian when he was the upstart, unblooded caesar in Gallia. Julian arrived up there full of himself. He was disrespectful to old veterans—military and civilian. They gave it right back to him for as long as they could.'

'All right, Marcus.'

'Wait, Ahenobarbus. If you think this is about Gallus, let's go talk to Apodemius right now. It's the best hour of his working day.'

'We're not to take business to the old man anymore, Marcus. Strict orders from *Magister* Otho.'

'Even if your theory affects him more than anyone?'

'Strictest orders.'

Ahenobarbus pulled on his cloak. 'Please don't tell anyone we talked like this. Or we might find ourselves writing yet another report.'

'Not even the canteen baker.'

He managed a weak smile and, pulling his hood low, dodged back out into the heavy rain.

※※※

The rain clouds dispersed in fresh gusts of winds howling like fallen gods through the *fora* and whistling through the bare trees overhanging our walls.

I closed my eyes but heard each man's name, one after another, read off the warrants of my imagination. One minute these names sounded like the pounding of marching feet approaching in the dark. Then the names fell like the dripping of a broken fountain in an abandoned villa. Taurus, Florentius, Florentius Nigrinianus, Evagrius, Saturninus, Cyrinus, Palladius—all civil servants of varying character but unswerving loyalty to Constantius. Not one was guilty of wanton cruelty like Paulus Catena.

Getting up was better than this tormented doze. I crept out of the *agentes*' dormitory unremarked. My hooded cloak disguised me from nosy minions. The quieter eye of the storm had passed and the rain was worse than before. I crossed the courtyard and crouched in an alcove of old stone below the familiar window of Apodemius' study.

Behind a grille, his thick glass pane distorted a lamp flame moving around his rooms. I couldn't detect a figure but I guessed from the shifting shadows our old *magister* was crisscrossing his cluttered rooms with unusual agility.

—THE BURNING STAKES—

Should I disobey Ahenobarbus and Otho? Could I pay my own 'courtesy call' in these small hours of the night?

Footsteps on stone—probably hobnailed *caligae*—warned me someone was about to discover my guilty vigil. I hunkered down under my hood and pressed myself deeper into the alcove like the guilty slave boy stealing kitchen treats I had once been. I felt ridiculous hiding like a thief within the confines of our own Castra. When had I ever felt such apprehension within our headquarters? I should just stand up and face the passerby, but I couldn't.'

I waited, listening. The footsteps halted right behind me.

A thick hand gripped my shoulder. I stiffened.

'*Io, Saturnalia*! You can't be hiding from me, Numi—dani—dian—ius.'

It was *Biarchus* Cassius, worse for drink.

'*Io*, Cassius. Where have you been?'

'Subura and other neighborhoods. Nobody around here will dice with me any more.'

'I hardly wonder.'

'Because I always win.'

'Because you always cheat.'

'Good news!' He lifted his face to the downpour and washed off his sweat with an end of his tunic. 'I found a new *popina*, The Tavern of the Sailing Flea, near the Porta Ostiensis. They don't know me.'

'That won't last long.' I dragged him under the eaves.

Cassius gave a clumsy tug to his loosened belt. 'Why are we whispering?'

I gestured up at Apodemius' window. 'I want to talk to the Old Man again.'

He glanced up at the window. 'Really?'

Thank the gods the interloper was underhanded Cassius, never the kind of *agens* to parrot rubbish that Apodemius was 'off limits.'

'And given Otho's new rulebook, I might need a witness. Follow me, Cassius.'

We mounted the creaking steps that led to the upper floor. The building wasn't empty by any means. Otho seemed to have set an army of slaves working all night to wash away centuries of grime. One of his cleaning slaves, a grumbling old woman bristling with buckets, broom, and scrub brushes, squeezed past us down the stairs. Her dirty water splashed our boots. We hid our faces in our hoods, mindful the crone might be yet another in-house spy for Otho and not as dim-witted as she acted, muttering away under her moth-eaten *palla*.

We reached Apodemius' empty outer office. Cassius gave a polite tap at the door with his toe. There was no lamplight leaking through the warped oak planks. In the old days, both his trusted clerk and his deaf masseur might have been sitting there, Cerberus-like. But tonight, the outer office was empty.

'He's working alone inside.' I tapped on the inner office door but there was no sound there either. We tapped again.

No answer.

'Good gods—' I glanced at Cassius, fearing the worst. Cassius was about to break in the door, when I tested the handle. The door opened with a creak to wake the entire headquarters.

We looked around.

Apodemius had disappeared. Otho's copied reports sat in a neat stack. The rest of the room bore few traces of the old man, barring stains of liniment oil underneath the massage couch.

But that was hardly why we stared, dumbstruck. His wall map was cleared of all its pins and flags. The strongbox in which Apodemius stored his copies of the Empire's most dangerous and sensitive documents stood open—and emptied.

'He's been seized for his papers,' Cassius whispered. 'We must alert *Magister* Otho right away.'

'No.' I gripped his arm.

'What?' Cassius narrowed his eyes, concentrating hard.

'At Trajan's Baths, I overheard Otho say he was to spend most of tonight politicking for our *schola* at a banquet for the city's highest and slyest.'

'But—?'

'Remember that his new social visibility is at Apodemius' own suggestion. We can't put Otho in a difficult position now, implying that his time would be better spent babysitting a doddering old man.'

'Numidianus—!' Cassius stared at me through the shadows.

'Shush, Cassius. Let me think.'

—THE BURNING STAKES—

Cassius tiptoed into the room, looking under the few pieces of furniture.

'You're a trained observer, drunk or sober, Cassius. No signs of any scuffle? No torn scraps of cloth or papyrus?'

'No spilled wine cup. No overturned lamp oil.'

'But someone was just here. I saw a moving light. They must have left some trace.'

We prowled in a circle around the small space, sniffing for anything more than the usual stink of lamp oil, candle wax, massage lotions, and packets from all over the known world.

Cassius puffed out a gust of protest. 'They must have coerced him without any struggle. Blackmailed him. Threatened him. Forced him to unlock his safe box.'

'Cassius, who could get past our gate undetected at this time of night?'

'Me.'

'Besides you.'

'Don't sound so cocky, Numidianus. You can't be sure Apodemius hasn't been kidnapped. Otho *has* to know right away.'

Cassius could be a slippery customer and not just at the dicing table. He wanted to win points with our new chief, cook up some story about his keen observation from the courtyard spotting trouble in time. I had to be cautious. I could hardly confide to Cassius any of Apodemius' deep worries about Constantius II's missing rescindment letter returning to haunt us both.

I pointed to the empty space underneath Apodemius' battered map.

'Kidnapped? Cassius, think straight. Did you ever hear of kidnappers who let their victim take his pet mice along for the ride?'

We slipped back out of the building and dashed for my cell through a deluge so thick Neptune himself might have been emptying the Tiberis onto Castra roofs. Though Cassius hardly needed more wine, I offered him the last of my beaker and a stool still wet from Ahenobarbus' midnight visit.

'Well, something's wrong.' Cassius warmed my tin cup over the lamp flame, but then set the drink aside untouched.

'I agree. He stripped the office clean of anything significant.'
'Maybe he's retired for good to his family home.'
'Family? Cassius, we are his family.'
'Where does he live then? Where does he spend all his days?'
'No one ever knew. No one ever asked.'
'Surely after so many decades, people noticed his routine, where he headed each—'
'Cassius, that cleaning lady.'
'Who?'
'That old Gorgon loaded down with mops.'
'You think she knows something?'
'Ha! Of course *she* knows! When I first met Apodemius in 348, in a sleazy dressing room in Numidia, he was disguised as an acrobat master. In 354, when he saved my life in Constantinopolis, he was unrecognizable, even to me, until I was a few feet away.'
'But—?'
'Apodemius knows Otho has the cleaning and repair staff reporting on our movements and conversations so he can take stock of our efficiency or time-wasting. The old man wanted to slip away unseen. He *was* that cleaning woman.'
'*Apodemius*? He's too crippled to wander very far through the city carrying all that clanking crap.'
'He hired a litter.'

It was still some hours before the Roman winter relinquished another night to chilly dawn. With Cassius on my heels, we dodged across the courtyard on the far side of the dormitory to a side gate in the outer wall. This exit was little used and lightly guarded as it backed smack into the insalubrious underbelly of the Aqua Claudia aqueduct. One of our sentries confirmed that tonight—and not for the first time—he'd unbolted its narrow opening for a smelly crone laden with filthy water to donate to the commonweal of our fellow citizens in a nearby gutter.

I was using instinct rather than common sense. But I knew that only yards away, litter bearers congregated here between rides to rest, eat snacks, and trade traffic congestion tips.

Their vehicles stood parked nearby. There were no brocade curtains or gold-painted feet on these conveyances. There were no six or eight man *lecticae*, cushioned and curtained for customers, say, a lady caked in make-up reclining in privacy as she swung above the heads of the street dwellers, or a powerful politician flanked alongside by his groveling *comites* and *togati*.

Battered third-hand *sellae* stood crushed in a jumble, one against another, no more than common two-man sedan chairs flaking cheap paint and broken curtain rails. Here was the low-rent version of Roman transportation, ready to resume the human burdens of another chilly day.

'Interrogate every man here,' I ordered Cassius.

Cassius plunged in, jingling the *nummi* in his belt purse to elicit indiscretion. I chose another tack, simply laying hand on my *pugio* hilt and addressing each miserable man in rags as a fellow Roman too proud to be bought.

We ranged back and forth, interrogating every ragged bearer, beggar, and lowlife we found resting or washing in the shadows of the ancient arches.

Neither money nor honor made a dent in their sullen indifference to our single question—had any man carried off an old cleaning lady? We wasted, by my glance at the sky, more than an hour questioning all the teams and even a few haggard females stirring a thin broth over an open fire.

Cassius took a last look at the brightening sky.

'Numidianus, we have to quit. The morning meeting will start soon. Otho takes attendance now.'

'I'm staying here.'

'The roll master will notice you're missing.'

'Better Otho should notice Apodemius is missing. But say nothing. Let him find out in good time.'

'What if he wants you?'

Cassius was right. Otho intended to dispatch me as escort with Consul Taurus at any time. All the more reason to grab my last chance to make sure Apodemius knew Palladius was next to be hauled before Julian's tribunal.

'Tell Otho I've gone up the Esquiline to bid my family farewell. Say you can't find me—say anything. Just give me time to find the *Magister*.'

It was a thankless task to carry on alone through those unwashed, illiterate dregs of empire reduced to the existence of oxen and mules. I'd been raised very young by a mule trainer in

Numidia. I knew how stubborn such beasts could be, but these men were worse.

Their flyblown, mucus-filled eyes glowered up at me from under lowered brows. Their grimy muscles rippled with wordless threats. If they wanted to, a dozen of them could strip me of purse and weapons like a volt of vultures. Or they might simply kick me to a pulp with their formidable legs before the *aediles* watching more honest streets would know where to answer my cries for rescue.

I'd exhausted their curiosity and patience too long without success. Their clusters began to thin out as dawn finally broke. Two by two, they trotted away in search of busier intersections and looser purse strings.

I refused to give up. Some inner logic told me that Apodemius had not risked limping into the crowds, either in disguise or in normal garb, carrying a treasure trove of valuable documents and a cage of beloved pets.

I squatted a stone's throw from their camp and waited. Slaves learn young how to watch their masters and mistresses for hours on end, marking the idle hours with dreams of fig tarts or freedom, depending on age and mood. I no longer dreamed of pastries like a child. I'd risked everything to win my freedom from a hardened, lonely father. So what should I dream of while I followed my hunch, squatting on this foul curbside?

I'd dream of two middle-aged litter bearers appearing at the end of the alley, their short second-hand army *saga* so worn of sheep lanolin, the soggy wool sagged heavy with rainwater. Their pitiful sandals were thick with fresh wet mud. I'd dream of one bearer kind enough to take out a glass bottle of something foul-smelling to rub along his partner's sore shoulder with professional courtesy. I'd dream of the two bearers splitting their takings and retiring to separate makeshift shelters under the indifferent stone arches.

I rose from my haunches and extended a hand, even before the older of the two had settled himself down for a rest.

'Just finished a long journey? You free to take another?'

'Try another team.'

'I want the same team who carried an old woman away from the Castra side gate over there.'

—THE BURNING STAKES—

He shrugged and turned onto his side, stretching himself out on a hemp pallet scarcely inches above a stinking gutter running with sewage.

'I told you, *Agens*, try another team. Let me rest my sore knees.'

'I'll pay whatever you ask.'

'Nothing can buy the sleep I need.'

'I could force you.' I laid my hand on my *spatha*'s hilt.

'You can't force me. I can't help you.'

What was the point of bribing the wrong man or running him through?

'You must know something. I can see it. I could haul you into the Castra for questioning.'

He gave a bitter chuckle. 'You can't do that either. I know your rules only too well.'

'Let me in on the joke, Bearer.'

'My only son was a recruit to that Castra up there. They made him all kinds of promises, taught him all kinds of skills and secrets. Made his mother proud to see him shaved and bathed and wearing the riding helmet of your lot.'

'What happened? Stationed far away?'

'If you call crossing the Styx far enough.'

'That's a route no *agens* wants.'

'He was one of your postal riders. Got caught along the Danuvius by some roving Trevingi savages who wanted his horse.'

'He got killed for his mount?'

He gave me a sour smile. 'I hardly think they wanted to read through his mailbag.'

'You have my respect, Bearer.'

'My name is Pluto. I would rather my poor Gaius had your prayers. His mother went to your temple, the one you can see just behind the front gate? Asked them to perform rites for her son— our only boy! But your temple was bolted. Pagan rites for dead *agentes* is out of bounds.'

His story was strange. His anger was real enough. And my hunch had paid off. Who had been able to recruit the quick-footed son of an illiterate bearer so close to our side gate, but been powerless to unbolt the Temple of Jupiter Redux closed under orders from Constantius?

I crouched low and searched his angry eyes.

'I make you a promise, Pluto. You tell me the old cleaning woman's destination and as soon as I can, I'll take you and your woman into the Temple of Jupiter Redux and personally manage the rites and sacrifices due your son for his loyal service. It's possible now under Emperor Julian.'

I unsheathed my *spatha* and laid it at his calloused feet.

The rain had abated. The sun crested the wet, shiny roofs of Roma. Pluto refused to carry me himself. But he explained the details of my destination. I saw he'd been bound to secrecy and feared discovery. Only love for his dead son could overcome an intense loyalty to someone still alive.

So I set off to exit the Collina Porta out of the city and down the suburban Via Nomentana lined with *mausolea* housing the noble dead of a great city.

As Pluto gave me the address, we said no more about our pact, but I had never felt a greater debt to a fellow *agens*—dead or alive.

Chapter 7, A *Schola* of Virgins

—THE VIA NOMENTANA—

As the sun rose, I trotted past hundreds of upturned sleepy faces stretching out between shutters and stalls to measure the dispersing clouds. A grateful city was waking up to clearing skies. Housewives, schoolmasters, shopkeepers, and basilica slaves set about unclogging the sewers and gutters collecting pools of filth outside their doors.

I searched out a *stabulum* at the Porta Collina to rent a decent nag. Thousands of suburban market farmers jostled with bewildered pilgrims anxious for a bed for the holidays—a crush that slowed any exit through the great gates in the Aurelian Walls. They were pushed aside by impatient soldiers starting a short leave and canny traders of all kinds bringing in wares from more distant eastern hubs—animal, vegetable, and human.

The press of humanity thinned out once I'd threaded my way over the Ponte Nomentana and reached the miles of market gardens stretching out on all sides of the *Cursus* and lying under the looming arches of great aqueducts reaching across the landscape toward the capital.

I rode past the city folks' great mausoleums large and small lining both sides of the state road. Each bore some verse or salutation from the living to the dead and vice versa, engraved after the letters 'DM.' *Dis Manibus*, yes, no Roman alive dare omit this sinister endearment to the spirits of the underworld that belied the thin sunshine warming the stones underneath my horse's hooves. Serried funerary urns tucked into *columbaria*, like marble or granite doves at rest, chilled my spirit.

Pluto had withheld nothing from me, but his instructions were vague nonetheless. I was to look for a villa not far past the former estate of the great Constantine's half-sister Eutropia where *Augusta* Constantia, fiend-wife to the doomed Gallus, had once sheltered.

Aunt Eutropia had married into the Nepotianii, an aristocratic Roman clan that could stare down any impertinent imperial eunuch or upstart Pannonian general. Their *gens* had already produced two consuls—including Eutropia's own husband—while I was still a slave.

Built at the edge of a rise overlooking the state road, Eutropia's villa was now a mockery of the family's former greatness. The late emperor's property-obsessed Lord Chamberlain Eusebius had confiscated it after the Nepotiani uprising and then abandoned it to the whims of weeds and weevils. Slime coated a pond sunk into swamp grass behind a lawn run riot with ugly vines. The high bronze gates bearing proud grille work in the shape of the family's standard Chi Rho had turned as green as the overgrowth masking the front portals of the main house.

I bestowed that ruin a bitter smile. Let it rot into worm-infested compost. Nepotianus had buttressed his claim to power by setting the city's felons and maddened thugs free of their shackles and chains to plunder and massacre Roman elites clinging to imperial loyalty.

My grandfather, the Senator, a blind man of fame and lineage, had died at their hands trying to protect his precious library from their violent rampage, mere minutes too early for me to rescue him.

I squinted into the dawn. No longer an eager young rider going post-haste from town to town like a tireless Mercury, I was a very human *centenarius* some years over thirty suffering the sandy-dry eyes of a sleepless night.

And I was beginning to fear that my bereaved litter bearer snoring under the Aqua Claudia had played a vengeful trick on me. I was nearly to the ninth milestone where the first state *mutatio* would offer layover services to travelers using the *Cursus*—more than halfway to Nomentum where my trail must end—yet there was no sign of my destination.

I scanned the left side of the road for a south-facing pink-washed villa. The *pars urbana* should be lined with cypress trees for summer shade, beyond which raised pathways would cut across a D-shaped lawn dotted with plane trees, their ancient trunks smothered under ivy. Waist-high statues of the gods would encircle a large and well-stocked fishpond closer to the villa.

There should also be a recent shrine to some saint my bearer didn't recognize in his haste to avoid the fishpond. Apparently even Roman lowlife knew Seneca's tale of the slave boy whom an irate Pollia threatened to throw to his carnivorous lampreys. That legendary fishpond had terrified me too as a slave reading out loud from a great scroll to the Senator. I'd kept glancing up at my listener to make sure the temptation had never crossed his severe mind. And I know I asked the Lady Laetitia whether our own modest atrium fountain basin had ever contained any lampreys, making her laugh for days afterward.

It appeared, at last, just before a frustrated curse reached the tip of my tongue. The villa stood pink-washed and gleaming in the fresh light, as if the sun's rays favored that property more than any other along this historic thoroughfare. I mounted the slope and found the outer gates unlocked. Passing between the stand of cypresses, I found the walkways, statues, and pond just as promised, set around a 'D'-shaped manicured lawn. I tethered my horse at the saint's shrine with suitable irreverence and approached high, carved doors flanked by columns overhung with a generous balcony overlooking the passing traffic below.

A slave opened the door just enough for me to see he was a head taller than myself, his tunic far too short for his brown legs, and his proud profile and high brow unsuited to the gold collar marking him as property.

He was a Berber.

'What do you want?' he asked with that telltale lisp of a mushy 's' typical of North Africans speaking Latin. I felt in luck. My mother and even Kahina, though not from nomad tribes, had never been able to entirely rid themselves of it. Surely a fellow provincial, especially as lowly as this one, would favor a Roman of my status extending a friendly gesture in his native tongue.

'*Barkit yawm, Cexer.* Blessing of the day, Gatekeeper,' I said in my rusty Punic. '*Ircit ra'c bet.* I desire the head of the household.'

He shook his head, saying '*Ruh, la ' xakkar*. Go away and do not disturb us.'

He slammed the door in my face and slid a bolt into place. Through its thick oak planks, I heard the jingle of bells tied to his ankles retreating through the villa's *fauces*. I knew as a former slave that there was no point in arguing with such strict instructions.

I circled the villa grounds until I reached the walls of the *pars rusticana*, that second courtyard where farm tools, unwanted old mattresses, and slave trunks would be stashed out of sight. It was easy to vault into the neglected space unseen. I searched out one of the many small back doors left unlocked for slaves fetching produce from the kitchen garden or taking a moment of privacy behind parked wagons.

The eerie calm of this proud estate got on my nerves. From the interior of the house, I heard more tinkling of ankle bells. I slipped through the outdoor *triclinium*, bare of any draperies, cushions, or signs of a meal during this chilly season. I found a corridor leading past three or four closed chambers toward the public peristyle courtyard.

Then I reeled. The elegant columned courtyard was bordered with the usual covered walkway, but a ghoulish population adorned its walls. Hundreds of *imagines*—painted wax and plaster faces of the dead—eyed me with wordless accusation. There had been, perhaps centuries before, some effort to arrange these mementoes and their identifying plaques and tributes in a kind of chronology. But this redoubtable Roman clan had outgrown that nicety long ago. The silent courtyard was a disembodied but crowded assembly room devoted to forgotten fame.

This must be no ordinary household. Even the Manlius family tree could boast only a fraction of such illustrious forebears. The house was occupied—yet it felt more dead than alive. It gave off an air of well-kept suspension.

As I peered into various unheated rooms, I kept my ears open for the warning of little bells. They were a peculiar innovation. Most Romans preferred that their slaves come and go in silence.

—THE BURNING STAKES—

The largest chamber was a winter *triclinium* with gilt and upholstered sofas lined in a horseshoe shape over an exquisite mosaic floor. The walls boasted exquisite murals hung with priceless treasures from across the Empire. I could not have identified half the items on display, but I knew one dagger had been won from a Persian warlord. I'd seen such a bejeweled weapon brandished by General Ursicinus in anger at the Mediolanum *consistoriani* during his treason hearing in 355.

But the dagger was the least of it. There was an ivory triptych, a standing screen embossed with gold figures depicting the Hunt of Diana, window hangings hemmed with gold-threaded embroidery, a priceless coin collection, and large ceremonial plates of hammered silver resting on a sideboard.

The swish of a thick hem dragged across the floor under a soft-slippered footstep heading my way.

I hid behind the stately couches. A figure stepping out of the pages of history swept past, headed for the *lararium* near the entrance of the atrium.

A stoop-shouldered old woman steadied her gait with hands slightly outstretched until she reached her goal. Her withered hand picked up a waiting oil lamp prepared by her slaves for a ritual lighting of the shrine to the gods.

Rough hands seized me from behind and throttled my neck. I smelled cheap body oil as I was punched and kicked to the floor by feet whose ankle bells were silenced by a pair of fine-knitted socks.

The Berber kicked me again and again under my ribs, determined to subdue me while the tinkle of myriad bells from all sides of the open courtyard warned I'd soon be overpowered by more minions. I fought myself back up to my knees by twisting one of his legs until I was sure his kneecap would pull right out of its sinews, but I was too late. Other hands pushed me down and flipped me onto my stomach. A long bare foot pressed my nose hard into the precious *tesserae*. I felt another foot press at the back of my nape. I was seconds away from a broken neck. I panicked. I knew from the battlefield that there's no recovering normal life after a broken neck.

'Stop that! What is it?' the old woman croaked. In a timid voice, a small girl-slave explained my intrusion.

My spine was saved, for the moment. The Berber hoisted me back on my feet and tossed me full length onto my stomach again near the woman's feet clothed in slippers of fine black goat suede.

'Who are you?' she asked, head held high.

'Marcus Gregorianus Numidianus, *Centenarius*, Upper Class, *schola* of the *agentes in rebus*. I was turned away at your door. I couldn't abandon my search to deliver an urgent message to someone I traced to your gates.'

'You traced whom?'

'Apodemius, *magister* of our schola.'

'A man of ill repute, according to all respectable Romans.'

'A man of honor whom I believe to be in serious danger.'

'Get up.'

Hundreds of dead painted eyes scrutinized me. I felt myself judged as dishonorable, disrespectful, and unworthy of my manumission. I even felt I recognized one particular face glaring dead and sightless from behind the old woman's extraordinary headdress.

I could hardly believe my eyes.

For she wore the encumbering coiffure of truly ancient times. The *suffibulum*, a rectangular cloth edged in purple and fixed at the bosom, covered the *insula* turban-like head-wrapping over looping ribbons or cords of *vittae* tying up braided hair. A broad coil of wool wrapped with thin wiry gray hair must once have been a magnificent thick roll of glistening tresses.

This elaborate *Seni Crines* hairstyle marked out the half-dozen virgin priestesses dedicated to the goddess of the hearth, Vesta. The Vestal Virgins were a sisterhood dating back some nine hundred years and lingering into our modern days like a human echo of far nobler times.

'You are a Vestal, *Domina*?'

'I was. Of course, I'm retired now.'

She didn't look me in the face. The woman registered my voice and smell, but she looked past me with eyes clouded white. Those tinkling bells alerted her to the approach of underlings.

'Where am I?'

'In a great house. You must leave.'

'Has Apodemius been here?'

'A notorious *curiosus* breach our privacy?' she scoffed.

—THE BURNING STAKES—

'*Domina*, hear me out, I beg you. I harbor deep worries for Apodemius' safety. He may fall victim to false charges laid by a military hearing sanctioned by our new emperor but already marked by prejudice and injustice. Day by day, our speediest couriers arrive at the gates of the Castra Peregrina with warrants for the arrest of civil servants long loyal to Constantius. A net is being cast over innocent men as if trapped by an invisible *retiarius* with a hidden purpose.'

'*Retiarius* with a hidden—my gods, *Agens*, your eloquence is wasted on me! Apodemius is not here. Political shifts no longer trouble our ancient walls. Look on these faces all around you. They have known far worse than the whims of upstart Pannonians in purple and their ungrateful Constantine offspring.'

I guessed where I was. I had indeed recognized the features of one face. A wash of nostalgic affection flooded my soul.

'You have retired to guard the country seat of the late Justus, son of Consul Vettius Justus, related to the Constantines, and himself once Governor of Picenum,' I said in a whisper. 'Those are his features over there.'

The Vestal could not deny it, so I continued:

'Justus fathered Justina, empress to the Usurper Magnentius. Justus Picenus killed himself when accused by Constantius of treason—for merely dreaming he drew a cloth of purple from his side.'

'His was an honorable suicide,' the Vestal said.

'But this doesn't look like a Pannonian house of recent fortune. So this must be the home of Justus' mother, an aristocrat of the venerable Roman *gens* of Neratius.'

She gasped and laid a hand on the edge of her shrine to steady herself. 'You speak like a friend of the family.'

'I was. I am. I'm the bastard son of Commander Atticus Manlius Gregorius who joined the uprising of reformers against Emperor Constans. Apodemius assigned me to watch the self-proclaimed emperor Magnentius' rebel court.'

'I see. So how would you describe the Empress Justina? A lady of maturity well-matched to her robust veteran hero?'

I chuckled. 'You jest with me, *Domina*.'

'You may call me Tullia.'

'Or perhaps you test me, Tullia? Commander Gregorius and I escorted Justina Picenus, still cradling her dolly Rosina, to be married off to the Usurper Magnentius. I passed many a privileged hour in her company while Magnentius' court occupied Aquileia. She was a beautiful and brave little girl, an innocent *dominula* unsuited to partner such a vulgar general. She was widowed, still virgin at thirteen, during the great Civil War. We can only be grateful Magnentius' primitive decency left that child unsullied.'

'Yet the years have been less than kind to one they called empress.'

'Justina is still young and, one presumes, a most beautiful woman now. She once confided to me a childish dream—a presentiment of being an empress and giving birth to an emperor—but not one sired by Magnentius. She called it a kind of oracle.'

The Vestal's eyelids flickered. Omens and dreams were the very stuff of her vocation. She knew as well as I that the gods bestowed hints and shades of the future to those prudent enough to listen.

'Justina serves as an obscure waiting lady on Marina Severa, wife of General Valentinian in Cibalae.'

'Only a day's easy ride from my base in Sirmium! When I return to my posting, may I relay the news that her home is well-guarded and that I have found its guardian well?'

'Justina's *domus* is safe.'

'*With a garden and a library, one has everything one needs,*' I quoted.

She gave a rueful chuckle. 'Sadly, our dear Cicero forgot to add, one needs eyes with which to read.'

'Have you no one here to read to you out loud? Even Cicero employed many slaves to read out loud to him—and his eyes were as sharp as *stili*.'

She scowled under the thick layers of cloth cushioning her brow. There was a hint of bruised pride at her physical decline. Vestal candidates had to be physically perfect pre-pubescent girls to make the final six.

'Excuse my rude candor, *Domina*. My task as a boy was to read for hours to Senator Manlius, afflicted in old age as you are.'

—THE BURNING STAKES—

Her practiced fingers searched out a twisted figurine of a god lying on his side where a slave had swept the ashes before dawn.

'I've tried but the household attendants here are either too old, too busy, too foreign, or to ignorant to spend hours on literature.'

'I would happily review the great texts with you myself in exchange for the insights your rare calling bestows.'

'I suppose you and I are a bit alike,' she said. 'You might say that the female priesthood of Vesta is a kind of *schola*, but unlike your disreputable department, ours is a *schola* of upright virgins.'

'We *agentes* do share a brotherhood and hold ourselves separate from the intrigues of the day for the protection of the Empire at the behest of the Emperor.'

'Hah! Emperors come and go. Temporal power is fleeting. We Vestals listen to the eternal gods themselves and pray for those who dismiss us as powerless women.'

'Powerful in your own sense of duty and perhaps to be returned to respect and usefulness under Emperor Julian?'

'Julian comes too late for me.' Her defeated air was painful to witness. 'You must go. Return to your duties. Give up your search for your former *magister*.'

'I owe him too much.'

She turned her back on me. With both hands patting the *lararium* shelf, she located more figurines and positioned them in a circle facing us.

'You're still there, *Agens*?'

'Yes. Apodemius needs my help.'

'I don't know you. I can't see your expression. Apodemius is hated by many for his cunning and independence. You all are. How can I be sure he's not in danger from you yourself?'

'Because I make you a promise on the Manlius name, Tullia, out of respect for this house. When I've warned the *Magister* in time and the nightmare of this tribunal is safely behind us, I'll return here to read to you.'

She gave a wry smile. 'A pretty but empty promise if you are based in Sirmium.'

'Not much longer, I hope. If my years in the Pannonian capital are to be rewarded, I intend to return to Roma for good. I have heavy responsibilities to the Manlius estate. Seeing that pond outside reminded me of the country properties I should be paying more attention to on behalf of my underage ward.'

'Our pond is well-stocked with fish.'

'Not lampreys, I hope?'

'Hah, Seneca's angry Pollia!' Tullia laughed. 'And the comedies of Plautus—how wonderful it would be to hear my favorites again . . . But no. I wish I could help you, Numidianus. But you understand I cannot.'

'That is too bad. Then I'll go now.'

She fingered a small ivory Hera. 'It is too bad. Suppose Apodemius had left Roma—for Mediolanum, for example? But then, why should your chief travel north? Isn't that what our Greek friends would dismiss as an empty ὑπόθεσις, a pure hypothesis? An unfounded supposition?'

I turned back to face her. 'What if he'd traveled north? What if I found him there?'

'I would ask you a small favor—to ask Apodemius to convey a message to the Marble Vestal, reassuring her that our Veiled Vestal is safe in Cibalae.'

'If he'd gone to Mediolanum—?'

'Only *if* he'd gone to Mediolanum, that is. Forgive me, we old women suffer from whimsies, I fear, but we hold our fellow sisters' welfare dear.'

I gave her my hand, watched over by dozens of silent death masks. This time I exited by the front door to cross the 'D'-shaped lawn with its busy fishpond.

No tickling bells molested my departure. No one threw me to the lampreys after all.

⚜⚜⚜

I dispatched messengers from the Porta Collina with verbal messages to Junius, Ahenobarbus, and Cassius to come singly by different routes to Cassius' latest 'hot tip,' the Tavern of the Sailing Flea.

This dive for men heading west for the Ostian docks turned out to be a place so dodgy that, if no one yet knew about Cassius' loaded dice, at least no self-respecting *agens* was likely to discover us here in debate either. The lavish revels of Saturnalia made little difference to the bankrupts of this Roman hole, though more than the usual number of candles fought the dark shadows where drunks snored over mind-numbing measures of undiluted *merum*.

There was no set menu, not even a placard advertising snacks and grilled meats on the wall over the smoking fire. The tables and partitions were slick with decades of greasy fumes. The low plaster ceiling flaked right into my cheap tin cup.

The toothless girls on offer were all around thirty—and that was being generous. But they were still alert enough to toss me chipped platters of fried whitebait.

Dodging under the low doorway lintil and searching me out through the smoky gloom, Ahenobarbus covered his nose.

'Why aren't we meeting at the Tavern of the Seven Sages or some other decent place?'

'Because we're not meeting, *Princeps*. Got it?'

He nodded with good-natured resignation, unsurprised by any subordination from me after all these years.

Junius and Cassius arrived, protesting that they'd cut their attendance at the First Morning Meeting short by five minutes and anxious they'd be marked delinquent. A hag with breasts listing wider than our table offered Junius a free turn out back before he even found a stool. Cassius tossed a friendly smile at some gamblers, but they turned their backs on him.

We ordered drinks. I filled them in on my interview with Tullia.

Ahenobarbus said, 'When I left the Castra, Otho still believed Apodemius was in the city, if no longer in his office.'

'And Apodemius probably still is around,' Cassius said. 'You look pretty wrung out, Numidianus.'

I rubbed my sore torso. 'I took some pretty vicious kicks from a Berber slave.'

'So drink up and think straight. You have no proof this blind old bird has kept her other senses any more than her sight. She's not certain sure Apodemius went to Mediolanum.'

'No, Cassius. I think Vestal Tullia gave her word to keep Apodemius' trip secret. Just like the bearer Pluto. So she conveyed it to me as a guess. Apodemius left this morning for

Mediolanum and I know why. The *Magister* hopes to pick up the trail of an important document there.'

I trusted these *agentes* huddled over that worn wooden table more than any others. But I'd learned that a secret shared is a secret lost.

I privately gave fresh weight to the offhand way Apodemius had described his 'last recruit,' that Benedictus. The boy was no doubt still tucked away in Mediolanum, far from Otho's new procedures that stripped Apodemius of his authority.

I didn't mention that the document in question might be a retraction of the Gallus killing from Constantius II. Such anxieties made me look too vulnerable in front of the junior men, though I suspect Ahenobarbus guessed from our previous night's conversation.

And why disclose Tullia's personal message about a 'Veiled Vestal safe in Cibalae?' It was unconnected to our worries for Apodemius. I didn't want to appear any more foolish than I felt.

Cassius ordered himself a second drink. 'A report came in this morning that Catena has fled to the wilds of Britannia. Happily for us, the rumor started in Mediolanum. If I'm the man to deliver The Chain to his fate, I should track down that story and I can hunt for Apodemius at the same time.'

'I'll ride with you,' I said. 'Catena is the most desperate man in the Empire at this moment. I can argue to Otho that I know Catena better than any of you. Someone else can escort poor Consul Taurus to the East.'

Ahenobarbus raised an eyebrow at Julian's wistful expression.

'If we're talking about Mediolanum, it's best you stay behind, Junius. You escaped that court as a wanted hostage and nothing has changed.'

'I disagree, *Princeps*,' I said. 'Constantius is dead. General Silvanus is dead. Julian *Augustus* has no need of any Silvanus family hostage. That chapter should be closed. It's time for Junius to return there and openly assert his freedom as a citizen.'

Ahenobarbus took a deep breath. 'Then that settles it for me. As *princeps* I'm pretty free to travel without Otho's say-so. I'm not saying I subscribe to your conclusions, Numidianus. I just want to use my standing in Mediolanum to ensure that Junius is no longer a political fugitive.'

'And help us look for Apodemius?'

He smiled at me. 'Why not? Your Vestal is our only lead. I care about the old man's safety on the road. The *Cursus* to Mediolanum might be snowed over in parts and he couldn't be that far ahead of us.'

In his healthier days, Apodemius had been an expert horseman who could outrace even me—but now? Common sense said that no old man could be so desperate for a piece of imperial vellum that he'd risk such a journey during the coldest days of lightless winter.

Yet the retired Vestal wasn't a woman to waste words or trust. She'd spoken as if she still tended the oracles of truth. Moreover, she was someone who wanted more than anything to hear me read out loud the lines of Cicero, Plautus, and Seneca.

Kindred booklovers like Tullia did not lie.

Chapter 8, The Scent of a Greek

—THE IMPERIAL PALACE, MEDIOLANUM—

Our speediest *agentes* could complete the postal run from Roma to Mediolanum in four to five days, depending on the season. I'd once counted myself among them but now? As we set off after a good night's sleep, Junius and I shared a hearty laugh about his first such race in my company back in 355, fleeing Constantius' court to confide his father General Silvanus' troubles to Apodemius. Junius had finished that marathon with fierce blisters on his palace-pampered backside.

Now it was Junius, hardened by his regular circuit rides south of Roma, who set the pace for our quartet with the impatient pride of youth.

We took four and a half days, stopping for a full night on the east coast at Fanum-Fortunae before tackling the busy northwest diagonal through Ariminum, Bononia, and Parma. We finished our last afternoon with a race from Placentia into the capital.

There was no reason for me to be so nervous. Between us, we'd ridden this route many dozens of times. Aside from Junius, ours were familiar faces at the *mansiones* and *mutationes* where we grabbed snacks and exchanged mounts. We were traveling during the culmination of the Saturnalia Festivities and our passage up the *Cursus* became easier by the hour as pilgrims and holiday-makers indifferent to our purpose reached their destinations and the crush thinned out.

We'd made plausible excuses to a pre-occupied Otho about Cassius picking up Catena's trail in the company of Ahenobarbus, Junius, and myself. The new *magister* didn't seem concerned that another man would replace me as Taurus' eastward escort. He seemed happy to think Catena's arrest was my priority for now.

Yet I was anxious, both for Apodemius' physical safety and for his secret that I still kept from the others. I wanted to attract no undue curiosity about our foray up to Mediolanum and I'd made sure that even the note sent to Kahina was very low-key. I didn't like drawing attention to our team, racing north offseason through inclement weather. I insisted we keep a low profile en route, eat in our rooms, and turn down dice games and the like in the common dining area (a particular hardship to Cassius.) We saddled up and rode off an hour before other travelers came down to breakfast.

At last the squat, twenty-four-sided watchtowers of Emperor Maximian's city walls hove into view. No doubt Constantius' Arian capital would also be celebrating a modern mix of Christmas spiced up with traditional Saturnalian follies and foods. But awaiting official clearance through its enormous gates, I felt submerged in dread. No hot, spiced wine or colorful figurine stalls could warm this cold, granite city. It had been the scene of too many betrayals, conspiracies, tortures, and deaths for me.

Striding behind Ahenobarbus to the *agentes*' residential wing nestled under a covered walkway at the base of the Financial Building, I recalled the vicious beating I'd received from Catena and his thugs outside *Ducenarius* Gaudentius' chamber. I pulled my short riding cloak over my nose. Was it my imagination or, even in December's frigid air, did the stench of Catena's cells beneath the courtyard paving stones seep up from grates that shed mere slivers of light on the horrors below?

Had Constantius' sudden death made much difference to Mediolanum?

Even though one emperor was gone and another reigned far away, the stolid capital churned along around us, fed by the military and commercial affairs of the Western Empire. We crossed palace courtyards—inner and outer—filled with men conducting pre-holiday business that couldn't wait until January. Hundreds of officials, all brandishing symbols of undiminished self-importance, crisscrossed from residential wings to courts and reception halls, from baths to offices and stables.

—THE BURNING STAKES—

The courtrooms looked as bustling as ever. Slander, larceny, bankruptcy, and violence took no vacation just because an emperor died. From within the serried hearing chambers, the clank of engraved silver balls dropped on the floor by the *primiscrinius* to mark the procedural hours echoed across the courtyard to our ears outside.

Querulous petitioners and their glossy advocates blocked our path under the bronze plaques advertising fees for lawsuit applications and hearings—so many *solidi* to register your complaint and another fee to get your opponent dragged into court.

But even during my short walk through the courtyards of the Palace of Mediolanum, my practiced eye spotted change. The *potestates excelsae*—the dozens of lofty persons who wielded influence on the imperial *proximi*, intimates who in turn held the Divinity's ear—were absent. What was left was not business as before, but business as necessary—provincial lawsuits, tax procedures, and military accounting—the machinery of imperial rule with all its cogs and gears grinding away.

The glitter and tension imposed by Constantius' court had vanished. You could practically reach out and grasp the *absence* of power lingering in the air. How could an ambitious official on the make 'sell the smoke' of perfumed access to Constantius if that useful person lay lifeless at the opposite end of the Empire in a marble bier?

The Pannonian 'divinity' was dead. His glamorous second empress, Eusebia, was dead. Her successor Flavia and her offspring, if it had arrived, was nowhere to be seen. The Lord Chamberlain Eusebius and the rest of the *consistoriani* had vanished eastward with them. And where was the late emperor's favorite *agens* of the Mediolanum court, Gaudentius, now? Reigning so confident in North Africa as the *notarius* running Constantius' anti-Julian blockade of supplies, where had Gaudentius fled?

At the sight of our insignia, low-ranking postal riders asked us few questions and made way for us to choose rooms, wash, and reconnoiter for our next move. Imperial barbers had just shaved each of us in turn when my own door burst open.

'Numidianus?'

Here was hearty Rufus, Gaudentius' replacement as senior *agens* in this abandoned imperial seat. I hadn't seen Rufus once since the aftermath of Argentoratum, but he hadn't changed much. There was the same wide, open brow and frank expression on his broad face under a thick shock of spiky black hair, as if he had just removed his *petanus* after a sweaty ride. He was still the straightforward Rufus who'd looked on with dismay as Cassius' dice cheated me near the gatehouse. I'd lost a lot of pay over many distracted hours that sweltering day in 355 while I waited to testify in the Gallus treason trials. And he was still the loyal Rufus who'd helped me expose skillful forgeries on reused vellum that had doomed General Silvanus as a traitor later that year.

'No fair warning to welcome you and the *Princeps* properly? Our new *magister* Otho is so big on reports from us these days. Why didn't I get a heads-up from the Castra?'

'I'm not here on an inspection tour, Rufus.'

'Then what mission brings you to this mossy heap? Don't tell me Julian's going to set up court here? He's an Athenian at heart.'

'Don't worry. Julian hates the place.'

'Good. The routine is nice and quiet now.'

'It'll stay quiet. You're welcome to don whatever leftover purple rag you find lying around and sport yourself in Constantius' private baths all you wish.'

'Explain yourself, you North African bastard.' He dragged a wooden stool to my side as I rested my weary backside on a spare mattress.

'A source up here tipped us off that The Chain has fled to Britannia. We need details. Cassius is carrying the warrant to send him to justice at a trial in Chalcedon.'

Rufus frowned. 'I can confirm no such source, Numidianus.'

He fingered a wet shaving towel hanging off my basin in the corner. 'Are you sure this Britannia report is reliable—or even likely? After the Magnentius persecutions Catena conducted up there, how long could he hide, even in thick fog? The colonials on that island hate his guts.'

'I agree. It's a strange rumor. Perhaps one he spread himself.'

'Even if it's true, I say, save yourselves the chase. Better to let solid Roman colonials drive him into some bottomless bog like a rabid dog.' Rufus made a rude sucking noise.

—THE BURNING STAKES—

'That dog is due the honor of a full trial. You're not paying attention to Julian's great reckoning in Chalcedon? Trials of the consuls Florentius and Taurus, of Catena, and other top civil servants?'

Rufus shivered. 'That sort of thing gives me chills. Catena could die in Londinium or Mauretania Tingitana, for all I care. I just want to do a good job up here, keep things running smoothly, and make a good impression on *Magister* Otho.'

'You do read the reports coming in as well as write your own, I trust?'

'Oh, I read the reports but I don't publicize them too much. Of course the courtiers love political gossip but I don't want to feed yet more rumors that only turn each civil servant against his fellow.'

'You too good-hearted, Rufus, but you can't change human nature.'

'I know but why spread fear? Listen for yourself. Try the Baths of Hercules tomorrow afternoon. It's all whispers behind curtains and partitions, lowered eyes and muffled greetings, fingers pointing, and names murmured in secret.'

'It must stop soon.' I didn't confide my worries for Apodemius, not yet.

Rufus squirmed. 'I hope it does. Constantius is gone, leaving a hollowed out court, Numidianus, but what's left? A nest swarming with hundreds of idle eunuchs, chefs, and leftover priests still haggling in the steam rooms over the nature of Christ.'

'At least Catena's atrocities underground are a thing of the past.'

'We should pour burning brimstone down those steps from the main *consistorium* hall into Catena's Hades. The steps from which no one returns . . .'

'You forget, Rufus, I returned once—with Adjutant Proculus in my arms—or what remained alive of him.'

I saw that, unruly hair aside, a well-manicured resignation had settled over Rufus' boyish, uncombed charm. We were all a little older now, looking into our futures clouded by the incense of the unknown.

'If Julian is nothing else, he's a blessing in that regard. With *Magister* Otho reorganizing us, weeding out the chaff, and putting new procedures in place, a new era seems afoot, right, Numidianus?'

My door opened after a token tap of a boot. Glancing up Rufus turned white. His mouth dropped open. I steadied him as he swayed on his stool.

'But—but—Silvanus' son is . . . dead!'

'Hah! Behold, Rufus, those Galileans are not the only ones who raise men from the dead. We've been calling Junius "Merovianus," since 355. Now he's a full-fledged *agens*, riding the southbound circuit from Roma.'

The two men stood laced already in a fierce embrace, tears in their eyes. Rufus had been a low-ranked postal rider during the days Junius skulked around Mediolanum's privileged corridors as a pimply adolescent, the Gallo-Roman prince captive to Constantius' permanent fears of upheaval and treason.

Having witnessed Rufus' shock, I rose and strapped my belt back on. 'I must warn your mother, Junius, before it's too late. With your candid ways, Rufus, it'll be no more than minutes before someone tells that poor woman they've sighted her son's ghost.'

Junius blocked my path to the door. 'No, Numidianus,' he said. 'My mother's waiting for me—'

'But—'

'—that is, waiting for a certain *Agens* Merovianus who brings news close to her heart regarding her lost Junius.'

'You've been officially dead now for six years. If you don't let me break it to her gently first, the mere glimpse of you may stop the poor woman's heart.'

'Then I intend that her last heartbeats are those of pure joy,' he said. 'Not even you, Numidianus will cheat me of this reunion.'

How the Frankish prince had grown up during my four years in Sirmium! I'd rescued, protected, and sheltered him through serious danger. But he no longer needed a big brother of any kind. With discretion, Rufus pretended to adjust a loose bootlace until Junius had left for the women's quarters across the courtyard.

'Stop hiding, Rufus. Was I wrong in bringing Junius out from cover so soon after Constantius' death?'

Rufus shrugged. 'None of Constantius' leftovers will bother contesting Junius' freedom. They have bigger worries for themselves. If anything, the Frankish contingent guarding the Palace will celebrate the return of Silvanus' heir too much. Worry about that!'

'So why look troubled, Rufus?'

'Because the shock is for Junius. The taint of treason hanging over Silvanus' death combined with the loss of her only son aged his mother beyond recognition.'

'She was always a nervous, nagging woman—'

'—now white-haired and mute from years of hiding herself away. I don't lay eyes on the poor thing for months at a time.'

'Sad, but she was hardly the only victim of Arbitio's conspiracy.'

I thought of my lost friend Roxana. Once the faithful mistress of Silvanus in Agrippina, she'd been crippled defending her lover from assassins' blades. After braving interrogation and torture before Constantius and his *consistoriani*, she'd fled imperial retribution forever. Where had she hid herself? Was she even alive? Roxana wouldn't be safe in any Roman society until the jealous General Arbitio's craving for her was extinguished.

I gulped down some warm *conditum* from a pitcher at hand. 'Rufus, to business. Has Apodemius been here?'

'*Apodemius*? No.'

'Sure?'

'Of course I'm sure.'

I didn't expect it to be easy, but I couldn't question his startled expression. 'Then, tell me, who's the "Marble Vestal"?'

'I'm no religious man, Numidianus.'

'Fair enough. Then do you know a certain Benedictus in the *scrinia*?'

He chuckled. 'Hardly. I leave the Secretariat to its own devices. Their Vesuvius of papyrus is of no interest to me until it's addressed, sealed, and in my mail sack—'

'Think, Rufus. I need this Benedictus. You must have had some contact with him. Apodemius praised him to me as a recruit.'

'A recruit from among the *scriniarii*? Oh, please, pull the other boot. You know what they are—hundreds of bobbing and bowing little mice-men in old-fashioned robes, scooting in and out of dusty archives—'

'Take me over there, Rufus.'

'Take you where? Which *scrinium*? The *a secretis*? *Scrinium memoriae*? *Scrinium epistularum*? *Libellorum*? The Greek archives?'

'Well, I don't know, not yet.'

'So ask the *chartularius*—no, he's prick—bribe the *cornicularius*, he's in charge—just don't ask me.'

'While Cassius is hunting down his source about Catena, we're going to find this Benedictus.'

Rufus groaned. 'I hope you have a month or two. There are over two thousand guys over there and not a few named Benedictus, I'll wager—'

'Save your bets for Cassius,' I said, pushing him into our walkway.

We wrapped ourselves tight against Mediolanum's frozen air and crossed the main courtyard. The city streets approaching the Palace had seemed festive enough, despite the gray and cheerless low skies, but within the palace walls, there was a deeper, more unnerving cold—the clammy grip of a dead emperor's shadow.

☙☙☙

Rufus was right, of course.

The palace walls still housed a hive of bureaucrats—not just scribes and *notarii*, but also *protectores domestici*. Apart from a river of snoots shod in polished black leather *campagi* under long white tunics festooned with *segmenta* and *orbiculi* set off by wide, bejeweled belts, we passed stagnant pools of eunuchs, barbers, laundry slaves, and dining room attendants left idle by the disappearance of Constantius and his Eastern entourage.

We started our inquiry at the offices of the *magister officiorum* and then the *magister memoriae*, but no one could help us. We tried the truculent *chartularius* and bribed the *cornicularius* on duty, but clearly not enough. If Benedictus was employed as a scribe, he must be a lowly copyist indeed—just a *scriba librarius* trainee.

We decided to tackle the musty archival offices ourselves—the *sacra scrinia* behind the judicial buildings. Two hours of circulating from one *scrinium* to another produced no Benedictus.

'He must have used the name Benedictus with us for discretion and another name here,' Rufus said. 'We've known undercover informants to do it before.'

'Who would notice anyone in this sea of bent heads and bowed backs?' I asked.

I gestured at dozens of writing tables populated by colorless men bristling with writing instruments. '*A pale boy like a Christian martyr, huge eyes rolling heavenward,* was our *Magister*'s description.'

'Let's try the eunuchs,' Rufus said. 'They'd notice a kid like that.'

'No, Rufus. Leave them out of this. Anyone but the eunuchs.'

'But the eunuchs notice everyone. Whether you like them or not, Numidianus, they watch us normal men with an avidity that gives me the creeps. Put their beady eyes to good use for once.'

I was glad I hadn't confided more of my purpose to him. Trustworthy but disingenuous, Rufus might slip up. He was already racing with impatience ahead of me down a main corridor past the Palace public rooms to make a last stab. He intended to ask the acting head of the *praepositi sacri cubiculi* for help from any of the minor *cubicularii* tending the personal needs of the senior scribes.

Should I explain to Rufus that it was Eusebius, the most powerful of the eunuchs' tribe, that Apodemius feared most in this affair? For, like *agentes* and Vestals, the eunuchs formed a brotherhood of their own, but a tightly bound network far more sinister, underhanded, venal, and sly.

For better or worse, Rufus struck gold as fast as a corrupt Roman governor newly posted to Asturia.

Eusebius' high-ranked deputy affected indifference to our question. But a soft-cheeked eunuch named Chryseros with elongated limbs robed in deep umber brocade, was eavesdropping on our inquiry.

'That sounds like Bellator,' Chryseros told his superior in a high, hissing whisper. 'Our *agentes* friends will find him in the last chamber off Room XIII of the *sacra memoriae*, that building, over there.'

Rufus was already speeding ahead of me when the eunuch grabbed my arm. 'Some coin to know your business in the archives, *Agens*.'

'None worth your concern or coin,' I answered, pulling my sleeve free. 'We keep records in Roma, too. Just routine inquiries to close some Castra files on the previous reign, that's all.'

'One gold *solidi*.' He took my sleeve again, this time with more insistence.

'I know nothing worth such hard-earned savings,' I said, prying off his long fingers. 'Thanks for the tip to the Britannian all the same.'

⚜⚜⚜

I couldn't detect the wondrous potential Apodemius attributed to this sullen Bellator, or Benedictus, or whatever his name was. His wide green eyes, feathery lashes, and stubby nose lent him an androgynous and feline air. I could see why he'd caught the scrutiny of Chryseros. He avoided our eyes as we asked permission of his superior for a quiet conversation. He fixed his gaze on the cold paving as Rufus and I led him outdoors into the thin shadow of the building.

The winter's weak daylight was nearly gone. We two *agentes* shivered in our weatherproofed cloaks. Benedictus wore only a hand-me-down wool tunic shorn of its previous embroidery but he must be used to colder climes. His bare white forearms popped not so much as a single goosebump. He seemed to be made of the same frost that covers his bleak and waterlogged home. He waited with fingers distended from copying clasped at his waist.

'We believe you know our former *magister*, Apodemius.'

Benedictus looked straight ahead at the bustling crowd around the judiciary with an impassive expression.

'Well, do you?' Rufus said, seizing one hairless forearm.

'Please describe this stranger.'

—THE BURNING STAKES—

I laid a restraining hand on Rufus' hand. 'We're wasting our time. The *Magister* used too many disguises and too many names. Benedictus, we need access to the imperial records of Constantius' directives of 354.'

'The *a secretis* files? You mean, the Emperor's personal correspondence?'

'Yes. We're not the first to ask this, are we?'

The boy betrayed nothing. Under repeated questioning, he confessed no knowledge of Apodemius or any previous request to view such imperial documents. Either this waif was wary of betraying the old man or ignorant of our purpose.

Perhaps Apodemius had warned him to trust no one—not even the *agentes* themselves. Did we even have the correct Benedictus? If we had the wrong boy, it was dangerous to press an innocent scribe much harder.

'*Agentes*, you make too much of me. Place an application, pay the fee, and one of the senior scribes will assist you.'

'No, we ask it of you, Benedictus. You know that section of the *a secretis* records, don't you?'

'I've delivered some documents for filing there.'

'I thought so.' I tossed Rufus a glance of satisfaction. 'Take us to the correct archive room. We'll pay any fee or fill in any—'

'There are certain permissions required—'

'*Imperator* Constantius is *dead*, Benedictus. The records must be examined immediately.' My voice softened, 'We assume full responsibility to your superiors.'

Benedictus relented. He led us into another building and with soft and silent steps, mounted two flights of stairs, past myriad offices rustling with scribes and filing clerks. We plunged deeper and deeper down corridors reeking of old papyrus, tanned vellum, decrepit men, and vital secrets.

Palatine sentries guarded various rooms, but Benedictus drew no glance from them. It seemed that scribes, especially as humble as the Britannian, moved invisibly through their realm. Only Rufus and myself—outsized, cloaked, armed, and nervous—attracted the hostile attention of a few standing duty.

'Perhaps this is the room you require,' Benedictus said with a slight bow. He opened a narrow paneled door at the end of a quiet corridor.

'Stay with him here,' I ordered Rufus.

The archivist, a small, bald man over forty, sat on duty. He rose from a stool and straightened his tunic. Flakes of crumbling papyrus drifted off his shoulders like a shower of dandruff.

'You want to see rescripts? There are fees, hefty fees, for calling up the details of the *cottidiana*,' he warned, sniffing into a handkerchief.

'Constantius' decrees are a matter of public record and reference, aren't they?'

'Yes, my fine *agens*, but they don't file and number themselves, do they? Someone has to prevent abuse of the Imperial Signature.'

'All right. How much?'

'A half-*solidus* for the search and another half for a stamped affidavit post-viewing.' He pointed at his painted signboard listing fees and regulations, just like the one outside the courtrooms.

'That's robbery. And for an official copy of the text?'

He shook his bald pate. 'No extra copies allowed. Our official copies are numbered and indexed. That's it.'

Apodemius had good reason to be wary about his alleged copy back in Roma. It looked more and more like a forgery.

'I'll need a chit for expenses back in Roma.'

'Of course,' he said, suddenly gracious. I paid the fee and signed my long-dead recruiter's name—Leontus Longus Flavius—on an expenses claim. He countersigned the receipt in a weirdly perfect square hand.

'It's only fair, *Agens*. I paid dearly for this post as *instrumentarius*. How do you expect a civil servant to live? Working for you for *free*? Nothing happens within these walls without fees.'

He blew his nose again, a victim of the marble chill and non-existent upstairs heating. 'I'm surprised you people don't check our records more often. What with the Emperor's signature floating all over the Empire on the bottom of one rescript or another—abuse was *rife*—people ripping his signature off the bottom of one appeal and reattaching it to some other—'

'I'm not tracing a *rescript*,' I corrected him.

He nodded, eager to do Constantius' famous work ethic full credit: 'Between five and ten decisions a day, when this court was in full throttle.'

'Yes, yes, I need to see your archived copy and messenger's receipt for an order *initiated* by his Divinity, Our Eternity *Imperator* Constantius himself. It would have been dispatched eastward to Pula, Istria in 354 and probably addressed to *Praepositus* Eusebius or the *Notarius* Pentadius, possibly to *Magister Apodemius* of our *schola*. Were such orders filed loose in a box or bound into a legal *codex*?'

The old Senator Manlius had often spoken of a definitive legal collection composed entirely of imperial rescripts, the Codex Hermogenianus, published around sixty years ago.

Flaky's eyes blinked rapidly. 'I know which volume you seek.' He shuffled away and returned, far too quickly to deserve half a *solidus*.

I took the heavy binding of thick papyri into my arms and spread it out on a side table. It was a masterpiece of bureaucracy. Folding back each neatly lettered document, my mind's eyes conjured up that heavy-lidded Constantine presiding over his court with scribes busy on either side, recording each phrase.

I waded through weeks of his rulings from that awful year. It was painful to revisit. Beset by fears of treason, worries about succession, and struggles with his Arian conscience, the late emperor had labored to do his duty. He summoned experts on religious squabbles and provincial tax disputes and issued one repetitious military order after another that did little to save Gallia or Rhaetia from barbarian incursions or the East from Persian depredations.

I finally reached the weeks in question—that is, between the day that Apodemius joined me to escort Gallus from Constantinopolis for secret interrogation and the day of Gallus' miserable beheading in Pula.

I found nothing. I flipped back and forth, back and forth. The bald clerk watched me from under lowered eyes.

'Isn't there some docket or index? You mentioned a *cottidiana*?'

'Of course.'

Flaky fetched a thinner register of daily business and laid it on the table.

I ran my index finger up and down the entries. I turned one page after another. I was coming close and then—the record jumped two weeks. I checked back and forward, over and over. The index leaped over the two weeks preceding Gallus' gruesome end.

I turned on him, furious. 'These files have been filleted like a banquet turbot.'

'No, no!'

'Someone requested this volume before me. Someone has been in here asking the same thing—don't bother denying it. I saw it in your eyes a moment ago. You had the volume too ready to hand. Who corrupted your records?'

I forced his trembling finger down the torn fibers at the spine where one sheet had been extracted from Flaky's exquisite binding.

I'd wasted over half an hour. I wrapped both hands around his greedy little neck. 'You know that an *agens* is never tried for his actions in the course of duty, don't you?'

He gurgled and nodded and got out something like, 'A Greek,' so I loosened my grip and let him catch his breath. 'A Greek legal official was in here. Made the same request two days ago."

'How do you know he was Greek?'

'He wore many layers of Eastern travel robes, very expensive damask you don't see in these parts, and gold-embroidered gloves. He had a thick accent, but was very high-handed. I didn't like him. His breath stank of retsina and goat's cheese.'

'Name?' I gave his neck another warning squeeze. 'You issued him a receipt like mine?'

'No name. He refused to pay the fee. When I told him off, he presented a search warrant issued from the court in Constantinopolis.'

My stomach churned. 'Signed by whom?'

Flaky coughed and rubbed his neck. 'Praetorian Prefect for the East, Secundus Salutius, presiding over some inquiry in Chalcedon. The official said the matter was confidential and that Salutius required evidence.'

—THE BURNING STAKES—

'It's no inquiry—it's a political purge, you fool!'

I flung the miserable man back against a bench in frustration. If there were a record of any rescindment or any clue to the person keeping it from us, it should have been buried here, waiting to be found.

If Constantius had lied to me to ease his conscience and in fact had never issued a retraction, this room should have provided the meticulous record-keeping to prove that.

But I was too late. Even as I left Julian in Naissus weeks ago with the warrants for the two consuls, Secundus Salutius had already been tapped as tribunal chief. He must have dispatched this Greek legal official here to investigate the same question. Where had Benedictus obtained Apodemius' 'copy'? I intended to pummel the truth out of that pale statue of a boy.

The corridor was empty.

Rufus and Benedictus were gone.

※※※

The sun had set behind the walls of the main Palace courtyard. Torches with staves the length of a man burned from sconces secured to the walls overhead. The shadows they cast were long, but their sulfurous flames did little to warm the winter air.

The guards patrolling the *scrinium* corridors had hustled Rufus and the colorless scribe back outside. Rufus had been wise not to alert them of my activity inside the solid carved office door. But now—where had they gone?

Again, the reek of Catena's sewers hit my nostrils from a nearby grate. I crouched down and, through the thick mist, my fingers found one of those apertures to Hades. I sniffed, but in addition to the foulness of decades of shit and vomit I also smelt . . . stew.

I continued back toward the Financial Building through the traffic usual for this hour: some officials heading late to the Palace Baths, day clerks hustling away to their cramped and seedy *insulae* rooms outside the imperial grounds, and a few off-duty laundry slaves tittering their way back from running errands in the city's market.

Then I saw someone who chilled me to my bones, a bloodless man more bluish-gray than white and more sinister than any Easterner stinking of feta.

As I shrank back to watch him lope past me, he paused and scowled, shielding his blinking eyes from the blaze of the nearest torch. But I'd seen him before tonight and then he was grinning wide-eyed at the sight of fresh blood and pus.

This evening he carried flatbreads and dried sausages from the marketplace in a basket as ordinary as that looped over the arms of the laundry girls returning with their cheap purchases a few yards ahead of him.

He hunched over, his skull cowering underneath his *cucullus* from the chilly breeze. But I knew him well enough.

It was the Worm—Catena's right hand man in the torture cells below ground. Few knew of his existence or had ever seen him during all his years of Constantius' reign, because to find yourself in his workplace meant no return to the life above.

Catena wasn't in Londinium.

He wasn't far away at all.

Chapter 9, Smashing Links

—The Palace, Mediolanum—

Ahenobarbus was returning to the *agentes*' rooms from a long afternoon spent in the Palace executive offices.

He shook his head: 'I've checked every single department within these walls. No one has seen Apodemius here. Your Vestal Tullia steered you in the wrong direction for reasons we can only guess. What's wrong, Numidianus?'

'Where's Rufus? Where's Cassius? We need them fast. I've spotted the Worm.'

Ahenobarbus curled his lips with distaste. 'Catena's assistant?'

'The creature himself, as innocent as a Christian acolyte, toting a basket of sausages back from the market.'

'Cassius is packing for the ride north. He couldn't locate his source, so he figures the only thing is to hurry via Lutetia to Londinium and see if he can pick up Catena's trail there.'

'Stop him. It's a ruse, a false rumor—bait to send our swiftest riders to the farthest reaches of Roman territory until things cool down for him.'

'Why—?'

'—because Catena is the most reviled man in the Empire, right? In what corner could he hide those notorious, lopsided features before someone turned him in—a widow, a relative, an embittered officer, a simple foot soldier? Why, there must be thousands of victims who lost someone to his cooked-up interrogations.'

'You think Catena's here? Protected by the Worm?'

'Under our boots as we speak. I can lead you now to a grate near the *sacra scrinia* leaking the stink of his warm stew.'

We found Rufus alone in his cell.

'Where's Junius?'

'Still with *mater*, I reckon.'

'What did you do with Benedictus?'

'Someone fetched him away and escorted me out of the corridor in the other direction. Did you get that document you needed?'

'No. Worse. Prefect Secundius Salutius sent someone to grab it first as evidence for Chalcedon.'

Ahenobarbus was already next door, rousing Cassius: 'Drop your bag. Numidianus thinks your man is hiding in the torture chambers right below ground. He saw the Worm returning from the market.'

'The *Worm*? Running errands? This place has a thousand slaves. The Worm would never leave his netherworld for anyone,' Cassius said, staring at us now crowding his doorway.

'Except Catena,' I countered.

Cassius dropped his travel sack. 'You're right. Let's go. Under your own nose, Rufus! Neptune's Balls!'

'Don't we need Junius?' I asked.

'As *princeps*, I order we leave the boy out of this,' Ahenobarbus said.

He seized both *spatha* and *pugio* and we followed suit. We filed back through the pillar shadows of the main courtyard toward the Palace. We made our way through minor reception rooms and echoing conference alcoves until we reached Constantius' great *consistorium*.

I'd never seen this assembly room completely empty before, devoid even of guards or cleaning slaves. The hulking incense burners and braziers sat on their tripods, dark and cold. The wall sconces were cold. Constantius' wide, armed *cathedra*, before which generals and bishops had prostrated themselves, waited on the dais in vain. It was no more than a vacant piece of old furniture.

Was I the only man tonight who thought he glimpsed the ghosts of Lampadius, Eusebius, and Arbitio along that great marble table totally bare of documents? Or those wide stools on which only the very loftiest of *consistoriani* were permitted to sit in the Divinity's presence?

—THE BURNING STAKES—

Ahenobarbus was first to reach the door at the end of the long room leading to steps descending to the tunnels below. We glanced into each other's eyes with the revulsion of men crossing the Styx to visit the dead.

I pointed to a slight wet patch on the floor where the Worm's leather slipper had crossed this sinister threshold.

'Wait, are there other exits or passages that must be secured?' I asked.

'I know of one,' Rufus said, 'a narrow tunnel, hardly the width of a man, giving on the alley not ten steps behind the Baths.'

Cassius nodded, 'Wait! There's a second—not a door, just a battered trap. The Worm fed their victims' corpses through it for incineration outside the city walls.'

'Then you two man those exits, so Ahenobarbus and I can trap these two in the bowels.'

'Sure you can handle him, Numidianus?' Rufus was proud of his broad physique, honed daily in the Palace gymnasium. He saw me as middle-aged.

'You've both been trained at the Castra, but you're riders, not fighters. Ahenobarbus and I have combat experience as well as the seniority to rope him in.'

They were to summon palatine guards as backup and show them Cassius' warrant. I whispered these orders to the younger duo with confidence, but still... Ahenobarbus had betrayed his years in the race up to Mediolanum and I'd spent four years behind a desk in Sirmium without wielding a weapon at anyone at all, much less anyone as desperate as a cornered Catena.

We measured the rise of the moon to allow Rufus and Cassius half an hour to position themselves. Then Ahenobarbus opened the door through which so many condemned to 'questioning' had disappeared forever. Pitch darkness waited below. I seized a wall torch from its sconce and held it over the *princeps*' head to illuminate the cracked stone steps that dropped steeply out of sight.

'In all these years, I never once went down there,' Ahenobarbus said, almost to himself. His boots froze in place.

'Come on,' I nudged him. 'Slaves go down all the time to fix the hypocaust piping.'

'But they say no citizen ever came back up.'

'It's just the plumbing system now. Catena took possession of an extension of the original heating and sewage passages. There's a sequence of central interrogation rooms with corridors of holding cells radiating outwards. I'll go first.'

I handed him the torch and stepped down ahead, balancing my left hand along granite thick with mossy slime. Ahenobarbus ducked his head and followed, the flame dancing behind his outstretched arm. We cast two unnatural silhouettes across the filthy stones underfoot.

We hadn't even reached level ground when a fierce and fetid aroma of stale vomit, blood, and shit invaded our nostrils. No doubt one of the Worm's responsibilities was to swab and sweep off the leavings of a day's work, but nothing could truly cleanse Catena's underworld. Even when he appeared in daylight, The Chain always gave off a repellent aroma of expensive bath oils masking human diarrhea. It clung to the soles of his high-cuffed *calcei* and the leather of his pigskin gloves, not to mention the sweeping ornate hem of his exaggerated *paenula*.

After passing through what I recognized as a rough antechamber, I padded ahead to a larger stone-walled space I knew to house a frame for strapping victims during interrogation. The image of faithful Proculus stretched to his limits, still protesting the integrity of Silvanus' command, roiled my stomach anew. I fought back nausea.

The rough-hewn walls caught my moving flare.

'Oh, the gods, the gods save us,' Ahenobarbus gasped, looking upwards.

Polished tools and weapons on racks—hatchets to amputate fingers and genitals, razors for slicing, and pokers and irons for searing and blinding—glinted back.

'Catena's so-called inner office', I whispered.

'Did Constantius realize? I knew him to be fearful but never perverse.'

'Did any soul, innocent or guilty, ever return to tell him? Quick, snuff out the light—'

A faint glow drew us forward down one of the corridors leading off Catena's interrogation hall. A low voice murmured. A grating rasp answered with the only sound possible for Catena's voice box after I garroted him in his Sirmium Palace dungeon a decade ago.

We crept forward like cats, our pupils widening on that glow, in search of the rat's hole. When we reached an abrupt narrowing of the passage that led away, Ahenobarbus unsheathed his *spatha*.

The sword's metal tip scraped the stone inches from his side. Its ringing sound betrayed us.

The faint glow ahead fell black. Without our own torch we stood blinded in a void that only our prey knew by touch.

There was no going back. I inched forward. Ahenobarbus followed. After a few seconds, my ears and nose seemed to have gained powers lost to my eyes.

Every sound grew louder—Ahenobarbus' nervous panting behind me, the crunch of loose gravel underfoot, the repeated plink-plink-plink of a broken Palace bath pipe dripping water from Mediolanum's vast plumbing network overhead.

The quiet shuffling of other boots pulled us along the passage almost against our wills. Catena might try to flee, but he wouldn't get past us by this route.

My nose caught a wisp of musky incense. Catena was using smoke from a censer to cleanse the rank and stagnant air in which he lived. Nostrils flaring, we traced this thread of perfume leading forward.

Another scuffling sound, then pounding footsteps thundered away. He'd broken into a run but the gods only knew where. We sped up, our knuckles grazing jutting cement work, following the growing reek until the walls fell away from our fingertips. We groped around in open space, ears and weapons poised for a sudden ambush.

A fresh clank of metal ricocheted far off—was that Rufus or Cassius bringing the *palatinae* forward?

Or Catena escaping?

I stumbled on an uneven stone and overturned a tripod. Metal rattled and rolled in a singing hum around our ankles, spraying the last of Catena's stew over my boots. We'd reached his lair, as empty and black as the passage, but giving off the stench and heat of an unwashed fugitive.

More bootsteps returned but at a steady, confident pace. The glow of a fresh torch became a bright flame held aloft by Cassius, backed by half a dozen guards, weapons extended and faces muffled from the stink by swathes of wool scarves.

'I saw his face!' Cassius burst out when he saw me crouching, ready for attack, in front of him. 'He tried the trap exit—it had to be him—then he turned and dodged back down. Where is he? We must have had him between us.'

A *domesticus* glistened with nervous sweat. His eyes still bulged with the shock of Catena's misshapen features looming up at him.

'Then he's headed for Rufus! The alleyway to the Baths! We'll re-secure the main steps,' I said.

Cassius and his guards lifted their torches to illuminate the walls of this miserable chamber until Ahenobarbus spotted another narrow aperture some ten feet away in the stone leading off in what we guessed was the direction of the Baths.

I took one torch off Cassius' party and, with more confidence now, Ahenobarbus and I squeezed ourselves around to face the opposite direction. I followed him on the return to guard the *consistorium* steps.

How the darkness had been kind to us! We hadn't realized on the inward journey that the walls were broken at regular intervals by cruel and windowless 'cells' that had interred Catena's victims in living *sarcophagi*.

We made a second awful discovery: what I'd taken in the dark for gravel under our boots was the crumbling detritus of torture victims littering the path to and from the detention holes—bits of bone or buckle that the conscientious Worm's mop and broom had missed.

But we'd underestimated the *notarius*, if in fact, that was really what the Dacian had ever been. A large iron grille now obstructed our safe passage to the last anteroom and the ascent back up to the *consistorium* hall. I flailed with both hands in a futile search for a bolt to draw back when a sudden lurch of a dark figure slinking along a wall behind a jutting boulder became Catena himself.

—THE BURNING STAKES—

He leered at me, his right arm already thrown tight around Ahenobarbus' shoulders and his *pugio*'s razor-sharp edge laid across the *princeps*' throat.

'I'll do to him what you did to me,' he rasped. 'Only worse.'

Ahenobarbus choked under his grip.

'You can't escape Emperor Julian's warrant for your arrest.'

'Sure I can. Tell your little bastard *agentes* to rip up the warrant or this—he slid his blade across Ahenobarbus' neck with a faint pressure. A thin line of red appeared.

'They'll issue another.'

'I'll take that chance—from Armenia.'

I banged my *spatha* on the grille bars to summon reinforcements. But Catena laughed. 'You'll regret that, my friend.'

I stabbed at him with the flaming head of the torch, but couldn't risk setting both men alight.

'Let me pass up those steps now, before we have an audience,' Catena hissed.

'I want an audience.'

'No, you don't.'

'I'm not afraid of you, Catena.'

'But you know very well you should be, Regicide.'

Ahenobarbus' eyes stared wide at me. He tried in vain to squirm free of the bulky torturer's vise-like hold.

Catena sliced the blade again across Ahenobarbus' neck, cutting very slightly deeper. A stream of blood began to run down the *princeps*' chest. Ahenobarbus gave a powerful jab with his elbow into Catena's stomach, but only hit the jewels of the notary's strutted belt.

'You toss down your weapons, one by one, Numidianus—with the torch—into that corner there and stand on the other side of the room while your friend and I return upstairs.'

With his foot he kicked aside a bolt positioned low to the ground. The grille swung open.

I had to act quickly to save Ahenobarbus. Catena would stop just short of finishing him off at the top of the stairs and drop him dying in the doorway to delay me and thwart our pursuit.

His hostage was as tall and wide as he. How could I swing at that tangle of legs or clutching arms without hurting the wrong man? Why had the *domestici* not answered the clatter of my sword?

Ahenobarbus was struggling but blood loss was dizzying him—his unfocused eyes rolled in disbelief through the gloom.

And now here was an ally to help Catena escape. The wraithlike silhouette of the Worm, armed with a poker, emerged from the shadows of the very corner Catena had designated my retreat. Catena must have known all along that the Worm was lurking there, waiting to run me through.

But the poker was long and precise, exactly what I needed. Tossing the flaming torch into the Worm's face, I seized my moment to wrest the long rod out of his grasp. If I moved quickly, I could reach past Ahenobarbus and pierce Catena with the precision my sword lacked. I would kill off the bastard with the guilty pleasure one feels sticking a javelin into an ugly, long-fanged boar.

Catena chuckled.

'That's right—kill me, Numidianus. Defy the new regime. See how Julian likes his orders disobeyed,' he taunted, his small nose and uneven eyebrows dripping sweat. He jerked hold of Ahenobarbus tighter. 'You have seconds left. Stand back.'

'You'll get a fair trial, Catena.'

'Then I'll make sure you follow me,' he hissed. 'Because my testimony will be against you—the murderer of Emperor Constans and the slaughterer of Caesar Gallus. If I fall, so do you, Numidianus. And your precious House of Manlius falls forever.'

'Lies, libel!'

I held off the Worm with my *spatha* in my left hand and jockeyed for a better aim with the poker at Catena's larger eye, blinking fast through rivulets of sweat.

'Lies?' he rasped. 'You escaped justice for Constans because Silvanus lied for you. You escaped justice for Gallus by blaming Barbatio! It was you, you fucking little freedman, who slew one Constantine after another. That's what the tribunal will hear from me and Julian will love every word. He hated your *schola* and so do I. You *agentes* traitors stick like shit to my boots. They call me The Chain because I forged links between men—'

'Linking one lie to another—'

'But go ahead. Turn me in. Once my accusations hang around your neck, shackling you will be easy. My grateful new emperor will reward me. You'll curse the day you sent me to Chalcedon.'

Years of brooding underground had fermented his curdled hatreds into vintage poison. He gave a high-pitched, rasping laugh. 'Still think I should wait around?'

He was right. All Julian's tribunal needed was to hear all those old charges revived against me, so untrue and yet only a hair's breadth from truth. My execution order would be sealed, the *schola*'s interests fatally wounded, and Apodemius doomed for trusting me within a mile of a Constantine ruler for so many years.

Let Catena go, then? I took a last look at his mismatched eyes, that pinched nose too small for his heft, and the swarthy cheeks and neck marked by the deep scar I'd left.

Why not let him take his accusations against me into the Armenian wastes? He sowed hatred wherever he went. Sooner or later, others would slay him for me. Let him die like a parched reptile on some bleached and uncharted steppe past the last civilized hamlet.

My hesitation proved lethal. Out of the shadows the Worm rose to his full height, his moon-white arms glistening like the underbelly of a snake, making for me.

I gasped. I lifted my sword, but I was too slow.

He surged past my swinging weapon and slipped like a thread of mercury to Catena's side. He would bar my way to let Catena escape, dragging away Ahenobarbus, soaked red and drowning in his own blood, up, up, up the steep stairs to freedom.

The Worm reached up and flung a loop of thick rope over Catena's head. He yanked back, banging the Dacian's thick skull fast to the iron bars of the grille. Catena dangled, choking, and hoisted up until his toes barely reached the floor.

I fell back, stunned.

Catena's hold on Ahenobarbus loosened. The *princeps* fell forward onto the ground between us. He clutched for purchase on the worn stones, to lift himself as a hero might, for a last chance to attack The Chain.

'I am a slave,' the Worm said in a low, flat voice. 'I always obey. I do not disobey Emperor Julian's warrant.'

Catena gurgled and reached with futile, claw-like swings to get hold of us, then wrestled with the rope cutting into his bristles, but to no avail. The Worm winched it tighter.

Only a few minutes had passed, but the clatter of boots arriving from distant passages heralded what felt like another day. The *domestici* used Catena's own chains and fetters to weigh down his ankles and wrists. They clamped a collar of lead thick as my wrist around his neck before shoving him into the nearest cell to await conveyance to the East.

'Pray that Nemesis protects you all the way to Chalcedon,' I advised Cassius. 'He'll need watching night and day. Let no one—man, woman or child—come near him, for only the gods know what tricks he'll try to escape.'

In my heart, I knew that this might be wishful thinking on my part. Before they slammed the solid door shut on Catena, I saw him break into a wide smile. He'd already started feeding his strange addiction to suffering with the unfamiliar fuel of his own incarceration. In his overheated mind, he was nearly to Chalcedon, laying out his half-rehearsed stories and forging new links in a chain of incriminating rumors—about that singular traitor against Emperor Julian's family—*Centenarius* Marcus Gregorianus Numidianus.

※※※

Two guard medics refused to operate on Ahenobarbus in the *agentes'* under-lit rooms. Gagging on blood under a makeshift tourniquet, Ahenobarbus rode on a stretcher across the court to one of the minor imperial suites. Long emptied of ladies and slaves by the departure of Constantius' busy court, dozens of rooms sat vacant in the residential wing of the Palace.

We raced an imperial physician to Ahenobarbus' bedside. He cleansed the wound with biting *acetum* and stitched up its gaping edges. Catena had not pierced his windpipe but there was drastic loss of blood.

By now another December evening was upon us. The courtyard's massive marble sundial stood useless in a blanket of mist. The hellish minutes underground has passed like hours. I'd read whole volumes in the frightened eyes of Ahenobarbus, the wild-eyed leer of Paulus Catena, and the inhuman compliance of the slavish Worm.

Yet no one above ground had noticed a thing.

Behind a pillar near the secretariat, a last cluster of officials wrapped themselves up to their earlobes under thick woolen hoods. They exchanged final words setting out the next day's agenda before breaking off by two and threes for their banquets.

It seemed incredible how these courtiers, archivists, advocates, scribes, and slaves went about their routine business. But of course, that had long been the way of Constantius' reign. The senses of decent citizens became inured over many years to disquieting noises or unpleasant smells seeping up from grates and plumbing conduits.

Hadn't 'Our Eternity,' *Imperator* Constantius himself set an example of hardened deafness to what happened beyond those stairs leading down from his council chamber?

But then, it seemed I was wrong. A young voice piped up: 'The *domestici* are whispering among themselves outside the Secretariat.'

The Britannian at my side lifted his fresh, reddened cheeks to a rising breeze.

'You were fetched away before I could ask you further questions.'

'Here I am.'

'Explain why our *magister* referred us to you.'

'I do not know him. But I understand more now.'

'Why?'

'Because I overheard Chryseros talk to your fellow *agens*.'

With precision that would have impressed a Castra trainer, Benedictus described Cassius perfectly, right down to the quick twitch of the mouth and the habit of hitching his riding trousers.

'What else?'

'Your man took a purse of coins from the eunuch.'

I heaved a disappointed sigh. Always in need of a fresh allowance to gamble and cheat into a sackload of *solidi*, Cassius had fallen victim to the soft-spoken seductions of Chryseros and told him—what exactly?

Cassius knew we were searching for Apodemius, but nothing of the suspicious loss of any imperial rescindment order. I was thankful that I'd kept so much of Apodemius' troubles to myself.

But news that the old man had gone missing could be damaging enough in the wrong hands. I was glad that, as someone had to leave our band to escort Catena, it turned out in the end to be Cassius—the one *agens* whose Achilles Heel at the dice table made him too weak to trust much further.

'So you know our former *magister* has disappeared.'

He nodded.

'I know you provided him a copy of a precious letter.'

The wise boy looked at his thin slippers and waited, saying nothing. I admired his aplomb but he didn't deny assisting Apodemius either.

'Where's Apodemius?'

'I know nothing that can help you, *Centenarie*.'

'Because you can't be sure of me. That's it, isn't it? So you remain loyal, discreet, and prudent—'

'I assure you, *Centenarie*—'

'Don't waste your breath, boy. It's obvious. Someone instructed you well. So I will only ask you a separate question. Who is the "Marble Vestal"?'

Startled, Benedictus looked up at me with a less clouded expression. 'But the Vestals serve in Roma, *Centenarie*. Even the stupidest Pict slave knows that.'

'Perhaps this so-called Marble Vestal is retired?'

'I know of no such person,' he said. But his bunion'ed writing fingers twisted the rough brown weave of his tunic.

'Too bad, because I carry a private message for this woman. It may be important. I don't know. We *agentes* often find ourselves in that position. Our delivery of a message can mean nothing to us—but everything to its recipient.'

I didn't hide my confusion. As I hoped, the boy's fiddling fingers relaxed. He'd stopped worrying about betraying Apodemius. He looked all around the emptying courtyard to make sure he wasn't overheard. In his fluting voice, he said, 'Perhaps you should ask Flavia.'

'Where will I find her?'

He drew back, puzzled. 'But surely your companions would know. There's already another *agens* with her, or at least, that's what I've hear.'

'Another *agens*? Where is this Flavia?' My hand gripped his shoulder too hard. He winced.

'The old Temple of Minerva behind the Imperial Baths.'

'It's been bolted up for years.'

'Flavia's a recluse, hiding herself in rooms opposite the temple entrance.'

'Why do you know about her?'

'I've never seen her. But stories go around the court. Copying is a boring task. The old scribes—the pagans—speculated about her last week. For so many decades our Christian court has had no use for her, so maybe now she'll take her revenge and show how little use she has for us.'

'You're a Christian?'

An anxious frown creased his pale brow. 'Is it true Emperor Julian is going to reverse everything? Will he re-open the temples and raze the basilicas? Will he persecute us followers of the Savior?'

How fast these fearful rumors were flying, from Kahina's gaggle of society ladies with their charitable organizations to a stalwart green colonial who'd barely spent ten minutes at court!

'No,' I said, patting a shoulder hunched by hours over a desk. 'Julian is not so stupid as to create martyrs. He'll let you Galileans devour each other, one faction against the other, like beasts in the arena.'

Benedictus recoiled. I suspected more than ever that Apodemius had indeed met him. What if he'd earned the lad's trust with a guarantee of our *schola*'s protection?

'We *agentes* keep our promises,' I said without asking him what promises had been made. 'You won't come to harm, Benedictus. Now, go inside before the night chills even your sturdy northern bones.'

Chapter 10, The Sword of Honos

—THE PALACE OF MEDIOLANUM—

'Don't try to talk, *Princeps*.' Rufus said as Ahenobarbus rallied. He woke up from an opiate-induced doze with a neck full of thick black stitches, healing salve, and boiled linen already dark brown with his stiffened blood.

At his bedside, surgical tools bathed in a bin of *acetum*, in case more stitching or scraping was required.

'I'm glad to see you awake,' I gestured for Rufus to wait in the anteroom outside.

'That scribe Benedictus told me that there's a Vestal in the old Temple of Minerva out in the Forum,' I whispered, 'who's sheltering an *agens*.'

'Apo—?' He struggled.

'Shhh.' I nodded, 'It has to be him. I'm convinced the boy swore to protect Apodemius but decided to give me enough hints to keep us on the trail. Because I mentioned the "Marble Vestal", he took a chance on me.'

Ahenobarbus scowled, but whether from pain or disagreement, he was too weak to do more than mutter. But I could see that he was determined to warn me of something. I put my ear close to his lips.

'You haven't . . . seen how Apodemius worked over this last year—secretive, mistrustful, short-tempered.' His wheezing words were distressing to decipher. 'He's changed. He's not the *magister* you left . . .'

'Perhaps, but that doesn't deter me from finding him.'

I rested a calming hand on Ahenobarbus' bare arm before continuing:

'I see three possibilities: Apodemius came up here to verify the authenticity of a copy of the rescindment order you heard Constantius announce with your own ears in 354. Or second, he fled Roma in some other direction because of quite a different threat unknown to us. We know there have been attempts on his life before. Or—.'

'— third. He . . . just . . . retired.'

Ahenobarbus managed a thin smile. It was typical of my superior, the most straightforward *agens* I'd ever reported to, to convert a mystery to the mundane.

'You mean, just collected his papers and mice and . . . disappeared?'

'Trust Otho to handle it,' Ahenobarbus murmured. 'He knows what's at stake for the *schola*'s future.'

'Remember that huge curtain they used to hang across the *consistorium* sometimes so that lowlier officials couldn't watch Constantius on the dais at work?'

He nodded.

'I feel like *something* is happening behind the curtain,' I insisted. 'A Greek official from the East was in the *sacra scrinia* ahead of me with a warrant from Salutius. He must be the person who tampered with the index.'

Ahenobarbus closed his eyes and heaved a painful sigh through his constricted air pipe.

'Why did Salutius send an official all the way here to do that? You see why? These pages would prove or disprove Constantius' claims to me in Mopsucrenae that he sent a last-minute order to Eusebius to save Caesar Gallus. Now only the tribunal knows Constantius' orders during those weeks in 354.'

'Even if an order's indexed, it might not show what Constantius' order *said*. Two and two do not make—' he coughed and sank deeper into his pillow.

The *princeps* was right. I was leaping to a dangerous assumption—that Apodemius' copy in Roma was of the document registered in the gutted index.

But now that I knew where Apodemius was hiding, half my problem was solved.

'By tonight, this nightmare will be over. So now I'm going to collect him out of hiding at the temple. As soon as you're well enough to travel, we'll take Apodemius back with us to the Castra. We won't leave his side again until we've solved the mystery of this rescindment to stay the execution—fraudulent or real.'

Ahenobarbus breathed slowly. The doctors had given him a powerful tonic but he saw through me, nonetheless.

'Numidianus, you're afraid for yourself.'

It was ignoble to hide behind a show of worry for Apodemius.

I nodded, ashamed. 'You heard what Catena said?'

'So it's true? You . . . did kill Emperor Constans? General Silvanus gave false testimony to absolve you?'

It was hard to let the truth surface, even to a man as trustworthy as the *princeps* lying panting on his sickbed.

'Silvanus had betrayed Commander Gregorius and all the rebels under Magnentius. Perhaps the morning after the battle at Mursa, he felt how much he owed me, Gregorius' freedman Numidianus. When he saw the imperial *spatha* lifted over my neck, he stepped forward and challenged Catena's accusation. At least he did the Manlius House that much honor.'

'So Catena was right?'

'No! No! No, I didn't assassinate Emperor Constans in cold blood! We'd hunted him down at the temple in Vicus Helena. Constans was cornered like a rat. I was covering Lieutenant Gaiso's back. He rushed at Gaiso from behind with his ceremonial sword, a pathetic parade piece. I . . . I . . . was only defending a superior officer. I didn't think straight until it was too late and . . . a son of Constantine lay there, bleeding to death on my boots.'

He was losing his battle with sleep. I hurried with the rest:

'Ahenobarbus, listen to me. You know I didn't slaughter Caesar Gallus in Pula. You know it was Barbatio who carried out Constantius' order. But this is what you don't know. Before he died, Barbatio laid a curse on my head. He called on the gods to revenge themselves on me.'

'Don't be afraid of empty curses. Trust Otho. He knows . . . what's at stake . . . for the *schola*.' He turned his face away as he fell asleep.

Rufus resented waiting outside like a schoolboy. I surprised him leaning too close to the door trying to eavesdrop. I entrusted the *princeps* to Rufus' watchful eye. But I didn't explain why I left the sickroom with an expression more unsettled than when I'd arrived.

It was nothing I could explain to the junior officer. It wasn't just that I realized Ahenobarbus still lay in danger. It was a realization that had been creeping into my soul since my arrival at Otho's reorganized Castra. This truth now stood before me as plain as the sentry guarding the exit overlooking the great steps of the Palace as I returned to the Financial Building.

It was this: The years were exacting their natural toll and stripping me of my protectors and mentors. The men who'd witnessed events as they really happened were slipping away, one by one.

The last of the troops who had followed my horse in pursuit of Emperor Constans to his final redoubt were lost to me as defenders.

Both Generals Silvanus and Barbatio had been executed for treason—real or imagined. Recent politics and ambition had painted over old history with a fresh coat of imperial power. Even had they survived, any word of exoneration on my behalf from Silvanus or Barbatio in a tribunal today might have been downright dangerous to me.

Only the Lord Chamberlain Eusebius—whose very sinews were twisted from fibrous lies—was still among us. He'd been in Pula that night. He knew the truth about Barbatio and Gallus. But Eusebius would rather lie and name me the assassin, if only to use me as an accessory to trap my *magister*.

And Constantius, the devout but fearful emperor, who listed from side to side like a ship buffeted by a tempest of rumors? He might have had the patience to hear the truth. He'd even promised me a fresh inquiry. But he was a corpse in Constantinopolis.

And Apodemius, who'd followed orders and signaled Barbatio to bring his sword down on Gallus' neck? He must be found.

I shook off my gloom like a dog coming in from the rain. For one thing, why assume the missing index page registered any *rescindment*? Might Salutius not read proof there was *no* order sent to Pula that week? That Constantius lied to me in Mopsucrenae? And that what Apodemius held in his safe box was pure fabrication?

Anyway, I comforted myself with one desperate hope. Was Julian's jury of hardened army veterans likely to believe the ravings of a doomed lunatic named Paulus Catena?

※※※

Mediolanum's main forum was a long rectangle with the Temple of Minerva at the northern end. Some attempt had been made under Constantius to convert it to a church. But in the end, the straight, clean space of the Temple didn't accommodate the late Pannonian emperor's ornate Eastern tastes in Christian ritual.

There were other basilicas across the capital more suited to the crowds of clerics attending Constantius' endless round of religious synods—the *Basilica Major*, *Basilica Martyrorium*, *Basilica Apostolorium* and, of course, the *Basilica Palatina*.

I crossed the crowded forum this evening thinking that, now Constantius was dead, the city's powerful Bishop Auxentius must be reveling in uncontested management of so many valuable properties.

The Temple of Minerva was a sorry sight. A collection of public scribes' stalls, vendors' displays, and a pyramid of bolts of imported cloth obscured its holy facade.

The tall, carved doors of the temple stood bolted fast and padlocked together for good measure. Surely, this couldn't be the sanctuary of Apodemius. But I didn't give up. I threaded myself past a merchant's tinkling curtain of dangling pottery Saturnalia gods and goddesses. There was the narrowest of passages between the temple's side and a state building built next to it.

But I found no access into the temple itself and emerged out the other end of the alley into the Via Moneta behind the state mint headquarters.

A solid wall of granite rose up to meet an elegant pitched roof surrounded along the top of its columns by a frieze. Our ancient and imperturbable gods and goddesses gazed down from the eaves of the roof onto the bustling stalls and hovels, *insulae*, and shops jostling for their precious feet of frontage.

An old man sat on a stool with his dog at the edge of the curb. Neither man nor beast seemed particularly worried about catching the mud of preoccupied passersby or the dangers of a fuller's overflowing urine vat a few yards away.

I asked him in a low voice if he knew of a retired Vestal Flavia? Without a word, the wily sage pointed with his knobby walking stick to a crumbling three-story apartment across the street—the least desirable real estate on the block.

I thanked him with a fistful of *nummi*. Within the half-open shutters of the apartment, I glimpsed a man's long *paenula* draped across a string to catch the winter sun that had sunk out of sight hours ago. A pair of thick woolen socks dried on a string—man's socks. A lamp lit up inside to greet the evening chill.

A hand reached out and closed the shutters but too fast for me to be sure—was it a man's hand? Was it arthritic and knobby?

The ground floor of the building housed a popular *taberna* doing brisk business filling dinner orders. The aromas floating into the street dizzied me.

A gaggle of chattering slaves waited up and down the sidewalk. With arms wrapped around empty red ware casseroles, they waited to plop the lid down on a batch of fresh-cooked stew or roasted rabbit. Mediolanum might be a younger city, but it was nearly as flammable as ancient Roma. Few living on the upper floors of these shoddy *insulae* dared to heat an oven or boil a pot.

Just then, an elegant young man with an air of purpose emerged from the laundry shop behind me. He carried a string bag of fresh vegetables on top of a thick stack of linens lined with gold braid and tied with a canvas belt. He dodged into the *taberna* with a familiar wave to the aproned proprietor tending the meat grill. I followed him up the steps at the back of the dining room—the access to the very apartment I sought.

—THE BURNING STAKES—

The slave realized I was following him. When he reached the first landing, he noticed my insignia, and thought better of stopping me up the next flight of steps.

He hesitated outside the uppermost door. Then, pushing it open with his shoe, he tried to slip in with his bundle. I pushed past him without apology into the front room of a frugal apartment. On my left was that cloak, still hanging like a room separator over a long thin string tied to crude hooks in the walls.

A man sat in shadow at the far end of the room. He stirred up red sparks in a brazier to warm up the place.

'Put her laundry in the back room,' he said, scarcely looking up at the slave. But his rough Neapolitan accent, shaven head, powerful shoulders bent over the bronze burner—these fixed me, shocked, in the doorway.

No, it was not the retired *magister agentium in rebus* I'd unearthed here.

It was Constantius' other missing *notarius*.

I found my voice. 'What are you doing here, Gaudentius?'

He jumped up, grabbing a *pugio* lying next to a half-loaf of bread. It had run many a man through before today. He backed up against the far wall, crouching and ready.

'Resting up. It's a long way from Africa.'

'Don't tell me this is your new home?'

'No, I'm a guest.'

'Of the retired Vestal?'

'No business of yours, Numidianus.'

'How do you know Flavia?'

'You forget I was chief *agens* of Constantius' court in this city. There isn't a man, woman, slave or dog worth knowing who hasn't landed at least once in my reports to headquarters. Now it's your turn, Freedman. What in Hades brings you to this nasty little corner?'

'I heard an *agens* was hiding out here.'

'A *former* agent. Now get your ass out of here.'

'The Castra thinks you're on the run. Didn't Africa agree with you?'

I pulled up a wooden stool, refusing to exit quite as fast as that. 'I heard your blockade was a great success—Julian was desperate for months.'

The hand clutching the dagger lowered an inch.

'Africa? Nothing but farmers and dye merchants. But I told that Count Cretio and the other commanders what needed to be done and they listened to me. It was I who assembled the bravest soldiers from every unit on hand. I brought over light-armed skirmishers from both the Mauritanian provinces.'

He flexed his chest. 'It was Gaudentius who made sure that the shores lying opposite to Aquitania and Italia were guarded tighter than a virgin's—'

'My, my, Gaudentius. You missed your true calling. Instead of utterly failing as a spy on Julian in Gallia, you should have joined the army.'

'You can smirk, Numidianus, but Constantius made no mistake in putting me in charge. For so long as "Our Eternity" lived, none of Julian's troops landed on that coast or touched its riches. Not that he didn't try! He had forces posted all down the coast of Sicilia, from Lilybaeum to Pachynum, the bastards just waiting to cross over the minute I let down my guard.'

'You were so sure Constantius would win?'

'Oh, let's hear it, your usual insinuations that I'm not only unlettered, but stupid.'

He leaned over, his glistening scalp reflecting the brazier's red glow.

'*We all were sure he'd win.* You included, Numidianus. Don't deny it! So I did my job—cut off Julian's grain and oil.'

'You did fine.'

He bristled, 'And His Divinity would have rewarded me well if—'

'Julian's in charge now and since you weren't one of his favorites up in Gallia—.'

'—I'll rejoin the *schola*.' He sat down to slice himself some bread.

'Back to the Castra? You know the rules. You'd have to start over again at the bottom. Surely not such a demotion for the self-made Neapolitan?'

'I climbed up once. I can do it again. I'll run rings around this new man, Otto.'

—THE BURNING STAKES—

'*Otho*. He won't have you. He's running a new shop. Lots of paperwork and meetings. Not your style, Gaudentius. Go back to North Africa. Try farming.'

'He'll have to take me in. I know too much.'

'Hah!'

I was eking some enjoyment out of Gaudentius' discomfort. I pulled off my cloak. I had little to fear from a man so out of touch.

'Know too much? Not about Otho. In fact, nobody knows much about Otho—except that he comes from doing tax inspections in Palaestina. His people, the Atia, are plebeians. Even his cognomen Otho means "unknown." He likes morning meetings, daily reports, and clean procedure. And that's really not your style, is it, as Governor Africanus and his dinner guests learned to their regret?'

More than once, Gaudentius had interrogated, reported, betrayed, and arrested men with the express aim of jumping over Apodemius' head and flaunting his maverick displays of loyalty to Constantius. Exaggerating the banquet boasts of some drunken provincials into treasonous crimes, Gaudentius had won the Emperor's trust, leapfrogged over Ahenobarbus and other senior *agentes*, and reveled in his abrupt promotion out of our *schola* altogether.

I wasn't the only *agens* who'd never again trust Gaudentius. His untrammeled ambition was so devouring, I'd once suspected him of attempting murder in 355. As he guarded an ailing Apodemius in Agrippina, I'd worried that the stinking tonics Gaudentius measured out were doing the old man more harm than good—he was *that* close to filling Apodemius' shoes.

Years of bitterness hadn't made Gaudentius' pitted, doughy features any handsomer. The North African plateau had burnt his face and neck an unseasonal mahogany. I couldn't see the manicured Otho welcoming the return of Gaudentius to the Castra one bit.

'*Agentes* are made of muscle and persistence—not bureaucracy, Numidianus. I don't need this Otho or your help. I'll go straight to the old man. I saved his life up there in Agrippina. Apodemius has to work me back in. He'll find a way.'

'The old man is gone, Gaudentius,' I spit out with frustration.

This trail was leading me nowhere near to Apodemius in time to warn him of the tribunal's deliberations.

There was a long silence as that thug poked at the brazier like a newlywed housewife.

'So where is he? I need him.'

I didn't answer. Gaudentius leapt up and pointed his *pugio* at me again. 'I asked you, where did he go?'

'I don't know. I thought he was here.' I kept my eyes steady and voice calm. He pulled back his blade.

'I thought you'd come to arrest me,' he admitted. 'There are strange rumors floating through the city.'

'They're true. Both consuls are named, Taurus already arrested, and Florentius on the run. It looks like a show trial for the army with Arbitio going for Constantius' civil servants.'

Gaudentius stabbed his *pugio* hard into the wooden tabletop.

'This afternoon we excavated Catena,' I said, 'hiding in the Palace hypocaust tunnels. Cassius leaves tomorrow morning for Chalcedon with that monster wearing a set of his own chains.'

'Maybe I'm next,' Gaudentius said with guttural resignation, 'unless I can produce some golden gift to bribe myself back into Julian's favor.'

He shot me a wary glance, still afraid to expose his back. I might suddenly clamp an iron shackle around his bull neck.

I was ravenous and grabbed a piece of bread. 'Where's your hostess?'

'Well, I tell you, there's one person in this city happy to see Julian take power. She's cleaning out the temple with her slaves in readiness for the imminent restitution of the true gods.'

'I have a message for her.'

'A message? Surely not from Catena?' Gaudentius had never been a wit, but at least he had the mettle to joke. 'Will you be back for me on your way to the Castra?'

I shook my head, no. He'd never been a friend to me and had no right to ask me to take up his hopeless cause.

'Think you're too good, Freedman? Too good for the gutter boy from Neapolis? I can make it worth your while,' he sneered.

—THE BURNING STAKES—

As the door slammed behind me, I marveled that a retired Vestal could tolerate his company for an hour, much less a day or week. Perhaps he'd once done Flavia some favor during her years of social exile under the Arian grandees of Constantius' Christian court.

Gaudentius was not entirely incapable of being true to his singular idea of loyalty.

⚜⚜⚜

I discovered a door on the opposite side of the temple. It stood ajar beside a gutter running with rubbish and excrement. Flavia's laundry deliverer was wielding a broom over a couple of marble steps leading inside.

The cold, stuffy air that gripped my face inside the temple was a shock, even after the bracing chill of the December night.

And equally shocking, I'd stumbled into an assembly of a hundred rigid figures. A secret synod of colorful gods was underway. Dozens of brightly painted orbs stared past me, over me, and through me, but not a lip quivered.

The goddess Minerva had exercised no discrimination in her invitation between major and minor divinities. Their outstretched hands hailed, saluted, remonstrated, and guided me forward into the recesses of the temple.

And everything else that greeted me was also cement or marble—a cracked *labrum* to catch the blood of ritual sacrifice, a circle of low blocks that marked out an inner circle for the absent *flamen* and his praying attendants, and the pillars that lined the long rectangular outer walls—all freezing to the touch.

There was a faint brushing sound at the far end of this eerie 'gathering.'

Then one figure draped in ivory to her ankles sprang to life and turned to study me on behalf of her motionless companions.

She was a tall woman of late middle age. The hair over her forehead was lifted up from her high brow and wrapped around a thick invisible cord fastened in a circular tube ending at her nape. The rest of her hair hid under a turban-like *infula*. But what hair I saw was striped black, gray, and white like the streaked marble of the ancient floors that echoed under my boot steps.

Two little slave girls scuttled around on their knees, scrubbing decades of grime out of the crevices between the Verona flagstones. Their mistress might keep them working until midnight.

She saw my insignia. '*Agens?*' Her expression was as stony as her surroundings.

'*Centenarius* Marcus Numidianus Gregorianus. I bring a message from a retired Vestal in Roma, Tullia. The lady is old and blind—'

'I know the person. Deliver your message.' Her voice was hard.

'The Veiled Vestal is safe in Cibalae.'

She stared at me, unblinking. The statues watching us from all sides of the long chamber showed more animation, painted though they were, than this long-scorned priestess.

'It's late for business. If that's all, you may go.'

Her implacable façade congealed any response hanging on my lips. She rotated with almost inhuman grace, like a column of wool, linen, and unyielding muscle, to resume her supervision of the children.

With an effort, I shook off her chilly spell. 'This is a very beautiful temple, *Domina* Flavia. It's a shame to see it used as a storeroom. Under Emperor Julian, may it come back to life.'

'You believe in the true gods? You're a *cultor deorum?*'

She didn't face me, but her voice seemed a sliver softer.

'With all my heart. I grew up a slave in a mixed family, a respected Roman pagan *domus* run by a Christian convert mistress.'

'The usual modern solution,' she said with a sniff. 'They try to keep the family protected on all theological fronts, like those gamblers in the *taberna* downstairs, hedging their bets. No one can trick the *Parcae* that way. The Fates will always weave a man's life the way they choose.'

I walked over to a statue of an armored god, neither young nor old, with one boot poised on a globe. He held a lance in one hand and a cornucopia in the other.

—THE BURNING STAKES—

'This is Honos, the god of chivalry, honor, and military justice?'

'So he is. That statue was moved in here from the Forum some years ago. As was Virtus, over there. Many were shifted from public spaces shortly after Constantius brought his court to reside in Mediolanum. Of course, he left the great emperors in the Forum, but one by one, these statues were consigned here for "cleaning and repairs." And never saw sunlight again.'

'Honos should be moved to Chalcedon.'

'So the rumors are true?' She still didn't face me.

'The accused must answer for actions committed while in Constantius' civil service. Yet it's a military court and those charged will find themselves at the mercy of military justice, such as it is. I've served as a *volo* in military camps and I've seen the kind of justice meted out in tents and barracks.'

She turned at last. I'd interested her. She scrutinized me. 'Then let's hope they find Honos bestowing his chivalry and honor in the East.'

'We've arrested Paulus Catena.'

'Paulus Catena? Hardly a "civil" servant.'

She had a sense of humor. Could I play on that?

I walked over to a towering figure of Nemesis, the Greek goddess of revenge and retribution, holding out a set of scales.

'Perhaps we could dispatch this lady goddess as one of his escorts under the command of my fellow *agens*, Biarchus Cassius?'

'Indeed. Nemesis consoles the spirits of those who have met a violent end. And she balances the random chance of Lady Fortuna's whims. No one can avoid Nemesis.'

I walked within a few feet of that grave face drawn with heavy lines and said to her, 'The tyrant King Polycrates tried hard enough. He tossed his most precious ring into the sea as a bribe—'

'—which then returned in the belly of a fish served at his royal table.'

Flavia shooed away the two little girls to join the slave sweeping outside the door. Their relieved giggles warmed the frosty air.

Flavia scrutinized my features with the frightening light-blue eyes of a wolf. 'What are you doing here, *Curiose*?'

'I delivered that message.'

'Now you linger. What do you want in return?'

'I'm looking for *Magister Agentium-in-Rebus* Apodemius.'

She paused for many minutes. I waited.

Finally she asked, 'What do you know about the Veiled Vestal?'

'Zero. *Nullus*.'

She laid a large but graceful hand on the shoulder of a gold-plated Apollo, as if needing support.

'I was expecting one of you, sooner or later. Oh, not that southerner using my outer room. I've known him for many years. He's not evil, only brutish and ambitious, thinking only of how to save himself.'

'So whom were you expecting?'

'I don't know. The gods did not reveal his name. He might be the most loyal or sentimental. Or the toughest or smartest or most ambitious. Are you one who protects—or one who betrays?'

'Your oracles are a mystery to me. What can you tell me of this Veiled Vestal?'

'Only this much, purely as a warning for your safety. No one can look on her face. Though much younger than any of our retired sisterhood, misfortune drove her into a sheltered life.'

'And is there any connection with *Magister* Apodemius?'

I lost patience and grabbed her solid arm, so cool and firm. '*Domina*, I must know!'

'Apodemius has been her guardian ever since her enforced seclusion. Her misfortune was not his fault, but you might say it was his responsibility.'

'What misfortune?

'Her family home was attacked one night. Everything—house and all its inhabitants from elders to slaves—all burnt to ashes. The neighbors could only stand by, helpless to put out the flames, for this fire exploded into an inferno executed with the precision of a military mind bent on revenge.'

'And this virgin?'

—THE BURNING STAKES—

'Only she survived, a baby carried to safety in the arms of a fire-fighting *vigil*—survived just. Since then, she has had to veil her features.'

'But all the Vestals are chosen for their beauty as well as—'

Flavia cut me off with a slow nod that explained nothing. 'If you ever meet this sad creature, remember to leave her the dignity of her veil and know that whatever lies beneath that curtain of plain linen, only pure goodness, not recrimination, dwells in her heart.'

'*If* I meet her? Why should I meet her?'

The thought of facing such a forlorn, disfigured victim, even veiled, was hardly appealing.

'I'm sorry. Of course she's not the one you seek. You have your mission to find Apodemius, don't you?'

'I fear he's in danger from Julian's tribunal for a crime he didn't commit.'

'Then I'll make an offering to Honos on your *magister*'s behalf. Now, *Agens* Numidianus, leave me to my duties. We have much to do. It has been too long since Saturnalia has been properly celebrated at this neglected altar.'

I touched my *spatha* hilt and bowed my head with respect.

'Delay your duties no longer,' she ordered with an emphatic wave. 'Delay nothing.'

I felt the lingering sting of her insult *curiosus* as I passed the slaves packing up their brushes and buckets for the night. Yet there had been an equal hint, glancing but distinct, of a thaw as she referred to my search for Apodemius.

I raced back through the forum to check on Ahenobarbus. She was right. It was important to delay nothing—yet how was I to find out what that 'nothing' was?

Chapter 11, Restitution

—The Imperial Residential Wing, Mediolanum Palace—

At least one thing was clear. The Vestals Tullia and Flavia knew something they weren't free to divulge. This was the second occasion, only after some circuitous testing of my personal *bona fides*, that one dropped hints that kept me inching ahead.

They did not quite trust me. But could I trust them? Were they sending me in the right direction? Were they not pagan, and therefore the natural allies of Julian's new order?

I knew for certain, thanks to Benedictus' help, that Salutius' Eastern envoy was ahead of me in removing any evidence that Constantius' last-ditch effort to save Gallus' neck had—or had not—been issued.

And second, I knew that Apodemius was linked by some debt to this strange sisterhood of retired Vestals, including a younger Vestal injured in a Roman conflagration.

I raced down the crowded *cardo* back to the Palace to repeat my conversation with Flavia to Ahenobarbus. As I passed through the echoing halls of the public imperial halls, I considered: Should I comb through more of the *scrinia* archives without the aid of the gutted index for more clues? Or once I'd accompanied Ahenobarbus and Junius back to Roma, should I continue immediately to Sirmium by way of Cibalae?

Was this chase all for naught? Was Apodemius using the Vestals to plant a false trail? Would a visit to Cibalae be a meaningless detour from my duties in Pannonia reporting to Otho?

Otho had seemed so sure—almost complacent—that he could navigate our *schola* through this perilous transition from a strong protector like Constantius to Julian who held our service in contempt. Otho was relying on stricter procedure, closer communication, tighter enforcement of hierarchy and regulations—and all of it handled in that grand open meeting room to air out the Castra's cobwebs. By night, I knew, he lobbied to bolster our support among Roma's most powerful politicians and families.

But even with tireless politicking and tightened management across our network, how could Otho stay so confident? He was an unknown to the Roman patrician class. Without Constantius backing our *schola*'s longstanding freedoms from vengeful prosecutions and political interference, how well could we function? Who would sponsor us now against Julian?

In the meantime, I would hurry back to the Castra with Junius and Ahenobarbus. I would fulfill my trustee's duties to Kahina, Leo, and the Manlius estates before the New Year began.

As for tracking down the old man, I must make sure I'd missed no clue in the Eternal City before returning to Sirmium. I didn't want to make a fool of myself. Perhaps his disappearance was innocent after all. He was old, retired, and unwell. Perhaps he was already accounted for this minute, easing his joint pains in some luxury resort south of Baiae.

I slowed my race back to Ahenobarbus, trying to convince myself that I was manufacturing dangers out of nothing. I wandered for a time through the Palace public rooms. Moonlight shimmered through the gold fretwork of the grille behind which Empress Eusebia used to listen to Constantius' proceedings. Silver, obsidian, turquoise, and other semi-precious *tesserae* set into the mosaics under my feet glinted under the odd torchlight. My suspicions must be infected by the old regime—that world of accusations, treason, and intrigue that Julian was determined to wash away.

Surely, Apodemius' departure was nothing to worry about. He'd taken his mice and—

No... no! He'd emptied his strongbox of *all* his papers when he should have archived them with the Castra secretaries as was proper. And only I knew that the 'copy' of the rescindment had gone with them. Only I knew, whatever excuses Otho swallowed, that Apodemius had worried about nothing so much as Constantius' lost stay-of-execution.

—THE BURNING STAKES—

I was in no rush to obey Otho's order that I simply resume my pedestrian tasks in Sirmium. Filing reports and supervising the postal hub of Pannonia wasn't going to save our old *magister* from Arbitio and Salutius' court—nor would it salvage my reputation in Chalcedon once Catena had unloaded his lethal charges of regicide on my vulnerable head.

My ears picked up the marching departure of Palace *domestici* and then the murmur of idle eunuchs in brocade slippers moving up and down the corridors of the residential wing. The eunuchs had their own channels of information. What were their sinister whisperings? What were their fears? Surely they suspected as well as I that Julian's tribunal had not yet finished with the court of Constantius.

I didn't know where Gaudentius would turn next. I didn't care. Perhaps my career was ending, too. Should I take up Kahina's suggestion and return with her to Numidia? I felt like an uneasy guest finding himself at a banquet where neither the smiling host nor his food can be trusted.

But any noble Roman didn't run from any such banquet—even one offered by rivals, enemies, or newly installed emperors. One tasted. One watched. One waited. One couldn't rise from the host's couch after only one course. We'd seen only the *prima mensa* of this political transition—I felt it in my stomach. The consuls Florentius and Taurus and the others—like Evagrius? Florentius Nigrinianus? They were only *hors d'oeuvres*.

The main course still waited in the wings.

I reached the busy sickroom exuding an aroma of medical tonics, cleansing acetum, and warm blood.

Ahenobarbus lay surrounded by a circle of new physicians. Half a dozen large lamps held by mute slaves flooded the *princeps*' chamber with bright light casting elongated shadows across a ceiling painted with scenes of famous lovers. Two military *capsarii*—probably from units left behind by Julian to secure the capital—were cleaning and re-stitching Ahenobarbus' throat.

Cassius joined me in the empty corridor outside.

'Where is Rufus?'

'I relieved him so he could eat something.'

'What's happening in there?'

'The palace doctor knew some army surgeons who are better at nasty wounds like this. He's developed a fever.'

'I'll take over. It's so late. You'd better get back to your packing if you hope to leave at dawn. Catena won't be a pleasant traveling companion. Get some sleep and leave the all-night dicing for Roma.'

'I can't wait to hand that animal over to the Eastern escorts. This means a promotion, for sure!' Cassius rubbed his unshaven chin.

I strained to see how Ahenobarbus was faring but heard only a worrying groan.

'Just get the job done, Cassius. Worry about promotion later.'

'You're in a sour mood, Numidianus, considering we caught the beast only a few hours ago. Today's action saved me a month's ride to the wastes of Londinium. I intend to celebrate, maybe for the rest of the night. It's my business, not yours.'

'I'm angry because you told that eunuch our mission.'

I slapped Cassius' heavy purse freshly filled with the coins of Chryseros' bribe. 'I don't promote blabbermouths.'

'What a bastard you are, Numidianus! That eunuch helped you find your Britannian scribe, right? Anyway, the whole Castra knows Apodemius has fled by now—count on it. Why shouldn't I profit from telling the son of a bitch what everyone up here will learn from postal riders within a week? It's natural we'd be looking for the old man.'

He started to walk away but hadn't quite finished yet. 'Don't be so righteous, Numidianus. Why should you scold me? You think Rufus is more discreet?'

'More loyal perhaps.'

Cassius shrugged. 'Fair enough. Loyal? Right! Loyal to whom? That's the question you should ask your apple-cheeked Rufus.'

I bit back further reprimands. Cassius had a point. I'd underestimated how his long years serving here in Mediolanum as one of the chief circuit riders had forged longstanding ties between the *agentes* at the Palace gates and the court's most assiduous informants within the perfumed suites.

Rufus turned a corner and hurried up to us.

'Is he any better?'

He gave Cassius some details about the cohort commissioned to protect him and Catena out of the Porta Nova and off to the East in only a few hours' time.

Suddenly, Cassius' bravado over delivering Catena wilted. 'Numidianus, you're sure you can't ride out with us as far as Sirmium?'

'Oh, Cassius, why would I rob you of all that glory? I have to help Junius get Ahenobarbus safely back to the Castra. Where in Hades is Junius?'

A strange gagging nose erupted from the sickbed. The doctors, heads bent low, argued between themselves. A new smell made us three *agentes* step a few paces away from the bedchamber. A slave emerged from inside, carrying a basin sloshing with red water.

⚵⚵⚵

I cornered the elusive Junius as he crossed the main palace courtyard. As tall as he was now, he wore the same worried expression I recalled in the fifteen-year-old.

'You've finished with your mother, Junius? Ready to ride out as soon as Ahenobarbus can be moved?'

'Would you please see her, Numidianus?'

'Junius, I'm exhausted. It's very late.'

'She wishes to thank you for protecting me during the conspiracy against my father—though that's not how she'll phrase it.'

'No?'

'She'll hail you for bringing me back from the dead. That's how she experienced my return—like a Lazarus from his grave.'

'The Christians' tale of Lazarus is a moving myth.'

I slung my arm over his shoulder.

'But keeping you secluded at the Manlius house in Roma was hardly burying you before your time... It's good to see you laugh. You looked far too grave just now for a young man in his prime. Fine, take me to her. And while she's showering me with her blessings, pack up your things and bid farewell to any other old Frankish friends whom you've shocked with your miraculous resurrection.'

'No, I'd better come with you, Numidianus.'

I'd seen Junius' mother only in fleeting moments during the crisis that trapped her husband into an imperial acclamation and his inevitable assassination as a traitor. The wife of General Silvanus was nothing like his mistress, the fearless girl Roxana who'd served as an *agens* before following Silvanus to his northern redoubt in Agrippina.

When I first laid eyes on Junius' mother six years ago, she must have been about forty—over-protective, self-obscuring, wary, and as it turned out, prudent to be all those things while she and her son were Constantius' hostages at the Palace.

She was free to go now but instead she chose to rattle around this drafty shrine to the late emperor's fear-ridden court. Why?

Junius ushered me down narrowing passages to a tawdry set of imperial chambers furnished with faded damask curtains and commonplace, dented braziers sitting cold and ashy.

'I believe the *Domina* is expecting me?' I told a lady's maid.

Junius cleared his throat, alerting his mother within of our approach.

'Marcus Gregorianus Numidianus, I introduce you to my mother, the widow of General Silvanus, lately *magister equitum* of the Western Roman Army and a loyal servant of the Empire.'

But this could not be! How had the Fates been so cruel to this woman? Her deterioration was more than misfortune. What curse had reduced a healthy, if nervous middle-aged female to a wizened crone in six short years?

Her hair had gone white. Her complexion was like a dried prune. Her spine had curved into an archer's bow rising behind her shoulders. Leaning on a stout stick with a knob of bronze molded into a bejeweled bear cub, she hobbled toward me. I pitied her.

'Thank you for the return of my son, Numidianus,' she said.

I didn't doubt her sincerity but her brusque tone surprised me. Junius must have told her of his years in Roma as a hideaway in the Manlius townhouse and how I'd sponsored his secret conversion under an assumed name into an *agens* she could be proud of.

But after Junius' build-up, her actual thanks sounded flat. I waited. She could muster no more. The exhaustion of her son's sudden reappearance must have been as great a shock as it was a joy. All emotion, including true gratitude, seemed drained away.

'He's a great credit to our service and the Empire, *Domina*.'

'Of course he is. Had the course of events gone otherwise, his father would be ruling all of Gallia today. Junius would be recognized as his heir, a prince among Franco-Romans. Now he's no more than a postal delivery boy.'

'Surely more than that, *Domina*. He may rise someday to be *princeps officii* to an urban prefect, commanding the respect and honors due a high official.'

She coughed up some green phlegm and spat it on the floor just in front of my boots.

'Respect? I never saw this court pay that hound of a man, *Ducenarius* Gaudentius, any respect. Honors? When every decent official shuns your kind? Condemns your arrogance?'

There was certainly no gratitude in this, only bitter resentment. I straightened my shoulders and nodded, determined to take none of her nasty remarks to heart.

How cruel such unflinching maternal pride could be! She'd mourned both father and son as heroes challenging the Constantines' mercurial, fearful rule. Silvanus had commanded the loyalty of thousands marching behind his standard into barbarian-ridden Gallia. He'd been cheered in the wastes left by Frankish invaders' depredations. He'd been acclaimed when he donned the purple.

This young man was to have inherited that acclaim. And here was a woman who'd lost the love of her husband, but still clung to her fantasy of reigning again at the side of her young prince.

Junius avoided my glance. I wouldn't hold him responsible. The illness eating his mother's body and soul was obvious. She couldn't celebrate the return of a low-ranked *agens* unheralded by her northern people. She actually mourned losing the honor of a son martyred to the family's nobility. She didn't want to go home without more.

I closed my eyes, flooded with memories of Silvanus racing up to our party on his stallion on the fields of Agrippina, extending his welcome with bravado and smiles. He was a man of calculating vacillation and the charm of a hundred Apollos. But he was also the man who'd betrayed my father, Commander Gregorianus, and all his compatriots who brought down the corrupt Emperor Constans.

'*Domina*, I'm sorry not to find you in better health. Junius and I must leave you for Roma to resume our duties.'

I shifted my riding helmet from one arm to the other as I searched for more comforting words. 'Your son is respected and beloved by all his fellows for his *Romanitas* in service. May his return bring you renewed happiness.'

'Return? Hah! You owe me restitution!'

This time her spit hit my boot square. 'I needed my son! And you stole him without a word of explanation. You owe me!'

This was insolence. I could no longer contain myself. '*Domina*, have you forgotten your status in this Palace? Have you forgotten your husband's usurpation? Junius was a hostage to be killed at the first sign of such treachery. Constantius had to believe the boy was dead! Junius had to be hidden!'

Junius laid a warning hand on my arm. He shook his head, hoping I would desist. I nodded and turned my back on the widow.

'Bid your poor mother good-bye, Junius. Give her the reassurances she needs. No woman was more protective or fearful for her child than she was. She was the last person the Fates should have maddened in this way.'

'Maddened by the Fates!' she screeched, hoarse as peeling tree bark. 'The Fates? It was you, Numidianus, who took the boy to hide like a coward behind the walls of a fine Roman mansion, to shelter him among the friends of my husband's whore!'

Oh, the gods, why did I not understand until now? She realized I was one of Roxana's few friends in the world. It was not the flight of her son that had pickled her like last year's plums. It was jealousy of Roxana—brave, clever, and as upright as a Sagittarian's arrowshot—that had eaten her up. I couldn't stomach this without doing Roxana's memory justice.

'*Whore?*'

'You heard me. I said *whore*.'

—THE BURNING STAKES—

'Your husband's friend Roxana seized an assassin's blade with her bare hands to defend his life. I also fought his murderers, thrust for thrust, and saw Roxana cut down. I also saw one of our finest *agentes* butchered by these murderers sent to punish your vain husband for his refusal to heed my own advice.'

'Bahhh.'

'Those of us who defended your precious Silvanus didn't idealize him. We fought for justice for a man wronged, for a fair hearing—not for some Franco-Roman hero hoping for a plinth in the Forum. I'm leaving now. I'll wait for you outside, Junius.'

Ashen-faced, he joined me after ten long minutes. We walked together back toward the Financial Building.

Just before we joined Rufus and Cassius, he stopped me. 'Marcus, I don't share her feelings.'

'I know, Junius.'

'She's dying. She begged me to take her north to visit my father's gravesite. She wants me settled in Agrippina to claim what she imagines is my rightful place up there.'

'She's conjuring delusions, Junius. The tribal Franks across the Rhenus will only seize you as a hostage for themselves. No one will ransom you. The Franco-Romans left in control of Agrippina by Julian have no need of another Silvanus to complicate their leadership rivalries.'

'Still, *Mater* wants to die among her people.'

'Let her go. But you're bound to our *schola* now.'

'She said if I leave with you for Roma, she'll kill herself.'

I stared into his green eyes, detecting echoes of Silvanus. 'Do you want to be released from our service? Was that grief-stricken performance back there stage-managed by you?'

'No, but—'

'Are you just like your father? One minute fidelity to your promises, your duties, your debt to the Empire and the next, lured away by visions of glory dangled before your eyes?'

'No, Marcus! No! No! But she's my mother! You have to understand—'

I grabbed him by the collar and shook him very hard. 'It takes courage and an iron will to put the Empire first, to serve the *schola* even when it causes suffering to those we love. It takes courage to serve the truth when others call us liars and sneaks. It takes guts to keep going when people hiss at our backs and spit at our boots because we pursue justice instead of favor or glory. Face it now, Junius. History will never be kind to the *agentes in rebus*.'

He was no longer a boy now but an indignant young man. He jerked himself free of my grip and straightened his tunic. I'd scared him as well as scolded him but he wouldn't let it show.

He trotted away to join the others without another word.

⚜⚜⚜

We four rose before dawn to see off Cassius and his cohort of *protectores* riders with their prisoner in tow. I'd instructed that Catena be gagged and was satisfied when he emerged from detention with his crooked little mouth bound up tight. Although I couldn't mute his accusations once he appeared before Arbitio and the military jurists in Chalcedon, no rasping curses that I was a regicide would be heard in the courtyard of Mediolanum Palace today.

I was free to stand there in the pre-dawn dark of a winter morning and heap on his head whatever insults came to mind. Instead I stayed silent as they saddled up. When it came to the moment of watching Cassius' horse lead their party through the Palace's outer gates, I felt unmoved to dignify that defanged dog with any curse of my own.

One bid farewell to men, not to animals.

'Ahenobarbus no better?' Rufus asked as we turned to see the first pinkish-gray rays outline the roofs and walls of the Palace compound.

'I'll speak to his doctors.'

The doctors were sleeping. A slave rose from the floor at the foot of Ahenobarbus' bed and backed away. The patient slept peacefully, but last night's fresh bandages rendered him as mute as Catena. His dark auburn hair curled on the pillow and the stubble on his face ended in an abrupt line where the surgeons had shaved him to re-stitch his wound.

I pulled up a stool to and listened to his labored breathing. How had the Fates allowed one more honorable Roman to be wounded by Catena at the very instant of his capture? How much I cared about the fate of Ahenobarbus and how I dismissed the uncertain destiny of Gaudentius brooding in that shabby *insula* less than a mile away!

The *princeps* woke up. When he saw me there, he tried to smile. I laid my hand on his forehead. It was still too warm.

The slave started to feed him broth. I took over the sponge and bowl and dismissed the boy.

'We'll stay in Mediolanum until you're ready to ride.' I said. But my assurance sounded as useless as a soldier's wet flint in a rainy tent.

He frowned, 'no,' and waggled his fingers in a gesture meant to send me back to the Castra.

'It wasn't Apodemius hiding at the Temple of Minerva. It was Gaudentius. He wants to be reinstated with us.'

That amused Ahenobarbus, I could see. Gaudentius and he had served side by side through too many seasons in this court for Ahenobarbus not to know the trouble the Neapolitan stirred up wherever he went.

'Shhh. Don't talk.'

It wasn't just loyalty that had made me hope we could return to Roma together. I needed Ahenobarbus' advice. He alone of my fellow *agentes* knew the full stakes of this mission to Mediolanum. He alone had witnessed Apodemius' delivering the executed Gallus' slippers to Constantius. He alone had seen the shock on the *Magister*'s face as the Emperor announced he'd changed his mind about condemning his cousin to death.

The *princeps* waved his fingers again. This time, I had to accept it as an order from an *agens* senior to me, not the wish of friend of longstanding fellowship.

'Perhaps I should take Rufus back with us to Roma to present the big briefing on Catena to Otho? It's too quiet for him here. He'd enjoy a chance to shine at headquarters with the new *magister*. Or do you need Rufus here with you?'

Ahenobarbus' lips moved, 'no.' He smiled to say he'd be fine and waved me away again.

I didn't dare tire him with more argument. Ahenobarbus knew, as do I, that a man's lifespan is measured in those invisible threads spun and woven into the fabric of every human's life by the three *Parcae*. Nona spins the thread of life from her distaff onto her spindle; Decima measures the thread of life with her rod; and Morta cuts the thread of life and chooses the manner of a person's death.

I couldn't change Morta's whims by sitting there, squeezing chicken broth between Ahenobarbus' lips.

Rufus, Junius, and I left Mediolanum not long after. I was right about Rufus—he'd seized on the offer to impress Otho with his role in the arrest of The Chain.

The weather was chilly and gray, but at least the roads out of Mediolanum were dry. The townspeople's gaudy holiday trappings flapped and dangled from the streetside stalls, arches, and doorways as we approached the Porta Romana for the Via Porticata and the great Arcus marking our route south.

I worried about leaving Ahenobarbus, but felt otherwise relieved as soon as we exited the city's last gates.

We reached Placentia without incident and decided that we'd press on after a short night. With fresh horses, Rufus told Junius, we could expect to be back in the Eternal City in time for the last day of Saturnalia festivities and a welcome return to routine.

I didn't dampen their youthful cheer with worries about Ahenobarbus or Apodemius.

But was I surprised the second morning when Rufus and I rose from our *mansio* beds, washed, and descended to set off again down the *Cursus* to find ourselves waiting for Junius in the cold?

Junius' tardiness irritated me but then I wasn't a Franco-Roman prince. I'd been raised a slave in the household in the camp of a military commander and served as his personal *volo* on campaign. At home and in camp, punctuality was all.

We two collected our food packed for the day. The day's journey should get us as far as Parma or even farther. Two horses waited, saddled and tethered, outside the stable. They were sturdy state animals in good shape but I gave the sleepy groom no tip.

'We handed over three horses. We expect three fresh mounts back,' I ordered the boy.

'Your third rider collected his horse twenty minutes ago,' the sulky groom shot back.

—THE BURNING STAKES—

I looked at Rufus. His stunned expression proclaimed complete innocence.

'Which direction?' I asked, guessing the answer before the groom had even lifted his arm to point the way we'd come.

Junius had ridden north.

Chapter 12, A Roll Call of Revenge

—Sigillaria, Roma, December 23, 361 AD—

Rufus and I reached Roma on the last day of the festival. We stabled our horses at the Porta Flaminia, registered ourselves as *agentes* entering the capital as the law required, and headed for the Castra.

'Sigillaria' referred to the figurines handed out as gifts, but also to the day culminating all the Saturnalia feasting. It always brought back a flood of childhood memories.

Christianity as a state cult was still quite new to contemporaries of the Senator and his son. Meanwhile pagan Saturnalia remained popular for good reason. Roman slaves saw no reason to celebrate the birth of Christ if it meant relinquishing ten days or more of turning tables—literally—on their masters.

In the old days, the Manlius' reception rooms had filled up all day with the Senator's prestigious clients. After dusk, it was the turn of the Commander's officer friends. They brought wives who were more than eager to escape their slaves' glee at the 'reversal' games and rituals overturning the order of each Roman household.

The streets were busy but had a tattered air. The winter revels had passed their fevered pitch and subsided into a celebration of satiation. The harvest's best fruits and vegetables had been sold off, leaving the minor markets with bruised squashes and black-spotted carrots. The effects of Gaudentius' blockade on supplies from North Africa were still in evidence. Until the regular shipping traffic resumed in the spring, housewives were at the mercy of black marketeers or their own frostbitten kitchen gardens.

The narrower streets were clogged with temporary stalls that had popped up, hawking cheap pagan dollies and silver-plated souvenirs 'gifts' that the poor exchanged.

A *sigillarius* desperate to unload his leftover merchandise yanked Rufus' arm; 'Only two *nummi* for five gods!'

I pulled Rufus away. 'We're in a hurry. Aren't you keen to see Otho's face when you announce Catena is on his way to trial?'

I was even keener to see whether Apodemius had returned with his valuable papers to the Castra.

He had not.

I discovered his office completely emptied of all its furnishings. I stood gaping into the inner room, watching painters whitewash a wall denuded of his old map. This doorway was so familiar to me. It was the threshold where, time and again, I'd waited for the old man's summons to brief him on my completed missions. For thirteen years I'd battled with jangled nerves before entering this room—nerves frayed by a sleepless ride lasting days and nights or jittery under the burden of sensitive information to be disclosed to him only.

Otho appeared at my shoulder, come to check on the workmen before holding his morning meeting.

'What do you think, Numidianus? Looks better already, doesn't it?'

'What's it going to become? Your own office?'

He laughed. 'Hardly. For one thing, I still smell mouse droppings, don't you? For another, I'm sticking with my own system, sitting among the other officers, exchanging information, and collecting everyone's opinion with an open mind.'

'Very modern, Otho. Is it working?'

A bell signaled time to convene.

'It'll take time for older officers like yourself to adapt to simple and rational work methods.'

'Apodemius was rational enough. Do you think there's no reason to worry his whereabouts?'

'I'll admit to you, I grow a little concerned, but only because of his age and frailty. You don't have any idea where's he got to, do you?'

—THE BURNING STAKES—

Otho stole a sidelong glance at me as we passed the new sundial with its polished bowls dripping, dripping, dripping away the minutes.

'No.'

'Just like him! Always so secretive! Stealing seals to break open mail. Changing codes every season for the smallest memorandum. You know, I used to sit there in my office in Palaestina deciphering codes signed with the sketch of a mouse only to find out the message was quite mundane! Come on, Numidianus, admit it. Who did he think he was fooling?'

'The man who ruled a corrupt empire.'

'You speak ill of the dead,' Otho warned, 'which is unfair to our late emperor, failed as he may—'

'I refer to the Lord Chamberlain, Eusebius.'

Otho stared. He hadn't expected a frank answer.

But if I meant to earn his trust with candor, why was I so tightlipped? Shouldn't I tell him I'd tried and failed to track Apodemius to Mediolanum? Shouldn't I tell him about the hints from the Blind Vestal and the Marble Vestal regarding Apodemius' unnamed responsibilities to a third virgin? Or shouldn't I confide the whole story of the suspect rescindment, Salutius' Greek envoy, and the damaged register?

Yet I held back.

'Well, well, we may pay for Apodemius' secretive habits yet.' Otho waved at an over-eager *circitor* waiting to usher him into the meeting. 'It would have been nice if you'd stumbled across him in Mediolanum and brought him back to safety.'

'Safety? So you are worried. What news from Chalcedon?'

He shook his head. 'With Catena's arrival, the cells will be bulging with Constantius' loyalists.'

I ticked off the accused on my fingers as we walked across the courtyard: 'Consul Taurus, Consul Florentius, *Magister Officiorum* Palladius, Count of the Privy Purse Evagrius, Palace Steward Saturninus, Notary Cyrinus, *Magister Officiorum* Florentius Nigrinianus and—?

'Notary Pentadius and ... Ursulus, Count of the Sacred Largesse.' He raised his eyebrows to convey his own surprise at this roster of government heavyweights.

'Pentadius? And Ursulus! *Ursulus*? Have they lost their minds? Ursulus was one of the finest citizens to ever prostrate himself at Constantius' hem. What could be the charge against that noble man?'

Otho shrugged, rubbing his clean-shaven jaw. 'I, too, was shocked to see Ursulus named. Do you know whether Emperor Julian holds a grudge against him, as he does against Consul Florentius?'

'On the contrary! When Constantius refused Caesar Julian the funds to pay his soldiers, Ursulus defied Constantius. He wrote to the officer in charge of the Gallia treasury to release the sum Julian required. Why—'

I felt like ramming my sword through a sack of laundry waiting for pickup nearby. 'Julian should *promote* Ursulus, not try him! This tribunal makes no sense!'

Otho listened with an impassive expression, impatient to call his meeting to order. But I didn't care who overheard my outburst—the assembled *agentes* or the pimply cadets from the training school.

'Is Julian trying to strike fear into everyone's heart? This isn't the caesar I knew in Gallia! If he mixes the fate of a honorable Roman like Ursulus with that of a slime-trailing reptile like Catena, no one is safe in his bed.'

I had no appetite to sit through any meeting. I begged off, happy to leave Rufus to enact the excitement of Catena's arrest to an audience of enraptured junior *agentes*.

Otho saw I was riled. He excused me with generous indulgence:

'I apologize, Numidianus. I've been remiss. I should have said congratulations for apprehending Catena as soon as we met upstairs. Well done. That's a report I look forward to reading. But first, get some rest. You need it.'

'Let *Biarchus* Rufus hog the whole show. My report won't be sent in until Ahenobarbus is back on his feet.'

I said it with bad grace. Otho remained unruffled.

'I'm sure the *princeps* will recover. Take all the time you need. Send your report to me from Sirmium, whenever you can pull it together.'

—THE BURNING STAKES—

Otho was overlooking my insubordinate attitude. I wondered why.

'Are you sure you didn't pick up any lead whatsoever on Apodemius?' he called as I stalked away.

I shook my head.

Until I heard the name of Ursulus, I could have dismissed the roster of Chalcedon victims as a predictable roll call of the military's petty targets among Constantius' courtiers. Ignoble of Julian to let General Arbitio get away with it, yes, surely, and even more ignoble of Salutius commissioned with cleansing the Constantius stables.

But *Ursulus*?

The arrest of Ursulus—neither a craven Constantius loyalist like Florentius and Taurus nor a man Julian might have reason to punish for deeds unnamed—upended all my hopes that Chalcedon was a limited political exercise.

On the other hand, Ursulus had no link to my greatest fear— that Julian might exploit Chalcedon to wreak revenge on anyone associated with his half-brother's Gallus' death.

No, Ursulus had had nothing to do with Gallus. Perhaps Apodemius was safe after all. Perhaps I was safe. Perhaps Barbatio's curse on my head was the empty wail of a doomed man—no more.

Everything felt upside down.

But after all, this was the last day of the festival of 'reversal.'

There was nothing to do but go home and celebrate it.

⚜⚜⚜

I took the side exit out the Castra's enclosure to see if the litter bearer Pluto was anywhere about. I'd promised to offer up ritual prayers for the soul of his dead *agens* son, Gaius. I never forget my debts, especially as Pluto's tip had steered me halfway down the trail to the elusive Veiled Vestal and her debtor, Apodemius.

His brother bearers said Pluto wasn't there and hadn't been seen for a week or more. I left a message with them explaining that the Temple of Jupiter Redux was unbolted and soon would be ready for devotions again.

They shrugged with indifference but I knew he'd get my message on his return. I certainly tipped them enough.

Someone less cooperative was next on my list of holiday stops. Soren sat outside his Subura shop, inveigling passersby to invest in a valuable book as a Saturnalia gift.

'No one can resist Juvenal's verse,' he barked at a loving couple walking arm in arm past his shop. 'Even married folk might discover a few bed tricks they haven't tried!'

'Save that for the whoremongers,' the man said in disgust.

I leaned over his stool. 'Business not so good?'

'Still looking for your *Cicero*?'

'Spit it out. You've heard something.'

'I've heard of a *Cicero*—'

'With the Senator's marginalia?'

'Calm down. I haven't checked it out.'

'You wouldn't mention it if you hadn't, Soren. You're not a man to waste your breath.'

'Are you so sure you want to trace this scroll? Why not buy a fresh copy with carved rollers in an inlaid *arca* imported from Greece? Or bound into an embossed leather *codex* for easy reading?'

'Why shouldn't I want to recover what's ours?'

'Because it isn't yours any more, is it?'

'Stolen goods—'

'Why assume it's stolen? What if your precious *Cicero* was sold, fair and square?'

'By the thief? Don't quibble if you know something.'

Soren pulled at his stubbly jowls. He stank of rotting papyrus and repair glue.

'And if I know something I think you don't want to know?'

I wanted to shake him. 'I want our *Cicero* back! I don't care how it left the house or who profited from it.'

The old man stood up and pushed me away.

'I'm not dealing with an ass of a bully, not even Senator Manlius' freedman. With that attitude, you'll never get your *Cicero* back. What's more, you'd better be prepared to see more *volumina* walk out of the house from under your very nose.'

—THE BURNING STAKES—

He disappeared into his shop and closed his rattling shutters. I heard the snap of a padlock.

He didn't have our scroll, not yet. Or he would have sold it back to me then and there. But he knew where it was. I was sure of it.

⚵⚵⚵

Our cherished Latin poet Catullus described Saturnalia week as 'the best of days.'

Kahina was wearing our cook's shabby tunic and stola with fake embroidered jewels around the neckline. Meanwhile, our cook was parading around the atrium garden in one of Kahina's finest ensembles, a tunic of deep rose silk overlaid with a stola of palest pink embroidered in gold thread along the hem and sleeves. Kahina had asked her chambermaid to dress the cook's thinning gray hair around a headdress of thick pink cord laid over her crown and tied at the back.

The elaborate hairdo make the cook look ridiculous but reminded me a little of the Vestals. I wondered how Tullia and Flavia were celebrating the return of a pagan emperor, a true 'reversal' none of us Romans clinging to our non-Christian traditions would have dared pray for, even two months ago.

To see the entire Manlius household gathered together all at once set me back for an instant. For years, as we labored to rebuild the Manlius fortunes after the civil war, I'd kept track of our growing household. The servants' quarters had seemed so haunted and vast when the civil war ended and only the nursemaid Lavinia, Verus, and the cook had presided over a handful of part-time minions.

Now their part of the house was overdue for refurbishing and extending. Tonight there were more than fifty carousing in the main rooms. Most of them were little more than names and upkeep to me.

A pretty slave girl just entering womanhood scampered past me through the kitchen corridor.

'Io, Saturnalia?' I greeted her with a jerk of my head as query.

'Drusilla, Freedman Numidianus,' she answered, 'daughter of Gardener Bulbus.' She wasn't astonished I didn't recognize her— why should I? But for some reason, she seemed particularly amused this evening.

Drusilla was soon prancing around the garden with her elders. Thirteen? Maybe fourteen, she was late to the party, delayed by changing into her costume—Leo's athletic tunic. She was cradling his *harpastum* ball in her thin, bare arms. She had started in on a parody of the scion of the house by quoting team scores to anyone who would listen.

The servants starting to point at Drusilla who was flushing with the unfamiliar attention. Her pubescent nipples swelled with excitement through the boy's shirt. Her grubby little feet sloshed around in Leo's sporting boots.

But of course the joke was really on Leo as he watched his slaves push Drusilla away with taunts of, 'Boring, boring, grow up and get yourself a bride!'

Soon they grew tired of mocking Leo's sports obsession. So Drusilla launched into bold declamations of bawdy poetry. Her audience hooted as her babyish lips recited Martial: *Mentula tam magna est, tantus tibi, Papyle, nasus ut possis, quotiens arrigis, olfacere!* Your hard-on's so big, Paplyus, you can smell it with your own big nose!'

Everyone roared louder. Our household was getting tipsy.

I would have pulled the girl away but for a sudden glance at the target of her comedy.

Leo had just winked at Drusilla. She returned his wink. I listened more closely. Drusilla knew not just Leo's favorite authors, but even his favorite verses. How could the slave girl know this if not for—?

I blushed deep purple for Leo and turned away from the merry crowd to find myself facing his mother. Through the raucous banter all around us, Kahina gave me a slow, complicit nod. She and I shared that moment all parents know too well— our precocious Leo was leaving childhood behind. Sometime since last year's Saturnalia, Leo had discovered Drusilla's skinny charms and everyone in the house had known it but me.

—THE BURNING STAKES—

How far had things gone?

I only wished Leo had confided in me, taken his 'freedman's' advice about toying with the slaves. If I'd been free to declare myself his natural father, I would have collared him without a second's apology and dragged him off to the Baths for a man-to-man warning.

But what would I have said? This had been Roma's way between masters and slaves since the beginning of recorded time. I had no doubt this would be the custom for another thousand years. Leo might someday have to take greater responsibility for little Drusilla.

It was just as well he was soon leaving right away for the chaste classroom of Ausonius. I resolved to have a serious word with him if the opportunity presented itself.

I stepped over a pair of Kahina's litter bearers, two youths dicing with the Commander's inlaid *fritullus*, an inlaid box he'd brought back from his tour in North Africa. North Africa . . . where he'd dallied with a lowborn young woman, my mother . . .

'By Jupiter, when's our supper, you lowlife? Bring me my supper, you half-humans!'

Verus slouched and shouted from his place of honor on the central couch of three fanned in a half-circle in the winter *triclinium*. His braying call as 'Senator' for food was my cue, for I was playing one of the kitchen stewards taking orders tonight from our pretend 'Verus'—played by Leo.

Leo was thoroughly enjoying himself mimicking our elderly *dispensator*. He had donned Verus' shiny, stained leather work tunic and mastered a limp that would have been cruel if it hadn't been so exaggerated, sending him in circles, around and around, and tripping over the prettiest of our laundry slaves.

'Keep your loincloth on, Senator!' Leo shouted, rubbing his chin in that way Verus had. 'Jupiter's Balls, I'm not as young as I was, that's for certain. And I'm too busy drinking all your best wine to see that you get any!'

Everyone loved this. They laughed even harder when Verus gave Leo's muscular behind a solid whack with the Senator's stout walking stick.

'Useless, useless man, that stupid Verus!' Verus boomed out in a stentorian baritone. 'And *soooo* arrogant! He thinks he holds this whole household together through the bad times and the good—'

'That you have, Verus, that you have!' shouted one of our estate managers, clutching the expensive silver pitcher Kahina had just awarded him for a year's faithful delivery of our hams and produce.

'Shush, you ungrateful rogue!' our mock 'Senator Manlius' shouted back. 'For I suspects that you give that old cripple Verus big cuts off the best Manlius beef sides and pork ribs and he devours these delicacies behind my noble, fucking aristocratic back, 'cause I can't see nothing! What do you answer to that, eh, "Verus"?'

And Verus gave Leo another affectionate *thwack* on his bottom.

I ran to mop up the wine Leo spilled before it stained the black and white tiles so expensively restored and re-grouted after the depredations of our former tenant, the Lady Laetitia's louche nephew Clodius.

'And where's Freedman Numidianus?' Verus shouted.

Leo's *rhetor*, Drusus, suddenly marched into the room in full armor, one arm crooked around my most battered riding *petanus* salvaged from a storeroom. He'd found some riding trousers and Kahina had lent him one of my own worn tunics discarded for a slave. In a pair of outsized riding boots with flapping, broken soles, he paraded himself for the delight of his audience.

Drusus then braced his feet wide apart and drew a huge round of applause for thrusting out his narrow, scholar's chest. It was almost completely covered by an enormous *agens* insignia improvised from coarsely embroidered toweling from the kitchen.

'*Io, Saturnalia*, Here I am!' he cried. 'Why, don't look so puzzled, my friends. Don't you know me? I am Marcus Gregorianus Numidianus, come to check the accounts, give Leo a lecture, and then disappear for another year without any explanation whatsoever!'

Fair enough.

I laughed along, but glimpsed Kahina's sad eyes looking at me over the heads of our slaves, retainers, clients, and employees. It was all there to read on her face—the naïve girl I'd embraced in

—THE BURNING STAKES—

the Numidian desert, the ambitious society bride of the Commander determined to forget her love for me and accept her future as mother of the heir to the Manlius house, and finally, the tired matron and mother who sought comfort in the embrace of Christ, her 'Savior.'

'Oh, we wouldn't want to be stuck with Numidianus all year round,' I shouted into the crowd.

'That's true, you thief of a steward, because I, the *curiosus*, would investigate your accounts every single week!' answered Drusus. 'And then we'd find out what happens to the Manlius fortune, wouldn't we?'

Kahina had hired musicians for this final night of Saturnalia. I wasn't very musical. When the banging cymbals and bleating flutes started up, I longed for the quiet of the Castra dormitory where only the snores of riders and rattle of midnight dicing interrupted my troubled dreams.

Amidst all the eating and joking, not to mention the guzzling of our second-best wine at a rate that dizzied the mind, I noticed our 'Senator' Verus slump down on his couch between two chubby slaves in Kahina's discarded tunics pretending to be 'society' flirts.

He lost his grip on the Senator's precious stick. It clattered across the tiles, rolling in a wide circle.

The *triclinium* fell into silence, though servants in the atrium garden kept up their drunken betting game of 'even, uneven' until someone shushed them up.

Kahina and her two lady attendants rushed to the couch, then made way for me to lift the old man into my arms. Drusus and Leo cleared my path toward the servants' quarters. I told Drusus and Kahina, 'Send a slave to rouse the doctor Sofus.'

Sofus would be getting on himself by now, but at least he knew the garrulous Verus well. He'd perceive immediately that a dumbstruck Verus was more than drunk. And it was essential that in his state, Verus cooperate and trust everyone around him.

We laid blankets over him. Verus tried to say something. His sounds were more gibberish than words. His right arm hung limp off the side of his bed, though his left clutched in vain at the mattress. He tried to right himself but couldn't sit up.

'No, Verus, lie still. Here, sip some wine.'

'I think he's had enough,' said Drusus.

'Would someone pay those idiotic musicians to pack up and go home?' I ordered.

Verus panicked. He tried to speak, but again, the usually voluble old man could produce nothing sensible. His eyes widened in terrified appeal.

'Shh, just rest,' Kahina said.

Verus was frantic, realizing that his tongue would not obey his mind. With his good left hand he kept reaching for his useless right, but Kahina tried to soothe him with a warm, wet cloth on his forehead.

I reached for her arm. 'Stop it, Kahina! He's not feverish. His brain has suffered some kind of attack.'

Verus' wide eyes stared up at us with frustration. Could he understand what we were saying? He looked bewildered.

Twenty minutes later we heard pounding on our gate—not a polite tap of a boot toe, but a rude, insistent fist rattling the hinges.

'Can that be Sofus so soon? I asked Drusus. 'Tell someone to bring him in. Make way for the doctor.'

We cleared the slaves that were clogging the passage to Verus' door.

I expected to see the avuncular medical man we'd often consulted during those darkest days of Kahina's wounded, dazed return from her enslavement in Hispania.

But it wasn't the old medic with his wooden box of tonics, pinchers and little cauterizing irons who pressed himself into Verus' tiny space.

It was *Biarchus* Rufus, white-faced and panting.

'It arrived by rider an hour ago. Otho called in half a dozen of the senior men still at the Castra. I didn't count, blast the bastard and all his so-called "openness," but I found out all the same and raced here to tell you.'

He crumpled over in two, stomach cramped by his breathless race up the Esquiline.

'What's happened? What came?'

'The Chalcedon warrant. For Apodemius.'

I dragged Rufus out of Verus' doorway just in time to see Sofus drop his *paenula* in the foyer and bang his heavy wooden box against a precious statue of Apollo pushed out of position during the party games.

'Charged with what?'

'Just called for questioning, like the others. But that's the form—even for Catena. I don't like it, Numidianus.'

I exhaled with almost perverse relief. The doubt had been agonizing, like waiting for your *contubernalis* to drop his second boot long after you've struggled to fall asleep in your tent.

'Calm down, Rufus. Calm down.'

'Don't you understand?' He grabbed my arm. 'This means the *agentes* aren't safe!'

'That's been Otho's mistake all along, Rufus. The *agentes* haven't been safe since the day Julian took power.'

Chapter 13, The Veiled Vestal

—TO CIBALAE—

It seemed one of the longest nights of the year in more ways than one. Sofus' tonic helped Verus drop off to sleep. The doctor left Kahina with careful instructions but I wondered how much she took in. Distress over Verus' collapse eclipsed even her sadness at Leo's imminent leave-taking.

Saturnalia was over for the Manlius household. Before dawn, Drusus checked the boy's luggage one more time, then his own. I restored calm and obedience among our servants. Their mistress Kahina was going to need their discipline and efficiency more than ever without old Verus to brandish his broom like a commander's sword at their heels.

My old friend, the retired soldier Cornelius arrived under our fig tree not long afterwards with two litters that would take them to a carriage station in the suburbs. I had recommended him to accompany Drusus and Leo safely to Burdigala and wangled the trio three *evectiones diplomatae* to use the *Cursus*.

This was, frankly, less than legal on my part, but what father wouldn't do the same?

By the lamplight, the old veteran looked more battered by life than ever. I could have predicted his retirement savings would trickle out of his badly mended pockets too fast to make much of his army land pension.

'You ready to travel?'

'Light as a *tiro*.' Cornelius patted a limp army satchel. It probably held only his shaving tackle, a cup and cooking pot, a 'good' tunic, and some dried biscuit. 'But I need an advance on that fee you promised,' he mumbled.

'That's your second advance since we made the deal. Where did the first go so fast?'

He gave me a sheepish shrug. 'Spent last night with Delicia at the *Seven Sages*. She's hard up these days, Numidianus. Not all the customers appreciate a tender lady with useful experience.'

I didn't begrudge the tired bargirl something to keep her going. The best client of her bed-alcove would be traveling with my son. But my 'advances' were sure to be forever lost in the vacuum that was Cornelius' mental accounting.

Leo appeared in his travel clothes—riding trousers topped by a bleached tunic under a sturdy new leather tunic trimmed with expensive stitching and decorative braiding. He'd managed to keep one slave sober enough last night to shave away his sparse fuzz. Apart from a broken pimple leaving a mean red lump on his temple, and the dark circles under his eyes, he looked like a young god. He'd inherited so much of the old Senator—gestures and facial expressions—but now that he was starting to fill out, I detected promise of the powerful Commander in shoulders broadened by afternoons on the *harpastum* field.

I flushed with pride as he straightened his belt and attached a *pugio*, my farewell gift. And what else did he inherit from me? Were there traits betraying our family secret? That glint of copper in his hair? His sudden height? The easy swing in the hip that his Numidian grandmother, the forgotten seamstress slave, would have recognized?

Happily, whatever North African features shone in his handsome face were easily explained away. For now his Numidian mother rushed out of the house to the gate, her face streaming with tears. She held onto her boy as if she could squeeze some part of him off to stay with her. She was exhausted to her very soul by worries large and small. Finding no words to express her grief at this inevitable separation, she buried her face in the cook's bedraggled *palla* and left us again, sobbing her way back to Verus' bedside.

Drusus patted his shoulder. 'Don't look so distressed, Leo. Mothers sending sons off to study always take it hard'

'But with Verus so bad—?' Leo looked as stricken by the unlucky timing as Kahina.

'You must be in Burdigala as close to the beginning of the New Year as possible. Put your mind on your studies,' I said.

—THE BURNING STAKES—

He took a deep breath, braced for my good-bye. In his travel boots, the boy stood even with myself. Year after year and mission after mission, I'd left this precocious sprout in his mother's care. I'd never once asked myself if he worried about me or woke up some mornings missing the family's freedman Numidianus.

But now, my own boy, my dear, dear Leo was leaving us, leaving *me*. The sturdy mosaic floor shifted underneath my steward's house slippers. He looked anxious to get moving, yet fearful to go. He betrayed apprehension, excitement, and determination to live up to a daunting family history.

I started, 'If the Commander were here—' paying lip service to the Commander's public status as Leo's father. I stopped short. I couldn't go on. I was his father and the Commander he never knew was his grandfather.

Yet I held my silence. I must remain mute, the awkward bastard interrupting the family line. I should never bequeath to this innocent youth the misery of legal doubts or public scorn.

Seeing me tongue-tied, Leo's face suddenly crumpled. He threw himself into my arms and embraced me, smothering his sobs of 'Marcus, Marcus,' in my borrowed tunic. 'Thank you for letting me go. I won't let you down. I'll be the best student Ausonius ever had.'

This was too hard, too hard. Once, long ago, the Commander had broken his promise to free me, so desperate was he to keep his bastard at his side. I would not hang on. I must send Leo off into the world with no hint of hesitation.

That impatient lout Cornelius was clicking some buckle. Leo got into the first litter.

Drusus gave me a nod, taking in hand the *diplomatae* that would see them treated well at every layover between Roma and Burdigala. I felt comforted that an educated man like the teacher was in charge of their trip. But documents, no matter how well penned, can be inadequate weapons.

I was more comforted when Cornelius, seated next to Leo's modest baggage in the second litter, stuck his unsheathed *spatha* high into the pinkish dawn and waved his reliable blade in farewell.

Magister Otho agreed that Rufus could accompany me to assist in Sirmium. If only it were spring, the *biarchus* and I could cut across the Adriatic by boat, but sailing was still suspended for another month. I figured the land trip to Pannonia would take about a week. Non-stop relay riders, with fresh horses, could make the journey in about five days. We were in a hurry, but we still needed sleep. What we hadn't reckoned with was an astonishing post-holiday traffic jam slowing our eastward progress.

At this time of year, there were always thousands upon thousands of Romans returning to their responsibilities outside the Eternal City—to far-flung garrisons or trading centers, mints and armories, tax collection hubs, and all the other junctions for imperial business.

But this wasn't just the usual traffic of trade wagons replenishing Roma's depleted markets. Or the resumption of incoming slave caravans or outgoing army units clogging the suburban gates and arteries.

No, the startling crush that had Rufus cursing under his breath on the horse ahead of mine was caused by convoys of masonry, statuary, marble basins, and altars. This was the astonishing consequence of Emperor Julian's new order to restore the Empire's temples.

The architecture of paganism was to rise from the rubble—and fast—and the *Cursus* was straining under the unexpected load.

There is nothing more frustrating to a seasoned *agens* commanding the soft verge of the *Cursus* to save wear and tear on his horse's hooves than having to slow his pace. Our horses dodged huge columns lashed perpendicular to rickety oxcart beds or bronze figures of Apollo with feet the size of baby baskets poised to trip us up as we galloped to the right or left.

It was bad north of Ravenna. It got worse after Patavius. We had hoped to reach Aquileia before nightfall on the fourth day but . . . ?

'I know a shortcut, unpaved, but all ours,' Rufus suggested.

'After the mill and the saddle factory?'

He nodded. 'That's the one.'

'Then we'll need horses that can do that leg without a changeover.'

With a bribe at the next *mansio*, we traded our two weary mounts for superior animals reserved for some traveling bishops expected through in an hour or two.

'You told any of our teams in Roma that you were taking the mail this time?' I asked Rufus, as God's chosen animals were being saddled for us in a guilty hurry.

'Yes. Why?' He tucked a packet of dried meat and fruit into his satchel.

'Because I thought I saw two *agentes* a few hilltops back.'

'We're carrying all the mail for the stations as far as Aquileia.' A stable groom dragged two heavy mailbags behind Rufus and tossed them over the horse's back.

'You didn't see two riders?'

Rufus shrugged. 'Probably just a couple of officers returning to their unit.'

He hitched up his wide strutted belt with exaggerated authority. 'When I tell any *circitores* I'm taking over the next shift, they stay put.'

We stopped at a rise to let our horses drink from a cattle trough by the roadside.

'Rufus, turn around. Look over there. See them? They're not cavalry-trained. Look at their seat in the saddle.'

He squinted down the slope. 'One's a hardened racer. But the second looks . . .'

'Downright clumsy. So we forget about them.'

Only, when we shifted off the *Cursus* and cantered down Rufus' shortcut, rutted by farmers' carts and fetid with dropped produce and ox shit covered in flies, the two riders took the same turning and stayed on our track.

We rode on for six more days. For half our journey, this cloaked pair trailed us carefully, moving in close, then moving back, keeping half a mile between us.

After Rufus dropped the Aquileian mailbags at the postal hub, we skipped our rest and rode on faster, hunched under lanolin-coated *saga* through a pouring rain.

Just where the Savus, Colapsis, and Odra currents converge, we hid behind a suburban villa in the suburbs of Siscia and waited for our mysterious shadows to pass us by.

But they hung back and didn't fall for the bait. When we reached Siscia's state mint, we looked back and saw our duo were still there. I didn't doubt now that civil servants of some kind—one a veteran of years on horseback, the other a complete amateur—were tracking us.

Rufus and I reached the crossroads outside Cibalae.

'You go ahead to Sirmium,' I ordered him. He should settle himself into my office at the rear of the state buildings near Constantine's old Pannonian palace and get started on the postal backlog ahead of my arrival. 'But first, get those two off our backs. Take them around in circles, if you have to, then lose them for good.'

'Where are you going, Numidianus?'

'A social call.'

'A social call.' He puffed out his squat chest. 'You act as if you don't trust me. Who's in Cibalae? Only that old drunk, the rebel traitor *Comes* Gratian.'

'Not Gratian. A long overdue visit to a very old friend.'

'Jupiter's Balls! You dragged me to Pannonia on a feeble excuse to Otho for nothing? I hoped you had some secret lead to Apodemius in Sirmium! You really are just headed back to base to sort mail?'

'I didn't lie to you, Rufus. I didn't make any promises. I just don't want to bore you with some family business with old friends of Commander Gregorius.'

Rufus sat there in his saddle like a disgruntled toad. He wrapped his *sagum* tighter under his chin against the wet winds blowing in from the coast.

I seized up my reins and turned my horse due north up a lesser state road forking off the main West-East *Cursus*.

'Just make sure those two bastards don't follow me from this point on. That's not a favor, Rufus. It's an order.'

⚜⚜⚜

—THE BURNING STAKES—

Why was I so sure of my destination? And why would I not explain—even to Rufus?

Because that phrase, *the Veiled Vestal is safe in Cibalae*, haunted me.

Yes, Gratian was in Cibalae, but he wasn't alone. Every city in the Empire was the sum of its people, ghosts, stories, pagan legends, and modern saints. Ugly little Cibalae was no different. It even boasted a discarded empress.

A humble granite milestone marked the distance to Colonial Aurelia Cibalae. Wasn't this the spot where the lumbering Cart of History turned its wheels of Fortune toward the Constantines? This was their birthplace, their crib, and the graveyard of so many they led to the black banks of the River Styx.

It was a grim plateau to those who knew their history. On these broad slopes within earshot of the cold, rapids of the Colapsis, Constantine had invaded his co-emperor Licinius' territory forty-seven years ago. After a savage day of close combat, Constantine had led the charge that broke Licinius' lines. Licinius' survivors fled, leaving twenty thousand fellow soldiers bleeding into the night.

Ten years ago, I'd survived a nightmare on the plains of Mursa not far north. Constantine's son Constantius battled the usurper Emperor Magnentius, my father the Commander, and all the noble rebels. The bones of those fifty-four thousand lay buried in Pannonia, too.

With Rufus gone, I rode harder from demons only I could see rising from the earth beneath my horse's hooves. I closed my eyes, trying to shut out the clash of metal, the neighing horses, and shrieks of wounded through a black night. When I opened my eyes again, it was ordinary daylight. Storm-tossed fields lay fallow and furrowed for the coming spring seeding.

Why did the gods curse these plains, the altar on which Constantines sacrificed faithful Roman souls?

Cibalae had one ghost towering over them all, but he was only dead politically. The ugly walls ahead marked the hometown of Gratian 'Funarius', a grasping rope salesman who had crawled his way up to become the great Constantine's *protector domesticus*. As *Comes* of Africa, he had embezzled funds and retired in shame. Then he pitched up again as Constantine's *Comes* in Britannia.

My horse slowed and picked his way through vineyards that had once belonged to Gratian. Someone else tilled them now because—just when Gratian's reputation, wealth, and vulgar happiness had seemed secure—he'd taken one fatal career misstep.

He'd let the usurping Emperor Magnentius lead his rebel forces through his vast estate to the showdown with Constantius II in Mursa. Worse, he'd hosted Magnentius and his officers to dinner at that villa now looming up ahead of me. He'd even hinted at support for the rebels. He'd smiled over his wine cup at the possibility of a Constantine's downfall.

So when Constantius II had slaughtered Magnentius' Western Roman Army, he had confiscated Gratian's lands as punishment.

Gratian's sons Valens and Valentinian had been struggling ever since to restore the family's reputation. We *agentes* heard in Sirmium that these heirs to suspicion were strengthening their ties with Pannonian notables and elders—including Varronian, the father of Emperor Julian's ally Jovian and his father-in-law Lucillianus.

The sun was setting behind me as I crossed a landscape of utter desuetude.

The villa's tiles hung loose. The orchard needed pruning. Broken irrigation channels flooded gushing rainwater onto the olive tree on a rise behind the house.

A pack of sniffing dogs circled my horse but why should we slow our gait for decrepit hounds with missing teeth and drooling gums? I dismounted, entered a front garden gagging on untrimmed ivy, and circled a cracked, silent fountain.

'Who's that?'

A thick voice shouted at me from behind a shuttered window. 'I asked, who's there?'

The villa's front door opened a crack at my approach.

I expected some light-slippered Illyrian maid or shy boy to admit me. Instead, a slovenly, middle-aged man and woman looked me up and down. Both wore heavy lead collars.

—THE BURNING STAKES—

Behind them, a giant of a man, unshaven and stinking of undiluted wine, blocked my stepping any farther past the two slaves and into the public rooms.

I made sure this unwashed brute saw my *schola* insignia.

'I've come to call on the Lady Justina, *Domine*.'

'No one visits that lady,' the old reprobate slurred. 'I'm in charge. No one visits anyone in my house. If you want to speak to the *Tribunus*, he's not here either.'

'I do know Tribune Valentinian, but I've come from Roma. I'd like to speak with Justina Picenus, privately.'

There was a swish of skirts coming from the atrium behind his hulking shoulders. Around a chipped pillar appeared a short matron in a simple housedress of bleached wool under a *palla* of faded crimson.

Half the Illyrian's height, she took Gratian's sleeve and tugged him away. '*Pater*, back to your cups.'

The disgraced veteran stepped back from the entrance with a whimper that he was hungry and his *cena* mustn't be delayed by the visit of any damned *curiosus* from Roma.

'I'm Tribune Valentinian's wife, Marina Severa. We don't dabble in politics in this house. We're a loyal military family. What's your business with my trusted companion?'

'Only social courtesy, *Domina*. I'm a freedman, Marcus Gregorianus Numidianus. My late master, Commander Atticus Manlius Gregorius, served in the court of Magnentius.'

'More fool he,' was Severa's dry retort.

An infant's screech came from the unseen depths of the house. The echoes spoke of empty rooms, lost furnishings, and light supervision.

Severa smiled with one side of her mouth. 'Excuse my child, young Gratian. Winter weather offers a toddler little freedom for his raucous games.'

'My own Leo raised our Roman roof with his indoor ball games,' I laughed. 'We've just sent him to study in Burdigala with the scholar Ausonius.'

'A wise choice, Marcus,' said a bell-like voice. 'Your wicked pagan superstitions must at last give way to a good Christian education for a boy so bright and good. Perhaps our energetic little Gratian should attend Ausonius' school someday?'

Severa's mouth dropped open as I fell to my knees.

'It's good to see you so well, *Domina* Justina.'

And it was good, as if the storms outside had blessed us with an early spring. The blushing features of the child, so charming in their even clarity, had become a picture of staggering womanly beauty. I'd seen hints of this during a brief reunion at the deathbed of her wealthy uncle, but this—!

There was a pleasing fullness of form and an inviting glow to her round cheeks. At last she'd attained full height and proportion, almost Greek in its perfection.

This was the unlucky noblewoman I would have been happiest serving as my empress.

'My dear protector, Marcus! Have you found my lost doll, Rosina, at last? Shall we poke our bare feet into the frozen rain barrel outside and see who lasts longest?'

'Propose any competition. I know your stamina. You'll always win, Lady.'

A subdued Severa instructed a slave to bring us snacks. The tribune's wife wore a perplexed expression as she disappeared into the private wing of her father-in-law's villa.

'You dreamt once, Justina, that you would be empress and give birth to an heir—but not one sired by Magnentius. How can this oracle be fulfilled if you hide here all your days?'

She laughed. 'Who knows what God holds out for the unlucky Justina? Emperor Julian is a bachelor but I'm hardly to his taste for all-night pagan debates! My dreams are postponed. What dreams bring you here after so many years?'

'I dreamt of a Veiled Vestal, hidden away.'

Justina paled. She retreated some steps.

'Not you, Marcus. I could not believe it of you. You could not change that much.'

'What do you mean, Justina?' I whispered. A couple of sluggish slaves lurked and listened at the rear of the atrium.

She steadied herself with one hand on a pillar and sighed. 'Are they so clever, to send you, of all people, to revenge themselves?'

'No one sent me, Justina. Our retired *magister* Apodemius might be in danger. Yet no one heeds my alarm. I'm on my own in search of him, with no clue but two retired Vestals telling me that a third is safe somewhere in Cibalae. But where? What's her name? Can she help me? Can you?'

'You know nothing else?'

'Yes. One said that Apodemius is responsible for this priestess' protection, but I assure you, Justina, it's Apodemius who needs my protection. There's a warrant for his arrest and questioning by an army tribunal in Chalcedon.'

She settled on a small inlaid bench. 'Are you alone, Numidianus?'

'Yes. I sent my *biarchus* ahead to our office in Sirmium. He only knows that Apodemius fled Roma.'

'But others may be following you?'

'There were two already on our trail.'

She shot to her feet. 'Oh, Marcus, you fool! You've led enemies straight to our door!'

She paced the airy chamber, her tunic hems sweeping worn, chipped tiles. I sat suspended, unable to touch sweetmeats laid on a tray by yet another collared slave.

She twisted the thick silver braid hemming her *palla*. After many minutes, she turned to face me square. All affection for her old friend had vanished.

'Marcus, if men are on your track, they mustn't find Apollonia here.'

'Apollonia? So she's in this very house? Hide her away if you must.'

'They would have the run of this shabby place. Old Gratian would do anything to curry favor and Severa must cooperate to protect Valentinian's rising reputation.'

'If they come, let me put them off.'

'No! No! Your very presence—your horse, your insignia—signal something unusual. Leave at once. Everything must look as normal as possible—'

'Those men are following me, not your Vestal.'

'But if Apollonia is found here, *Magister* Apodemius is truly lost, not just missing or hiding. I have no choice now but to trust you. I owe him that much. He couldn't protect my father from accusations of treason or the shame of suicide. But Apodemius used all his influence, even blackmail, to protect my virgin reputation safe from the consequences of Magnentius' downfall.'

'Then of course, we must save this Vestal Apollonia.'

'I'll entrust her to you, but you must first make me solemn promises. And if you betray this lady, you betray your *magister* and your *schola*. But most of all, you betray an oath I've given before God.'

'Shall I take her to my base in Sirmium and hide her somehow?'

'Yes, the very crossroads of imperial communications. You monitor everything passing from East to West, don't you? The sooner you're back in place the better.'

'If it means serving the *schola*, as well as Apodemius.'

Justina raised an eyebrow.

'Rumors say the great chamberlain, Eusebius, sits in Sirmium now. He keeps his finger in the air, testing the political winds. Do you avoid him?'

'On the contrary, *Domina*, Praepositus Eusebius is an old enemy. If I can spy on his moves, I do. One learns nothing useful by watching only friends.'

For a long minute, she paced the room, waving aside a bent-backed slave sweeping the atrium tiles. The childish giggles of the tiny Gratian in a nearby room grated on my nerves.

'I've decided. I have no choice. You leave here now in Severa's closed carriage. We hitch up your horse in harness with ours. Severa is taller so you'll wear her clothes. Apollonia will be disguised in mine.'

'And if someone questions you? Questions me?'

'You've never been here, Marcus. We've never spoken. I don't even wish to know Apollonia's hiding place and I don't wish our driver to know. When you've hidden her in Sirmium where they will never, ever find her, send the carriage back under cover of night.'

Justina shooed away a cluster of slave children and led me to a set of chambers nestled behind Gratian's dusty study. She sent maids running to collect suitable disguises.

I let her fasten a faded *stola* in dark red with two bronze *fibulae* carved into pheasants over a long ivory tunic. It bore subtle darning where time or moths had had their way. She found no gloves to fit me, so used two matching gold cuff bracelets carved with the facade of a Greek temple to disguise my sturdy wrists.

Slaves changed the harness and saddle on my *Cursus* horse to the tarnished livery of Gratian's faded estate with a second horse similarly trapped out.

I stuffed my *petanus* in the back of the carriage and let Justina arrange a long, warm *palla* over my shoulders, fixing it low over my brow and masking my dark jaw by tucking the ends high across my chin and then fixed underneath each shoulder pin.

'Oh, we nearly forgot your socks and boots!'

A pair of Gratian's unseasonal sandals was scavenged from a summer trunk. Without my riding trousers and leather over-tunic, I started shivering as they powdered and rouged my telltale features. But Justina's stony cool was of a different variety.

Shunted aside to wait in the vestibule, I listened to Justina, Severa, and others murmur for an excruciating ten minutes. Justina re-appeared in the atrium.

'She's ready. The carriage waits behind the villa. Take the road behind the house and go past the oil presses and stables. Then turn right on a mule trail that leads back to the main road to Sirmium. The driver's a dullard but loyal. He knows the way.'

Her trembling fingers held my arm fast. 'Marcus, promise me never to lift her veil. Never look on her fateful features. Her face is the Cross she carries for life. She bears up well, but don't press her on her past misfortune.'

'I promise. Will I see you again, Justina?'

'That would be unwise, Marcus. Marina Severa is good to me, but she's hardly sentimental. I survive here as a nobody and under the reign of Emperor Julian a nobody I must remain.'

A female appeared in the archway. She wore a long *paenula*, goatskin travel shoes, and fine-knitted socks against the cold. Justina had removed any telltale headdress or hair coils of the Vestal order and re-covered her head with a teal-blue *palla* monogrammed with 'JP,' and finally, a dark brown linen veil over her face.

This female nodded at Justina's rushed introduction and answered my greeting, 'Were circumstances different, perhaps we'd enjoy this journey as old friends, Marcus Gregorianus Numidianus.'

An old slave covered her mouth with her rags, trying not to laugh out loud at my getup. Angered by her insolence, Justina ordered the hag to take Apollonia to the waiting carriage.

Now Justina shivered. 'I pray to God we do the right thing, Marcus. If you can find her, so might others. So you must do everything short of burying her alive.'

'I know a place where no one will search for a Vestal."

'Good.' Justina nodded. 'Apollonia's the worthiest girl I know, Marcus. Her goodness is as pure as Kahina's. Her courage greater than Roxana's.'

'Sadly, her beauty nothing like her sponsor's.'

Justina blushed. 'Beauty has never served me well. Now promise me one last thing.'

'Anything, *Domina*.'

'That you will not be a fool and lose your simple heart to a mystery even you can never solve.'

It was the strangest of farewells.

Apollonia and I rode away in the high-roofed carriage from the Gratian estate. After half an hour she spoke in a quiet, clear voice muffled by her veil.

'*Domina* Justina says you are not the usual North African freedman.'

'How so?'

'She says you are educated and sentimental. Not what one expects of *curiosi*.'

'That is because you know Apodemius, our retired *magister*. Certainly he's not sentimental.'

She fell silent. She would not be drawn so easily on the subject of Apodemius.

After another quarter of an hour, she said, 'Justina says you've memorized many great books. As a girl, I wept over the death of Dido on her pyre.'

'Yes?'

'Queen Dido wanted to be loyal to the memory of Sychaus and to dedicate herself to the great city she'd built. But she was conquered by love for Aeneas instead.'

We listened to the crunch of wheels on the paving stones.

—THE BURNING STAKES—

I recalled Vergilius' tragic stanzas describing the lovesick Dido. '*What use are prayers or shrines to the impassioned? Meanwhile her tender marrow is aflame and a silent wound is alive in her breast. She wanders like an unwary deer—*'

Apollonia laughed, 'No, not quite, Numidianus! You forgot, she burns. *Wretched Dido burns and wanders frenzied through the city like an unwary deer struck by an arrow—*'

'*that a shepherd hunting with his bow has fired from a distance in the Cretan woods—*'

'*—leaving the winged steel in her, without knowing.*'

I bit my tongue. Wretched Dido burned to death for love. Who knew better than this poor woman the price of cruel fire? Was it Dido's broken heart that made the child Apollonia weep? Or the abandoned Carthaginian queen building her own funeral pyre so its flames could devour her dying body?

The carriage wheels squeaked underneath our rocking wooden cabin.

'Have you forgotten the rest, Numidianus?'

'No, no, *Dominula*. What man does not feel guilt when the unfaithful Aeneas looks from his ship back to Carthago and sees the flames of Dido's funeral pyre rising like a plume into the sky?'

'Perhaps you men take too much on your conscience.'

Was she thinking of Apodemius? Hadn't he assumed responsibility for the criminal arson against her family?

She added, 'You couldn't have foreseen the fates of ones you loved.'

Beneath my disguise, my jaw dropped. How could this stranger allude with such confidence to my personal failures?

I looked sidelong at the contained figure swaying gently with the rhythm of the vehicle. I could see nothing of her but two graceful hands with long fingers and neat, shining nails. She smelled of sweet almond oil, a pathetic reminder she was denied all the other toilet vanities of normal women.

How could Apollonia read my loss and guilt for Kahina's mind and spirit damaged by years of enslavement? How could she know how often I'd relived those last moments defending General Silvanus when I should have saved Roxana first from harm? How could she divine the torture I still suffered from doubt over Gunda's lonely death on the Rhenus while I served the Empire first?

What did Apollonia know of the fates of women I'd cared for and failed? Justina could not have told her any of this. Was this maimed creature not only a priestess, but also an oracle?

Chapter 14, Office Routine

—Sirmium, Pannonia—

The Pannonians call their capital Sirmium, 'The Glorious Mother of Cities.' Of course, they're completely deluded. Even a seven-hundred-year-old city of 100,000 citizens is nothing to Roma.

Roma is the mother of cities.

Roma is the mother of the world.

It isn't a bad capital, as Roman cities go. Perhaps I will go so far as to admit, say, to a Pannonian paying for my drink, that Sirmium enjoys a good view over the Savus River. My post as *centenarius* in charge of Sirmium's communications, road permits, account inspections, and whatever espionage was needed, might be considered a plum assignment.

Some might even call it a privilege for a pagan like me competing for promotion against favored Christians under the Arian, Emperor Constantius. Sirmium boasted a powerful bishop and had hosted many church councils. Any *agens* who had access to all that postal traffic had to be a man with whom parties of all faiths could co-exist.

Thus far, no one had found fault with me.

More to my taste than churches were Sirmium's horseracing arena, mint, two theaters, workshops, and modern baths, not to mention dozens of temples soon to be restored—all surrounded by more minor palaces and luxury villas.

My routine involved a lot of economic as well as religious surveillance. Commercial traffic offered a refreshing rest from the political upheavals of my thirteen years of service to date. Sirmium's mint was connected with the mints in Salona and Siscia, all of them in constant communication down the Via Argentaria to the Fortress Ad Drium with its silver mines nestled in Mount Dinara closer to the coast.

The country folk reported that those mountain peaks were infested with giants. But giants were of no concern to me—at least not until they requested mail service.

Sirmium had another spot of local interest especially useful to me this particular evening.

I directed Severa's driver to steer his battered carriage around the corner of the city walls embracing the western end of the racing track. We would sneak into Sirmium by a gate on the northern side giving onto the slums lining the river docks.

Controls over entry seemed unusually tight this evening. I even knew the two guards on duty but the disguise of modest eye-makeup and cheek powder saw me safe through. It was amusing when they waved me into the city as the sleepier of two veiled travellers from the Gratian household.

Our carriage drew up at an obscure corner I chose for its dim torchlight. Apollonia and I were headed for a humble but thriving establishment where I'd once hidden myself away for many weeks during the civil war. It wasn't a place I dared even name to my companion nor an address I reckoned Severa's slaves might have recognized. But anywhere more respectable was risky.

Still wearing Severa's ludicrous-fitting *stola* and *palla*, I shuffled in Gratian's sloppy slippers up the side street through the chilly evening to make advance arrangements for my ward's new hiding place.

The proprietress, Optata, looked in fine form this evening. She reigned over her main reception room off the street in a flowing winter gown of garnet wool under an embroidered *palla* of ochre flowers on deep silk. Her hair was a veritable siege tower of black curls lacquered to lean forward over her brow. Her sharp black eyes lined with Egyptian kohl penetrated my slapdash disguise within seconds.

To her credit, she didn't burst out laughing. She knew I was a senior *agens* and it paid well to assist an *agens* without hesitation—however smudged his eyeliner. With efficient calm, she promised me everything would be perfect for her unusual veiled guest—perfect discretion, perfect privacy, and perfect anonymity—all for a perfectly outrageous price.

Quiet was another matter, but there was nothing one could do about that. I secured Apollonia the best room at the back.

Unlike many of the more popular 'rooms,' my guest's must be hung with a curtain for privacy, I explained.

'The lady is tragically disfigured. The sight of her could be bad for your business.'

Hearing that, Optata doubled her room rate. I changed back into my own clothes, paid up a week in advance, and installed Apollonia, still covered head to toe, in her new 'home.' I promised to return as soon as I could—provided I wasn't followed.

One lead after another brought me no closer to Apodemius. But as far as the Vestals were concerned, I'd done my duty. For her part, Apollonia must have been scared, either for herself or for Apodemius, because she after a moment's hesitation on the threshold of Optata's boisterous reception room, she made no protest over my unorthodox arrangements for her safety.

Quite the contrary.

'Rest assured, Numidianus, I'll find my new room a novel change from Severa's pious and martial domesticity,' she said through her face covering. 'I smelled a delicious dinner downstairs, *Domina* Optata. Please send me a tray whenever it's convenient. My former hostess Marina Severa of Cibalae was generous in many things, but very, very stingy with her *garum* sauce.'

To be compared so favorably with a Pannonian tribune's consort was flattering honey to Optata who rushed off to her cook.

'The food may be hearty, but you'll have trouble sleeping through the noise,' I warned Apollonia.'

'You've never shared a house with Gratian the Younger,' she quipped.

Understated humor seemed to be Apollonia's trusty weapon against the tragedy of her existence.

She squeezed my hand with both of hers, eager to show me her courage and confidence in me.

I left Optata's with the faint whiff of sweet almonds lingering in my nostrils.

☙☙☙

After an exhausted sleep in my familiar narrow bed, I grabbed a shave from the corner street barber and went straight through the dawn to the Palace grounds.

A cluster of sleepy slaves loitered outside the *agentes*' office suite. They were waiting for my staff to process applications for road warrants for masters claiming 'official' business in distant parts. Most were legitimate requests, but this morning I turned a blind eye to a couple of bribes easing the travel of two minor officials' wives. A little grease helped the gears of state keep turning.

Rufus was already at work inside, helping a deputy *eques* unload satchels of imperial correspondence that had arrived during my absence.

I bolted the door of our main workroom against the clamor of idle folk sleeping, snacking, and chattering in the Palace corridor.

'Did you do as I asked, Rufus? Did you lose those two riders tracking us?'

'No.'

His stolid, open features gave nothing away.

'Rufus? What happened to them?'

Surely he heard my note of alarm. But Rufus fixed his attention on deciphering scribbled addresses.

'Rufus, did you let me down?'

'No, Numidianus, I did not fail your instructions. As soon as I arrived, I gave orders in your name that all city gatekeepers were to cross-examine any suspicious riders from the west. And I exerted all my authority so that every piece of identification was checked for forgery.'

'So that was why security coming in was so tight last night. Well done.' I gave a relieved sigh. 'So you lost them, right?'

'Hardly.'

Rufus kicked open the door to my inner alcove where I kept a wooden cot, washbasin, and backup riding gear. Someone was sleeping on my mattress. He lay blanketed under the same patched *paenula* I'd spotted hanging inside Flavia's shuttered window.

—THE BURNING STAKES—

With an angry sweep of my arm, I uncovered the snoring Gaudentius. At his feet, the boy scribe Benedictus, curled up like a napping kitten, blinked himself awake.

'Bastard! What are you doing here?'

Gaudentius stretched and collected his truculent overconfidence. 'A warrant for Apodemius has gone out.'

'I heard. For questioning only.'

Gaudentius stood up and emptied the contents of my washbasin in a few swallows. 'Come on, Numidianus. You don't believe that's all. Neither do I.'

'You followed me here?' I shook my head at Rufus, who shrugged and kept on sorting mail.

'I reckoned you were heading straight for Apodemius,' Gaudentius said with a grunt.

'He's not here!' I gestured around my shabby workplace.

'I'm disappointed, sure. But that doesn't change much. Sooner or later, you'll find him. I'll help you. He's got to get me back into the *schola*.'

'Only Otho could do that, but I told you, you're not his type. And what's the scribe doing here?'

'He sent you to me, didn't he? Back in Mediolanum?'

'I wasn't looking for you.'

'So you claim. You were looking for Apodemius. He only wants to be useful.'

'And you're so very good at using people.'

I was furious. I returned to my desk and tossed Rufus a stern glance. When I'd ridden up to Mediolanum with Cassius and Ahenobarbus, I'd managed to keep the sensitive matter of the missing Gallus execution rescindment a secret between the *princeps* and myself.

Would I have to confide now in Rufus and Gaudentius? How much did this feeble reed of a Britannian understand? This was not the 'team' I would have assembled had I not been a victim of bad luck thus far.

'Jupiter's Balls! Have a look at this, Numidianus.' Rufus' normally ruddy face flushed deeper.

He pushed aside the pile of ragtag correspondence and routine reports mounting around our opened postal bags. His thick fingers dangled a heavy vellum packet from a pristine purple and gold ribbon, its imperial seal cracked into two. He scanned the contents before I could snatch it from his grasp.

'These are instructions from Chalcedon for the *curiales* to post their convictions in the usual public places.'

'Julian's jurists haven't wasted an hour.' Rufus read my thoughts.

'New year—new regime.' Gaudentius poured more water from a pitcher into my basin, rinsed off his face, and pulled on one of my spare tunics. Thanks to his blockade of grain and oil, he'd obviously eaten better in North Africa over the last year than any Roman; the struts of my second-best *cingulum* strained like palisade posts across his hard belly.

'Read it out loud, African.' The Neapolitan dried off his shaved scalp and scraped a wooden stool forward for himself.

Wearing little more than his socks, Benedictus squatted on his haunches like a litter bearer at the notary's feet in the inner doorway. Though Rufus had all the braziers going, I felt cold just looking at the boy's snow-white ribcage.

I scanned the first page. It was grilled with the straight lines and even lettering of *litterae caelestes*—specialized court handwriting permitted only to *sacra scrinia* officials—spelling its message out in impenetrable technical legal phrases. Thus did our machine of state keep a thousand superfluous men employed.

'Bad news; Consul Taurus has been exiled to Vercellae for dereliction of duty.'

Rufus said, 'Bad news? A day's ride from Mediolanum? He's got off easy. So, they had nothing against him in the end, except working for Constantius.'

Indeed, it could have turned out far worse for the trembling consul begging me for protection from the dank shadows of the Temple of Jupiter Redux.

'Consul and Praetorian Prefect Florentius,' I continued, 'condemned to death *in absentia*, for dereliction of duty.'

'Only because he ran away, like a coward.' Gaudentius said with a disdainful jerk of his formidable shoulders. 'Florentius gave Julian a bitch of a time up in Gallia. And it was Florentius' bright idea that Constantius remove Julian's crack troops to the Persian front. Florentius knew he was in for it if Julian found out.'

—THE BURNING STAKES—

'Well, at least he's safe for the time being—wherever he is.' I read on: '*Magister Officiorum* Florentius Nigrinianus—deported to Bua Island off the Dalmatian coast. Oh, Olympus! He was an honest man.'

Benedictus blinked heavy-lashed eyes still puffy with sleep. 'Nigrinianus was much beloved by the older scribes. They said his filing was exquisite.'

I thrust the vellum aside for a moment, remembering the conscientious official working overtime on arrangements for Constantius' religious synod. I suddenly felt twice as old as my thirty-some winters.

'What you don't know, Scribbler, is that Florentius Nigrinianus was responsible, at my behest, for calling in the imperial *quaestores* and exposing a plot against General Silvanus in Agrippina in 355, a plot in which our chief Chalcedon jurist General Arbitio was complicit.'

'In short, boy, Nigrinianus knows too much army dirt,' Gaudentius said.

So did Gaudentius himself. Then-*Ducenarius* Gaudentius had been at my side as we spied through a chapel window on the Emperor praying. We'd observed treasonous forgeries attributed to the innocent Silvanus passed to Constantius in front of his private altar. We'd watched the military conspire to assassinate one of their own.

'Is that it?' Rufus asked.

'Hardly. Two more pages.'

I read on with a tighter throat. 'Evagrius, Count of the Privy Purse, exiled. Former Steward of the Palace, Saturninus, exiled. Ex-*notarius* Cyrinus, exiled—all for dereliction of duty.'

'All for show,' Gaudentius scoffed. 'Anyway, in a few years old loyalties will be forgiven and forgotten. They'll be back on their comfy estates and I'll be—'

I continued: 'Ursulus, Count of the Sacred Largesse—Death by burning.'

'How can that be?' Rufus whispered. 'Ursulus was good to Julian. Ursulus disobeyed Constantius' orders. He wrote to the treasury to get Julian funds—'

I waved a hand, 'I know, I know.'

Rufus groaned. 'For show? You think this is just for show, Gaudentius? Julian's tribunal is a danger for the future of the state! For all of us! Where are the rules of evidence? Where are the witnesses? Where are Ursulus' lawyers?'

I had to be careful how I answered Rufus. Many a man had died for treason, regretting that the ambitious Gaudentius had overheard his careless criticisms.

'General Arbitio cares little for Roman law, Rufus. But has our new emperor no gratitude? Can a devout pagan sovereign be so blind to Justice? With my own ears, I've heard Julian say that an emperor should increase the number of his friends by clemency.'

Rufus gave me a pained expression. 'Perhaps you favor Julian too much, Numidianus. Executing Count Ursulus is not clemency.' He looked down at Benedictus. 'I once heard Cassius joke that Ursulus was so honest, you could play "Rock, Scissors, Paper" with him in pitch blackness and still win.'

I smiled at the image of the upright Ursulus making 'scissors' in the dark.

'It doesn't matter what we think, Rufus. What matters is the judgment of the gods. This is not the hand of Honos but of Nemesis—but why?'

Gaudentius muttered. 'Honos? Nemesis? Come down to earth, Numidianus. Julian isn't even in charge of this show. Obviously, Ursulus' death sentence is the revenge of the Ioviani and Herculiani.'

'I don't understand, Gaudentius.'

The disgraced notary gave me a sour, superior chuckle. 'I obeyed Constantius' orders, right? I cut off supplies to the western ports. And I listened in North Africa. I listened to Artemius, that bastard *dux* devouring Egypt's rich pickings. I listened to the vice-regent of North Africa and to the fat *curiales* at their banquets in every inland trading hub. I listened to the bickering grain merchants on the docks. I listened to the army officers in the baths in Carthago—'

'You listened, all right, and you heard something about Ursulus?' Rufus prompted.

'That's right. For the honor of the Roman army, Ursulus must now pay with his life for uttering *a single phrase*.'

—THE BURNING STAKES—

Benedictus' pale, feline eyes stared up at Gaudentius, who continued:

'It happened last year, just after the autumnal equinox. Count Ursulus toured the front with Constantius and his army. They crossed the Euphrates and halted at Edessa for the arrival of other divisions and supplies. The Emperor set out to inspect what was left of our beloved Amida and found the Persians had left nothing but ruins, corpses, and smoking ashes.'

Gaudentius looked up at me. 'Constantius took it hard. He wept!'

I had to correct such a tall tale. 'Constantius? Weeping? The man never betrayed any single emotion so long as I—'

Gaudentius shot up from the stool. 'I'm telling you, Numidianus, *he wept hot tears*. He finally realized Roma's shame, the Empire's shame, *our* shame—when his fancy boots had to walk through his citizens' vulture-picked bones.'

'But what about Count Ursulus?' Benedictus pressed him.

'When Ursulus saw Constantius breaking down, he knew it was bad for morale. He forgot his place. He shouted right in the officers' faces, right in front of their troops: *What courage! So this is how our cities are defended by men whom the Empire goes broke paying?*'

I could imagine the scene all too well. The humiliating loss of our fortress city Amida to the Persian king Shapur had broken the career of veteran General Ursicinus, forced into shameful retirement. But those in the know blamed the fall of Amida on General Sabinian who resisted Ursicinus' pleas and strategies to lift the Persian siege. Suspicious rumors blamed Sabinian's fatal inaction on secret instructions from Lord Chamberlain Eusebius, who remained as determined as ever to rob Ursicinus of any glory or influence over Constantius to rival his own.

With every passing day, this unpredictable Chalcedon tribunal looked like a settling of old scores. With Ursulus doomed to the stake, any man would be wise to scour his past for clues to his chance of survival.

Including Gaudentius; disliked by Julian as he was, Gaudentius had never had time either for Arbitio, Eusebius, or Constantius' courtiers in Mediolanum on whom he'd spied for years. *Notarius* Gaudentius might fall victim to the anti-

Constantius cleansing underway as readily as any crooked *consistorianus*.

Yet he was no guiltier than any man convicted so far. He'd only done Constantius' bidding.

On the bright side, the Roman army held no grudge against Gaudentius. Neither did the army have anything against Apodemius. Apodemius' questioning might turn out no worse than that of Consul Taurus.

My heart felt lighter. Rufus was right. Vercellae was only a day's ride from Mediolanum. The Manlius estates included beehives, oyster beds, and pasturing farther from Roma than Vercellae.

'Is there more?' Benedictus asked.

I turned to the last page. 'Former *Magister Officiorum* Palladius, dereliction of duty, exiled to Britannia.'

Benedictus laughed. 'Britannia! That's no punishment! I'd go home with him today if I could!'

Then my stomach lurched.

'—for poisoning the mind of Emperor Constantius II against the Caesar Gallus while serving in the court of Antiochia .' Well, Ahenobarbus had warned me.

'Go on, Marcus.' Rufus was oblivious to my drying throat.

'Sorry. Notarius Pentadius, charged with taking notes during the Gallus interrogation in Pula—acquitted.'

I exhaled.

'Anything about Paulus Catena?' Benedictus asked.

'Too soon, boy,' Rufus said. 'Cassius and the escort won't dawdle but they don't have wings . . . '

I hardly heard the rest of their conversation. My mind raced. Two men had been called up on charges related to Gallus' death. One convicted. One acquitted! If only Ahenobarbus were here . . .

Rufus reached into the tumbling mess of mail. 'Here's another one, Marcus.'

Impatient, I broke a thick wax seal bearing a startling impression of our new emperor's profile with a pagan philosopher's beard.

'A piece of good news, I suppose.' I looked at three waiting faces, each man so different from the next.

—THE BURNING STAKES—

I spread the new missive out on the table for all to read. 'It's our warrant for the arrest of the Lord Chamberlain, *Praepositus Sacri Cubiculi*, Eusebius.'

'More *questioning*?' Gaudentius laughed.

'Hardly,' I gave him a satisfied grin. 'The State charges as follows: one, judicial fraud committed by the Lord Chamberlain Eusebius against General Ursicinus over the loss of the Roman city Amida; two, financial fraud and illegal dealing in Church and private property obtained by blackmail or other dishonest means; and three, political treason against the throne. Any and all properties in the possession of the Lord Chamberlain are to be immediately impounded by state agents, registered, and held in trust for the throne until further notice from the court of Chalcedon.'

'So maybe it's not a complete farce after all, Gaudentius?' Rufus tackled the rest of the mail, humming to himself.

He could afford to hum. He hadn't been in that cell in Pula the night Caesar Gallus' head rolled at my feet.

※※※

In Sirmium—as in the forum and bathhouse of every other city and town across the wide empire—the decrees of the Chalcedon jurists over men deemed innocent or guilty would be public knowledge sooner or later.

But the warrant for the great eunuch, swathed in his comfortable damask maroon robes and brocade slippers nearby, was ours to relish in secret until we had him safely in custody.

'Where is he now?' Rufus asked me.

'He'll be keeping to himself in his suite on the other side of the Palace complex,' I told the others. 'Knowing that spider of a man, he's plotting his next move back toward the center of power under Julian—but how? He spent too many years weaving himself into the fabric of the wealthy Church to reclaim his pagan ways.'

'I know the greasy bastard only too well from Mediolanum,' Gaudentius muttered. 'One slipup on our part, one whisper of this warrant, and he'll disappear from view on those quilted slippers of his, patting his sweaty forehead with a square of silk.'

'It would be easy enough to escape us, even with his blubbery girt,' I agreed. 'Eusebius controls thousands of eunuch allies, in every dark corridor of every imperial palace. We've all seen them swishing and slithering through the wings of suites from Treverorum to Mediolanum to Nicomedia to Antiochia. They answer to no loyalty but their own greed and resentment. They'll hide Eusebius, lie for him, maybe even die for him.'

'They're half-dead men already,' Benedictus said. 'Sometime I feel sorry for them.'

'What do you know about being a man?' Gaudentius said with a chuckle.

I shook my head. 'Don't waste your compassion. Even if Julian were to cleanse Constantinopolis of his like, burn the great Palace down to its foundations, the very ground is infected with them.'

'They're like hairless gray worms threading through the soil under our boots,' Rufus told the scribe with a grimace. 'Let's move on Eusebius—now!' He slammed an impatient palm down on the table.

Gaudentius grabbed his shoulder. 'It's not that easy, Rufus. The very sight of Numidianus or me approaching his staff will put him to flight. He saw often enough what *agentes* can do during treason trials. Once or twice, he even helped me do it.'

I studied Rufus, trembling with excitement. Should we send the *biarchus* with the warrant? Eusebius might have forgotten the humble, open-faced rider rushing to and fro at the postal hub housed at Mediolanum Palace's outer gates.

But even now, even with his promotion, did Rufus possess the required *gravitas*? If he could get close enough to corner Eusebius, could Rufus arrest a wily and formidable politician over whom it was always said, 'Constantius II wielded a *little* influence?'

No. I couldn't risk sending Rufus to bluster straight into Eusebius' realm, though later, I might need all available manpower at my disposal.

—THE BURNING STAKES—

We sat, hungry and over-excited, unsure how to beach the great whale once and for all. I sent one of our slaves for cold ham pie and a pitcher of diluted wine to wash it down. I could not think of any way to get physically close enough to Eusebius, even with the help of a unit of Palace enforcers, without triggering his escape down some imperial rabbit hole.

Still hunched in the archway between my two rooms, Benedictus ate and listened to us strategize how to move in on Eusebius by stealth. Though he was no match for Gaudentius' bulk or Rufus' hearty appetite, the boy devoured twice as much pie as the rest of us. Where did he store it all on that slim frame?

The food was almost gone when the scribe brushed crust off his long, thin fingers and interrupted our debate.

'The solution is very simple, *Agentes*. The Lord Chamberlain has never met me. Obviously, I am the man to deliver the warrant.'

Chapter 15, A Social Visit

—SIRMIUM—

'I'll deliver the warrant into the eunuch's hands on your authority. Then the rest of you close in on him and make the arrest,' the boy said with startling authority.

We stared at the Britannian's narrow shoulders, bent from months of copying.

'Oh, of course he will still try to flee,' he added in the low tone favored by the wizened old men of the *scrinia*, 'but it seems obvious to me that if you anticipate his escape path correctly, you can position the guards from the *domestici* to wait for him in a trap.'

Trapping seemed better than attacking. I thought of Ahenobarbus' ugly wound incurred by Catena before he was felled. This seemed a better plan, though the eunuch's weapons were poison and guile, not blades or hot pokers. He would run from the boy, but in which direction?

Then I recalled my time in Sirmium during Magnentius' uprising a decade ago. I'd found myself trying to escape Paulus Catena through the underground bowels of this very palace. I'd dashed around a network of dark maintenance and storage tunnels housing the hypocaust heating system and the imperial baths' drainage. In my black panic escaping Catena's dogs, a faint whiff of Eusebius' sickeningly sweet body oil had led me to a set of stone steps and smack through a door into the Lord Chamberlain's private office.

'If he thinks we have all the gates and corridors blocked,' I told my fellow *agentes*, 'he'll take the one route left to him. And that's where we'll wait.'

We set about our stealthy preparations. Many of my regular riders were on the *Cursus* right now, directions east and south. So Gaudentius and Rufus solicited the help of the remaining junior officers and Palace guards I judged trustworthy to help their descent into that Hades of old torture cells and stony passages zigzagging underneath the exquisite mosaic Palace flooring.

Benedictus swapped his shabby scribe's tunic and borrowed riding trousers for a suitably refined palace ensemble to slip unremarked into the eunuchs' aromatic and fashionable wing.

I resealed the warrant and handed it over to Benedictus with an ironic smile. Across the Empire, similar calls had gone out to detain Apodemius for questioning—to no avail. Apodemius had seen the hands of the gods writing in the clouds and made his way to a place of safety in time.

Eusebius had been unable to tear himself away from the comforts of his perfumed sanctuary. I would have Apodemius' longtime enemy in shackles before Apollo made another circuit of the sky.

But the Fates don't like to be bored. No sooner had my fellow *agentes* dispersed to set our trap than the gods played an enormous joke on me.

There was a polite tap of a well-soled slipper outside. Even before I could open my outer door, an unctuous mix of sweet jasmine and musk that sickened the mind as well as the stomach seeped into my rooms.

The Lord Chamberlain's impassable bulk filled my doorway.

'Marcus Gregorianus Numidianus,' he cooed, patting his damp forehead with a pink silk handkerchief. 'I haven't laid eyes on you since the fateful day of our beloved Divinity's death on that scrubby plain outside Mopsucrenae.'

'Please come in, Lord Chamberlain.'

'I've forgotten, is it too late to wish a pagan *Io, Saturnalia*?' He gazed around my small domain. 'Family well? Roma as licentious and irrelevant as ever?'

I thrust the pages of the Chalcedon convictions under my tunic. It was too soon to announce his personal fate. Our trap was an hour or more from readiness.

—THE BURNING STAKES—

I pulled the curtain of my inner alcove closed to hid the disorder left by Gaudentius and Benedictus. I offered him Gaudentius' stool—far too narrow for his enormous buttocks.

He shammed embarrassment at the consequence of his gluttony. 'May I take that more comfortable seat over there?'

Before I could protest, he'd lowered himself into my own chair behind the long table still scattered with half-sorted piles of mail.

He smiled at the clutter. 'I've often wondered, in my simple fashion, how it is you *agentes* maintain the lines of communication so well? From such a towering, teetering mess as this? It's a Babylonian ziggurat!'

'Is this a social call, Lord Chamberlain?'

'I was merely passing by.'

'You are always welcome to pass by.' Passing wind of a political sort was more like it but I would happily detain him here today. I gave him a warm nod but not so warm as to raise suspicion. Let him linger, confident that he was imposing himself on me. Eusebius' absence from the eunuchs' usual haunts made Benedictus' job that much easier.

'I'm sure you find my rooms rough to your taste, *Praeposite*,' I said. Years ago, I'd seen the expensive tapestries and decorations of his offices on the far side of the Palace. The property-avid obscenity overflowing my chair had only become wealthier since.

'You sort all this yourself? By department? Route? Priority?'

'I have staff.'

'And you make copies, surely, illicit copies? For dossiers at the Castra?'

'I cannot admit to being that clever, Lord Chamberlain.'

'Oh, I disagree. You're clever enough not to admit it. But I know your *magister*'s ways. Or rather, I did. How do you find this new chief—Otho Something, isn't it?'

'How do I find Otho? As the joke goes, turn left at Aquileia and ride on toward Roma.'

With pudgy fingers laden with bulging gold rings popping with rubies, carnelians, and diamonds, the eunuch played with my paperwork. He read an address or two, flicked a military factory report this way, a mint inventory that way. He was distracting me as best he could—almost flirting with me.

'Is he settling in? The men like him?'

'*Magister* Otho is very competent and popular. He receives all ranks as equals.'

'He'll have to be more than competent to reverse Julian's distaste for you *curiosi*. He'll have to be very clever. I'd advise Otho to promote educated and handsome pagans like you to win over our young sovereign.'

I recalled Eusebius' attempt to brand Julian with treason in an attempt to knock the gauche and stuttering philosophy student out of competition for influence over Constantius at court. Surely Julian hadn't forgotten Eusebius' enmity. Perhaps today's warrant for Eusebius was definitive proof.

It was so tempting to announce the charges against my guest. But not yet . . . no . . . I was alone with him. I had no witnesses, no back-up. Benedictus carried the warrant. It was not yet the moment to spring our trap.

So I kept our 'social visit' cordial.

'And how does Julian regard your own vast empire, Lord Chamberlain?'

Eusebius gave an uneasy chuckle.

'My empire, you call it? I'm only a glorified bath attendant—a back-scraper, a nosehair-plucker—and out of a job, it seems. What empire? You were always a saucy freedman, Numidianus. You know, I could have had you hauled in time and time again, but you amuse me more than annoy me. Only powerful men get under my skin—never slaves and certainly never *ex-slaves*.'

I could have grabbed him by his triple chins and heavy necklaces and slammed the Chalcedon warrant down his gullet then and there. But I held back, resorting to my slave boy's patience—watching, waiting, while the spider twisted some unseen, sticky web. His thick perfume was coating my premises. How much longer before our trap was set?

'Well, perhaps it's too early to assess your new *magister*, Numidianus. But you're not withholding valuable information from me? Please don't underestimate our long acquaintance.'

'That I do not.'

He sighed as he toyed with my mail. Was he searching for something?

'And Apodemius? Off to Chalcedon—tsk, tsk—hardly the retirement he so richly deserved. Any updates here from the East? Have they lit his pyre yet?'

'Your information is premature, *Praeposite*. A warrant for questioning cannot be served on a man who can't be found.'

'Not found?' His fingers stopped their fumbling for an instant, then flicked some sealing wax crumbs off his ornate sleeve cuff.

'Perhaps lost for good.'

Eusebius wheezed his regret. 'All the better for the poor old man. And that girl, that *agens* Roxana—you know the female—the lithe brunette who once beguiled me into thinking she could be of some service to my poor self.'

'Roxana?'

'Oh, don't look so blank, Numidianus. You and that girl were very close at one time. My *domestici* spied on you in bed once in a slum hovel in Antiochia. They said you two made a pretty couple that hot afternoon. Any idea where I might find her now? Or is she also . . . "lost"?'

'Roxana was seriously wounded while fighting General Silvanus' assassins.'

'Ah, yes, I recall. She had to be carried into trial to testify. *Magister* Apodemius prevented Catena from torturing her into the truth. But that was six years ago. Did she not recover? Did she lose the leg?'

'She limped off to an obscure life. Some think she died.'

'Died? Oh, I do hope not. General Arbitio was very fond of that lady—far fonder than yourself—in his particular way.'

Eusebius' thick jowls gave a sudden jiggle as his bulging eyes darted at the closed door. 'Numidianus—is someone listening outside?'

I checked the corridor. No one was eavesdropping, only a slave or two retreating from the far end of the corridor into a courtyard beyond. Eusebius' jangled nerves unnerved me. Had he caught wind of his imminent arrest? Was the trap ready yet?

'What was I saying, Numidianus?' he continued when I returned.

'You were talking about Roxana.'

'Oh, yes, Roxana. You're a Numidian, you must know how the Egyptians in Heliopolis worship a cat god who embodies nine lives?'

'Atum-Ra, I think he's called.'

'Atum-Ra? Yes. Roxana was a bit of a cat, don't you think? Always landing on her feet, a cat of many lives . . . you might even say an alley cat with a colorful past.'

'We never discussed her past. The *schola* requires we divorce ourselves from our past to devote ourselves to the service.'

'But once you retire?' he continued, snapping the corner pages of a bound ledger on my desk. 'Hoping our Roxana has survived, where would you guess she'd choose to live out this so-called "obscure" existence?'

Still harping on Roxana.

'As I said, the *schola* assumes a sadder fate. Roxana has disappeared without trace.'

Was this his purpose in making a 'social call?' Eusebius' humming and fiddling didn't fool me. The spider's finished web swung visible now. He was a eunuch in a hurry. He'd come to my office hunting for a pawn, a bribe, a *latrunculi* piece to play on the game board of shifting court power.

Eusebius and Arbitio had been political allies for years. Together they'd helped bring down General Silvanus using forged papers, then General Ursicinus using his rival General Sabinian at Amida. Together Eusebius and Arbitio had conducted months of interrogations and purges in the wake of each political rival's downfall.

But now? How weak Eusebius found his new position!

Julian needed the Eastern Army as well as the Western and General Arbitio had the crack Ioviani and Herculiani behind him, whereas Eusebius' 'troops' were only legions of castrated chamberlains. Julian despised his ranks.

I began to follow Eusebius' desperate plan. He wanted to offer the pawn Roxana to ingratiate himself with his lost ally, General Arbitio, who enjoyed such fresh bargaining power with Julian. If Eusebius could satisfy Arbitio's frustrated lust for the lovely Roxana, their frayed alliance might be repaired. The glory-

—THE BURNING STAKES—

seeking Julian could be waved off to new battlefronts while the old Eusebius-Arbitio alliance raked in the profits at home.

Eusebius might reign over an empire from the bath chambers once again.

'I truly cannot help you, Lord Chamberlain. The Empire is huge. Roxana is indeed lost forever.'

He hoisted his jelly-like torso up from my chair and waddled to the door I held open for him. He reeked like a concubine's toilet box. He laid that collection of sparkling nuggets on my shoulder to give me a fraternal pat.

'The Empire is not as big as all that, African and, thanks to the successes of King Shapur, shrinking every week. I fear it's already too small for a visionary like our boy Julian.'

☙☙☙

We kept tabs on Eusebius for the rest of the afternoon. For an hour at the imperial baths, he soaked and scraped his lardy stomach clean and layered a fresh coat of Eastern oils on his juddering thighs. He took a solitary meal: veal escalopes with raisins, preserved turnips, chicken in garlic sauce, and fruit tarts in his private rooms. Then he returned to work in his office, right where we wanted him.

It was all going according to plan. Hidden unseen right beneath his padding slippers, I waited in the dark with Rufus and Gaudentius in a narrowed passage hacked out of rock. We listened to Eusebius' heavy footfall, shuffling this way and that as he reviewed his affairs.

We heard the arrival of one after another of his fellow eunuchs, the high-pitch of their various exchanges as they reported the unremarkable proceedings of a palace shorn of imperial clients. Constantius had filled all his residences with hordes of eunuchs, cooks, barbers, slaves, and secretaries. And all across Roman territory, these thousands hung about—idled and waiting.

I'd been very careful to name only Palace guards I could trust not to confide the news of the warrant to a single *domesticus* among the eunuchs. In the end, we had only ten men we could be sure of poised in the tunnel and a scant dozen more blocking the public exits of the palace.

There was a sudden, sharp knock in the room overhead. Through the worn planks and elaborate tiling of the old Palace floor, we heard a muffled echo of Benedictus' clipped salutation.

Our trap would spring in a few seconds.

Fear for the boy shot up my spine. We should have armed Benedictus somehow. He was on his own against one of the most ruthless men of the Empire. Even an old eunuch—if facing death at a burning stake or by live burial—might ignore his distaste for personal violence and bring the boy down with a blow or dagger. But it was too late now.

Two needles of Eusebius' lamplight cut through the flooring of the rooms above and landed on Gaudentius' gleaming forehead a few inches from where I hid. The *notarius* braced himself for Eusebius' sudden plunge through the door hidden behind a curtain near his desk and down into our midst.

Eusebius said something brusque to our scribe—probably that he knew of no business with Benedictus. He dismissed our envoy with a curt good-bye. Benedictus' feathery footsteps moved back toward the door.

Perhaps Eusebius dropped his eyes back down to his work. Perhaps he watched the scribe leaving. Benedictus' steps halted. There was another exchange, too low to catch. We heard a rustle, the boy's voice, another rustle, a few steps, the scrape of Eusebius' heavy *cathedra* shoved away from his desk, the boy again, and an abrupt rebuttal from the Lord Chamberlain.

Another quiet, firm word from Benedictus followed.

Eusebius shouted, hoarse with shock, for eunuch underlings to remove Benedictus. His shouts filtered right through the floor and silk carpets overhead. But my men were ready to block any eunuchs' path to his rescue. No one could slither past us to his indignant side.

After a few seconds of futile waiting, the Lord Chamberlain must have realized his options had been reduced to only one.

Benedictus cried out. There was a scuffle of slippers and shoes as the hefty eunuch seemed to be pushing Benedictus out of his sight. He tried to slam his heavy oak door on the boy. We

—THE BURNING STAKES—

heard a whelp of pain as Benedictus used his foot to keep the door open.

We heard a body hit the floor.

We fought off our fears for Benedictus, extinguished our torches, and waited. Eusebius was too wise to shout for help again. He must realize he had little time to take stock of his files, secrets, treasures, deeds, and dossiers.

There would be time to recover all that later. First he must elude detention. He'd make his way to fellow eunuchs far from Sirmium. Or if he couldn't trust his brethren snakes—he'd secrete himself away in any one of dozens of religious properties or secluded villas he'd confiscated during years of blackmail and coercion.

Yes, he must buy time by disappearing—just like Apodemius— until Julian's regime had settled its scores.

Eusebius would now escape by the one route no one had used for years.

He'd resort to Catena's old maze. He must, I told myself, he must.

We waited through the pregnant silence overhead. No footfall, no shout, no groan—what was he doing?

Suddenly a bolt slid and the wooden door above us flew open. The square of office lamplight from above outlined the terrified eunuch's enormous silhouette. Then he tumbled heavily down the steps—right into Gaudentius' firm embrace.

Shaken by such sudden success, I admired the coldblooded flick of Gaudentius' wrists as he snapped thick iron shackles around Eusebius' fat ankles.

'I told the guards to bring the largest pair in stock,' the Neapolitan grunted. He knelt in the filth of the tunnel and tested the locks to make sure the catches were fast.

Eusebius flailed, but his trunk-like legs were weighed down as never before. He gave out a sudden, ear-piercing squeal, the like of which I haven't heard since I went boar hunting with the late Lieutenant Gaiso in the wilds outside Treverorum.

Gaudentius moved away so our guards could take custody of the prisoner. Young Benedictus' pale face appeared framed in the square of light above our heads. His thin arm handed down the opened warrant. Following the Castra's time-honored training in arrest procedures, I read the state document out loud before the witnesses in the tunnel.

But Eusebius didn't hear me. He was whimpering and, we realized in that closed and fetid passage, emptying his bowels with fear into the thick damask folds of his under-robes. Hardened soldiers surrounding him winced with disgust.

'That is the decree. Your hearing starts as soon as you arrive, Lord Chamberlain,' I said. 'All your property is to be collected by the state for assessment and judicial redistribution. I think, before you leave us for a cell not far down this passage, we'll start by removing all your rings.'

⚜⚜⚜

Delivering Eusebius would be the highest priority of our *schola*, yet we couldn't delay his departure for the East just to inform Roma of his arrest—the eunuch should be nearing Constantinopolis by the time our relay-message landed on Otho's desk back at the Castra.

We lost valuable hours with the Palace *tribunus stabili* arguing over whether the *Cursus* animals could bear Eusebius' weight from Sirmium to Constantinopolis without risking damage to state property. The alternative was a state carriage—Eusebius' preferred mode of transport—which would add days of delay to serving him up to his former ally General Arbitio.

And which *agentes* on hand should supervise his escort to trial as prescribed by Roman law?

'Certainly not I,' Gaudentius said. He was changing his clothes before going out into the back alleys of Sirmium for the night. He said he needed drink and whores, so I tipped him off where to go—as far in the opposite direction from Apollonia's hideaway at Optata's as the walls of Sirmium allowed.

'But you know his wiles, Gaudentius. And as *notarius* you're ranked higher than any of us.'

'No. Julian despises me. Escort is the *schola*'s job and I'm not going if I'm not reinstated yet. Only Apodemius can get me back into the Castra—'

—THE BURNING STAKES—

'Don't count on him.'

He shrugged those muscle-bound shoulders. 'Anyway, landing Eusebius will help argue my case. Thanks for that, at least, but perhaps you're right. The time's not ripe.'

'Thank me properly by finishing the job. I can't leave my post. Julian may think better of you with Eusebius in tow.'

I argued because it seemed the perfect way to rid myself of Gaudentius' presence. I needed time on my own to win over the Veiled Vestal's trust and find Apodemius before Otho's 'new men' arrested the old man.

To do that, I had to protect Apollonia from discovery until the safety of Apodemius was guaranteed. It was a riddle as black and deep as the Styx. I shared Justina's palpable terror. Though I remained half in the dark, I had guessed this much: anyone controlling that lady whom no one could view was within reach of Apodemius.

This afternoon, as on previous occasions, Gaudentius and I had worked well enough together but I knew what and who he was at heart. The Veiled Vestal hiding on the other side of Sirmium was none of Gaudentius' business. The street-hardened notary was not above delivering Apodemius himself to the tribunal if that would guarantee him restitution and good standing in Julian's new court.

Gaudentius still balked: 'Can't risk it.'

'But I can't delay delivery of Eusebius waiting for backup from Roma. Then Rufus will have to take him.'

'Rufus will find some excuse to stay here. Bet on it.'

'Why do you say that?'

'He needs to stay here.'

'What are you talking about?'

'The morning the kid and I arrived, he was filing a long report. Sealed it fast. Sent it out with your *eques* heading in the direction of Roma.'

'A report? On what? On who?'

'On *whom*,' Gaudentius corrected my grammar with a facetious sneer. 'Why, Numidianus, I never knew you to be so modest.'

I felt sick to my stomach. Rufus was watching *me* all the time? Was he fulfilling some duty to Otho's new 'procedures' where *agentes* watched each other as hard as they spied on everyone else?

'Did Rufus report on my trip to Mediolanum?'

'Sure.'

'My meeting with the Marble Vestal, Flavia?'

'He tried grilling me, but what did I know?'

'Did he question Benedictus, too?'

'Probably.'

'Then it's settled. He conducts Eusebius on the road.'

Gaudentius gathered up his shabby *paenula* and a money purse that would return after dawn either empty or doubled. A junior *eques* arrived from the Eastern route via Singidunum and dumped the last mailbag of the day in the doorway. I entered it in the registry, he co-signed, and then went off for a much-needed bath and shave.

There wasn't much mail. I shook out the contents and was just about to call another staffer to sort it, when a folded papyrus with the telltale purple and gold ribbon fixed by Julian's imperial seal slipped to the floor under my table.

I said nothing to Gaudentius. I picked it up only once the *notarius* was safely gone.

It was from the *scrinia* in Constantinopolis. 'Sirmium,' had been added in a second hand, as no doubt were the names of other cities on identical packets moving all over the Empire. It looked like yet another general announcement for the officer in charge of each station.

I cracked a bright green imperial seal and unfolded the single page. My stomach dropped to my knees. I swayed. I steadied myself with one palm on the tumbling mess of mail.

It was from Chalcedon, not Constantinopolis. It was a warrant for yet another arrest.

It was a warrant for *Centenarius* Marcus Gregorianus Numidianus—for 'questioning.'

Gaudentius burst back into my office. 'I forgot to ask you for the name of a good whore who likes to—'

He saw the lettering, the broken seal, and the dangling ribbon. He wrenched the warrant from my hand. I closed my eyes and waited as his crude mind deciphered the formal palace wording.

—THE BURNING STAKES—

Now Gaudentius had no choice but to arrest me. This shaven-headed brute would have to pack me off in that same Chalcedon-bound carriage, gagging on the sickly stench of my fellow prisoner.

He folded the warrant back into three. He wrapped the pristine ribbon back around its center. A crumb of hard sealing wax fell on his boots.

'It's started snowing, Numidianus. That's why your office is so cold. Your brazier needs topping up.'

He thrust the warrant into the red ashes of my heater and stoked them in silence for an endless minute until the ribbon caught flame.

'I can't burn every copy between Roma and Antiochia, but at least that buys you a day.'

I stared into his humorless, weathered eyes.

He hissed, 'Run for it, you bastard, run.'

Chapter 16, A Family Brothel

—OPTATA'S, SIRMIUM—

Which nearby cities had received warrants bearing my name by now? Which roads were blocked already? Which gates manned on alert?

I don't recall much of that race for the docks. Where else could I go? I trotted through the falling snow, hardly knowing where I was, until I leaned against the wall of a familiar street corner. When I reached the depths of Optata's stinking back corridors lined with busy, open alcoves, I fell panting and panicked on the hard cement of an absent whore's spare platform 'bed.'

Every week Sirmium's city collectors dropped in to tax at the rate equal to one trick per prostitute. The *aediles* would appear at the first sign of disruptions. Any of these fellow officials might recognize my familiar face, whatever their 'business' here. I paid Optata well to keep her mouth shut and warn me of any strange visitors. I needed the proprietress to stay on my side. I needed every one of her employees—from her youngest child whore to the crippled and ancient scouring hag—to look right through me. I would have paid off every last 'Thais' and 'Lais' in person, only Optata warned me off.

'Leave the staff to me. You don't want to raise suspicion and invite blackmail.'

'You trust every one of them?'

'Most of them. You staying for weeks on end, like last time?'

'I doubt I'll have that pleasure. You'll be paid, sooner or later—provided I survive.'

'I could get used to this,' Optata said, jingling my heavy coins in her palm. 'Maybe I should upgrade my business—retire the sluts and hide political stowaways instead.'

Once she'd cleared away a pile of dirtied blankets and a box of contraceptive sponges and vials of vinegar, she brought me a pitcher of warm *conditum* to quench my thirst. The spice burnt the back of my throat. I drank it down, turning my back on the parade of shivering half-naked boys and girls in little more than breast bands and loincloths plying their trade up and down the open corridor just outside.

Huddled against a flaking plaster wall covered with crude erotic paintings, I collected my racing thoughts. I'd hurtled through the shivering crowds thronging Sirmium's evening market without a moment to consider my next move. Escaping with nothing more than what I could carry on me, I realized what must have happened in the East.

The warrant came days too soon to be the result of Catena's threatened revenge. I said nothing about my stabbing Emperor Constans outside the temple in Vicus Helena in 350—the accusation Catena dangled over my head.

No, the Chalcedon tribunal's interest in me must be tied to something or someone else. The testimony of Notary Pentadius? It must be Pentadius. I'd felt there was something askew with the Chalcedon convictions that arrived earlier in the day. There were two men on that list associated with Caesar Gallus' execution: Pentadius and Palladius.

The tribunal had ruled that Palladius had poisoned Constantius' mind against the sick caesar's reign. Palladius was convicted.

But what was mere gossiping as a crime compared to actually *participating* in Gallus' death? Pentadius had been *there* as a witness in Gallus' dungeon cell in Pula that terrible night. He'd sat next to the eunuch Eusebius during Gallus' secret 'hearing.' He'd even served as the required court scribe sent from Mediolanum to take official notes for Constantius back at court.

Pentadius had watched and listened while Apodemius interrogated Gallus on charges of misadministration and the unlawful murder of Roman citizens and statesmen. Pentadius had witnessed Master of the Guards Barbatio lift his *spatha* and sever the Constantine's head from his quaking body on his imperial cousin's order.

—THE BURNING STAKES—

And yet? Pentadius, not Palladius, got off. Was it not suspicious that so far *Notarius* Pentadius was the only man to testify before Chalcedon's military jurists and walk out of their chamber *a free man*?

What phantasms of accusations against Apodemius and myself had Pentadius concocted to satisfy Julian, sitting across the watery strait from Chalcedon, secluded and aloof in his vast new palace?

I started shaking, despite myself. I put my head between my knees and pulled my cloak tighter around my shoulders. How much had Pentadius' acquittal cost the rest of us in betrayals and outright lies? How far had his falsehoods gone? Barbatio was dead—there was no satisfaction to be gained for the army in blaming a man already buried as a convicted traitor. Fresh names and reputations must be sacrificed in Chalcedon if Nemesis was to be appeased.

Cleaning slaves and snack vendors shuffled up and down Optata's corridors behind me. Her establishment was about as private as the Sirmium Forum, but all the more determinedly anonymous. I pressed my fingers into my ears to block out the grunting of a customer next door and watched as a crooked-backed old woman dragged her pail of dirty water along the broken flagstones fronting the alcove arches.

After a long time getting my bearings, I took stock of my surroundings. Apollonia was not in the room I'd arranged. I found it being used for the kind of activities Roman wives were not supposed to know about—even though such entertainments were advertised and illustrated, position by position, fee by fee, above the street entrance outside the reception room.

'Where's the veiled woman I brought here?' I asked Optata when she brought me a brazier against the freezing evening. I shoved it underneath my brick bed and waited for the room to thaw out.

'I had to take her into my quarters,' she muttered. 'A stupid rumor went around my girls that one of our customers cut off her nose for insulting his dick. They wouldn't go back to work until I got her out of the way.'

'Is she comfortable?'

'More comfortable than me. She's napping on my bed right now. When's she leaving?'

'Be patient. I'll make it worth your while.'

She patted her towering coiffure and waved it off.

'Triple your rate and I'll shut up. No, that's all right—pay me later. I trust you. Now drink this and sleep. No, don't argue with me. Nobody disturbs my customers unless I say so. You're turning blue and shaking. Get under this blanket and rest. I'll wait you in an hour. I know every face, and a lot more besides, about pretty much every man and woman in this town. So you're safe here for now.'

Her wine was heavy and rough. The room warmed up.

※※※

'... so I just ran here. I'm sorry, Apollonia. I can't protect you any longer. I can't even protect myself. The best thing is for you to return to Gratian's estate.'

I hunched over Optata's small inlaid table and stirred a bowl of curds and lentils around and around without appetite.

From behind her veil, Apollonia listened. Her perfect, graceful hands lay folded in her lap, but I could read nothing in them. I wished she trusted me more.

Optata had tried to wake me, she said, twice, and failed.

It'd stopped snowing before dawn. I rose, stiff from the bare brick bed, hours before the tired whores and their snoring customers woke up.

By the fading red ashes of cooling braziers flanking the walls, I'd found Apollonia's sanctuary at the better end of the building without difficulty. The proprietress' two-room retreat was separated from the brothel by a stout door with a bolt. Admitted inside by a limping old woman, I'd found Apollonia on a stool, giving a black kitten a saucer of milk laced with *garum*.

'She likes the fishy taste,' Apollonia said in an amused tone.

We faced a glass window sealed against the weather with lengths of thick robe stuck with wax around the frame. The wintry morning light was like gray flannel and the noise of the

—THE BURNING STAKES—

brothel muffled by a thick door that made sleep possible for Optata through the busy, profitable nights.

'Justina can make sure you're safe.'

Apollonia shook her head. 'I can't go back to Severa's, though I trust those two ladies with my life. I can never be sure who may talk or gossip and who might be listening for a clue to my trail.'

She glanced behind to make sure that Optata's slaves weren't listening, even here.

'Why? Apollonia? There are kind people in this world. Loving people.'

'This life of hiding has taught me many things. Never retrace your steps. Never seek the past.'

'Tell me what happened, please. You told Justina. And Justina entrusted you to me.'

I waited, imaging her hesitation under that linen covering.

'I can tell you some of it. I was born into a powerful Republican family, one of the oldest in Roma's long history. I know you were raised in the Manlius *domus*, but your venerable senator's line was plebian by our standards. The bickering of mere senators was nothing to us when we boasted so many consuls, provincial governors, and generals.'

Who told her that I was raised by Commander Gregorianus and his father Senator Manlius? From Justina?

She chuckled, 'They say that there were so many marble busts and wax *imagines* of ancestors in our house that my parents knew only a tenth of their names or histories. The walls of our atrium were lined with dozens upon dozens of plaques and dedications to our *Romanitas* and *meritum*.'

'But your family made enemies?'

She nodded. 'Jealous and dangerous enemies. It's not a very complicated story. It started when my mother, a great beauty at thirteen, received an offer to marry the scion of another powerful clan. He was sixteen, good-looking, and rich. His family took my mother's acceptance for granted.'

'Something went wrong?'

'Yes. Although it was an attractive opportunity with many advantages, they were 'new' Romans, flush with vulgar loot from eastern conquests. But don't misunderstand me. It wasn't snobbery on our part but self-protection. Their *pater familias* was a powerful politician whom we knew to be guilty of financial corruption and bribery in high office.'

'So your family declined?'

'My mother's refusal was awkward and very public. Finally, my grandfather put a definitive end to this family's angry threats by marrying my mother off to someone else. This man, my father, was a courageous tribune serving under Constantius, but hardly an aristocrat, not even born to Roman *honestiores*. He was a man of noble spirit and great physical courage. It was a loving marriage by all accounts . . .'

Her voice trailed off. She gazed through Optata's curtains into the hazy daylight of the window at our shoulders.

'Such things happen among highborn families,' I said.

'But the failed bidders for my mother's hand weren't highborn enough to swallow our rebuff with good grace. They couldn't afford it. They had counted on it and took this public setback very hard. They spread rumors about us—false libels and slanders—to show we weren't worthy of *them*. Something had to be done.'

She halted again and secured her veil a little tighter. Her hand shook.

'What did your family do?'

She gave a wry chuckle. 'Nothing, at first. Every offense they accused us of was a public hint of their own crimes. If they murmured around the Forum that my uncle was guilty of tax evasion, we soon heard they cheated every year on their own assessments. When they suggested at the Baths that we were party to a conspiracy to seize the throne, there was soon a clue that there *was* such a failed plot—which they'd been tempted to join.'

'They didn't have any imagination.'

'Not much. Defending our reputation, we took the family to court, armed with irrefutable evidence—written documents, and unassailable witnesses. The court found against them. We'd "won." Our reputation was restored. Theirs was ruined forever. Their great house on the Caelian Hill was emptied of booty. Their warehouses, workshops, country estates, and savings became state property.'

—THE BURNING STAKES—

She fell silent, distracted by the slave with the rattling pail mopping in Optata's second room. But this was a rare chance to understand Apollonia's sad history, so I pressed on.

'I understand as much as you've told me but—was this their revenge?' I touched the hem of her veil.

She nodded. 'Nearly everyone in our great house was burnt alive. Roman *vigiles* are used to putting out conflagrations in the Subura. Flimsy apartment blocks catch fire all the time in the slums. Wagons stand ready for the alarm with tanks full of water and hooks for pulling down neighboring buildings nearby to control the blaze—'

I nodded. I'd seen the *vigiles* teams risking their lives to save whole entire neighborhoods.

'—but we didn't live in the Subura. The wagons couldn't get up to us fast enough, a sturdy townhouse of solid granite and marble surrounded by gardens behind thick walls that had stood for two hundred years. Why should such a house catch fire?'

'Why indeed?'

'When I woke up in a strange wet nurse's crib, my parents were probably already dead. Dozens of our slaves and freedmen burned alive, trapped inside our walls. You see, no one could escape. In the middle of the night, after the curfew on heavy cargo was lifted, the arsonists had blockaded all our exits with cheap carts and old carriages.'

She paused, as if choosing each word carefully. 'From then on, I had to hide.'

'And *Magister* Apodemius took responsibility for your loss?'

She shook her head, yes.

'Please explain to me. Why?'

'Because Apodemius shared his dossiers from the Castra with my father.'

'He provided the crucial evidence against your enemies in court?'

She nodded.

'But he was trying to help.'

'With terrible consequences.'

I seized both her hands in mine.

'Could I at least see your eyes, Apollonia? I'm not afraid.'

'No, you may not.'

I'd seen hundreds of atrocities on the battlefields of Mursa and Argentoratum. I'd seen the 'lucky' wounded groaning in medics' tents across the Empire—not to mention the everyday horrors that lined the Roman streets where beggars clustered. Was there any misfortune in our cosmopolitan world that a Roman my age hadn't seen firsthand? Could Apollonia's mutilation be so shocking between two people who needed each other now?

Despite the racket of the brothel's business picking up outside, it was hard to deny the spell of intimacy growing with each passing minute between Apollonia and myself.

For a few minutes, we didn't speak. The bolted door could not completely muffle the unremarkable noises of human coupling seeping through. Optata reprimanded a customer for some misdemeanor. Some panting, a slap, a laugh, or a grunt reminded us of where we sat but such noises seemed removed in spirit from our quiet confidences.

A veteran soldier with a thick Dacian accent broke out in sobs in his whore's embrace not far away. A second whore came to her friend's rescue and helped soothe the weeping man a little. Closer by, one of Optata's youngest 'employees' could be heard whining he had earned himself a sweet pastry. Everywhere there were sluts and slaves, miserable souls, but here I sat next to this graceful mystery.

I remembered Justina's warning.

The old cleaning lady was scrubbing hard on her knees in the room behind us. She was a distraction, but I determined she would not slow my progress with gentle Apollonia. For I knew now I was making progress. Apollonia leaned a little closer to me now. I smelled sweet almonds through her veil and a whiff of something else . . .

'Apollonia, you're not really a Vestal, are you? I mean, you might be a virgin, but you're not a proper, initiated priestess, right?'

She broke out in a rueful laugh. 'Why do you doubt it, Numidianus?'

'Because, with all respect, Roma's handful of Vestals is selected for their unparalleled beauty as well as their virtue.'

Apollonia threw up her hands in mock helplessness.

—THE BURNING STAKES—

'Oh, well, I'm welcomed by those ladies—though no one can ever compare me to Aphrodite, I assure you. Apodemius arranged my education and shelter among their sisterhood because . . . I suppose . . . because the *magister agentium in rebus* felt sorry for me. After all, you *agentes* gather information to serve the Empire, not to ruin the faces and future of innocent girls. But yes, you're right, Apodemius couldn't turn me from this into a beauty.'

'If Justina trusts me, why can't you?'

'I've sworn not to reveal my face out of consideration for both strangers and friends alike. Respect my privacy, please. Leave me my dignity. It's a kind of duty you cannot understand, Numidianus. You cannot imagine the consequences.'

'You aren't helping me.'

'How I wish things were otherwise.'

My hand crept toward the protective brown linen.

I lowered my voice. I spoke words for her ears only: 'You say it's a duty? Did Dido not put aside her duty to her people in revealing her heart to Aeneas?'

'Dido was a queen,' Apollonia whispered back. 'And Dido was a beauty. I am neither.'

My fingers had got hold of the hem of her veil. I was within seconds of yanking it away.

'Your voice is incomparably beautiful, Apollonia. Your hands are exquisite. Your mind is educated. Your soul is noble. Your gait is graceful and your posture is like a queen's. That is a great deal. After all, what woman is perfect?'

I braced myself to see the worst—the melted nose, missing lips, scarred eyelids, melted ears or missing hair—whatever the fire had claimed from the infant Apollonia.

'Stop!'

An arthritic hand wrenched away my arm. I looked up at the old cleaning hag glaring down at me.

'Then take off your own disguise, *Magister*,' I said, lifting his tunic skirts to expose his knobby ankles above the familiar goatskin travel boots.

Speechless, Apodemius glared at me, his rheumy eyes lined with red.

I gave him an innocent shrug. 'You trained me,' I said.

I lifted off his crone's greasy *palla* and a particularly nasty wig the texture of a dead rat.

'No one else in the entire empire uses such foul-smelling liniment. It's rubbed off on Apollonia's *palla*. And you really must do something about that ugly new growth on your chin.'

Apodemius slumped his crooked self down on Optata's neat bed. He stared for a moment at the broken *tesserae* underfoot.

I was as shocked as he, but it would have been cruel to tell him why.

I had suspected 'she' was Apodemius as soon as I recognized the trace of his liniment on Apollonia's sleeve. But I hadn't perceived what I detected on his face now. It was obvious from his gray complexion, the yellow and red streaks discoloring his eyes, and the horrible cough that seized him, that Apodemius was fighting like a gladiator in his old man's private arena—with Death.

⚜⚜⚜

He took a few drops of that same tonic that had relieved his pain back in Roma. We helped him stretch out his bent limbs on Optata's cushioned bed. The long minutes of scrubbing mosaics nearby had left his joints red and swollen.

'. . . At first I only sensed danger was coming, Numidianus, but I didn't know when it would strike or from whom. Of course, there was always Eusebius' treachery to worry about. But there were so many others, too. We've thwarted many careers. The ambitious and avaricious stand ready to pounce on our *schola* during uncertain times.'

'You always measured its success by the frustration of its enemies.'

He coughed heavily. Finally, he asked, 'How did you know it was me, Numidianus?'

'First, a simple piece of logic. If Apollonia's whereabouts were so rigorously protected, would I be left alone for long to guard her? Not likely. Someone would join her. Was she in a position to send word to Cibalae from here after she arrived? She wouldn't risk it. Therefore, the people in Cibalae entrusting her to my care were already confident they could guess where I was taking her. How could Justina, Gratian, or Marina Severa be sure of that?'

He smiled.

'Second, in Cibalae, I noticed Gratian's slaves. They wore cruel collars of soldered lead reading, *Return this ungrateful wretch to Gratian. He's a runaway.* And *This Heredis is stolen property. Return to Severa Gratianus.* But as Justina and I talked, I noticed an eavesdropper, a doddering old biddy with a broom. She wore no collar.'

He laid his head back on a pillow. 'Slaves are like furniture and cattle. Nobody notices slaves.'

'Trust an ex-slave to spot an impostor.'

'I've lost my touch.'

'I recalled the cleaning woman who brushed past Cassius and me when we were racing up to your offices at the Castra. Her buckets were full, weren't they—of secret files?'

He nodded.

'But a cleaning lady can't march into the *sacred scrinia* or the *a secretis* in Mediolanum with a fat coin purse to pay off a greedy scribe, can she? So you covered your telltale liniment stink with heavy Eastern perfumes and disguised your crippled hands with expensive travel gloves. You were the Greek with a forged warrant from Salutius, weren't you?'

'And I wasn't happy with what I found. Constantius was telling you the truth before he died. He did give a rescindment order, Numidianus. The Emperor signed two actual documents— one to be sent to us in Pula and a copy archived and indexed in the imperial files. I found such a decision was recorded in the *cottidiana* index ten days before we executed Gallus in Pula—just as Benedictus had discovered on my instructions months before.'

'Ten days? Then we should have received it.'

'But when I returned and searched the archives for the original document in purple ink from which the boy had made the copy I showed you in my office, it was gone.'

'So you were left with only the index page? You destroyed it?'

'For self-protection, I had no choice! Someone was building a case against me—collecting proof of Constantius' change of heart that I'd—'

'We'd—'

'*Allegedly* ignored. And this person or persons had left nothing else I could tamper with, nothing I could reword or rewrite, even had I wished. Someone now had the *scrinia*'s official copy and, for all I knew, the original dispatched by Constantius to Pula. The question remains, what next?'

I paced at the end of the bed and thought out loud:

'If the rescindment turns up in Chalcedon, you and I must find some way to tell the truth about Pula. We must argue with as much confidence as Notary Pentadius who is acquitted.'

'Acquitted?'

'Yes, take heart, *Magister*. Pentadius has walked free. And after all, why would anyone still have this document seven years after the event? Wouldn't such an elaborate conspiracy speak against itself?'

Apodemius shook his head, discouraged. Pentadius' acquittal didn't impress him as much as I hoped.

'We did *not* receive Constantius' rescindment in time. That is the truth—whatever Pentadius has claimed to buy himself freedom.'

'This Numidian would charge the Minotaur in his Maze,' Apodemius commented to Apollonia.

'But did you train him to ignore sense, *Magister*?' she asked with a note of mischief.

'He was never my brightest,' Apodemius said, 'but he was the most stubborn, persistent, mule-like *agens* in the entire Castra. I should have known it would be you, Numidianus, who would doggedly track me.'

'You trust the Vestals more than your own service?'

Apodemius ran gnarled fingers through his wig-flattened white hair.

'Oh, ho! Should I trust Gaudentius yet again? Already he once vaulted over my authority straight to the Emperor to condemn foolish drunken revelers for "treason". Or should I trust little Rufus, so impressed with Otho's newfangled reporting procedures? I saw enough of that before I fled the Castra! Oh, the gods, how the younger *agentes* welcomed all his so-called modern systems. You'd have thought Otho was as scientific as Aristotle! Or Galen!'

'And Ahenobarbus, so faithful and honest?'

'Half-retired, half-exhausted by decades of service?'

'Even me? You couldn't trust me?'

'I could trust you to be observant and consistent, certainly. I needed less than a day in Cibalae to figure out where you'd hidden away Apollonia. You hadn't told anyone, even Severa's driver. But I recalled our debriefing in 351. You'd gone missing. I got no coded explanations sent back to the Castra and no apologies between the lines. Then you turned up in one piece! You'd hidden away for weeks on end from Barbatio's attack dogs and Eusebius' intrigues—in a Sirmium brothel. How could I forget the detail that even Catena himself had come here as a regular customer—and never noticed you working around him as a slave?'

He smiled at the veiled girl next to us. 'And here she was.'

Apollonia squeezed the old man's trembling fingers.

'But now, *Magister*, no one is safe,' I said. 'Not even Eusebius. We arrested him just before the warrant with my name arrived.'

'Ah!' He slapped his shaking hands together as if in prayer. 'Then we still have hope, Numidianus! Perhaps Eusebius is our man and perhaps Eusebius has made a mistake. Perhaps he has left us a clue. He's not infallible.'

'Can we trust that innocent scribe Benedictus?'

He closed his eyes and murmured, 'We must trust someone. Even though he seems guileless, he shows promise.'

'Call an innocent scribe to this place?' Apollonia disagreed. 'No. With those obscene murals in the front room?'

Apodemius caught her graceful hand mid-protest. 'It's all right, dear. You've recovered quickly enough. So can Benedictus. We're well fed here and, thanks to Numidianus, well hidden for the moment. Try to think of this place as . . . our friendly, family brothel.'

He laid his skeletal head down on Optata's thick pillow cushions. 'Summon Benedictus, Numidianus, somehow. Quickly.'

Chapter 17, A New Management Plan

— Optata's Private Rooms, Sirmium —

Apodemius insisted on seeing Benedictus alone. I caught a glimpse of the boy as he hurried down the corridor and passed my room where Apollonia and I waited, huddling for warmth over a large pottery brazier standing between us.

I had hardly recognized the scribe when he arrived from his slog through the driving blizzard filling Sirmium's alleys with snow. He was covered from pale face to borrowed boots in a crude Britannian garment of beaver pelts stitched together, complete with original heads and tails. I'd noticed a pile of animal fur among his things in my office, but assumed it a bedcover of some sort. It was hardly something an *agens* avoiding attention in Pannonia might wear.

The Vestal and I waited for a signal from the *magister* to join them. She was quiet, thoughtful, and disinclined to more conversation. A whore next door to us broke into raucous laughter and a baritone growled back in bearish play.

'Someone sounds happy in her work,' Apollonia commented.

'Or happy in her pay. Optata treats her merchandise better than many businesswomen do.'

'You know this place well, *Agens*?'

'I'm no prude, *Dominula*.'

'*Domina*, please—for contrary to what you might think, I'm a grown woman. I'm not such an innocent to the ways of the world.'

'Well, after another week here, I won't doubt it.'

Half an hour later, a slave said we should return to Optata's rooms. Benedictus had already gone.

'It was safer the boy knew nothing about you two,' Apodemius explained, still lying on Optata's bed. 'I avoided his eye when he told me you'd disappeared without explanation, Numidianus. Apparently Gaudentius announced he would hunt for you at another whorehouse you recommended—'

'—on the far side of Sirmium. The ladies there are talented and Gaudentius wants to give me time to escape. His "search" for me is bound to take a good while.'

'Excellent. Benedictus asked not one impertinent question,' the old man continued with a satisfied wheeze, 'but took good note of my instructions. I expect him to return to us in an hour or two.'

'With what?'

'Well, the rescindment, I hope.'

He ignored my dumbfounded expression. A series of gleeful slaps on naked buttocks somewhere nearby gave the old man shivers.

'Apollo's Chariot, how could anyone willingly disrobe in such cold! Apollonia, please get us a pitcher of hot *conditum* and some sustenance. Even a bird needs seed.'

Lying there, Apodemius did resemble a scrawny fowl, his areole of white wisps on Optata's pillow like a wreath of chicken down. Was all this—the running, hiding, fighting, and spying—worth it to a man who looked like he had so little time left?

In the other room, I'd had time to reflect. Anyone could see that Emperor Julian was in a mood for vengeance, but certainly he was not an unfeeling monster. If I had to submit to questioning anyway, should I offer to go first to Chalcedon? If told Apodemius was going to cross the Styx soon enough, could Julian not display timely compassion or at least a modicum of respect for old age? After all, Apodemius' service to the Empire stretched back more decades and generations than any other *agentes* could measure.

I could plead with Julian that the *Magister*'s seniority had earned him the right to retirement in some quiet corner of—I paused. What and where did Apodemius call home?

But was I brave enough, even capable, to carry Apodemius' defense alone into Arbitio's arena?

—THE BURNING STAKES—

Bronze bowls of hot spelt grits covered in honey and curd cheese arrived, along with a platter of warm greens pureed with dried mint, oregano, peppercorns, and white wine. Optata had not forgotten generous amounts of *garum* sauce. A slave diluted a pitcher of hot wine with water and poured it into sturdy gold-lipped glasses. Mythical couples painted in eyesore-bright colors gamboled *in flagrante delicto* around the side of each glass.

'Optata has favored us with her best dinnerware,' Apodemius warned Apollonia with an amused sniff.

I swapped my glass with Apollonia, so that she sipped from the naked Pyramis and Thisbe united at last in face-to-face ecstasy.

Meanwhile, I used her glass, adorned with Zeus as the white bull stuffing a comically outsized erection into a capacious Europa who looked downright thrilled with the encounter.

The drink shot some needed color into Apodemius' cheeks. He seemed grateful to quit shuffling in that ridiculous wig carrying a bucket and mop up and down the freezing brothel corridor.

After gulping down his grits, he pulled himself more upright.

'Let's review from the beginning, Numidianus, from the time you completed your Gallic mission and took up residence here in Sirmium four years ago. Julian never liked our *schola*. He trusted your pagan leanings, but not your mission, not until you provided key information that saved him from disaster on the battlefield of Argentoratum. Thanks to you, perhaps he appreciated having the *agentes* on his side—well, at least for a week or two.'

'Then you assigned Gaudentius north to succeed me.'

'Not I. Emperor Constantius insisted on him. It was a huge mistake. Gaudentius became too haughty once he made *notarius*. He was too ham-fisted and shortsighted. He flouted orders from me to please one man only—Constantius. Meanwhile, he gave Julian nothing, *nothing* in the way of useful information! Worse—knowing that Constantius kept Julian short of money to pay his troops, Gaudentius insulted and slandered Julian in public for giving a few coins to a soldier who wanted to buy himself a shave. Idiotic!'

We three ate and sipped for a minute, listening to the rising tempest rattle the window covers. Apodemius needed to collect his breath or he'd start coughing again. He dribbled his wine. Apollonia gently wiped his chin with Optata's embroidered napkin without comment. She herself ate with delicacy underneath her veil.

Apodemius continued:

'By the time Julian expelled Gaudentius from his new court in Lutetia up on the Sequana, I had to resign myself to the damage done. Our pagan caesar was as hostile to the Castra as he was to everybody else—the *consistorani*, the generals he'd antagonized and shamed, the eunuch fraternity, the Church—Zeus! Did Julian hate everyone—apart from his precious Petulantes auxiliaries?'

Snowfall muffled the usual noise coming off the street at the front of the building. Behind Apollonia's silhouette, a faint gray horizontal line rose as the snow collected up the outside of Optata's windowsill and dimmed the already faint winter light.

Apollonia lit two oil lamps and placed them on a table next to Apodemius' bedside. He started coughing harder than ever. I fetched another blanket and wrapped him tighter. He felt like a bundle of brittle sticks.

'When Julian declared himself emperor last year, Constantius kept his calm. And why not? Over ten years, he'd seen off all his other rivals for the diadem—Magnentius, Nepotianus, Vetranio, Gallus, Silvanus—even Ursicinus. And poor Barbatio's fantasy of the *cathedra* was nothing more than a feeble after-dinner joke around Roma.'

Stupid Barbatio, felled by a love letter from his own wife, but not so stupid that his last bitter curse hadn't fallen on my unhappy head. Did Apodemius read my fears?

He continued:

' . . . the Persian army on our doorstep. He couldn't let Shapur carve up the East while he squabbled with his young cousin. Constantius had to take things in turn.'

I stoked the brazier's coals to keep us warm.

'And then came the exciting news that Empress Faustia was pregnant!' Apodemius gave a sour chuckle. 'Oh, the gods!'

'Julian saw his chances grow slimmer as Faustia's belly grew larger,' I said.

He wagged a finger under my nose. 'Yes, after three marriages, Constantius would have his heir at last. But sitting alone in Roma, Numidianus, I could not feel so sanguine. I stepped up my defensive moves. What I needed most was *time*. I needed a placeholder to free my hand to protect our department against a future under Julian. So I asked for sick leave.'

'You summoned Otho to take over?'

'No, not I. He was a hardworking, neutral choice from the East. I tried to unearth anything in his disfavor, but personnel files had little to say. The *schola*'s record of his work inspecting eastern tax hubs was sound. Most important, his nomination did not come from Julian's *magister officiorum*. I felt secure in stepping aside to "write my memoirs".'

'—assuming Constantius would hold on for years with a prince in the cradle. Instead, the diadem fell into Julian's lap without warning.'

'Gods! It was a blow!' Apodemius laid his head back on the pillow and closed his eyes.

Apollonia wiped feverish beads of sweat off his brow.

'I tried not to panic, Numidianus. The important thing was to guess how Julian would discredit our *schola* so completely that an entire imperial network could be closed down.'

'Corruption?'

'Corruption was diminishing. I'd been working hard for years to scrape out the dead wood and the rotten figs. I cut back on bureaucracy, meetings, and excess reporting. I dismissed or retired the stool-warmers. I limited the *agentes* holding a double post to only men who delivered useful information. I set a ceiling on bribes and fees. I listened harder to the complaints of prefects sharing an office with any of our *princeps officii*. I whittled down any bad practices during account inspections. I upgraded our animals and services on the *Cursus*, faster routes for the mail—'

He broke off into painful hacking and spat up a glob of blood-streaked green phlegm.

'Nothing changes that fast, *Magister*—'

'Nevertheless, a newly minted emperor could not close down the Castra without substantial grounds. Dereliction of duty? We worked around the sundial. Corruption? Abuses were under control. Road conditions? Why Julian had just sped his Western Army with their wives, children, slaves, and baggage like a bolt down *our* Cursus—he could hardly say we didn't keep the network in good repair!'

His voice rose with indignation. Apollonia checked no one was listening at our door. Her graceful discretion hardly interrupted the *magister*, but the lascivious panting and orgasmic cries we suffered when she briefly opened the door must have made her blush under her veil.

Apodemius grabbed my wrist as if he was afraid I'd lose the thread of his explanation:

'No, Numidianus, I came to the conclusion that Julian had no choice. He could discredit the *schola*—discredit *me*—only in one swift, fatal blow. He had to move quickly, before we made fresh allies in his new pagan court. I was not surprised his first move was to placate Constantius' generals with this Chalcedon farce.'

'*Magister*, Constantius' army knows to its cost that you're a dogged civil servant. They'd have to find you guilty of a heinous crime—nothing less than treason. What was left?'

'More than mere murder, certainly.' Apodemius nodded. 'One, killing a caesar. Two, killing a Constantine, Julian's own half-brother. And three, the essential key to any successful conviction against an *agens*—*not* doing it in the course of duty, but doing it *against* the express orders of the Emperor. If one were a Christian, one might call those charges the Fatal Trinity of Sins.'

The snow was falling harder than ever. Optata's braziers must be drawing fresh customers off the street into her main reception room in hope of warmth of any kind.

We rested for a while, waiting for Benedictus. Apollonia cleaned up our platters and handed them to a slave outside. Then she laid her heavy head with its thick coils, braids, and veil between arms crossed on the table. Apodemius began to snore. White stubble caught the old man's saliva dribbling down his open jaw.

Benedictus returned, cheeks bright and shoulders covered with snow. I roused the other two.

'Did anyone follow you?' Apodemius whispered.

'I saw no one. I went in circles, as you ordered, recognized no man behind me, doubled back on a diagonal, and cut through alleys. Only a bird overhead could have followed me.'

'Good. Did you find it?'

The scribe shook his head, no. Apodemius fell back on his pillow and closed his eyes.

'Did you look hard?' I pressed the boy against the wall.

'*Centenarie*, the Lord Chamberlain's office was in perfect order. It was easy to check every single document, every piece of writing, in the entire room. I did the same in his private bedchamber. I turned over his entire suite. There was nothing.'

Apodemius patted the boy's hand, blue with cold.

'Eusebius has done well,' he said with a wry chuckle. 'Differently, but well enough.'

'How do you mean?' Apollonia asked. 'He's on his way to trial.'

'I too knew my enemies could search my office right under Otho's nose. They could empty my safe box of every last secret and use something against me. The only way I could ensure nothing incriminating was planted on me was to make sure my premises were discovered empty. Every secret gone. My safe box cleaned out.'

'Which is how we found it,' I said. 'Yet, warrants have been issued for you and for me.'

'Exactly! *You*, Numidianus. The only *agens* who escorted Gallus from the safety of Antiochia Palace into my personal custody. What better proof that the case Julian prepares against me rests on events in Pula, Istria that fateful night? Clearly Pentadius has named you as a witness—'

'Or worse—'

'Otherwise why haul a *centenarius* all that way?'

'There was one other witness that night in Pula, *Magister*— the Frankish tribune, Mallobaudes.'

'Mallobaudes only accompanied Eusebius and Pentadius for bodyguard purposes. And now he's up in the boreal wilds of Gallia on the Rhenus, ruling over the Franks. For all intents and purposes he's a king among them. He won't interfere with

Chalcedon under any circumstances and even Julian can't make him.'

'Surely Eusebius would have destroyed the rescindment to avoid problems for himself as a witness,' Apollonia suggested.

'No, dear child, you have lived too long among good women. You underestimate the eunuch's venom. Eusebius is, first and last, a blackmailer. No blackmailer destroys something with such potential, though Eusebius wanted Gallus dead more than any of us.'

'But you said that Eusebius' blackmail operations in Antiochia depended on the stream of dirty gossip flowing through the imperial family's suite.' Apollonia's hands twisted in her lap.

'True, the eunuch encouraged Caesar Gallus to gather dirt on Antiochene elites for the purpose of "righting wrongs." The imperial duo were his pawns. But Eusebius saw it couldn't last. Don't forget, Gallus was a Constantine. He was starting to distrust Eusebius, even to believe he didn't need the eunuch. Any member of the imperial family, no matter how unstable or useful for a time, threatened Eusebius' grubby gasp on illegitimate power.'

Optata threw open the door without tapping. I hoped she didn't do this to her more 'active' clients. She trembled with cold—or fear—under her expensive *palla*.

'There's an official in the front room,' she said. 'Wearing your *schola*'s insignia.'

I wanted to run, but hid my panic and asked her, 'Bald, with a Neapolitan street accent?'

'I couldn't say in that crowd. He's wearing a *pileus* low over his eyes. He says he's here to take the old man back to Roma.'

'I'll deal with this,' I told Optata. 'Go offer our visitor a drink on my tab.' She nodded and left us.

I glanced at Apodemius. 'Somebody's been talking.'

'Not I!' Benedictus shot to his feet.

'It doesn't matter who. You must hide yourselves somewhere else, immediately.' I told them.

'But you'll be arrested, Numidianus!' I was moved by the clutch of tears in Apollonia's throat.

—THE BURNING STAKES—

'Maybe not, if it is Gaudentius. He let me escape once. He might turn his back on Apodemius—if I promise him a fat bribe. I'll stall him. Benedictus, scout out an exit through the kitchen door or a slave's window. Give me a signal somehow when you're sure they're safe.'

Benedictus stared at me. Apollonia was quicker, already lifting up Apodemius, blankets and all.

I shoved the scribe into action. 'Now—*move!*'

I waited a full five minutes, while they scurried out of Optata's rooms, long enough to gain time, but not so long our *agens* waiting out front would start searching the whores' chambers. I tightened my *cingulum* for courage and strode down the chilly corridor.

Optata's warm braziers and stained cushions had attracted many 'customers' now eating snacks at tables near a smoking grill. I scanned the jumble of wet hoods and heavy cloaks. A dark figure waited in the shadows of the curtained arch that gave onto the street. By the flickering light of bad-weather torches stuck into wall sconces above our heads, his riding helmet glistened with melting sleet. Clumps of fresh snow stuck to the toes of his polished black shoes. He wore a comfortable *paenula* fastened with thick leather toggles and decorated with embroidered *orbiculi,* rondels marking his station as a fresh member of the *clarissimi.*

I adjusted my belt and tunic, as if interrupted while sporting in bed. He spotted me. He elbowed his way through the huddling, chattering crowd. No one noticed the strength with which he seized my upper arm. I shook him off.

'Numidianus, please! I've come to help you.'

'How did you find me, *Magister*? You couldn't have tailed our little Britannian. The boy would have spotted you—such a handsome sight. In a neighborhood like this, you stick out like a one-man Triumph.'

'Of course I was invisible to him,' Otho replied, 'Because I wasn't there.'

'Someone else watched him?'

'Didn't have to. He left the Palace just before I arrived. I heard about his eventful visit to the Lord Chamberlain's suite of rooms. He's a boy worth interviewing. I simply followed his amusing tracks, those ridiculous animal tails zigzagging around in the fresh snow.'

Otho circled the steam of his breath in the frosty air with his index finger. 'He might as well have dropped a trail of dried peas for me. You aren't thinking of recruiting him, I hope?'

Otho's poise was masterful, considering the haste of his long race from the Castra and the frantic success with which he'd located me. Even when a drunken customer still wrapping up his naked behind bumped into him, Otho took a moment to steady the slobbering lout before turning back to me.

Did he notice I was imitating his languid manner? Did he realize I was playing for time?

'You just told the proprietress you came to escort Apodemius back to Roma. I don't understand.'

'We need to prepare his defense. Hire the best *assessores*. It's the least we can do.'

'First we'll have to find him.'

I considered my next move. Behind Otho's shoulder, I spotted Benedictus outside, jerking his head at me through the falling snow. Was this the signal that the other two had got away? His expression was wide-eyed with alarm.

'Otho, there's my beaverish little friend, as nosy as any *curiosus*. Let me get rid of him first.'

Otho warmed his hands over the red iron bars of the cooking grill. I ran outside.

'Are they safe?'

'Yes,' Benedictus said between chattering blue lips. 'They're on their way to an attic where Optata promises they'll never be found. That officer says he's taking you back to Roma?'

'As he can't find Apodemius, he'll have to settle for me. Why?'

'He stationed your escort around the corner, hiding out of sight, where the fullers' laundry vats collect the public piss—'

'An escort from the Castra? Wearing this insignia, like mine?'

'No, *Centenarie*, no!' Benedictus panted.

I glanced over my shoulder. The heavy weatherproof curtain drawn over the entranceway obscured most of Optata's customers inside, but I could catch a sliver of *Magister* Otho, gesturing in friendly fashion to the grill cook.

'Then who are they?'

'Eastern troops, in rich cloaks with red silk linings. Their *cinguli* are double your width and their *spathae* hilts groaning with jewels.'

'Their insignia? Can you remember?'

'Yes, of course. I've drawn those shields when copying *fabricae* inventory. They have black eagles on a dark red background, like this.'

With a bare finger and practiced eye, Benedictus traced the unmistakable image of Roma's supreme fighters in a snowdrift at our boots.

'*Herculiani?*'

He nodded. 'I think so. From Constantinopolis. Speaking Greek.'

So Otho was lying to me. The soldiers waiting to escort Apodemius were not headed westward to the Castra in Roma. They'd come from the East and rendezvoused here in Sirmium. They would return to the East.

'Run, Benedictus! Avoid them! Go back and help the Vestal and the old man. And for the gods' sake, pull those damn pelts free of the snow!'

Clearing my head with a bracing intake of clean, freezing air, I returned to the bustling tables in the fug and stink behind Optata's street curtains.

'There! I've got rid of the pest. It's cold out there.'

I rubbed my hands together. 'Don't you want another drink, *Magister*? What help could Castra lawyers be to Apodemius, anyway? Do you know the actual charges yet?'

'No. And before we discuss Chalcedon in detail, may I know where *Magister* Apodemius is hiding himself?'

I feigned surprise. 'That's what I don't understand. What makes you think he's in a dive like this? He's a little long in the tooth for this kind of pastime.'

'Enough, Numidianus. There's a warrant out for you, too, though you tried to burn it in a brazier. If Apodemius weren't somewhere around here requiring your assistance, you'd have fled Sirmium without delay—for the wilds of Dacia or over some gods-forsaken Alp for Rhaetia.'

I took a breath and bluffed it out. 'There must be some misunderstanding.'

'None.'

'Well, well. You've really ridden all this way, by yourself, to help the old man? Apodemius would be touched if he knew.'

Otho glanced around him. The bastard was so *neat*. He wanted to depart with us renegade colleagues in tow without a struggle that might leave cooking grease on his clean cloak. Could I use his sense of decorum to escape him?

'You surprise me, *Magister*. Your personal solicitude for Apodemius impresses me more than anything else—your modern clock or all your new management plans. After all, you're still new in the saddle of command. I would have thought any charges involving the Castra would rattle your nerves, put you on the back foot, have you staking out a safe distance from the old man's mistakes. But no, here you are, talking about hiring expensive legal advice. Backing Apodemius with Roman lawyers at the state's expense could bring the *schola* down around your ears.'

Otho dropped his smile. 'On the contrary, it'll bring down your *schola*.'

'What do you mean?'

'Marcus Gregorianus Numidianus, you're not as quick-witted as your evaluations say. You still don't understand? This is the new plan. Apodemius' Castra is to become a footnote of imperial history, just like the *frumentarii*.'

'Replaced by?'

'A completely different department—very trim, very efficient, based in Constantinopolis. A handful of Eastern officials reporting to Julian's *magister officiorum* will take charge of the *Cursus* and postal services. Say, two dozen.'

'Only two dozen? What about our information gathering? Language training and reconnaissance for border defense? Accounting lessons for cross-reporting on taxes and customs?'

'Your Apodemius built an illegal empire on the back of a bloated system of hangers-on and *curiosi* too idle and troublemaking to be of any credit to our new reign.'

'*Our* new reign?'

'Of course. Julian himself installed me, right under Apodemius' nose.'

'But you were an obscure tax specialist working out of Caesarea, Palaestina. How could you be installed by Julian when he was a world away on the Sequana River?'

'Remember all those letters Julian wrote to Libanius in Antiochia, Sallustius of Emesa, and all his brainy friends? He was lonely, wasn't he? He kept in touch with everyone, including me. You see, Julian and I were schoolmates, Numidianus. Long before you met him, I knew him as a stammering, goatish philosophy student, shaking in his rough *susurna* before Constantius' councilors.'

'Students? Where?'

'In Athina. The Emperor and I shared books, meals, even pranks when Julian wasn't being too high-minded or jabbering away about magic statues coming to life. But why try to explain such loyalties to you? You're only a freedman. An ex-slave can hardly understand the ways of the elite, Numidianus, no matter how many volumes he borrows from his master's shelves.'

'You arrogant—it was you who lured and betrayed Consul Taurus in the Castra temple, wasn't it?'

'True friendships forged by boys wearing matching school cloaks are never forgotten. And how easily the Castra's dossiers are edited! I expunged my education from my own dossier and Apodemius never connected me with Julian's classroom days.'

I turned my back, but Otho seized my arm again, with a vise-like grip, fingers hard as steel.

'You're wanted for questioning, *Centenarie*.'

I had to play along with Otho to give Apodemius and Apollonia time to escape. Apodemius may have been doomed, one way or another, but I had to bluff this out as long as I could—for her. I could not bear the idea of Otho's men harassing her, cross-examining her—or worse.

'I've nothing to fear from questioning—whatever Notary Pentadius alleged in Chalcedon, Otho.'

'In truth?' His chuckle turned my stomach. He gripped me tighter.

'I escorted Caesar Gallus to the dungeon in Pula, Istria as instructed. I witnessed his execution, as did Lord Chamberlain Eusebius, as did Pentadius himself. But I was not the Caesar's executioner, nor did I approve of Barbatio's obscene treatment of the imperial corpse.'

The image of Barbatio kicking Gallus' severed head over and over until it was a bloody ball of featureless pulp was nothing I wished to revive before others, even under oath.

'No one has accused you of abusing Gallus' corpse.'

'I'm relieved to hear it. If I did anything useful that night, it was presenting irrefutable proof gathered by senior Antiochene civil servants that the Lord Chamberlain was corrupt. Behind Constantius' back, Eusebius exploited Gallus and his *Augusta* to amass confiscated private property for himself.'

'Indeed, that charge is already on the books against Eusebius.'

Otho nodded as if we were on the same side. 'His appetite for luxury and property is known across the civilized world. Emperor Julian has ordered his ill-gotten goods be returned from the eunuch's possession to the rightful owners or heirs without delay.'

There was a long pause broken by the bumping, grunting, and sighs of professional lovemaking in the open alcoves along the corridor behind us.

Otho loosened his grip a jot. 'No one requires you to testify against Eusebius.'

'Without Apodemius in custody, I present a pathetic substitute. Are you proposing to take me back to the Castra for meetings with expensive lawyers?'

'Oh, Numidianus, I'm afraid there will be no possible legal defense for you.'

Otho leaned close to me, so that I would not mistake his next statement through the raucous banter drowning our conversation.

'When I found you'd disappeared from your office, we searched for a clue. You'd opened the warrant and panicked. Well you should. We searched all your papers. We found exactly what Pentadius promised to his jurists.'

My hand gripped the hilt of my *pugio*.

—THE BURNING STAKES—

'An imperial order, dated 354, and signed in purple ink by the Divinity, *Master of the World, Our Eternity* himself. The Emperor retracted his order to execute his cousin and commanded that Gallus be brought back alive to Mediolanum for a proper trial.'

Eusebius had won. And I guessed when.

How foolish to think his curiosity about Roxana's whereabouts was anything more than a ruse. He'd pulled off his real sleight of hand while fiddling with unopened letters and official packets. Was it any use to tell Otho how the eunuch had come to my office uninvited? That while my back was turned checking for listeners at the door, he'd planted his last and most powerful weapon against Apodemius—*on me*?

'I never saw such a document,' I whispered. 'It was hidden there by Eusebius.'

'No one will believe you.'

Otho smiled with feigned regret through his even, white teeth and rubbed his smooth chin. He stepped back as half a dozen smartly uniformed Herculiani legionaries cut through the crowd, dizzying drunken onlookers as they took my weapons and clamped my wrists behind my waist.

'You're escorting me to Chalcedon, Otho?'

'Of course not. I still have to find Apodemius and send him along behind you and Eusebius. And then I mop up my task in Roma—organizing the most important of the *schola*'s dossiers for Julian's perusal before dismantling the rest of the department. I'm not sure what we'll do with the Castra itself. I've restored it to good condition.'

'You'll be reporting my arrest tonight?'

'Yes. I'm sending the incriminating rescindment document ahead to the tribunal by twenty-four-hour relay couriers. Such invaluable evidence deserves the white feather of urgency. Your *Herculiani* escorts move a little more slowly, but I don't suppose you're in such a hurry, are you?'

'Then please send ahead a single message to Emperor Julian from me.'

'And that is?'

'Tell him *Argentoratum*. *Centenarius* Marcus Gregorianus Numidianus requests an urgent audience, in the name of Argentoratum.'

Chapter 18, 'Argentoratum'

—CONSTANTINOPOLIS—

So it was back to the East for *Centenarius* Marcus Gregorianus Numidianus, once a free man and for one day, even a trusted *proximus* of an emperor, allowed close conversation riding alongside his hallowed person on the plains outside Mopsucrenae.

And now? Stripped of weapons on which I might impale a guard or even myself, I traveled as a prisoner of the Empire. I didn't even enjoy the perverse companionship of escort by my fellow *agentes*, but instead traveled surrounded by stony-faced Herculiani under strict orders to speed a regicide to his punishment.

In the short distance between Sirmium and Singidunum, shackles had rubbed my ankles raw and bleeding. An iron collar absorbed the cold. It became a ring of ice battering my collarbone with each rocking movement in the saddle.

I'd put up no struggle. On the third day, the leg irons were removed while we rode with faces slammed by freezing winds but only because they were irritating my horse.

I slept in fits and starts, re-clamped to each new bedstead on our few stops. The *optio tribuni* in charge refused to remove my collar at any time, even after we'd crossed the Margus River and stopped for a full night in the old fort of Horreum Margi, far from any hope of rescue.

So I tossed and turned with a great wedge of cold metal strangling my nightmares. They took me back again to the slaughtering ground of Mursa. I saw the dead warriors beckoning to me with severed stumps for arms, their hacked and blinded faces smiling missing lips or noses as I neared my own judgment hour. One night, Apollonia lifted her veil and oh! horror! What a flat mask of featureless, thick scars grinned lipless with love for me!

Before leaving Naissus, we rode past that very spot where Julian and I had bid each other farewell in November—he speeding off for a brilliant new life to return the civilized world to the pagan glories of Hadrian and Marcus Aurelius, and me heading back to a Castra laden with disdain, suspicion, and finally betrayal.

Julian had ridden eastward that day with all the gods attendant on him. Had he not left even one minor deity facing the West to protect an innocent Numidian *libertus* from others' treachery?

All through my service, what had been the first lesson for the lowliest *eques*? Ride fast, faster than you've ever ridden before, son, so fast that if you risked looking over your shoulder, you'd see the god Mercury himself, crestfallen at your speed, folding his golden wings in defeat.

Ride through as many stations as you can without stopping. Don't give in—don't give up—not yet! Not until your stomach caves in on itself and your horse rears in protest at his aching fetlocks, and your mind is numbed by the very sight of the *Cursus* paving stretching forever underfoot and hoof.

As we thundered on and on, I prayed, I begged, that the ice-clogged tributaries parallel to our route would flood the road. Or that the *mutationes* would run short of fresh mounts. I imagined fierce hurricanes that might delay us until I could devise my escape. When we spotted another company riding in the far distance, I prayed they were not Romans, but a band of Goth brigands in cast-off Roman gear. They'd drag us away as prisoners over the imperial border, never to be seen again.

But the barbarians proved as unreliable as ever.

As we rode on from Serdica to Philippopolis, I comforted myself—there was one good reason to hasten to Chalcedon. Might Eusebius be persuaded somehow to tell the truth before they tied him to the executioner's stake? Was not Eusebius of late one of the Church's most powerful allies? Did he not fear his Christ's eternal hell for his sins? Could he be persuaded to make his confession?

I reviewed the six men who sat in judgment of me—Salutius, Mamertinus, and the four military career soldiers Arbitio,

Nevitta, Jovinus, and Agilo. Would any of those men believe a sweaty eunuch recanting just to save his blackened soul?

Only General Arbitio had been present in the *consistorium* that day in 354 when Apodemius and I reported Gallus' death. Triumphant from a record-breaking journey that had killed one *Cursus* animal right underneath his saddle, the *Magister* had stormed into the privileged chamber and tossed the dead caesar's red slippers to the foot of his imperial cousin's dais.

Yes, I recalled, General Arbitio had been present, but had he *witnessed*, had he *registered* for himself Apodemius' stunned expression as Constantius announced to the chamber that he'd changed his mind?

Could Arbitio's memory of Apodemius' innocent dismay save my life?

I kept my hopes to myself and swallowed the dry bread the soldiers gave me, feeling a fool to compose any happy ending for myself. As the hours drew us closer and closer to the eastern capital, I knew how futile it was. I was pinning my survival on two vicious men: Constantius' doomed Lord Chamberlain who harbored no loyalty to any man and an amoral general ready to do anything to appease Julian, his enemy in November and his commander in January.

We were making 'good' time, but as we dismounted at a *mansio* outside the walls of Hadrianopolis, my hope that Eusebius would still be alive when we reached Constantine's *Nova Roma* faded.

These Chalcedon proceedings were barely legal—none of the usual procedures pertained. Eusebius had no defense and no right of appeal. His condemnation by Arbitio's jury was certain. My guards gossiped among themselves—the local *curiales* were already returning Eusebius' stolen property to rightful local owners.

It seemed the venerable protections of Roman law bent and bowed to Julian's goal of military unification.

I thought of the good and innocent Treasurer Ursulus—dead already. How much time had transpired between his verdict and execution? Minutes? How much distance between the hearing hall and the stake? A hundred feet? Two hundred?

I must have been thinking out loud, because my watcher Loxios looked up from his mashed chickpeas in answer to my ruminations.

'What would you answer to that, Risto?' He wagged his spoon at a fellow rider. 'I'd reckon the distance between the tribunal chamber and the stakes is less than between this stable here and that fallow field over there, about to that row of olive trees?'

'No, a bit farther,' Loxios said. He spit out a bone. '*Magister Militum* Arbitio don't like the smell getting into the tribunal chamber. So he drove the stakes behind the far side of the forum, I'd say, at the end of that field, no closer. But didn't do no good. You can still smell it all day—smoke, fat, and ashes.'

We were only one day away from Constantinopolis when I rose from a rough pallet in an unheated room crowded with sleeping soldiers. I'd had no sleep at all. I resigned myself to watching the sun rise on my despair. I asked for a piece of something to write on, wanting to finish a letter to Kahina in time. A fellow *agens* riding the circuit westward had guaranteed delivery to her in the old house on the Esquiline Hill behind the fig tree overhanging the old gate.

. . . we will not meet again. Before I left Roma, you made clear how much you would prefer to retreat to a life of religious devotion and penance in Numidia. If ever a Christian soul was free of blemish, my dearest Kahina, it is yours and had I not rescued you from that martyr's death you sought so many years ago, your pagan friend Marcus Gregorianus Numidianus would not have been surprised to see you, among all those leaping off the cliffs, rise into the heavens unaided.

I preferred a life of service to the Empire. Despite your suffering, you have done much to make that possible. It once seemed possible, long ago, that we might live together, not only in deep friendship, but even more, but the Fates deemed otherwise. I see that your love of your Savior is profound, and greater than any human bond, excepting perhaps your love for Leo.

Now I am thankful, because as I write this farewell, I know that your faith will support you when I am gone.

But please, for my sake, delay your departure for a life of prayer and peace until Verus had made his own last journey across

—THE BURNING STAKES—

the River Styx. He has been the pillar of the Manlius House, more than a mere *dispensator*. I cannot go to my death thinking such a noble soul will die among underlings and slaves without due honors and the comfort of your care.

I write this as my testament, legal, and of free will. I bequeath all my possessions and rights as the appointed trustee of the Manlius estates to Leo, and ask that until he comes of legal age, *tutela impuberum* be transferred to his former rhetor Antonius Drusus.

Kahina, the last is hardest. You alone will understand. What I cannot risk in writing is engraved already on our hearts. When Leo comes of age and holds full legal possession of the Manlius estates and fortune, please return to Roma and tell him the entire truth. He is no less a Manlius for knowing.

Your oldest and most loving friend,
Marcus Gregorianus Numidianus

I gave this letter to the departing *agens* and, to the disgust of my hardened escorts, Risto and Loxios, wept hot tears until we approached Constantinopolis.

I would never see my beloved son again.

All too soon, the glistening domes and Constantine's impenetrable walls stretching from the Golden Horn on our left to the Sea of Marmara on our right appeared, basking pink and gold in the setting sun. Our *optio tribuni* halted so that the company could adjust belts, helmets, and pennants for entry through the city gates.

We rode up in a straight line eastward. From his pedestal feet fifty meters above the forum, a porphyry Constantine fashioned in the style of Apollo greeted us. He held out an orb containing, Christians claimed, a splinter of the so-called True Cross. Kahina would have loved that but I remained unmoved.

His great gates opened to receive our company.

I pulled myself upright under the weight of iron and rode toward the Palace. I recognized the gilded status of Flavius Philippus, Constantius' envoy who tried to save the Magnentius rebels with negotiation. There were dozens upon dozens of other marble figures staring down at our progress toward the Great Palace, most of them stolen by Constantine for his new city during my father's day.

The main boulevard was jammed with people headed for markets, races, meetings, and bathing. I spotted my new jail on a walled rise to the far east of the peninsula. We had to make our way up the ceremonial porticoed Regia flanked by the Baths of Zeuxippos, the Augustaeum market, and the Senate House.

Then we moved through the bronze doors of the Chalke and into a huge court called the Delphax with meeting chambers, past the Triklinos of the Nineteen Couches where foreign ambassadors feasted, the Basilica Magnaura open to the public, two *consistoria*, and the Daphne residential suites that communicated with the nearby hippodrome by a spiral staircase.

My fretful state reduced all this modern glory to a miserable, blinding haze of pleasure gardens, fountains, elevated and sunken passageways, Christian chapels, and yet more statuary—all of it mocking a doomed man's every step.

Of course none of this dazzling architecture was my destination: I was led past staff quarters, stables, and barracks for the palace guards to a set of half-submerged cells of hard granite and plain stone floors, with not a single mosaic tile in sight.

'I've sent word to the Emperor, a special greeting, and I hope he'll grant me an audience,' I reminded Loxios, mustering as much confidence as was left to me by my ordeal. Over my miserable week, I'd noticed that Loxios' *optio* was a stickler for procedure. An ambitious, conscientious officer couldn't ignore the possibility that Julian was waiting to examine me in person.

'Bad news and good news, *Centenarius*,' Loxios told me after an hour gone performing routine arrival procedures.

'Bad news? Is Julian too busy to see me now?'

'The Emperor sends no such permission. You'll obtain no audience.'

'Then what could be your good news?"

'It's too late to cross the Bosporus. You spend tonight in the Palace cells—but see how stout these doors are? Tonight you don't have to sleep in that collar.'

※※※

—THE BURNING STAKES—

I slept so deeply that one leg shackle was unlocked before I realized I was being roused from my bed and dressed to move.

'Is it dawn already?'

'No, no,' an unfamiliar *protector domesticus* grunted. 'Another two hours, maybe a little more. You're summoned to an imperial audience. Wash yourself in that basin while we fetch a clean tunic.'

Only when I stripped the stiff linen off my back did I see the streaks of brown blood crusting the back of the collar where the iron ring had worn painful sores into my nape. Imperial slaves murmured and stared by the lamplight at a dozen white, welted scars striping my bare back—the 'medals' of my first mission in Numidia pretending to be a runaway slave punished with an all-too genuine whip by my recruiter.

With my life at stake in my guise as an aspiring Circumcellion, I had had to convince committed religious suicide fanatics I was desperate to join their demented folly. I'd completed that mission and won myself a career in the *agentes in rebus*, but I'd borne these vivid mementoes of service across my shoulder blades ever since.

Someone poured hot, clean water into a bronze basin studded with engraved 'Chi Rho' picked out in jewels to symbolize Christ. It was far too elegant a utensil for a condemned man. The dead Galilean must have fallen abruptly out of favor in this palace. Given the religious leanings of the new landlord, perhaps Christian treasures all over this vast complex were being shunted and dumped into unused dusty corners.

I followed my escorts quickly through a still and starry winter night. We approached the most sacred wings of the Daphne compound.

Julian waited for me at the far end of a vast imperial reception room. He dismissed my guards and, once we were completely along, gave me a trusting smile.

'How do you find me, Numidianus, your new sovereign?'

He was dressed like an ancient Greek sage. He raised both arms and turned around in a circle to better display a floor-length white wool toga draped over one shoulder and falling to the mosaic floor over an equally old-fashioned under-tunic of snowy linen.

Even on this bitter January night, he wore simple sandals without any socks covering his hairy toes.

'*Auguste*,' I murmured as I fell to my knees and was about to stretch out in full, when Julian pulled me up short with a thick, hairy forearm.

'Look at me, Numidianus! Do you see any purple to worship? There'll be no more hem-kissing now. No more *proskynesis* for my interlocutors. And I may even come to prefer *basileus* in the Greek manner.'

I was astonished. His beard was fuller than I'd ever seen it. His student's round-shouldered posture had straightened up to meet the weight of his new power over the world.

'Resplendent,' I answered. 'You might pass for Socrates or Plato.'

I could only imagine what the courtiers of this palace thought. Gone was Constantius' embroidered velvet *pileus* or jeweled diadem. Gone was the silk tunic festooned with Christian symbols or dazzling rondels or *segmenta* of sparkling beads and jewels. Gone was the bejeweled crimson *cingulum* with its upright struts of gold.

Gone were the trousers of melting-soft kid suede. Gone were the royal cobblers' embossed *campagi,* whose blinding black polish was imitated by every magistrate or governor between Londinium and Carthago.

And gone was the heavy purple silk military-cut cloak lined in deep purple damask. How many times had I stood behind the crowd of *spectabili* and *clarissimi* assembled at Mediolanum's court to watch Constantius II rise and retreat from his audience, that weighty *chlamys* dragging a fortune in hand-woven gold braid behind his short-legged, rigid figure?

Julian waited for more praise.

I bowed my head to hide a dangerous impulse to smile. I'd preferred the unwashed student caesar wearing a rough *susurna* against the Gallic winds in his army tent. Like this, Emperor Julian did not look resplendent. He looked like a stocky, hirsute goat going to a fancy dress banquet. No one but old clerks in Syria or Egyptian scribes fending off a heat wave in Nubia had dressed like this for decades.

—THE BURNING STAKES—

Did Julian intend to reform all the customs of the last century? Even Roma's most battle-shy teacher garbed himself in the modern business costume based on Roman military uniform. Be he junior tax collector or harried sewage inspector, every official wore leg bindings or trousers, a long-sleeved tunic hemmed with embroidery and garnished with thick appliques of *orbiculi* designating rank and department. Even if he had never so much as plucked a chicken, any civil servant worth his stipend was sure to carry a sword or staff of office—though he might never use it on anyone but his laziest bath slave.

'Your journey from Sirmium wasn't too painful?' Julian broke the awkward silence. 'I had them remove your irons.'

'The ride was well conducted. I'm thankful I wasn't beaten or tortured.'

Julian stuttered, embarrassed, 'Oh, that. I recall Catena beating you badly that night in Mediolanum.'

'Do you recall other things, too, *Auguste*?'

'You mean your testimony defending me against Eusebius' accusations that I conspired with my half-brother?'

He'd mentioned Gallus. Was this a gloved invitation? Should I seize the moment and make my plea?

'You have not forgotten, then, gracious *Auguste*.'

'No, of course, I haven't, Numidianus. Stop being a sycophant. I'm not senile.'

'And Argentoratum?'

Julian wasn't listening to me. He had cocked his ear to something else. He turned back to face me.

'Notice how quiet it is?'

'Surely the Palace sleeps at this hour.'

'They didn't used to. I hate to waste time sleeping. But you know what I've done? Do sit down here. Let me boast a little to an old acquaintance.'

I took the seat indicated, one of those silk upholstered couches meant to flatter the reclining Empress Faustia. I thought how comely the turquoise brocade must have set off her legendary eyes. Where had the dethroned and widowed empress fled with her newborn now?

'I've dismissed the *entire court staff*.'

I wasn't sure I'd heard Julian right. He'd tossed thousands of court slaves and eunuchs to beg on the streets outside?

'Once the funeral was over and I'd been witnessed in my grief and disheveled distress by the population of the city at large, I called for a barber to cut my hair. The man arrived in a suit of gold, I swear to the true gods, dripping with rings and necklaces, perfumed up his behind, probably. I said, "I sent for a barber, not a treasury official".'

'You forgot he was a *court* barber, *Auguste*—'

Julian laughed. 'Indeed. I asked this fop what he earned from trimming hair all day. He said a daily take equal to twenty times the state bread *annona* and an equal amount of fodder for his beasts, on top of his annual court salary, and all the other perks of living here at court.'

'You dismissed him?'

'Then and there. I sent him and all the other hairdressers and barbers and bath slaves and chamberlains packing their bags. I ran all the eunuchs out of the palace, and over one thousand kitchen staffers. Would you believe, each of them protested he alone was Constantius' favorite cook.'

'And we know Constantius never took fruit, hardly touched meat, and was no gourmand.'

'Exactly.'

'Where have these thousands gone?'

Julian shrugged. 'I don't care. I'm setting a new course. I've summoned my best pagan friends here to form my new court. Some Christians, too. I've reopened the temples, offered thanks to the gods, and sacrificed many hecatombs of oxen already.'

'Let us hope the gods are pleased.'

'I start as I mean to continue. At Mamertinus' and Nevitta's installation ceremony as consuls later this month, I'll attend on foot with my new court walking beside me—not behind. And then, when the true religion has been firmly restored, Antiochia will be my base.'

'Antiochia, *Auguste*?'

'From Antiochia, I will be positioned to conquer the Persians, once and for all, and save the Empire. They shall add *Parthicus* to my name as I enthrone our old ally Prince Hormisdas in Shapur's place.'

—THE BURNING STAKES—

Dawn might be no more than an hour away.

Before he saved the Empire, I had to concentrate Julian's attention on saving me. I spoke in a gush of panic, pressing on him every word and insistent gesture.

'Those very consuls-elect, Mamertinus and Nevitta, will question me in Chalcedon today. I beg that Eusebius' execution be delayed or my life is lost, *Auguste*. Eusebius squirreled away Constantius' retraction of Gallus' death sentence. He committed a crime, betraying not only your family but also your family's loyal servants—Apodemius and myself. Apodemius acted out of duty only, in complete ignorance of this retraction. I was an escort—no more. Barbatio wielded the sword, but only under imperial order.'

Was Julian listening? I couldn't tell.

'*Auguste*, these events Eusebius witnessed and can confirm. *He must confess* under an oath to his adopted God, when confronted with the charge that he willfully planted Constantius' lost rescindment in my Sirmium offices to incriminate our *schola*. Otho was meant to find it there, meant by Eusebius in cahoots with Pentadius.'

Julian pulled at his wispy beard and didn't reply for an excruciating minute.

'The *schola* of the *agentes in rebus*—that's why I asked to see you tonight, Numidianus, before it's too late.'

I took a deep breath. He gathered up the dragging hem of his philosopher's garb and shifted on the couch, afraid of being overheard. Though the Palace seemed emptied of eavesdroppers and even those shushing *silentiarii*, Julian lowered his bleating voice.

'Otho has been reviewing the *schola* for me now for months—its efficiencies, inefficiencies, personalities, politics, and petty corruption.'

'*Magister* Otho's a very efficient man.'

'But he wasn't at the Castra during the old days.' Julian pressed his index finger on my chest. 'You were. I want you to tell me now how it all worked under Apodemius before he became so feeble and secretive.'

'But *Auguste*, Eusebius may be tied to a stake before my questioning even begins and I need him to stay alive. My hearing is only hours away.'

He bobbed his head like an eager student. 'Yes, we have many hours before you cross the water.'

For an instant, I recalled that boy with no tent mates in his army digs but the dead authors of well-thumbed *codices*.

Now the emperor who held my life in his hands was asking me for advice as his friend.

So I collected myself and started his briefing. Under the glow of a hundred flickering lamps and wall sconces reflecting off Constantius' gleaming dome and onto our two heads, I explained the *schola*'s system of service grades borrowed from the non-commissioned ranks of the cavalry. Then I described our recruitment process—how we took letters of *commendationes*, citing the *suffragium* or patronage, *meritum* or service records, the *potentia* and *gratia*, clout and connections, of the candidate's father, family, and referees.

But we relied on our own talent spotting, too, I explained. We measured integrity, rectitude, industry, and reliability. We knew what the Castra needed—not spoiled scions of powerful families, but quick-witted boys with stamina and loyalty. Our trainers whittled down each fresh litter of youngsters during their testing years in our junior school.

I explained the tedious years of riding the postal circuit that followed. Then there might be promotion from *eques* to *circitor*, then *biarchus*, and always, always, further training at the Castra.

Julian had seen the worst of our service in Gaudentius' meddling and tattling. He'd felt the sting of the Neapolitan's public insults in front of his ranks. Now I filled his eager ears with the serious breadth of our responsibilities:

There were the proper ways of registering and routing imperial mail. We liaised with imperial engineers and state veterinarians for the upkeep of the roads and imperial livestock servicing traffic at the thousands of franchised layover stations—oxen for the heavy cargo on the *Cursus Clabularis* and horses for relay service. In Sirmium, I'd been in constant contact with two imperial mints to coordinate secure delivery times of raw metals and finished coin.

—THE BURNING STAKES—

Some of our men learned the dialects spoken along our borders by the Goths, Alemanni, and Franks who supplied recruits for the army in exchange for the right as *laeti* to settle Roman land. They could be a valuable source of information on unrest or incursions in barbarian hinterland unexplored. Other *agentes*, like Otho, specialized in auditing tax inspections, armament orders, and treasury transfers.

Our men also studied the habits and hierarchies of our Persian enemies, or the peculiar customs of the vast eunuch brotherhood that ruled the imperial palaces, or the constant shifts in foreign policies between our various allies.

Then I moved on to the *quaestores*' regulations for arrest and escort procedures. Only briefly did I allude to less savory lessons in poisons and antidotes, unorthodox weapons, or assassination.

I even confided one of the Castra's darkest secrets of all—that strange caste of *arcani*, rumored agents choosing permanent exile, living outside all civilization where they roamed, listened, rode, and infiltrated the savage, unlettered tribes that swirled and swayed beyond our border garrisons. Occasionally we made contact with one and his report might well have come from another planet, so strange and primitive were his companions.

Julian listened with avid attention. He needed no notes. He'd always been an apt student. He had a mind long honed by disciplined study and wary observation. Now only thirty, he'd gone into battle memorizing battered volumes of old Julius Caesar and other war tomes to emerge from one fray after another victorious over both the enemy and his own jealous generals who'd failed to do as much homework as the green Constantine.

I paused for breath. I glanced up at the high windows for a hint of morning light. Where was Eusebius now? How much longer did I have?

Those drooping Constantinian eyelids narrowed. 'What about those double appointments I came across in Gallia?'

'Our *schola* boasts in total about a thousand, two hundred men—most operating openly. Only a few dozen reach that pinnacle of rank. The most senior *agentes*, like Ahenobarbus of your acquaintance in Mediolanum, might earn a second position as *princeps officii* reporting to an urban prefecture or attached to the *a secretis*, the emperor's personal *sacra scrinia*.'

'But the loyalty of such *agentes*? What I need to know is, to whom do those *agentes* really answer? Where does their loyalty rest?'

'With our *schola*,' I admitted. I owed Julian the uncomfortable truth. If I could please him tonight with my candor, I might even become too useful to be sacrificed to the army tribunal's maw. I might not even need Eusebius, sweating out his last hours on earth while Julian and I bent our heads together in trusting consultation.

Finally, I could think of nothing more to explain—from Apodemius' meticulous dossiers on every active official in imperial pay to secret histories of Roman families stretching back as far as the ancient Flavians.

Julian rose to his sandaled feet and summoned my escort to return. He scratched his beard and shot me a wry smile.

'You know what my friend, the Antiochene philosopher Libanius, calls you *agentes*? Sheepdogs who run the wolf pack. Troublemakers who terrorize law-abiding provincials. He says you blackmail innocent citizens with sensual boys and plant evidence of illegal magic practices. You're all liars, informants, snoopers.'

'*Auguste*, by the love we share for the true gods, give the service a chance to serve you well. I could show you records that disprove—'

'Records! That's why I installed *Magister* Otho at the Castra! He's gathered records for months. His conclusion is that I could run your whole network of postal roads with two dozen reliable tribunes.'

Four *protectores* crossed the echoing expanse of the vast reception hall. They claimed custody of me by both arms. Julian was already making for his exit by a private door at the rear of the empty dais.

'But *Auguste*, will you not recall the charges against me? Or at least command that Eusebius be examined on his possession of Constantius' retraction?'

Julian looked genuinely puzzled at my rising panic.

'*Auguste*, did you not grant me this audience in memory of "Argentoratum?" In Naissus, you promised to help me if I signaled, "Argentoratum." Didn't Otho keep his promise to send word? Isn't that why I was summoned here tonight?'

He cleared his throat and avoided my gaze.

'No, Numidianus, no one conveyed such a message to me, nor would it have made any difference.'

'Then why—?'

'I needed to hear how your *magister* held the loyalty and discipline of a thousand *curiosi*, a class of bad characters universally despised by all decent Romans.'

'And now you know.'

'Yes. Thanks to our chat, I see more fully how I can to transfer most of those duties to the regular forces.'

Had Julian understood nothing? I gave it one more try:

'Have I not explained how the *agentes* might serve you?'

'Come now, Numidianus, we both know our history books backwards. A hundred and fifty years ago, Emperor Diocletian knew when to disband the hated *frumentarii*. Why should I halt my own reforms at the gates of your beloved Castra Peregrina? After all, you serve the Empire, Numidianus, as do I. We both wait on the pleasure and guidance of the Divine.'

'I would trust the judgment of Nemesis and Honos. But you abandon an innocent man like me to a scoundrel politician like Arbitio?'

'You speak of the *magister equitum praesentalis* with such open contempt? Well, I admit I don't like him either. He is very ill read. But I cannot be seen by either the Fates or ordinary men to interfere with the army's independent decrees—particularly where the unhappy fa-fa-fa-te of my half-brother is concerned. General Arbitio, Salutius, Mamertinus, Nevitta, Jovinus, and Agilo—these must be your judges, not I.'

'But your word alone could—!'

'Unlike my late cousin, I will not claim to be divine. I pray for wisdom from others who have gone before me. Perhaps you too should offer more prayers to the gods.'

Though a mere Numidian freedman, I could not bring myself to beg this man who claimed such lofty standards, yet abused high-minded sophistry for his base revenge. If Julian had hoped I'd make some gesture of obeisance or prostration now, he could stand there in his ridiculous Socrates getup until Apollo's great orb froze in the sky.

He saw I offered no respectful or affectionate farewell.

'I hear my palace coming to life, Numidianus. I'll have to bathe, if only to refute those who say I dismissed a hundred barbers and bath slaves so that I could stay dirty.'

I didn't acknowledge his dud joke. Dawn came bursting through a dome window at that moment, shooting a blinding ray off a golden arch overhead.

My imperial audience was over. My imperial trial must now begin.

Chapter 19, City of the Blind

—Chalcedon—

Dawn broke bright and cold, promising the sort of winter morning an *agens* rider loves, the wind fresh at his back and the sun warm on his face.

I sat in shackles in the prow of an army skiff and watched the golden domes, impregnable walls, and colorful gates of Constantinopolis recede into the morning mist still blanketing the water. The great statue of Constantine basked in the rising sun on his pillar high above the city. He waved a motionless farewell.

We anchored at the opposite dock without fanfare or welcome. A week or two ago, the arrival of doomed imperial officials from Constantius' court might have caused excitement, but my clumsy scramble in irons onto the rough-hewn quay raised no eyebrows this morning.

The Emperor himself was never seen on this shore. How clever Julian was to stage his 'show' trial where there were no legal-minded critics or civilian powerbrokers, no expert *quaestores* or *assessores*, for an audience. General Arbitio and his jury could do what they pleased here.

Yet the lie that Julian was too far away to monitor or interfere was illustrated by this morning's easy commute from his residence to this miserable suburb.

Chalcedon wasn't the sort of town a man took any note of—unless he faced his death there. It was, a boatman told me coursing over the choppy Bosporus, a Megarian colony built in the seventh century before Christ. Its site was so obviously inferior to that of Constantinopolis on the opposite shore that the locals brazenly nicknamed it, the 'City of the Blind.'

I'd trudged through Chalcedon's narrow streets once before. Little had changed in seven years.

The gleaming capital, our 'Nova Roma' on the far shore, was the architectural glory of our century and the strong arm of our Eastern defenses. Chalcedon was its stinking, hairy armpit—fouled with open sewage and jammed with beasts of burden jostling with unwashed fishermen, merchants trimming their overheads, and prostitutes sidelined by disease or injury.

How appropriate that Julian chose Constantinopolis' dump—Chalcedon—to discard the debris of Constantius' court!

We left the docks behind, escaped the suffocating market, and reached the town center. To one side of the rectangular forum, Arbitio had set out the execution ground—stakes jutted up from behind the roofs of minor office buildings. On the periphery, a mob of the idle and curious circled like playgoers during the interval. There was even a boy not unlike Benedictus, a thin, underfed, forlorn figure, who wandered listlessly, waiting for the next act of Arbitio's production.

Soldiers barked at the locals to back away from slaves sweeping away human remains. A gaggle of concentrated ragamuffins scampered through ashes to retrieve belt struts for resale—once those of Count Ursulus?

'You're going in there,' said a guard, pointing to a *curiales'* office as rundown as the other municipal buildings fronting the modest forum. The judicial building sat facing my makeshift jail. Passing its open doors, I heard the murmur of formal proceedings underway.

'Who's on trial now?'

One guard shrugged. 'Makes no difference—either exile or death.'

'Notary Pentadius got acquitted.'

'If at least one guy doesn't walk free, the whole thing looks rigged, doesn't it?'

They shoved me down a few steps into a low-ceiling'ed storeroom, half sunk into the ground for the sake of keeping perishables cool. There was only one window, grilled and shuttered against rodents.

'I'm hungry.'

'Why waste good rations on a doomed man?' the second answered out of the side of his mouth, chewing on a wad of fresh-baked flatbread.

—THE BURNING STAKES—

The door slammed behind me. An iron bolt slid shut on the thick stench of sour perspiration. My eyes adjusted to the gloom. At the far end of the room, another man lay on the floor with his back turned to me. He rolled over on the rough stones and squinted at me.

'Numidianus,' Paulus Catena rasped.

I slammed my back against the wall so hard plaster showered my boot heels. The Herculiani guard had locked me in with a man-reptile. The stink of his loose bowels and fresh vomit nauseated me.

His legs stretched out full length behind him with his calves wrapped in loose linen soaked dark with blood. He pulled himself forward, elbows wide, like an Egyptian crocodile.

'What happened to you? You've been tried?'

'Yes.'

'And?'

'The stake. Any minute now.'

'Your legs, what—?'

'Tried to escape. Attacked the guards. Killed one. The other was a veteran, just back from Amida. Said the Persians had a way to keep Romans too sick or old to be prisoners from returning to their ruins. Bastard pulled out his knife and used it on me.'

I'd smelled his foul wounds as within seconds. Catena's feet lay limp and useless, his hamstrings sliced through. He would have to be dragged by both arms or carried on a litter to the stake. The rest of him was unchanged—that twisted mouth too tiny for its brutal, bristled face and the cruel expression in those mismatched eyes.

Less than twenty feet of empty storeroom separated us. Outside the door, two Herculiani chatted, their job done. Inside our dark hole, I crouched low and slipped back toward the door, ready to pound for help. However slow he was, if Catena tried a move on me, I'd demand my right to safety until my hearing.

'Numidianus?'

I waited. The Chain had nothing good to say to me.

'I need your help.'

I didn't answer.

'You there, *Agens*?'

'I intend to walk to my hearing, not crawl.'

'Help me!'
'There's no escape, Catena.'
'There's one for me.'
'None.'
'I need you to kill me.'

Appalled, I crouched lower in the moist, cold shadow. Even my silence was an invitation to the man.

'I saw how Ursulus burned—your eyes pop out, your hands swell up, feet go black,' he gasped. 'Your mouth opens wide with screams, but no sound comes out. Your butt crackles like the fat on a roasted boar but you're still not dead, even when your tongue—'

'Shut up.'

'You shut me up. I mean it. I want you to.' He dragged himself forward a few inches. 'You used to be so clever with your hidden toys.'

'They took my weapons.'

'Even your bootlace garrote? Your folding knife?'

'They took everything.'

'So here you are, defenseless, just like me.' Catena giggled.

Could I deny it?

'Then strangle me, Numidianus. Now. Fast. Before they tie me to that thing. I'm not afraid of death, but I want to go fast and sharp, not slow. I've seen too many die slow.'

I closed my eyes. I had no wish to get within five feet of him, much less touch him. But killing him? That was tempting, I admit.

'Making men die slowly was your specialty, wasn't it, Catena?'

'I'll make it worth your while.'

How I'd love to watch him twitch until he dropped limp between my hands—for Ahenobarbus' sake, for Proculus' sake . . .

'Listen, I'll recant my accusation—all right? I'll take it back—how you killed Emperor Constans in Vicus Helena in cold blood.'

'You knew it was a lie.'

'All the time. Isn't that my business? Weaving lies into links of a chain?' He was panting harder.

'A sick entertainment.'

—THE BURNING STAKES—

'I'll take it back! I promise! Then you kill me. Do we have a deal, Numidianus?'

After a long pause, I asked, 'You'll write it down?'

'Yes! Yes! Do it fast, right? Use your tunic sleeve, one good yank, tight around my throat? Quick? I won't struggle, I promise.'

I yelled to our guards that Catena had a legal statement to make. 'Bring us something to write on—anything.'

I could almost taste the delight of killing him but I had to be careful. I insisted, 'I'll draft it myself. You sign.'

'All right, all right.'

When they brought me a single sheet of coarse, gray *emporitica* that had wrapped dusty pottery goods, I brushed it clean with my sleeve.

With their cheap reed and black-gum ink, I scratched: *I, Notarius Paulus Catena, withdraw all accusations and charges against the Agens in Rebus Marcus Gregorianus Numidianus, including allegations of misconduct or dereliction of duty, of any manslaughter or illegal murder, and any other slanders, libels, or crimes I laid against his honorable name before this court. With a wish to go to my death with a clean conscience, I withdraw my false testimony against Centenarius Numidianus without reserve or hesitation.*

'Sign it,' I ordered.

His white fingers moved through the shadows so fast he almost ripped a hole in the cheap stuff. He handed it back to me.

How would it feel to eliminate a man who'd tortured so many thousands of innocent Roman citizens?

I summoned our guards.

'Catena has withdrawn his testimony against me. I demand you deliver his statement without delay to Saturninus Secundus Salutius.'

The guard took the retraction. With a short aside to his companion, he re-bolted the door. I sank back against the wall, as far from Catena as possible.

'Now do it!' he hissed. 'You promised.'

He stretched his neck forward like a lizard peering from under a rock. His eyes glinted by a sliver of light that shot between the shutter slats and cut across his path on the floor.

I stay where I was, my back pinned to the crumbling plaster.

'Kill me, fast, before they come for me!'

'No. It's time someone tortured you back. You must face the gods Nemesis and Honos for your crimes like every one of us. Why should I commit murder for you?'

'You promised!' It came out a hoarse, high screech. 'They'll come any minute! Now!'

He clawed the floor between us, but they hadn't fed him much for days.

'I lied, Catena. I lied. For the memory of those Romans you persecuted in Britannia—remember them? The mother of my son was one of them. She ran from your notorious purge to fall into a worse Hades. She was never the same again.'

'You call yourself an honorable man?' His voice cracked with terror of the waiting pyre. 'You tricked me into exonerating you?'

'Why shouldn't you clear my name? Why shouldn't I lie to you? You never valued truth, Catena. You preferred your games with knives, oil, torches, and claws. You think I've forgotten your Persian experiment in Sirmium, burying your victim up to the neck in a barrel collecting his own shit?'

Catena whimpered, scratching at the worn flagstones with his dirty nails.

'Remember Titus? You sliced off his ear for fun to entertain Constantius' party guests in Arelate. Remember General Silvanus' Adjutant Proculus? Wasn't Proculus an honorable man? You tore him to shreds, pulling off his skin, strip by strip. I carried his still-breathing remains in my arms to a more peaceful death. Yes, *I lied*, Catena, for Adjutant Proculus.'

'You stinking, freedman! You *curiosus* cunt! They always said you were a bastard. Kill me now or else I'll kill you!'

He couldn't move fast enough. He knew it. But he tried. He got himself moving forward, his useless feet dragging behind him. The grout in the stones tugged at the crude bandages around his calves. The festering wounds opened wider. He grunted and struggled, inch by inch.

He hated me now more than ever.

I rose to my feet and measured his progress. I moved to the door and readied myself to kick him away, but knew he'd grab my foot. I wasn't sure how much he could hurt me—

—THE BURNING STAKES—

The bolt slid and the door flew open, slamming me hard against the wall. Six Herculiani hoisted the sobbing Catena onto an army litter. They pushed deeper into the room and bound him tight with ropes and carried him away.

They bolted me in again. But I ran to the window and worked the shutter latches free with my fingers until they bled. The wooden planks separated just enough to see their retreating party and hear his strangled screams drowned by the welcome cheer of the impatient horde.

I could make out little more, but even over the rising excitement of hundreds of Chalcedonians, the barking orders of the Herculiani echoed off the forum's cracked facades.

Catena—his name was notorious across the world. Julian's philosopher friend Libanius had written that Notarius Paulus Catena deserved death in both Europe and Asia 'ten thousand times.' The loquacious Antiochene letter-writer was familiar to all postal officers for his exaggerated prose style, but in Catena's case, no hyperbole was enough.

Through the tumult, there was the sudden clanking of *spathae* on dozens of shields to herald and approve the tribunal's decision. Lit torches floated over the heads of the mob.

There was a great whoosh of sparks as the pyre's foundation caught fire. Hundreds of bodies pressed forward, drawn deeper toward the stake to catch every detail of Catena's painful end. I wished I had a better view, because who among those mere Chalcedonians deserved such satisfaction as much as someone like me, who'd circled Catena's tunnels and grates with a wary eye as I served from court to court?

The winds began to toy with their victim. They danced away from the stake, to the east, then west, then north, and south. The great charcoal plume of smoke swayed overhead, this way and that. The gods prolonged Catena's slow extinction with fickle interest in feeding the fire.

Catena's screaming, already hoarse, rose to a prolonged choking, and then fell into broken moans that silenced his audience for many long minutes.

Finally the crowd dispersed, clearing my line of vision to a blackened sack, still dripping and smoking, hanging loose from its chain bindings.

There was that boy again. He crossed the forum, with covered head, leaning into the breeze. He had the same hunched posture and the same white cheeks, but he wasn't my scribe. He wasn't wearing Benedictus' beaver cloak—just a plain brown tunic and trousers. Could the Empire be dotted with slope-shouldered Britannian boys? Or did the gods amuse themselves by mixing the terrors of the stake with phantoms of fresh-faced hope?

※※※

Saturninus Secundus Salutius arrived at my bolted door as dusk fell. Clasping Catena's last-minute confession of false testimony, the Praetorian Prefect of the East ordered my guards to bring two stools and some lamps. I might be a condemned man, but this was to be a civilized meeting. After all, we two had once dined and debated in a Gallic army camp among Julian's favored few.

He was by no means a young man but he'd kept himself fit. By the flickering lights, he looked oiled and scraped shiny from a session at whatever Chalcedon called its baths. As the most prominent pagan intellectual among Julian's jurists, he must be setting an example for his army colleagues of rougher stock—the famously vulgar new consul Nevitta or the taciturn, pockmarked Alemannic veteran Agilo. It was hard to imagine those two jurists this aromatic after a working afternoon.

'Sit down, Numidianus. We suspected Catena's accusations were just third-hand rumors that circulated the Treverorum court.'

'He didn't witness Constans' death.'

He gave me a measured smile. 'The Gallo-Hispanic border is indeed a long way from that forsaken capital.'

'Notary Catena has hated me ever since I was a junior rider, freshly manumitted, assigned to Treverorum in 351.'

'Hated you? Why?'

'He thought me arrogant. I was an ex-slave, less than nobody, yet I refused to collaborate with him. After he'd made his name by purges and persecutions of the rebel hiding in Britannia, I met him again, in 353, at the Arelate Palace. I ruined the evening of his most public triumph. He was presenting tortured Magnentius followers taken captive as his "birthday surprise" for Constantius.'

'Constantius had no taste for the Dacian's gifts?'

I shook my head. 'Unlike Julian, Constantius preferred very perfumed, decorous Eastern protocol. He employed Catena but kept him out of his courtiers' sight. That night Catena saw his "presents" had failed, but he didn't understand why.'

'He blamed you?'

'For interrupting his show. Empress Eusebia and her ladies were already nauseated when he confused the banquet hall with the arena. He started cutting off body parts. Catena's soul was never fully human. And he resented anyone with a modicum of education or integrity—or simple good taste.'

Salutius raised one plucked eyebrow. 'Like you? I would agree with Catena on one score. For a freedman in your position, you're hardly modest. But this retraction helps you.'

He folded the rough paper and tucked it away under his jeweled belt of office. 'I'll enter it into the record as genuine.'

'Of course it's genuine.'

'Well,' he gave a knowing chuckle, 'who knows what goes on between two desperate men locked up together?'

'Then I'm free to resume my post?' I rose from my stool.

'Oh, Numidianus, don't chafe at our hospitality! What *agens* serves so well as you for fifteen long years without crossing powerful men?' His voice hardened. 'I'm afraid there are other rumors that dog your reputation.'

'Such as?'

'Are you not only the freedman but also the bastard of the dead rebel commander Atticus Manlius Gregorius?'

'So? Tribune Valentinian serves in good standing as we speak, though his father Gratian fell from grace over the Usurper.'

'Gratian lent Magnentius a bed for one single night. Your father was the Usurper's *magister peditum* and died fighting Constantius at Mursa. You nearly died at Mursa yourself. You exceeded an *agens*' mission. You wielded weapons for the rebels against a Constantine.'

'I acted as a go-between for Roma's divided armies, as *agentes* must when ordered. Remind your jurists that I also joined in the hunt for Magnentius and his brother Caesar Decentius. Magnentius impaled himself on my own sword—before witnesses. So how could you condemn me as a rebel?'

My spirited defense displeased Salutius.

'There's more, Numidianus. For a man still struggling for promotion to *ducenarius*, how much your record surprises us! How do we explain your frequent proximity to the lofty *potestates excelsae* around the Constantines? It's as if you intentionally maneuvered yourself within reach of their persons, time and time again.'

'I'm guilty of no malice toward the Constantines. On the contrary, I followed my *schola*'s—'

'—You also served as escort for the Emperor's sister, the *Augusta* Constantia, in 354. She hurried from Antiochia to beg that Constantius spare Caesar Gallus' life. Only she never reached Constantius' court alive, did she? She died of a so-called mysterious fever at some desert post called Caeni Gallicani outside Bithynia—under your protection. The gossips blame poison.'

I jumped and kicked my stool against the wall. A guard slid back the bolt and checked to make sure Salutius was unharmed.

'I see. I *comprehend*, Salutius. Your prosecution is building up a completely false portrait of me—a colorful mural of lies that would cover the whole tribunal wall.'

'These are the facts before us.'

'Who's behind these so-called "facts"? Who needs to paint me as a diehard enemy of the Constantine family tree?'

'First Constans at Vicus Helena, then Constantius at Mursa, then Constantia in Bithynia, you admit, it looks . . . odd?'

'Who's my enemy here? Not you, Salutius. Or you wouldn't be sitting there, tracking Catena's pus on the soles of your polished *campagi*.'

'I may believe your explanations so far, but there's one more charge, not so easily dismissed from your record.'

'That was planted in my office. I swear it before all the gods.'

—THE BURNING STAKES—

'Planted? The original? Signed *Our Eternity* in Constantius' hand in purple ink? The jury has just heard the second day of testimony from the Lord Chamberlain—'

'Of sticky stories and fabulous falsehoods.'

'The eunuch swears before us that he suspected you of withholding the rescindment ever since that night in Istria.'

'Me? Why? *Why*? Surely he himself received it as Constantius' personal emissary to Pula. Eusebius withheld it, not I. Why would I disobey Constantius' orders? You didn't serve in his courts, Salutius. The late emperor vacillated, chopped, changed, sidestepped, prevaricated, hesitated in everything he presided over.'

Salutius' eyes narrowed but now I'd gone too far not to explain.

'The safest thing was to follow Constantius' orders to the letter. Why would I, a mid-ranked *biarchus*, make anything more complicated than it already was for our service?'

Salutius spoke with the placation of a confessor:

'But you see how the prosecution case against you fits? One, you killed Constans on the excuse of defending Lieutenant Gaiso, two, you opposed Constantius for as long as your father and the rebels held out, three, you poisoned Constantia when you had her unprotected in a gods-forsaken hamlet, and finally, you made sure that Julian's half-brother Gallus was beheaded.'

'To satisfy an inexplicable obsession with killing off the ruling family—?'

'The gods work through man in mystery ways, even through a freedman, perhaps. Can you not understand Emperor Julian's new court must clear all this up?'

I leaned into his earnest face. 'Salutius, do you believe any of this?'

He scraped some of Catena's glistening slime off his shoe.

I persisted: 'Look me in the eye, please! Why would a lowly freedman of the venerable Manlius *gens* ruin his career and their reputation trying to wipe out the House of Constantine? On the contrary, I did everything the *schola* asked of me, whether ordered by the *magister agentium in rebus*, or by the emperor himself, in person. Why? Because I was trained to serve the Empire!'

He glanced up at me. I'd caught his attention. I'd just fallen into a trap, a trap involving *Magister* Apodemius.

'Why do you phrase it that way, Numidianus?' He wheedled now, shifting me into position. He was foremost a writer first and a prefect second. Words mattered to him.

I had to dig myself out.

'The truth? You jurists really want to scrape the wax tablet smooth? You seek the truth? Here's the truth, Salutius. Constantius' court was a Hall of Mirrors: false evidence mistaken for *veritas*, right and wrong inverted, a show of "clemency" ended in cruelty, good men held back wise counsel for fear of perverse consequences. Why, I investigated crimes in Antiochia under Gallus and Constantia where decent citizens believed that even the walls of an empty villa had ears reporting to the Palace.'

'So you grew to dislike the Caesar there, I suppose?' He smiled.

'Don't insinuate. Gallus' death gained me nothing. But the Lord Chamberlain Eusebius was in it up to his wide waist. His property confiscations depended on Gallus' blackmail network and false convictions. But even Antiochia reached a point where the more honest courtiers couldn't stomach any more. Eusebius couldn't risk imminent exposure.'

By now I'd circled the claustrophobic storeroom, unable to control my anger and despair.

'Sit down again, Numidianus. Everything you say is correct.' He rose and laid a sympathetic hand on my shoulder to lead me back to my seat.

I shook it off. I didn't need an executioner's kindness—not yet.

'Why are you really here, Salutius?'

'To offer you a deal.'

I righted my stool. We sat down facing each other once more.

'Your observations are correct, Numidianus. Indeed, why you? You're no consul, no treasury chief, no prefect, or imperial chamberlain or steward. "Marcus Gregorianus Numidianus? Who's he?" Consul Nevitta asked us only earlier this week. Consul Mamertinus never heard of you. Agilo said he'd noticed you once, maybe twice, in service on the Rhenus—no more.'

'Catena was right. I'm nobody.' I glared at his clean-shaven features through the flickering lamplight.

'Oh, no, you're very, very important. You're not just a messenger boy, not just a Numidian freedman, you're a pawn on the game board.'

'A hostage?'

'You're a hostage. Or as those fishermen outside might put it, a little catch. We're prepared to toss you back into the sea in exchange for a bigger fish.'

'I have no idea where he is.'

'That's hard to believe. We're in communication with others who're convinced he may be near. They say sometimes he travels as a worn-out hag. A leather merchant from Hispania? A redware trader from Carthago? Sometimes as a circus master?'

'He's retired. That's all I know.'

'A Greek merchant on occasion?'

'Sometimes. He had a dozen disguises. And even if I knew, would you expect me to turn in Apodemius so we could burn together? That's no deal.'

'True.' Salutius leaned forward and whispered: 'Last night Emperor Julian told you he intends to disband the *schola*. He will reassign the *Cursus Publicus* and the imperial post to trusted members of his new court?'

'So?'

'You deliver Apodemius to us. Julian entrusts the new network to your command as tribune, Numidianus.'

'*Tribune?*'

He leaned back on his stool. 'It's an attractive offer. Don't deny it.'

'I can't give you Apodemius. I have no idea where he is. But you whisper for good reason, Salutius. Your very offer admits my innocence. And I hold you, honor bound, to repeat your faith in my innocence before witnesses in court.'

'Think it over tonight,' he said after a pause. 'Why should one Roman die because his double-dealing *magister* refuses to answer for himself before honest citizens?'

He turned at the door while waiting for a guard to escort him out. 'Did you witness Catena's end?'

'Too crowded.'

'Pity. I'll have you brought to observe Eusebius' hearing tomorrow. It may teach you where your interests lie. You'll see the futility of your gesture to a runaway courtier whose true master lies in a stony mausoleum across the water.'

※※※

I stretched out on the floor and despite the filth and discomfort, dozed off. I thought again of that boy—that twin of Benedictus—hunched, thin shoulders, pale face, and wide-eyed expression. But then, the world must be full of boys who turn white-faced when they watch their first public burning.

The storeroom flagstones were hard. Real sleep eluded me. I found myself fighting off the vision of myself promoted to tribune.

And anyway, wasn't Apodemius sick, a man with little time? What would my death serve? Without the *magister*, his knowledge, his secrets and his dedication, how could the *schola* survive Julian's assault? Did I really have to incinerate for a dying man and a doomed service?

I gave up on sleep and rose again to stare through the window. Beyond the rooftops surrounding the forum, the spike end of Catena's burnt stake sent up lingering wisps of smoke curling across the face of the low-hanging moon.

Two other stakes, roughhewn but still untouched by flame, stood silhouetted against the moonlight. Erect and ominous on either side of the smoldering wood, they waited for tomorrow's victims. One was for Eusebius.

And the other?

The idle hubbub of Chalcedon's natives burbled away, broken now and then by outbursts of laughter echoing off the forum facades.

I felt a surge of hatred for their carefree business. This was the noise of Roman citizens the empire over ending another ordinary day. For humans who aspired to nothing more than a cup of decent wine and a bowl of fresh fish stew, laughter near a winter hearth came so easy.

—THE BURNING STAKES—

They would laugh. They would frolic and make love, squabble, cheat, and barter. They would luxuriate in their ignorant wisdom and innocent sins and sleep together under soft blankets tonight. Tomorrow morning, between shopping, dicing, bathing, and trading, they would stop to enjoy another act in Julian's horror show.

Let them devour the awful sight of men who led them, managed them, even tortured their fellow citizens, as they melted and crisped into black and oily ashes—like so many helpless rabbits on a spit.

I was about to die for something even I'd lost sight of—some vague and shining thing I'd dropped on my long ride between *eques* taking up my duties in Treverorum and *centenarius* carried off in fetters from Sirmium.

I listened to those strangers laugh tonight, even if I could not. Or was it the invisible gods I heard chortling at me? And why shouldn't they laugh at my expense?

One way or another, our *schola* was up in smoke as well. Should I really die for something that was already dead?

Chapter 20, The Imperial Scapegoat

—CHALCEDON—

At dawn, my ankles were shackled again, linked by a heavy chain. I was given only a jug of water for my breakfast cum toilet. I marched on an empty stomach out of the storehouse cellar for the tribunal hall.

In principle I walked escorted by the same Herculiani guards assigned to all the condemned men. But in practice, I was hounded the length of the forum by a loud school of urchins who plucked at my tunic and spat on my feet.

Two muddy girls waged a contest to hit my face with crumbling mule turds, adding a circus touch to my plight. Halfway to the steps of the hall, I leaned over and gave one curly-haired sadist a wide grin. Her mother, terrified by the sight of my teeth, snatched up her daughter and ran.

I straightened up and scanned the crowd for any familiar face. I saw only merchants and farmers drawn to town by the excitement of the hearings. They jostled with sullen slave girls and chattering housewives for a better view of me. A party of Greek merchants elegantly garbed in glittering hemmed tunics and costly travel capes stood aloof from the fray.

Greek merchants! Would that one of those refined observers turned out to be Apodemius in his Mediolanum disguise, hiding arthritic knuckles in a pair of embroidered goat suede gloves.

But each of the merchants I passed stared at me with open-faced curiosity or ill-disguised contempt—nothing more.

Thus our gods tease men *in extremis* with phantoms born of wish thinking. There was no sign of the Britannian lookalike. No trace of a veiled Vestal, either. If I imagined that particular trio might have followed me all the way here, I was more than a fool.

We passed into the outer hall, past a phalanx of Ioviani restricting entry through two large inner doors, and into the hearing chamber.

The sun was fully up, the chamber already full. The sight of the waiting audience startled me—over a hundred brilliantly armored officers seated by rank—the Herculiani commanders and adjutants on the north side and their Ioviani counterparts facing them across an open space broken by a prosecutor's table and half a dozen scribes poised on a bench beneath the raised jury's raised dais.

Eusebius stood in the open area beside a wide stool provided to rest his weighty bulk when the process overwhelmed him. He had already withstood two days of rigorous questioning. His frame looked shriveled by the pressure.

His florid, sweaty face dripped with unseasonal perspiration. He'd lost his supply of silk handkerchiefs and smoothed and patted his fawn-colored hair down on his round skull with a pudgy palm. He looked as though he, too, had been denied food and the decency of a washbasin expected by any civilized Roman. His rank, unnatural odor fouled the room, even as far as the corner when I was told to stand between two sentries.

Next to me trembled the court timekeeper. He was nothing to match Mediolanum's *primiscrinius*, only a nervous local hustled from a clerk's office. He'd been instructed to drop his engraved metal balls marking each hour in imitation of the Empire's more exalted law courts. With the clank of his first sphere, Eusebius' ordeal resumed.

Within minutes, I felt grateful to have missed the preceding days of allegations. They'd finished examining Eusebius' connivances for Church property and ecclesiastical political information. Apparently, they'd ended the previous day with his denial of any hand in Gallus' actual execution and his vicious insistence he had no knowledge of any purple-inked rescindment. So I'd come in time to hear Gallus discussed.

'... having denied all charges so far. We've established your rise to power in the Sirmium Palace and the trust Constantius placed in you in assigning and training the network of imperial chamberlains to serve Caesar Gallus and his *augusta* when they set up court in Antiochia. This entailed ...'

—THE BURNING STAKES—

Nothing in the prosecutor's introduction held my attention. I knew the ways of Eusebius' nest of eunuch *cubicularii* in Antiochia Palace as well as every other imperial residence.

So I examined today's court instead.

As I'd feared, there was no defending *assessor* or advisory *quaestor*, only an army hack reading from notes handed to him by Salutius. This was an army farce, a burlesque of Roman justice.

General Arbitio sat next to Salutius in the very center of the bank of jurists. He gave me a hard glance when I stared at him. Salutius avoided my eye.

Roma's two new consuls Mamertinus and Nevitta looked distracted. *Magister Equitum* Jovinus and Agilo looked disgruntled. I don't think these squalid tales of Gallus in Antiochia or Church greed were as important to them as their immediate concerns; the unification of their divided army, the restoration of its reputation battered by Persian victories, and its future loyalties to an untried emperor.

General Arbitio focused hard on his jelly-like defendant. His frozen scrutiny of his former ally Eusebius could not be misread—but what irony! Eusebius was accused here of treason, yet it was Arbitio who had betrayed their long partnership.

We were watching a duel between two estranged and embittered allies. Arbitio was trying his own long-time co-conspirator.

And why should Eusebius stand trial and not Arbitio? Had not Arbitio just positioned his army against Julian in the field two months ago? Only because Arbitio commanded troops Julian sorely needed now for the Persian campaign to come was he sitting above us.

Eusebius commanded an army, too, but his units were half-men armed with *strigiles*, massage oils, and vicious tongues. What greater warning did Eusebius need that he would never leave Chalcedon alive?

But Eusebius was not quite finished yet. The great eunuch might still prove dangerous and Arbitio's wary expression showed he knew it. Everything concerning the eunuch's fate touched on Arbitio's exiting this hall more secure than when he entered it.

'...the trial of Clematius is our next problem, Lord Chamberlain. This wellborn Alexandrian was executed on Gallus' orders on false charges of forced sexual congress with his own mother-in-law—a vicious, dishonest, and jealous woman. You claimed ownership of the family's confiscated business before Clematius' body was cold. What was your hand in this travesty of justice?'

To the surprise of his judges, Eusebius smiled.

'I know little of that story. The Alexandrian's business fell into my unwilling lap. Why not ask that man, over there, for more details?'

He pointed at me and continued:

'—for I do know that a diamond necklace was the bribe to Augusta Constantia from the mother-in-law making the accusation against Clematius. The jewels ended up in the possession of Constantia's attendant, a certain Roxana who spied for a time for that prisoner's *schola*. You might well ask him what he knows about all that.'

Arbitio's jaw dropped. Eusebius allowed himself a smirk. He might have just saved himself from the stake, for he knew the fearless and elusive beauty Roxana was Arbitio's Achilles Heel.

I saw the general's impassive composure falter. Did Eusebius know where Roxana was? Arbitio couldn't be certain but he would pay dearly to know.

I admired Eusebius' bluff, despite myself. Roxana was dead to the world and safe from his vile games.

The startled prosecutor shuffled through his notes, but found no mention of Roxana. He demurred, 'This falls outside our line of questioning. We've established that Caesar Gallus collected dozens of complaints and accusations against innocent Antiochenes. You abetted their convictions and ensured the confiscation of each slandered victim's property for yourself. You accrued your corrupt wealth from hundreds of victims—all built on information passed to you in good faith by the gullible Gallus and his consort.'

And so it continued, case by case. The army's prosecutor droned on in this vein, to whitewash Gallus' appetite for rumor and libel while deepening the eunuch's guilt as instigator and abettor.

—THE BURNING STAKES—

Eusebius' shoulders sagged. He'd dangled Roxana as bait under Arbitio's nose but the general hadn't bitten.

'We now pass to your crimes in Mediolanum after the murder of Caesar Gallus. You deny knowledge of the rescindment order. But nonetheless, now safe from prosecution for crimes in Antiochia, you then aimed your engines of defamation against Flavius Julianus himself. You were the source of rumors that Julian and his half-brother had conspired together against Constantius. These tales were false but you attempted to portray Julian to his cousin as a plotter and deadly enemy of his throne.'

Eusebius muttered to himself.

'Meanwhile, you accompanied one of our jurists here, General Arbitio, to Aquileia to interrogate other officials accused of being associated in Antiochia with Gallus' errors in judgment. Many of the accused were innocent. Yet you drove some into exile—their names are entered on this document here—and without sufficient investigation, you personally tortured and executed others.'

Eusebius raised his bloodshot eyes to the dais. Arbitio had been his willing playmate in that Aquileian adventure. Arbitio must have even provided the prosecutor with this list of victims . . .

' . . . having filled the mausolea of Aquileia with ashes, you returned to report your so-called "success" to the impressionable Constantius. Of this episode, our esteemed General Arbitio washes his hands. He has submitted his written testimony as a witness to your crimes.'

One could almost pity Eusebius. His pleading eyes sought mercy from Arbitio who had never lifted his ambitious boot off the neck of any rival unlucky enough to stumble across his path.

'Lastly, to the dismay of all honorable Roman soldiers, you directed your poisonous energies to the destruction of General Ursicinus. You waved the image of Ursicinus before Constantius' fevered imagination like the proverbial Gorgon's Head.'

That was a nice rhetorical touch. The prosecutor stepped forward and spoke only inches away from Eusebius' dripping features.

'Lord Chamberlain, you fouled Constantius' mind. You suggested that his loyal *magister equitum* had returned to the Persian front boiling over with frustration and resentment, panting to seize the imperial *cathedra* for himself.'

Eusebius' anger exploded in spit into the prosecutor's face.

The prosecutor reeled back and wiped his face clean. Then he continued with words that might have come directly from any one of the assembled soldiers on the dais:

'Why? Because General Ursicinus was the only man in this empire who rose above your sycophantic *consistoriani*. Because when you demanded that Ursicinus either hand over his rich estate in Antiochia or else suffer the consequences of libel against his service and against his son Potentius, what did Ursicinus do? Ursicinus refused and defied you!'

The prosecutor toured the margin of the long, narrow chamber.

'Naturally, my fellow officers, our hero Ursicinus shrugged off this blubbery, pathetic *castratus*! So, defeated in your greed for his villa, orchards, slaves, and stables, you resorted to warning Constantius that Ursicinus was too dangerous to sit on his privy council. You whispered that Ursicinus must be forced into retirement! And so he was. A great soldier was sidelined into obscurity by this "man" who hardly deserves the label.'

The assembled command burst into deafening applause. Salutius let the clamor continue for over minute before raising his palm. In vain, the clerk dropped his next metal ball, swallowed up in noise. This was the army's long-awaited vindication of General Ursicinus. All Herculiani and Ioviani present were determined to relish it.

More accusations flowed until a third metal ball dropped and then a fourth. And with each loud clank on the floor, one hour less of my own life was marked and gone.

The prosecutor grew hoarse. Arbitio murmured to his colleagues on one side and then the other, cautioning the jurists to withhold sentence.

Withhold their sentence? Eusebius began to shake. Could he wangle life-in-exile for himself so easily? Had a few elaborate lies and a false lead to Roxana won him reprieve so easily? Would he end up in Bua, Britannia, or Vercellae, like *Magister Officiorum*

—THE BURNING STAKES—

Florentius Nigrinianus, Count of the Privy Purse Evagrius, Steward Saturninus, and Notary Cyrinus?

The delay in judgment overwhelmed the Lord Chamberlain. Again, Eusebius lost control of his bowels. He collapsed into a stinking heap, fainting dead away with relief. His limp tonnage was hoisted by soldiers onto a litter and carried from the tribunal to his detention place, mercifully far from my storehouse.

Another metal ball clanked on the floor. I was pushed to the center of the great room.

After completing the public downfall of the Empire's most powerful man out of uniform, my own questioning was bound to be a minor affair for the last hour preceding dinnertime. The prosecutor unrolled his accusations just as Salutius had predicted, almost as if reading from the same play script.

Catena's retraction was entered into the scribes' record but changed little. I had murdered Constans in cold blood on the Hispanic border. I had fought with Magnentius' rebels in Mursa to bring down the House of Constantine. I had poisoned Constantius' sister Constantia in a lonely Bithynian outpost. I had intercepted imperial orders to spare Caesar Gallus in that dungeon in Pula, Istria.

And behind every assertion lay the prosecutor's hissing implication; did you do this under orders from *Magister* Apodemius?

Uncomfortable with the allegations stacking up against me, some of the army officers shifted and murmured on their benches. Constans had so shamelessly dishonored the army, its honorable commanders had elevated one of their own to seize the purple. Caesar Gallus had started his reign well by leading Eastern troops against Jewish rebels, but he'd soon collapsed into self-loathing, decadence, and madness.

No soldier on this earth cared about the vicious Constantia.

I noticed their sympathetic glances. A little glimmer of hope sparked in my heart. Might I escape with exile?

Then the prosecutor's notes prompted a surprising embellishment:

'*Agens* Numidianus, you also personally unraveled the forgery implicating General Silvanus in a plot against Constantius, did you not?'

'I did. Silvanus started out an innocent man. He was an honorable and brave commander. He made one serious mistake.'

I looked General Arbitio in the eye. He'd known full well how his rival both in love and politics had been cornered into seizing the purple by the *consistoriani*. Arbitio had stood by and let Silvanus die, all in the hope that Roxana would return to his cruel bed.

The prosecutor could not believe his luck.

'*Agens*! You dare call an unabashed usurper, a claimant to Constantius' throne, "an innocent man"?'

I saw there were officers listening who were glad to hear me defend the hapless Silvanus.

'Accused falsely of the deed, he was cornered into it.'

'That statement is indefensible treason in itself!'

The prosecutor waved his notes in triumph. I'd been easy pickings. A pre-prandial snack. The jurists and officers could all retire early to their baths, banquets, and brothels.

'Wait.'

General Arbitio pressed down on me from his comfortable chair. 'And Silvanus' whore?'

'Silvanus kept no *whore*, General.'

'This woman Roxana, who took pearls off a dead *augusta* and cavorted with the married Silvanus in the north?'

'A lady devoted to the hero of Agrippina.'

Arbitio fought to contain himself.

'Where is she, Numidianus?'

'She's not on trial. Let her name rest in peace.'

All color drained from Arbitio's face. He'd already composed his underhanded offer to Eusebius, imagined Roxana's arrival in Constantinopolis, calculated the cost of jewels and villa to lure her helplessly back under his control. This wolf of a man had started tasting his prey already and now—?

The witless prosecutor pressed me. 'Rest in peace? Is this lady dead?'

I refused to answer. For the *schola*, her friends and enemies, Roxana was dead. I prayed she knew how to stay that way.

There was a final clank, the last of that wretched Chalcedonian's timekeeping spheres. Secundus Salutius gazed down at me with regret in his eyes. He hadn't forgotten my

—THE BURNING STAKES—

description of Constantius' reign as a Hall of Mirrors. Deflated and distracted, Arbitio gathered the indifferent accord of the other jurists.

Lord Chamberlain Eusebius was to die at the stake. All his bluffs and feints had failed. Arbitio would make him no offer of exile tonight.

The tribunal was also ready to pronounce sentence on me, the lowly *centenarius* still testifying—bar one legal nicety.

'Marcus Gregorianus Numidianus,' Salutius intoned. 'You killed three members of the imperial family. You blatantly endorsed the treason of a self-declared usurper. This is not mere dereliction of duty or petty corruption, for which we might offer exile.'

He paused. I'd entered the court a valuable pawn and would leave it an imperial scapegoat.

'We're obliged to condemn you to death for your crimes against the House of Constantine—with one caveat. Under Roman law, *agentes in rebus* are immune from prosecution when proven to have acted under the orders of the *magister agentium in rebus*. And who could confirm that but your former *magister* himself?'

I closed my eyes as Arbitio's words sunk in:

'Should Apodemius testify that you served entirely and consistently under his direct instructions, you would be acquitted. That not being possible, you bear responsibility for your actions and die tomorrow at the stake.'

My shuffling march back across the forum to the storeroom drew little notice. My guards were waiting, half drunk. I was faint with hunger, but didn't feel any pain. It was all going to burn away tomorrow.

My companions turned more raucous with each hour. Only after bringing in a couple of sluts and banging at them in the corridor within my earshot did the dreadful night settle into a quieter death vigil for me.

I thought of the goddess Athena reminding Aeneas of his duty to Roma. I thought of Leo safe with Ausonius. I thought of mute Verus, struggling in his bed. I thought of Kahina, praying for deliverance from her lonely duties so far from her beloved Numidian sunsets.

And I thought of Apollonia's soft voice, her graceful hands, her humor and warmth that day we fled Cibalae in Lady Marina Severa's carriage. I missed Apollonia, yet I had no idea what I wanted of her. All she begged from the world was privacy, discretion, and a veil.

I tried to imagine how bad her disfigurement could be. She had braved flames and survived. If she had borne the pain, so would I, though I would not survive. Fire would be the last thing we shared in common.

I crossed the storeroom in complete darkness and saw a sliver of light. The guards and their whores sprawled snoring outside the door.

They'd left my door ajar. I could escape, right now, unseen.

I slipped out the door, darted over their sleeping forms, and raced to the steps. I peered up across the empty forum. I raced to the great fountain the marked the center and crouched low, considering my next move.

Then I saw something shift in the moonlight: three dark silhouettes hiding behind a large statue of Trajan riding a giant horse at one end of the forum.

There was a long stillness. I waited for them to continue on their business. After ten minutes, I faced the worst—they were waiting for me. They intended to let me pass, steal food, a horse, a blanket, and a cloak to make my getaway.

And then? Those three and others like them would follow me as I far as I led them—tonight, and tomorrow, and the next day, until I reached Apodemius, their true quarry. It might take weeks, even months, but I would never lose them.

Yes, I could make a run for it. But it would only buy me time and, leading them to Apodemius sooner or later, I would doom the *schola*.

For the *schola* to survive somehow, Julian had to believe it had died with me. As ill as he seemed, *Magister* Apodemius had to survive—invisible and determined—long enough to outwit Emperor Julian's plans.

Fourteen years ago, the *schola* had engineered my manumission from slavery. In return, the service had asked only that I swear to serve the Empire. Nemesis? Honos? Which god or goddess watched over me now in my pitch-black despair?

—THE BURNING STAKES—

The open door had been a temptation and a trap.

Service for me tonight meant only one thing: sacrifice tomorrow of the highest order.

I returned to the darkness of the storeroom.

Chapter 21, The Burning Stakes

—CHALCEDON—

Salutius' jaw dropped when he saw me marched through the forum and past the audience of jurists and officers toward the waiting stakes. The Gallic prefect must have negotiated my intended escape with Arbitio and the others, probably arguing that my low status was an insignificant footnote to their imperial purge. My flight would prove more useful—within weeks or months at the latest, I would lead them to their true target.

Instead, I trudged between my guards past the curious mob with my stomach growling and my vision hazy with fatigue and failing courage.

Eusebius was brought out next. He waddled along, trussed with a web of thin ropes like a stuffed pheasant readied for the oven. He was to die first; he fought his executioners with surprising strength. But they mounted him at last in the center of the straw pyre and bound him to the towering wooden trunk.

The morning grew warmer. A breeze coming in off the docks dropped away. The crowd's jabber fell to awed, impatient silence.

Arbitio's soldiers laid their lit torches to the dry kindling. The beginnings of a fire crackled and sparked as a wisp of black smoke appeared at the edge of the straw and began creeping toward the eunuch's soft leather shoes. Eusebius' eyes widened and he tried to stomp out the flame, but to no avail. One shoe caught fire. The embossed seals of court on its upper curled in the heat, its threads turning from gold to black.

At first Eusebius clenched his lips tight. He was determined to give no one the satisfaction of measuring the depths of his agony. But as the fire nipped at his toes, he emitted his first scream. Then howling protests, 'Stop, stop, stop,' grew into a deafening roar. I recalled Catena's description of crackling fat, but the first smell of Eusebius that hit my nostrils was the incongruous aroma of perfumed bath oil rising into the air.

The great eunuch struggled, flailing with determination to break free. The ropes binding his knees began to scorch and fray. Before anyone could break his plunge, he'd wrenched himself loose from the stake with a burst of superhuman force. He scrambled down through the blazing straw and straight through a gaggle of toddlers, his flaming robes flapping within inches of their flushing cheeks.

The crowd parted as he shoved his way, lit up, to the public fountain. Rolling himself over its ledge, he clawed at the low waters pooled on the floor of the basin. Screaming all the while, he rolled to one side, then the other, and tried to extinguish the fire eating his nether region with desperate sweeps of his arms through the shallows.

A pack of Ioviani soldiers fell on top of him. They yanked his sopping tonnage out of the fountain. With solid boots, they stamped out the dangerous flames licking his smoldering hems.

I registered this as a lesson for myself—Eusebius had only prolonged his own torment. Catena was right on that score. I wouldn't be so foolish. Groaning from the pain of purplish white blisters puffing up from his legs and arms, he was dragged by his armpits across the flagstones. With a concerted heave by the soldiers, he was slammed against the blazing stake, roaring harder than ever into the sky.

Eusebius' head was quickly consumed, even while his stumpy legs still kicked and jerked. Through the blaze, I glimpsed his bulging eyes extrude from their sockets as if coming straight for me.

The screams stopped. The eunuch's fat began to sizzle like a roasting boar's and his costly maroon brocade robes crumpled, browned and flaked into black ashes.

I averted my eyes, straining to contain bowels turning watery with fear. The crowd could not tear their eyes away and their heartless laughter doubled. Some made rude gestures and pointed at Eusebius' obese groin and thighs. The empty humiliation of his lifelong mutilation, his castration, sagged into blackened flesh for these insatiable voyeurs to mock.

The reek of burnt flesh clogged my nostrils. The air turned sticky and fouled. Eusebius was a mass of greasy intestines, charred bones, and a boulder of charcoal for a head. Feathery ashes blinded my eyes.

My hands were bound. I couldn't wipe Eusebius away.

The onlookers coughed and covered their faces or turned away but they didn't disperse. Even with the unexpected suspense of his attempted escape, it was over too soon for the Chalcedonians. They wouldn't be sated until they'd seen how a robust North African from Roma endured the same ordeal. If their avidity for another human's suffering wasn't enough insult, I felt the irrelevant torment to my empty stomach of vendors moving through the throng hawking prawn snacks and fried squid rings.

They led me to the stake and bound me fast. I gazed out over their heads. I would end my days no more than just another spectacle in the average Roman's day. Across the breadth of our empire, taunting kids threw turds at chained prisoners, housewives compared notes on gladiators' muscles over cold chicken legs, and Greek merchants cast bets with each other from a cool distance under a wide awning.

There were more Greeks in the forum than yesterday. I stared hard at them. Arbitio followed my eyes. I'd admitted to Salutius that Apodemius had used a Greek disguise. Had Salutius mentioned that to Arbitio?

Arbitio raised a palm to halt the proceedings. He called a centurion to his side to pass an order. Four Herculiani dashed across the forum and pulled apart the cluster of Greeks. They shoved first one, then another, and then another forward for Arbitio's glance.

Oh, gods, had they captured Apodemius?

Arbitio selected the likeliest candidate, a venerable in a richly embroidered *pileus* and scarlet travel cloak trimmed in brown marten fur. The soldiers hustled the unfortunate trader, resisting and protesting over his shoulder to his friends, for the examination of the jurists.

They snatched off his hat and heavy cloak, revealing a familiar-looking man with snow-white hair and aged posture. From fifty feet away, I strained to get a better look at him. I wanted to believe, oh, how despite my brave and principled resolution, I wanted to believe in an impossible reprieve!

From where he stood ranked among his fellow jurists, Arbitio gave nothing away. After an approving nod from Salutius, he signaled one of the officers to cross-examine the indignant trader. I caught little of their conversation—the breeze rising off the seashore was against me. But I caught:

'Name?'

'Andris.'

'Home?'

'Athina.'

'Trade?'

'Let me go!' The Greek tugged his rich sleeve out of their clutches and stood his ground. 'Silks and spices from the eastern routes.'

'Bring him forward,' Arbitio shouted. The elderly Greek was pushed to his knees only a few feet from Agilo's pitted scowl. I looked to see how his supposed fellow merchants reacted. I confess I was disappointed—their heated, impotent outrage was so obviously genuine.

And well it should be, because from where I stood, I spotted the real Apodemius, leaning on the arm of Benedictus Bellator a few feet at the far end of the forum. Only the bronze rump of Trajan's horse kept Arbitio or the others from spotting that wispy halo of white hair floating in the breeze.

I forced my head back against the cruel stake. I closed my eyes and sucked in stinking smoke through clenched teeth. My gaze had already proved risky to an innocent bystander. The smoke from Eusebius' stake stung my eyes, but I pressed my eyelids shut all the tighter against the temptation to look across the forum one last time.

Last night I'd avoided the trap Salutius laid. I'd come this far and it would be over soon. I would not be the bait that caught Apodemius. For the hunt for Apodemius to end, the trail must go as cold as the fire that devoured me was hot. I trusted Apodemius to use his remaining time to save the *agentes* from destruction.

—THE BURNING STAKES—

'Open your eyes, *agens*, and look on your superior who sacrifices you for his own selfish ends!'

'You hold the wrong man,' I shouted so that everyone could hear me.

'You said yourself that Apodemius traveled disguised as a wealthy Greek—and here he is, the spitting image!'

'That is not Apodemius!' I shouted to Salutius.

'But the *Magister Equitum in Praesenti* just confirmed it is!'

To my horror, Arbitio had just recognized this innocent Greek as Apodemius, whom he may have seen barely once or twice during brief court consultations. For lack of other corroboration, Consul Mamertinus commented, 'He's awfully alike.'

'It's the wrong man!' I insisted.

'That bastard would defend his *magister* with his last breath,' Agilo growled. 'They stick together, those *curiosi*.'

'Better than some who once swore allegiance to the former emperor,' I shouted, cocking my head at Arbitio.

And now I knew that what I was doing was right. I'd sworn allegiance to defend the Empire, not an emperor or a *magister*, and if my death meant the *schola* had a chance of surviving, so be it.

Commander Gregorius had gone into battle on the plains of Mursa because he was convinced that reform was justified and that rebellion was not disloyalty. My grandfather Senator Manlius, blind and helpless as he was, had defended his library of great men's writings with the last futile wave of his walking stick, because it represented the Empire's legacy of law and learning against unlettered felons.

I would soon be crossing the Styx to join them, as much a Manlius as my Roman ancestors for gritting my teeth through a few minutes' pain rather than collaborate with Julian's political whores.

The Greek trader would not utter a word in my defense, swearing he would call down the gods on their heads for holding him a minute longer. Frustrated, Arbitio ordered the soldiers put their torches to the straw. I seized my last moment to beg Honos and Nemesis to forgive me, however I'd failed. Let them do me honor now.

'Absolve this *agens* of all your charges. I take on my shoulders responsibility for all his actions as charged.'

Apodemius had hobbled around the fountain, but no one heard him over the cheering crowd. He was too late. The blaze took hold.

Benedictus ran through the mob and grabbed Salutius by his broad belt and dragged the pagan prefect past my burning pyre. The boy pushed the towering Gaul at Apodemius.

'Absolve that *agens* of your charges. The *magister* takes on his shoulders responsibility for all Numidianus' actions as charged,' Benedictus was screaming with all the power of his lungs.

A bucketful of slop water drenched my head and doused the flames. But I felt no rush of gratitude, braced as I was for a quick end. Was I to suffer the same ironic marathon, the same stop-start prolonged death, as the unworthy eunuch?

Apodemius was led forward until he faced the jury lined up before us in full regalia, flanked on both sides by their Herculiani and Ioviani protectors. His resemblance to the defiant Greek trader was striking. But their differences were just as marked, especially the state of their health. More than one fellow jurist glanced over at Arbitio who blushed for his error.

'Release this Athenian,' the *Magister*'s voice quavered. 'I am Apodemius, *privatus*, former *magister agentium in rebus*. I assume full responsibility for the acts of our *schola* during my tenure in office. Let the *schola* be dissolved if the Emperor so wishes. Let his punishment, however undeserved, fall on my shoulders alone.'

'You murdered the Caesar Gallus?'

'No!' Apodemius began coughing hard. He spattered blood on the flagstones in front of his goat suede boots. 'You can't make me lie, Arbitio. No one puts lies in my mouth, especially not you, a weathervane masquerading as a general. I held an imperial execution order. I didn't receive Constantius' rescindment in time. Nor did this *agens*. I was there in Pula, at Numidianus' side, with him at all times.'

'So you don't accept the authority of this court?'

Apodemius burst into laughter. 'You call yourselves a Roman court? You think your verdict against this *centenarius* was

—THE BURNING STAKES—

based on sound evidence? You've been duped by the Lord Chamberlain for the whole Roman world to see! Where are his defending advocates? Who has enjoyed the right of appeal?'

'Shut this fart up,' Nevitta muttered.

'Count Ursulus was an honest man!' Apodemius hobbled on Benedictus' arm in a wide circle, addressing the muttering onlookers. 'An honest man!' He bellowed with what was left in his frail lungs. 'I tell you, people of Chalcedon, Treasurer Ursulus, Count of the Sacred Largesse, was an honest, noble, and generous man to Emperor Julian! These men have burned to death an innocent Roman citizen!'

Arbitio thundered, 'This jury has finished its deliberations. Do you understand, if you take responsibility for your *schola*, you accept our verdict?'

Apodemius shook his head. 'You enact the primitive revenge of family, Arbitio, not the business of our Roman state. Even the German barbarians do better than this—they accept payment of a *weregild* for the loss of a brother. If Emperor Julian exacts blood revenge like a savage, then it is I who must pay, not this innocent imperial servant, Marcus Gregorianus Numidianus. Let your scribes, such as they are, record his innocence.'

'I've finished with this,' Nevitta growled. 'They're scum. The *centenarius* is as guilty as the old man. I say both men burn and let their entire department—'

Salutius cut him off. 'Their *schola* is not on trial here, Consul Nevitta. The former *magister agentium in rebus* has taken full blame.'

'We're not cruel or barbaric men, Apodemius. You can still save yourself,' Arbitio interrupted Salutius. 'It's not too late to cooperate with this tribunal. Barter your life by giving us valuable information essential to the continued working and stability of the state.'

Apodemius answered Arbitio with nothing more than a tightlipped smile. Had the old man foreseen this offer? Was he tempted? I knew he needed more time. How would the *schola* survive without him? The postal service and road licenses were only a small part of our work. Without his decades' treasure of secret files and deep knowledge, what solid counsel could be given a rash young emperor who prayed for statues to spring alive?

Then Apodemius gave his answer.

He loosed Benedictus' hand from his arm and patted the scribe on the shoulder in farewell. He clambered up the pyre next to me.

He gave me the dismissive waggle of a knobby hand with which he had shooed me out of his study, time and again.

I was dragged away to one side—to safety—with not one second in which to exchange a word. Some hecklers at the front of the crowd jeered. Others looked confused or provoked or jostled for a better view.

Apodemius offered no resistance to four soldiers binding his stick-legs to my stake. He wiped some floating ashes off his forehead with the back of a gnarled hand. With the other hand he slipped something from under his tunic belt and inserted it between his lips. The soldiers busy bunching straw back into place took no notice. The onlookers might have thought he was merely wiping away a senile man's drool.

But I knew otherwise.

As they bound his wrists to the wood, the old man straightened his shoulders and lifted a calm face to the sky. He gave a sudden convulsion, then stood still. He seemed impervious to a serpent of flame inching up one of his dried leather bootlaces. Orange tongues began to lick the fine hem of his outer tunic.

Apodemius closed his eyes. He looked as though he was falling asleep. He even slumped, his knees bending and his back sliding down the stake into the waiting fire.

Arbitio leaned forward, peering through the rising smoke. He realized now as well as I did, seconds before the crowd: Apodemius had killed himself with ease. Julian's revenge on Apodemius for Gallus was thwarted. A dying man had just put himself to painless sleep.

I could have laughed at them all if my grief hadn't been cutting me in two. Those Chalcedon jurists holding their strict line backed by ranks of vengeful Herculiani and Ioviani commanders and aides—not to mention this ugly rabble of an audience—these hundreds were just staring at a corpse undergoing incineration.

But what I saw was a noble embodiment of the *schola* I loved crumpling into nothing. There was little flesh or fat on the old man. Soon he was only a blackened, shriveled collection of bones and black ashes. A wisp of white hair floated overhead, singed at one end. It settled like a tiny dove on my shoulder. I plucked it off and tucked it into my *cingulum*.

Arbitio lingered in the forum as the other jurists filed away to their baths and dinner. He looked at the three stakes with their corpses and spat on the paving.

The Chalcedon Tribunal was over. Arbitio had consolidated his political survival by betraying one Constantius loyalist after another. In November he had marched his Roman legions to confront Julian. Now he would lead them behind Julian.

Julian had won.

But he'd won by the most ignoble means—by slaking the army's lust for revenge on Constantius' *consistoriani*, both good and bad. Killing the honorable Ursulus was Julian's petty sop to the soldiery's humiliation at Amida. Exiling dutiful courtiers gave Arbitio and his ruthless friends a free hand in government to come.

But I pitied them their new master. I looked into the future and felt almost sorry for today's military 'victors.' They'd just accepted pitiful payment to wage Julian's campaign to come—marching Roman troops into the merciless Persian desert to flail away against King Shapur's Tigris and Euphrates strongholds.

Arbitio's wolfish expression in the fading daylight looked far from satisfied.

I suspected that Arbitio had harbored little appetite for exiling or burning old allies from Constantius' council. Even Julian's obsession with revenging Gallus was of little interest to Arbitio.

Arbitio leaned over the smoking straw. He stared at Apodemius' remains. Apodemius had stolen his most treasured possession. Apodemius had hidden away the one thing Arbitio truly wanted.

I didn't know Roxana's fate. But I was relieved I wouldn't spend the rest of my days a hunted man just because Arbitio thought I did.

In my ignorance, I was safe. I faced no more charges and no more convictions on the scribes' trailing records. Catena was dead. Eusebius was dead. Apodemius was dead. Constantius was dead. Arbitio strode out of the forum behind the others, the survivor and the loser.

Through the departing crowd, Salutius appeared a few feet behind me. He looked suddenly his true age and diminished by this last month's work.

'I don't expect we'll meet again, Numidianus. We're going now to the baths.'

'So all good Romans end their day, Saturninus Secundus Salutius, scraping off the muck that sticks to their consciences.'

He curled his lip. 'It had to be done. You'd do well yourself to wash away all memory of what happened here.'

'I will never forget. Lord Chamberlain Eusebius and Notary Paulus Catena deserved their fates. But many others were blameless civil servants. Julian could sacrifice all the hecatombs of cattle between here and Londinium and his devotions to our gods would ring hollow in my ears.'

Salutius' tone hardened. 'Keep such thoughts to yourself, Numidianus, for your own safety. Our empire will belong to Julian for decades to come. May he rule wisely. Take the advice of a man nearing the end of his useful career. Make the most of the time Apodemius has handed back to you. Forget the *agentes in rebus*. Make an honest new life for yourself.'

'I had an honest life already.'

'You nearly lost it. The Fates untwisted a rope around your neck today but their invisible weaving continues. Don't count on their kindness again.'

The officer ranks had filed out of the forum behind their commanders without so much as a glance at me. The crowd scattered away from their gruesome amusement and filed back toward the market stalls and alleys honeycombing the town.

I wandered the emptying forum in a daze, unable to collect myself or move on from the scene. Unlike these strangers, I had

—THE BURNING STAKES—

nothing more important to do but to honor the presence of Apodemius' remains.

The Britannian scribe found me on my knees, mumbling to myself, and sifting through Apodemius' ashes.

'You're cold and trembling, *Agens* Numidianus. You need a cloak. Let me help you find food and shelter. Let me take care of you.'

He dropped to his knees in the ashes next to me and thrust his freckled face into mine. 'Numidianus! You don't know yourself. What are you doing?'

'Looking for something to remember him by. Anything... anything.' I was swaying on my knees, my eyes clouded with tears and ashes. The heat scorched my fingers as they sifted—

'Stop, Numidianus! Stop! Come with me, please. You're fainting. I'll find you food—'

'Anything... help me look... this will have to do.'

I extracted a sooty, tarnished buckle from the smoking mess. It had held his *pugio* sheath to his unadorned belt. He'd worn his dagger hidden underneath his travel clothes the day we first met in Numidia in an oil merchant's private office. It was the first signal to me that the harmless old coot visiting the jovial Leontus Longus Flavius was far from harmless and that the North African oil merchant was more than a prosperous, provincial middleman.

I pocketed the relic. Its lingering heat imprinted a neat brown square onto my tunic linen.

'Where's Apollonia, Benedictus?'

'The Vestal Virgin is safe, back in Cibalae.'

Ah, yes, *the Vestal Virgin is safe in Cibalae*. I pictured her for the rest of her days, veiled as always, reading her beloved Vergilius. She faced a forlorn future, sheltered under the stalwart protection of Justina and Marina Severa. Apodemius was gone, but a life of disfigurement imprisoned her freedom forever. I wished with all my heart to see her at least once more. Her gentle voice, her sharp and educated wit, even her beautiful white hands, would have cheered and anchored me.

But she was gone, too.

Benedictus hurried off to collect my weapons from the guards. He buckled me back into my gear. He held out my boots.

'Must I return to the *scrinia* in Mediolanum? Take me back to Sirmium with you, Numidianus, please.'

'Neither, boy. My post in Sirmium no longer exists. The whole service will be shut down in weeks. Help me hurry by the fastest route back to Roma. There are things I must do before the Castra is bolted shut for good.'

Benedictus ran off to the market to wangle us travel supplies—by any means. I had to concentrate on more important things: the fate of Ahenobarbus, my promises to the litter bearer Pluto and the Blind Vestal Tullia, my care of Verus, and provisions for Kahina's desperate desire to leave the capital.

The gods who had stood by silent for so many long weeks finally whispered encouragements in my ear. The sun fell behind a cloud and a driving rain burst out over the forum all around me, swallowing up the fountain, Trajan and his horse, and the swirls of smoke spiraling up from the smoking stakes.

As I walked away, blind to whatever stood even twenty feet, I knew such clouds only needed time to lift. There was more for me to do. But as always, I lacked the patience Apodemius had always urged upon me to decode it.

At least now there still was a Marcus Gregorianus Numidianus who could listen to the gods and press patience on himself. Whatever waited to be tackled, I'd do it despite any obstacles.

I should feel grateful that I was still alive. Perhaps I'm an ingrate by nature, but within an hour of breathing clean air again, I was filled with anger, not thankfulness.

I refused to accept that I was no longer an *agens*. Julian could use Arbitio's jury to murder Apodemius on a trumped-up charge, but surely our service was more than one feisty old man. I couldn't believe Julian could kill off our service just like that, with a fraudulent trial, some purple ink, and a freshly-carved imperial seal.

My seamstress mother had always scolded me, saying I was as stubborn as one of the mules my Numidian stepfather tended.

She was right. Emperor Julian had brought out an Olympian mulishness in me today. If Julian intended to disband our *schola*, I was going to fight him until I was the last *agens* standing. But how?

Chapter 22, Verus' Testament

—Roma, March, 362 AD—

My last letter had terrified the entire household and my unannounced re-appearance at the gate deemed 'a miracle.'

I returned home to the sight of Verus lying very still in his narrow bed. He looked tiny under the thick blanket. One side of his mouth drooled, open and limp, as he snored.

On the small table next to his pillow stood an arsenal of tonics and sedative dilutions flanked by various-sized spoons for measuring and a wax tablet and *stilus* for recording each day's dosages.

Kahina had filled his windowsill with fresh flowers. But she'd also hung a small portrait of some pious saint on his wall over his beloved ivory statuette of Mars.

Commander Gregorius had given the Mars to Verus one Saturnalia during the war between Constantine II and Constans. Perhaps my father had understood even then that Verus was the pillar that propped us all up as the Senator lost his sight, Lady Laetitia her health, and my disappointed mother—the neglected seamstress slave—all hope and laughter.

I had always recognized the crude little Mars for the tacky field souvenir it was. Camp followers along the army palisades sold such figurines by the dozens to soldiers hoping for luck in battle. Verus had no notion of the gift's market value. He'd dusted and polished it ever since.

Kahina woke him up to welcome me home.

After a few seconds, Verus shook off his heavy dream and blinked up at me with huge, pleading eyes as I stood, still wearing my travel cloak, framed in his doorway.

He struggled in vain to wave his limp hand or speak a real word. So he clasped my right hand in his able one, shaking my whole arm to express relief at my return.

No one appreciated better than I that Verus had held our household together for many years during my long absences on mission for the *schola*. No one suffered more now, besides the *dispensator* himself, from his helplessness to guard our portal as before in my place.

A buxom, smiling slave came in with dishes of *puls* and mashed river fish. When he gave no reaction to the beaker of wine on his tray, I knew the cranky majordomo's spark was gone for good.

Kahina fed him spoonful by spoonful as I kept hold of his crabbed hand. Just to see one side of his face drooping slack and useless as he tried to get the food down was to break the heart of all who loved him. The cruel Fates had silenced the insolent, chirpy old fart lording it over our atrium like a Cerberus in a wine-stained leather apron.

Later, Kahina and I sat dejected in the kitchen, our heads bowed over the cook's battered table.

'Can the doctor do nothing more, Kahina?'

'Nothing. *That* was the liveliest I've seen him in weeks. He's getting worse. Don't leave us again, Marcus. If you're not here to say good-bye to him, you'll never forgive yourself as long as you live.'

'I won't go, Kahina.'

She hesitated before blurting out, 'Once he's gone, Marcus, I'll be free as well, won't I?'

'You mean to go home to Numidia?'

'Yes, Marcus, let me return home, please.'

The begging in her wide brown eyes was more wrenching to me than Verus' wordless struggle.

'Alone, Kahina? Your parents must be old or even gone by now. Leontus' twin daughters are grown and married off. Your African "home" is no more.'

'No. I still have a chance. I told you my plan. Some of us want to go to the Numidian plains—'

'—Roman holiday pilgrims! Religious tourism!'

'No! To go into the desert and live a simple Christian life.'

'Surely you're not going to rejoin those Circumcellions!'

She didn't see I was joking. She answered me carefully, as if explaining some dense ecclesiastical brief to a catechist of ten:

—THE BURNING STAKES—

'Marcus, you should embrace the truth of Christ, our Lord. Our community will live according to the creed proposed by the great Athanasius. We will follow the precepts set by the pioneering Egyptian fathers of the desert.'

I stroked her wrist. The ten-year-old wedges of scar tissue left by the Hispanic shackles of her slavery had softened with age.

'I was only joking, my dear.'

Looking at her, I measured the cost of her years in the Eternal City. She'd never succeeded in Roman society, neither as the young and fertile matron of the maimed hero Gregorianus, nor as the widow of Gregorius, the discredited rebel lost with the Usurper Magnentius.

Her lush North African figure had grown heavier over the years, but from the idle eating of unhappiness, not gluttony. No, never that sin, nor any other that I could detect.

She wore no jewelry. I suspected that long ago she'd donated her wedding jewels from the Commander to the city's poor.

She no longer dyed her hair a fashionable gold or red and had never understood fickle variations in ladies' makeup or crimped hairstyles. Finding herself always three seasons behind in Roman trends, she'd given up at last. Her unadorned tunics and *pallae* could not be dowdier.

When Leo grew too clever for his mother's simple conversation, she'd left him to *rhetor* Drusus and his football. She made new friends among other devotees of the Church. Of course, they weren't the glamorous society ladies who donated whole estates and made extravagant pilgrimages to Jerusalem. She was left to admire such celebrities from afar.

But at least some of her Church acquaintances seemed genuine in their faith and showed compassion for her simplicity with their companionship. My fears that some unscrupulous cleric would wangle the Manlius estates from Leo through a trick of theological seduction had faded by now.

'Would you leave this spring if Verus—?'

I couldn't bring myself to finish.

'Yes. I've already promised my friends that we could leave Roma and use the Ostia apartment while we wait for the right ship. Imagine, Marcus, if we had favorable winds, I'd be landing in Carthago only a few weeks from now.'

Her face lit up for an instant, then she frowned.

'That would be all right with you, wouldn't it, Marcus? If we used the Ostia rooms?'

'Of course, it would be all right, Kahina. The Ostia apartment is yours for as long as you want.'

'I was always happier by the sea, away from these crowds and confusion. Roma is so . . . so . . .'

I put a protective arm around her shoulder with a reassuring squeeze. What had happened to the lively Numidian girl who'd seduced the young *volo* Marcus one night among the wild Circumcellions in 347? Where had she gone, that would-be martyr who gave herself to my passionate embrace because she was about to die for her Christ?

In a way, Kahina had martyred herself anyway. For our unborn son, she'd made good on her Numidian parents' promise she would marry the Commander. She'd kept Leo's true parentage a closely held secret through years of lonely nights. She'd never blamed any of us for her years of bewildering abuse as a prisoner taken in civil war. She'd struggled on after her rescue with crippled ankles, a flayed back, and a blunted mind ever since.

Her Christ had suffered and sacrificed Himself for others and therefore so should she. I'd heard from various neighbors that 'Leo's mother' was often glimpsed on her rounds, tending the sick and destitute in Church institutions between the Esquiline and sanctuaries as far as the northeast side of the Tiberis.

If the Galilean's suffering comforted her somehow, she more than deserved the happiness in Numidia she longed for.

'Do you want me to come with you as far as Ostia?'

'No, thank you, Marcus. I prefer to travel with my friends.'

'Am I not even a friend to you, Kahina?' My voice cracked. 'I'm Leo's father, after all. Doesn't that make me your closest friend in the world?'

Tears streaked my tired face, but she merely shook her head and laid a roughened palm on my cheek.

'Of course, you're my friend and protector, Marcus, but you belong to your service. You always have. My closest friend is our Lord, Jesus Christ.'

—THE BURNING STAKES—

※※※

I hadn't forgotten my promise to the bereaved litter bearer Pluto, whose son had died in our service without recognition or honors paid.

Time was short with the Castra closing for good in a matter of days. *Magister* Otho had gone to Constantinopolis to collect his promotion for being so instrumental in engineering the end of the service. A detachment from Julian's Celtae auxiliaries had marched in formation across our courtyard to take possession of the dormitory cells.

Pluto was an elusive man to locate but I sent messages through a murky underground of bearers, starting with the brotherhood stationed under the arches of the Aqua Claudia and spreading through the great city from the Subura slums all the way out to the northeastern villas with their unsullied river views.

Eventually Pluto answered my invitation.

'Why were you no longer at your station?' I asked him when he appeared one night under our fig tree on the Esquiline Hill.

'I answered to only one customer,' Pluto replied, 'and now he's dead.'

Only then did I realize that this humble man with his scarred arms and calloused feet had served for many years as Apodemius' trusted means of slipping away from the Castra every single morning. Not only was his son a veteran of our service deserving of recognition—the father had been one of our most essential colleagues for decades—and none of us had ever known.

Before Julian's orders to evacuate the Castra could take full effect, I mustered some fifty *agentes* to attend a small memorial in the family's honor.

We lit incense and listened as our chief archivist, Arsenio, recited the few details of Gaius' short service as a cadet rider. He'd been killed on a lonely stretch along the Danubian shore for nothing more than his horse. His ashes had been interred by a *riparienses* unit in Posonium. One of our riders had brought the urn back to Roma at my request in time for our ceremony.

But no *agens* listening to the biography of the humble rider could deny that we might as well be interring the *agentes in rebus* service itself with our prayers.

Our eunuch instructor Einku applied a flame to the incense.

Ahenobarbus, still frail, said it would be his honor to nail up the bronze plaque I'd ordered for the Temple wall. Below the murdered Gaius' name, I'd added a quotation from Horatio, '*Eques ipso melior Bellerophonte,* A Better Horseman than Bellerophon himself.'

As I read it out, comparing his son to the master of the mythical horse Pegasus, tears coursed in deep rivulets down the bearer's cheeks as unhindered and unremarked as the man himself had trotted barefoot along our city streets all these years, anonymous and unrewarded.

We all embraced him in turn and, in a melancholic file, left the Temple of Jupiter Redux. We had dodged out of the blustery February wind and into this dark sanctuary as *agentes*. But within the next few days, we would all be required to turn in our identification papers and insignia for good.

Death, death, death—it was all around me, from the memory of the stench of Eusebius' melting lard lingering my nostrils to the grief I felt every day I returned home to see Verus waiting, wordless and immobile, for my day's 'news.'

One day, I was droning on with my tedious account of another day of watching the Castra being dismantled when I noticed Verus' eyelids drooping. His attention wandered. I broke off to tell him:

'Verus, listen to me. You awake? Good. Now that you can't stop me, I've made an unusual decision. Before our nine days of *novendialis* mourning for your stringy old carcass are up, I promise I'll order an *imago* of your face made in wax to hang out there on the atrium wall with all the Manlius ancestors.'

I laid a hand on his chest to calm him. 'No, no, stay put. You can't stop me now—I already ordered a bronze plaque with your *titulus* and years of service. It arrived from the engravers yesterday.'

He trembled with excitement.

'All right, I'll get it.'

I fetched the plaque still wrapped in the engraver's protective embroidered red flannel. Its sheen reflected the oil lamp flame as brightly as Kahina's toilet mirror. Verus traced his name with a finger and ran his roughed palm over the surface. His head bobbed uncontrollably as he clutched it to him with his good arm.

'So, I guess you'll be watching over us forever, hanging right there next to the *imagines* of the Commander and the old Senator. Whenever Leo, then his children, and then his grandchildren pass on their way to the winter *triclinium*, they'll say, *That old bird over there? That was Verus, the best dispensator the Manlius domus ever had.*'

Verus' good hand shook to let go of the plaque and reaching for me, waved in feeble protest. His eyes widened and with half of his mouth, he gave me thanks.

I laughed. 'Oh, I would have told you before this, but you're the kind of obstinate, old-fashioned coot who'd keep taking it down off the wall every time I left Roma, telling the staff it wasn't the "done thing".'

He gave a grunt for a laugh. I wiped the spit off his bristly chin. Then he held the plaque to his chest and closed his eyes.

I've heard it said that there is a moment in many lives when a peaceful man's soul beckons him to turn his face to the wall for release into the next world. The day I returned from the Temple of Jupiter Redux ceremony for the bearer's son, Kahina greeted me outside the gate. I looked at her face—a mix of relief and sorrow—and suspected what awaited me.

Verus had turned his face to the wall.

'He won't drink, Marcus. He won't eat. He won't even open his eyes. He just lies there, but he's not asleep. I know he isn't.'

'No, he's not asleep. He's breathing and his heart is steady.'

We sat on either side of the old man's bed. The spring evening's pink glow faded outside his window. One by one, the slaves came to see him one last time. The lithe Drusilla brought him a cup of wine, but he didn't respond to her insistence he take at least a sip or two.

After I was sure that everyone had had their chance to say good-bye, I drew the curtain on his window and Kahina lit a lamp on the table beside his pillow. It was too dark to see his features but still we sat there in silence, missing his gruff, bossy ways.

The doctor Sofas came, summoned by our cook.

'How long has he been like this?' he asked.

'Since yesterday afternoon,' Kahina said. 'He wouldn't take his evening meal and today—'

Sofus gave her a gentle smile. 'No, *Domina*, I meant, how long has Verus been dead?'

We'd sat there in a trance of grief so deep that Verus slipped across the River Styx as modestly as he'd served us all those decades.

This winter I'd seen Constantius II die overhearing the calculating whispers of sycophants outside this tent, Paulus Catena die abused like a mutilated animal, Eusebius die to the jeering laughter of coarse strangers, and Apodemius die in defiant, if dignified, self-sacrifice.

But who could not believe in our true gods when one saw they were kindest to deserving Verus?

I slipped a coin as 'Charon's obol' between Verus' dead lips to pay the ferryman rowing him to the underworld.

The satirist Lucian once joked that to avoid death, a clever Roman should just refuse to pay the fare. But Verus was beyond saving by mythical tricks. This very minute, he would be regaling the tireless boatman with a pointed introduction of how notable his passenger was, despite the stained leather apron, in the scheme of aristocratic Roman domestic history.

'You can take the rest of these medicines with you,' I told Sofus as I paid his outstanding fees, 'if they're of any use to your other patients.'

The doctor sorted through the tumble of vials and powders. He handed me the fanciest, a large blue glass bottle encased in gold filigree with a gilt cork stopper.

'This one isn't mine,' he said, 'People take it for painful hips and stiffening joints, but it is useless, overpriced huggermugger.'

'It looks expensive.'

He chuckled. 'That it is. I'm surprised at you, Numidianus. This stuff is from one of those quack magicians who takes in all the gullible *ignorami* of the Subura. Costs a small fortune and does no good at all.'

So that explained the clumsy 'theft' of our missing *Cicero* and Soren's reluctance to tell me the truth.

I cursed myself for having been such a blind fool. Kahina would never have got my permission to waste *solidi* on a quack's tonic. She knew better than to ask. Long ago, we'd settled on her allowance for Church donations on top of regular household expenses.

So desperate to ease Verus' suffering, she'd given up the Senator's treasure without a moment's hesitation for a blue bottle of sugar syrup.

⚜⚜⚜

Verus had no relative to seal the passing of his spirit, so Kahina performed the last kiss and closed his eyes. The servants began their lamentations, calling for Verus by name. After his body was prepared, he lay in state in the atrium for two days with his feet pointed toward the front gate, silent after a lifetime of filling the atrium with his good-natured curses and cusses.

Finally, it was time to prepare Verus' room for his successor. I put off the task for many weeks until, alone one evening while the household slept, I crept into his empty room and unlocked his dusty trunk with the key Kahina had entrusted to me the day she left.

Verus probably thought he would live forever, like some death-defying god sent to look after the rest of us. At any rate, he left no written will. It fell to me to examine his belongings for gifts to the household.

Thank the gods I was alone.

I leaned back on my haunches and closed my eyes in distress at the sight. Inside his simple chest lay my mother's long-forgotten festival tunic, worn on the days she curled her thinning black hair with the heated tongs of a *calamistrum* and traded her house slippers for what she always called with her Numidian lisp, 'city shoeth.'

I faltered for a moment, collected myself and then lifted out the garment still fragrant with lingering traces of her bath oil. I found her well-preserved street shoes underneath, then her single necklace of African obsidian, the one she wore in hope and excitement to the Roman slave market the day we two were sold.

It was the last day she believed my father was buying his Numidian lover and their son out of affection, rather than childless necessity.

'Oh, Verus,' I whispered. 'You loved her all these years?'

My mother's dreams had died in these back rooms. She'd treated Verus as the household rube, no more than a sidekick for the cook to spoil. Had he never dared to make his feelings know?

Underneath my mother's best belongings, carefully wrapped in unspoiled silk he must have spent weeks' of wages on, Verus had packed away some of my childhood toys.

Perhaps he had intended to pass them on to Leo? Had the moment slipped by as he watched the Commander spoil Leo with the best toys Roman markets could offer? Or perhaps he'd hoped someday to give them to a child of his own?

Here was the miniature centurion he and I had carved together from a block of soft wood he brought into the kitchen one day when I was no older than ten. Not a splinter had changed; the homemade glue holding the red scrap of cloak we tied over his uneven shoulders cracked as I fingered it.

And there was my boat, another homemade wooden toy that we launched in the fountain basin in the atrium when the house was empty of Manlius grandees. Lady Laetitia's nephew, the troublemaker Clodius, had stolen this boat once but we got it back. After that, Verus kept it hidden away for fear of more trouble.

Nobody in the Manlius family had made toys with Clodius. All his playthings were bought down in the expensive markets, then broken and discarded within months. How he'd hated me—the seamstress' slave boy, the Commander's *delicatus*. I was allowed to stay up late while Gregorius entertained his fellow officers. My thick bronze curls were ruffled by veterans' goodnatured paws as I refilled their ornate goblets.

At the bottom of Verus' trunk lay a set of 'best clothes' still bearing faint price marks inside the hems. Even during Saturnalia, Verus had never worn this fine linen tunic shirt, this shiny belt, or these silk underclothes. I spread the trousers out on his empty bed. They were made of goatskin pounded thin as papyrus, as good as any Eastern tribune's.

I guessed why he'd never unwrapped these treasures in wool and silk and suede. This was meant to be his wedding suit.

I understand as never before the pleading expression in those dying eyes as he gazed at me in the doorway the day I returned from Chalcedon. How he'd worried for me all these years spent guessing the dangers I faced and lying to Kahina and Leo that I was safe delivering some governor's mail.

In his mind, I might be the Commander's bastard, but in his heart, my mother was his great love and he saw himself as my father.

I whispered to his spirit filling the darkened room, 'Better than my real sire, you lovable old crank.'

There was a loud pounding on our gate but the *ostiarius* was fast asleep. Before anyone was roused, I tossed down the trousers and answered the door myself.

In the cool, peaceful breeze, the bookseller Soren waited under our looming fig tree. He'd wrapped up tight, but looked old, shivering in the dim circle of a street torch. He was rubbing his chin, wondering whether anyone was still up or whether he'd climbed the steep Esquiline for nothing.

'You ply your trade at odd hours these days!' I said, ushering him into the warm vestibule. 'If you think we're selling anything, someone's played you a hoax, Bookseller.'

He pulled a long package out from under his cloak and offered it to me.

I raised one inquiring eyebrow.

He nodded. It was Senator Manlius' *Cicero*.

'How much?'

He shrugged. 'Keep it.'

'I'm grateful but I don't want to owe you, Soren. I'm not asking for any favors.'

'Forget it. We're both getting old, Numidianus. You'll be looking at forty soon and I'm well past sixty. What did Cicero cry out to the Republican Senate in despair? *O, tempora, O Mores*? The times are indeed changing on us. Who would have thought I couldn't sell an original *Cicero* with Senator Manlius' *marginalia*?'

'I can't believe that.'

'The market's dying out from under me. I'll be retiring soon, leaving the stock in the luxury shop to my daughter, and moving south. This is my last winter in Roma.'

'*No one* would buy it?'

He chuckled and waved farewell as he loped back down the sleeping street toward his musty office.

I wanted to believe Soren was lying about the value of our *Cicero* out of backhanded generosity. Perhaps he'd heard rumors from neighborhood gossips or rival book collectors as to why Kahina wanted money on the sly. Perhaps he'd taken pity on the Manlius house.

It would be almost sadder if Soren weren't lying to me. I knew Soren's reputation as a ruthless dealer. Pity on any book collector fallen on hard times had never been his weakness.

The greatest minds of Roma no longer held their sway? I couldn't be sure Soren wasn't telling me the sorry truth.

Chapter 23, Apodemius' Legacy

—Roma, April, 362 AD—

As soon as I reached Roma, even before I had tackled the Manlius estates' neglected business affairs, I sent one of our most trusted slaves with a note to the Blind Vestal Tullia's echoing marble villa on the Via Nomentana. I hadn't forgotten my promise of December. I was ready to come and read to her as regularly as she liked. I invited her to name her first author. I would return to her, the child slave Marcus alive in my memory, reading to a sightless venerable once again.

Tullia didn't answer. For a few weeks, I was too busy to think more of it. But indeed, I intended to repay my debt and wrote her again at the end of February.

Again, there was no answer.

I began to worry. It's easy to forget how fragile our old people become after sixty. Tullia was possibly ill cared for, perhaps even friendless, in that great house with her skeletal staff. She might have even died during the harsh winter.

I wrote a third note, requesting any recipient of my letter explain her silence and insisting that, without a prompt reply, I would visit the Via Nomentana estate in person.

She sent back a note in handwriting I suspected belonged to her Numidian doorman.

'It is not yet opportune,' it read. I accepted that I must be patient until Tullia decided it was 'opportune.'

The moment came one blustery spring night. I was alone, wrapped in a thick blanket and reading in the Senator's old study, when one of the slave girls interrupted my peace to announce a 'Berber' outside our gate.

Tullia's Numidian stood barefoot in the wet fig leaves blown to the pavement by the snapping wind. Behind him waited the litter bearer Pluto and his partner. The slave handed me a note, hardly legible in the storm.

'This evening is opportune.'

Opportune for her perhaps, but it was a miserable night for social calls otherwise. Half of Roma was hiding in bed, taking any warm body near to hand. The other half huddled, drinking behind shuttered doors and pulled curtains, arguing and dicing away their spring sneezes and chills.

At last Pluto's litter reached the villa, looking as abandoned and dark as the tombs and *mausolea* lining that famous road.

Cypress trees along the curving drive up to the villa entrance swayed and whipped in the high wind. I scraped wet leaves off my boots before crossing the vestibule. The Numidian carried a small oil lamp to guide our steps. Ankles jingling as before, he led me along the peristyle courtyard awash with rain that extinguished his flame. We continued past an unused winter *triclinium* fitted out in last century's style and, finally, entered a small carpeted room. It was furnished with shabby couches and low cushioned benches warmed only by a brazier with red coals glowing like cat's eyes.

'Identify yourself,' said a woman's voice from the shadows.

'Is that you, *Domina Tullia*?'

Talking into a nearly black void reminded me too much of the storeroom I'd shared with the mad Catena.

'I'm glad to find you as before, *Domina*. I'll need more light than this to read by.'

'Leave him your lamp,' Tullia told her Numidian. He rekindled the flame and placed the shoe-shaped pottery on the floor before jingling away to a dry bed in the slaves' quarters. He'd trotted all those miles alongside my litter bearers and wanted no more of me.

'It's still not bright enough to read by, *Domina*.'

'You aren't here to read books, Numidianus. You couldn't visit before now because you were watched—you, your household, and all your friends and clients. You've been spied on since your return from the East by men selected from Julian's most trusted units left behind in the West.'

'A waste of effort.'

'And your innocent comportment has been utterly convincing. Apodemius trained you well.'

—THE BURNING STAKES—

'I've deceived no one. My days could not be more innocent. I tend the Manlius estates full time. When I leave Roma for a few days, it's for business concerning our docks and warehouses in Ostia or meetings with merchants halfway between our holdings in the south and north.'

'And now any suspicious are put to rest. You're deemed harmless.'

'I am harmless, *Domina*.'

Did I detect a slight smile on those shadowed features?

'With the service gone, my only duty is to the Manlius family.'

The Vestal turned on her bench and rubbed her knobby knuckles over the heat of her brazier.

'Well, I have summoned you here to read, Numidianus, but not Homer.' She chuckled, staring six inches above my eyebrows. 'Another time, perhaps. But I doubt you'll have the leisure from now on.'

'I'll always make time for you, *Domina Tullia*.'

'This wet weather makes an old woman's joints ache. Let me get to the point. For centuries, we Vestals have guarded the wills of great men—all the emperors, good and bad, but lesser men, too. *Magister* Apodemius entrusted his will to me. You're his only legal beneficiary, Marcus Gregorianus Numidianus. Take it from my hand, and read.'

The great villa was silent, except for rain pounding on the darkened atrium skylights. The bells tied to her slaves were stilled by sleep. Only the wet lashing of the towering cypresses filled the gardens outside with movement.

Tullia handed me a roll of papyrus tied with simple packing string and sealed with a plain blob of common red wax. No document could look more innocuous. It might have been a deed to a doghouse. I lifted the oil lamp closer and read a few paragraphs.

'But Apodemius writes here that he bequeaths me the *schola*—a government department that no longer exists and was never in his private possession. Was he well in his mind? Did he write this before he knew the extent of Otho's so-called reforms?'

'Well before.'

'And even if the Castra flourished in those days, this legacy or appointment isn't his to make. The *magister officiorum* always selected the new *magister agentium in rebus*.'

'Which will never happen under Emperor Julian,' she said with a sigh. 'So it is just as I suspected. Apodemius bequeaths you his job.'

'Then he bequeaths me nothing. Why?'

'One would think you don't see any better than I do, *Agens*! Months before Constantius died, Apodemius foresaw the inevitable. He knew full well that, if ever you held this in your hands as you do tonight, then the *schola* and he himself had been destroyed by Julian. I was told to keep this until the day I was sure his legacy could be conveyed to you in complete safety and secrecy.'

'And therefore, without the necessary legal witnesses?'

'You don't understand. This deep and unorthodox act is made necessary by our troubled times. Apodemius chose me as its guardian, not only because I was a Vestal, but because I'm blind and could not tamper with it without an accomplice. Finish reading.'

'He writes there is little physical property to be transferred to my custodianship. What remains is secured in trust. Here? By yourself?'

'No, Numidianus. Not here. I guard nothing else. Read on and perhaps we'll understand better.'

'He bequeaths to me the sole right and privilege as his chosen successor to rebuild the *schola*. But why me? And using what?'

'Perhaps it's enough for now that he's anointed you. He trusts you to find a way. For the sake of the service you loved, you must accept this honor.'

'But how? The Castra Peregrina is bolted against us. Military officers in the East have taken over the *Cursus* and postal hubs. Otho has gone on to greater glory serving Julian in Constantinopolis. Only one genuine *agens* will be appointed to liaise with his army officers taking our place—some twenty Petulantes. We await his nomination, but you can be certain it won't be me.'

—THE BURNING STAKES—

'Then for the moment, prepare. Gather only your most trusted fellow *agentes*. If Emperor Julian thinks he can replace the *schola* with a gaggle of untrained auxiliaries, you can start with half a dozen seasoned *agentes in rebus*, and build up from there.'

'In secret?'

'Until Julian sees the error of his arrogance or his reign is cut short by—'

'Stop. To say more would be treason, *Domina*. I'm still too fresh from the ordeal in Chalcedon to allow you to utter another word, even at midnight in an empty house.'

'You're right. The Fates will decide his reign. Is that all he writes?' Her voice warbled with age and fatigue.

I read on in silence. I was afraid that even her brazier had ears. The next paragraph referred to care of Apollonia. That was honor enough.

But a startling appendix followed the main body of his testament. It contained the darkest of secrets—the information for which Arbitio was ready to kill—the former *agens* Roxana was alive after all and Apodemius confided her hiding place.

The tightly lettered clauses explained what I had often suspected but never dared ask.

Roxana was not only the object of the late General Silvanus' illicit affection and General Arbitio's thwarted lust. She was not only what Apodemius had called with pained frustration, 'his failed experiment' in training a female *agens*.

Roxana was common, humble human property—but whose?

I knew that when fleeing General Arbitio's cruel habits, Roxana had begged our *schola* for shelter and training. Now I read why. She had hinted some of this in Agrippina during her happiest days as consort and empress-designate to General Silvanus. Apodemius' document filled in more sordid details: my old training partner had started life an enslaved child whoring in a down-at-heels *caupona*. The married Arbitio met her there while carousing one night with other slumming military bigwigs.

He bought her for his own singular pleasure—the pittance was specified.

Week by week and month by month, the balding, arrogant *consistorianus* had grown intoxicated with his enjoyment of the lithe, quick-witted brunette. Alarmed by his growing obsessions and mounting abuses, the barefoot girl had fled one night to our Castra gates with nothing more than a flimsy night tunic covering her bruised body.

Apodemius had advanced her money against her wages to purchase her freedom from Arbitio. But when Apodemius' packet of cash arrived at his door, Arbitio just pocketed it as 'partial compensation' for temporary 'loss and damages.' Arbitio wouldn't sell Roxana to any man or service, no matter how worthy.

Why did Apodemius' testament contain such astonishing details? Because what I also held in my hand were Apodemius' arguments and evidence for a longstanding lawsuit between our *schola* and General Arbitio over his missing property—one runaway, Roxana of Tarsus. The appeals and defenses had mushroomed into bitter legal warfare until, suddenly, real civil war had eclipsed their courtroom battles.

I glanced over at Tullia. She couldn't see my welling tears of pity for my friend and rival Roxana. Fifteen years ago, I'd known the exhilaration of earning my manumission, bloodied and embittered as it was, in the field.

Poor Roxana had served but been despised, loved even as she despaired. She, too, had strived but remained bound. Crippled for life by her brave actions in Agrippina and brokenhearted by the loss of her beloved Franco-Roman hero—even after all that, she was still not liberated.

I folded up the papers. Thanks to his political bargain with Emperor Julian and his triumph in Chalcedon over Eusebius and Apodemius, General Arbitio stood more powerful than ever. Roxana of Tarsus could never again breath freely on this side of the River Tiberis.

The Blind Vestal waited. The brazier's red glow gave her withered profile the look of a wise old bird crowned with coils of elaborate, braided feathers.

'Why do you sigh, *Agens*?'

'Apodemius bequeaths me mere women—one to be my helpless ward and one whom I now discover is a runaway slave.'

She snapped at me: '*Mere women*? Was Apodemius mistaken in his trust? Are you just another ignorant Roman male who sees women as lesser humans? Remember, Numidianus, please remember to whom you're speaking. Our history of proud service to the Empire has lasted many centuries longer than your precious line of *agentes*.'

'No, please, you misunderstand me, *Domina*. First, Apodemius appoints me *tutor mulierum* for Apollonia, the Veiled Vestal, until she marries. Some action of his harmed her family and personal prospects long ago.'

'Is that all you know?'

'That's enough. *Tutela mulierum*—that ancient custom is all but obsolete!'

'Yes, yes, but consider Apollonia's condition. He had to consign her to another man's protection under law sooner or later, though that must have been the hardest thing to do in his long life.'

'Apollonia is too great a responsibility for me. In her plight, her permanent disability, she needs constant assistance and companionship. Should we not place her with Flavia in Mediolanum?'

'No. We must trust Apodemius in this. And that young woman might prove far less helpless in future. In fact, I guarantee it. But that is for Apollonia to decide.'

'She's brave and formidable, I confess. She's so brave and surprising, she unsettles and confuses my emotions.'

'And the other?'

'The second woman I dare not name, even to you, *Domina*. She was one of the finest *agentes* I've ever known—always too much for me to handle. Beside her I felt a *mere* man. She outwitted all of us, even Apodemius. Once her heart had settled on a mate, she loved enough for two women. But I insist, she is too much for me, even now that I know how she suffers.'

Tullia straightened her shabby headdress with impatience. The noise of the storm tired her. My excuses and hesitation annoyed her. My obvious bewilderment confused her. It was late and she seemed to be asking herself: why had Apodemius ever entrusted his cherished legacy to such an incompetent nincompoop as this North African?

She stood up and rang a tiny bell that hung from her belt for assistance to her bed.

'You cannot refuse Apodemius' legacy. He chose you for reasons that will become clear soon enough.'

'Perhaps because he knew I had money at my disposal—far too much on hand for a freedman left idle.'

'True, rebuilding a secret service will cost something. But it can't be a question of funds alone. The only sort of man you should recruit would serve the Empire for free. No, it must be more than a question of money. Wait. And while you wait, study the situation and prepare your trusted team.'

※※※

I called our first meeting a month later in the busiest, least suspicious corner of Roma—Cassius' greasy *popina* where we jostled between the crush of our city's lowest caste of customers—coffin-makers, burglars, and beggars.

I'd chosen my co-conspirators guided by Apodemius' example: you don't favor men for their strengths alone. You select them for all their points—both good and bad. Then you exploit their weaknesses to best purpose.

For all men are human and flawed, even *agentes in rebus* trained by the best professionals in the civilized world. The *magister* who employs their faults for the good of the *schola* is well armed against enemies who aim first at our Achilles Heels.

Had not Apodemius flattered my pride in my memory for books so that I'd recite back stolen reports verbatim? Hadn't he exploited my inability to stay out of trouble only so as to have his man in the midst of any fray?

Who were my new *agentes*? How to manage them best?

Rufus arrived at the *popina* first, always a shade over-dutiful. He was a restless, insecure man whose weakness was excessive loyalty to authority. Yes, he'd spied and reported on my movements to Otho. But now I was his last genuine superior standing—not the discredited Otho. I harbored no more fears for Rufus' fidelity.

Rufus loved more than anything to travel far on horseback, so I'd offered him charge of gathering fresh assets, information, and even recruits stretching between our two western capitals just short of Sirmium—where Julian's East began.

Cassius arrived next and ordered himself a large pitcher of honeyed *mulsum* with a platter of greasy sausages. He apologized in hushed and hurried tones to me for the third time running. He still felt abashed at how his indiscretion with the eunuch Chryseros in Mediolanum had nearly cost me our vital contact with Apodemius.

Only the gods knew where Chryseros had fled, now that Julian had cleansed all the courts of eunuchs.

Meanwhile, Cassius remained sharp-eyed, at both dice and life. He would never change his stripes to become an upstanding *paterfamilias*. But unlike Gaudentius, Cassius was not a thug by nature. He had the soul of a casual, clever cheat, but not an assassin. He was better suited to haunting society's underbelly in hotter, more exotic Roman terrain than Italia.

For the time being, I decided, Cassius should enjoy putting his petty dishonesties to good use by testing the integrity of other men who might prove useful. He had agreed to be our regional man along the eastern Hispanic coast down to Carthago in Roman Africa. He would steer shy of Numidia's border with Egypt. Alexandria was a hotbed of religious gossip and geographically too close to Julian's network of loyalists to be safe for our new setup.

Moreover, I promised to back Cassius' gambling losses— within reason—out of the Manlius accounts to make sure no one would ever buy him again.

Ahenobarbus arrived, leaning on the arm of our young Britannian. There was a quiet steadiness to Ahenobarbus that I needed, complemented by an enthusiastic gratitude from the boy who would rejuvenate us all.

'Do we need this extra stool?' Benedictus asked.

'Leave it for the moment,' I said. 'I expect one more *agens*, brought out of retirement under a work name. To any of you who suspect this veteran's previous identity, I bind you to an oath to bury all knowledge of it.'

Ahenobarbus lifted an eyebrow at me. He knew only too well Gaudentius' high-end habits of careerism upsetting our plans— whatever his adopted work name.

A new man sat with us, a stranger to everyone but me. But Grifo's pedigree was beyond reproach. He'd been sent from Agrippina by our defector, the late General Silvanus' son Junius. All of us except Benedictus had known Grifo's esteemed father, Meroveus, a castrated ex-captive-of-war who'd served the *agentes* well and died fighting for truth.

I delegated Grifo to link our group to the corridor of garrisons along the volatile Rhenus up to the northern delta and over to the weakened capital of Treverorum.

To a man, each swore secrecy on his lost insignia. We waited, our conversation subdued on the margins of the anonymous hubbub around us. After some minutes, the others began to discuss division of their responsibilities, to compare notes on how best to evade detection, and whether this or that former *agens* could be brought into service on terms of partial or total trust.

The extra stool remained empty next to Benedictus, like a three-legged rebuke of my judgment.

The other five could see I'd made a mistake with that invitation. What we were planning was outright treason and putting our lives at stake. An invitation refused implied a possible breach in our security.

Were we already betrayed?

It was a stumble that didn't bode well for my leadership. It showed me to be susceptible to nostalgia for the heady days when the Castra corridor thrived with classes and the shabby canteen with comradeship.

I noticed as the minutes dripped off the *popina*'s crude water clock that no one spoke the one name foremost in our shared memory.

We missed his mice, his fumbling around his great map of the Empire, and his stinking liniments. Perhaps we didn't miss his nocturnal working hours. But no one wanted to hear again what I'd witnessed in Chalcedon. No one wanted to believe him dead. But there was nothing to do now but honor his trust. They translated their regard for his memory into respect for his written legacy to me.

One could not allow sentimental comparisons to weaken our precarious beginnings. For who knew how long Julian's reign would last? We faced many years of hard-nosed, stealthy labor, with no thanks from anyone. Our tiny band of impromptu *agentes* would require a steely, discreet resolve and ironclad trust.

'Right, let's begin,' I said in a low voice. I kicked the empty stool aside and we hunched together, half-a-dozen heads bent low over the table.

'Benedictus has agreed to start a new *scrinia* from what information we possess and can muster between ourselves—road guides, biographies of all officials and officers we've worked with, knowledge of regional Churchmen and *curiales* in any towns we know well, our glossaries of the border dialects, our lists of the men running the weapons *fabricae*, mints, tax collection hubs, regional markets—the lot.'

'In short, everything we've learned in our years of riding and working the *Cursus*?'

'Exactly, Rufus. We tell our scribe here everything or lend him whatever we've got. He'll copy and collate it.'

'That will take him months, if not years.' Rufus shifted in his stool. Reconstructing the Castra archives was not his idea of action.

'Ahenobarbus has put his name forward as the official liaison man advising Julian's team in Constantinopolis on its takeover of the postal and road management. Otho is sure to endorse him. As *princeps*, he made all the right contacts and kept his hands clean. Thanks to his arrest of Barbatio, he'll pass scrutiny easily and be our vital spy on the official system.'

Ahenobarbus gave an ironic, wry smile.

'So the rest of us must avoid visible contact with Ahenobarbus,' Cassius said. 'He mustn't be contaminated by association with us.'

Ahenobarbus nodded his agreement. He'd survived Catena's vicious blade, but the damage to his gullet was tragic. He had trouble speaking, eating, and even at times, breathing. Emperor Julian would be sure to underestimate the wit and guile of the *princeps officii* chosen as his disabled stoodge fronting for the transition.

We agreed to meet next on the Ides of July, at the same hour in a different city. I paid our hefty tab and looked at the empty stool with regret one last time.

The stool was seized by a reddened hand.

'Sorry I'm tardy. I had trouble with my horse.'

The latecomer plopped next to Cassius, pulled back the thick woolen *cucullus* of a Goth tribesman's hunting cloak from a weathered face, and offered Ahenobarbus a brave smile.

The *princeps* clasped her calloused hand to his lips in silent welcome. I would not have known her had I not recognized her voice.

'I thought we'd lost you,' Ahenobarbus croaked.

'I have lost myself among a strange people,' Roxana said. 'When I received Marcus' summons, I realized I might be useful to you now. Do any of you remember the old man's wall map of the unexplored lands and the uncivilized peoples north of the Danuvius?'

I said, 'Apodemius once warned me that the Gothic tribes—not the Persians—may pose the greatest danger to Roma. For unlike the Persians who have religion, art, literature, and history like ourselves, the Goths are not civilized, not as we understand the word. Yet in their straggling caravans and pathetic wagon trains, they rove along our borders, pushed from behind by other peoples of whom we know nothing.'

'Not civilized?' Benedictus saw only a coarsened, uneducated female across the table. 'But the great missionary Ufilas has converted many Goths with his translation of our Bible into their tongue!'

Roxana frowned down her nose at the boy's disdainful tone. She lifted his right hand to the lamplight.

'This little bunion on your third finger tells me you're a scribe. Perhaps you'll better understand if I explain that I survive among a people who would make your average Alemannic or Frankish brigand look like Marcus Aurelius.'

'You've become an *arcanus*, Roxana?' Cassius stared at her in awe.

Few *agentes* ever encountered this rare specimen of informant. *Arcani* took more risks than any of us. They spent their entire lives traveling incognito among savages and declared enemies outside the Empire.

Few were dispatched into such service and fewer excelled. Sooner or later, most were lost to the Castra forever, their communication links with Roma broken and their service unmemorialized.

'Please,' she corrected him, '*Arcana*.'

'You're a *Goth*?' Benedictus asked.

'No, I'm still a Roman, boy. But I am safer among those free men and women than here in this great city. I cannot stay long, Marcus. You understand why. But your group will not lose touch with me.'

I could see the Britannian was finding it hard to accept Roxana as one of us. But he dared not object when she continued:

'And brothers, I promise you the kind of information that haunts Roman nightmares—of Goth ambitions, Alan pillage and slaughter, and punishing raids on these two barbarian peoples by far more ferocious men riding in from vast plains beyond. The Goths and Alans flee these flat-eyed, cone-headed men who eat raw meat tenderizing under their saddles. They never sleep under roofs, only wagons. They're faster archers than any Sagittarian and such bow-legged horsemen from infancy, they can hardly walk on their own two feet.'

I nodded. 'Apodemius once called them the Xiong, but said they were a rumor, a myth.'

She gave me a wry smile. Her right incisor was broken.

'They're no rumor, Numidianus. I have fled them myself, twice. They are a civilized man's nightmare. Better Shapur himself sits in state over half our empire than these horsemen reach Roma.'

'That'll never happen!' Cassius scoffed.

'No? Thousands of Germans—whole tribes—talk of seeking safety within Roman borders. Even the bravest Goth shudders when he mentions them by another name—the *Huns*.'

I raised my cup to our traveler. 'As for names, let no one speak your true name, now or ever. How should we toast you from now on?'

'The deadliest female in Roman history was the *Augusta* Livia.'

'Then welcome to our secret *schola*, Livia,' I said.

One by one, we six men embraced her with all our hearts.

Chapter 24, Apollonia's Fire

—Roma, June, 362 AD—

I'd been traveling on business for three weeks, settling troublesome contract disputes with beef and ham merchants and whiling away too many hours buying drinks for tax collectors in the hope of lower assessments on our Baiae oyster beds. And always, on the sly, I kept my eyes open for potential *agentes* to propose at our July rendezvous.

When I returned home to the Esquiline Hill that summer night, I was ready for a large glass of good wine and a clean bed.

Our new *ostiarius* unbolted the great oak gates and told me a letter from Leo had arrived from Burdigala.

Nothing could ease my testy mood better than some fresh gossip about his social climbing teacher Ausonius and student life in the far Gallic west. The boy's rhetorical style was improving to my satisfaction, but it was his sketches of people and events that gave me the greatest joy. He'd learned much from reading the letters of great men in the Senator's study.

No sooner had I tossed my workaday *sagum* at the vestibule slave than I stubbed my toe on an enormous box left in the shadow of the archway leading to the wine cave.

Six similar travel trunks blocked my passage through the narrow *fauces* into the house.

'Clear these away. Deliveries come through the back gate into the kitchen or through the summer *triclinium*, as usual. You're lucky Verus isn't around any longer to discipline you.'

'A lady has arrived from Cibalae, *Domine*. The boxes are hers. Please tell us what to do with them.'

The two slaves looked at each other, wary and waiting. Extreme fatigue had made me short-tempered. We were a quiet household without Kahina, Leo, and Verus. Any unexpected guest was bound to unnerve them. When I glanced through the atrium, I saw why.

Apollonia stood at the far end of the public rooms. Tall and slender, she looked intimidating underneath her Vestal's elaborate coil, ribbons, and dark veil. She stood facing the old marble *lararium*, where the atrium archway gave onto the peristyle garden. She brushed off her hands after positioning our battered bronze and ivory figurines of gods and goddesses so long disdained and neglected by Kahina.

Leo's saucy playmate, the slave girl Drusilla, wore a somber expression tonight. She held out an oil lamp from which Apollonia lit a long taper and applied the flame to small bricks of incense in a tiny porcelain dish.

The two females looked like figures on an ancient frieze carved into the side of a temple ruin freshly disinterred after centuries of obscurity; Apollonia might have been a classical Republican matron teaching her attendant proper regard for our watchful deities.

They heard my approaching footsteps.

'Oh, at last, you're home! You don't mind me lighting your shrine, Marcus Numidianus? The gods kept me safe on a long and dangerous journey and I wanted to thank them. Your girl helped me clean out the old ashes to brighten it up.'

Her voice was unchanged. Pulling myself together, I greeted Apollonia warmly on behalf of the entire Manlius clan, but felt both awkward and ashamed. Hungry and untended, our poor traveler had been waiting in the atrium for over an hour before she found something and someone to occupy her time.

I ordered us food and drink from the kitchen. As I settled her in the summer *triclinium* at a small wicker table to wait for our meal, I hid my mounting discomfort.

After reading Apodemius' will in April and conveying his wishes to Justina for any comment and help, I'd waited in vain for guidance from Cibalae.

In the meantime, I'd come to a difficult conclusion: I meant to install Apollonia with the Blind Vestal Tullia on the Via Nomentana. I knew it was a depressing fate for a young woman, but what else? Could she live here alone with me, an unmarried freedman, and keep her reputation intact?

—THE BURNING STAKES—

Given time, observers might discern I was too fond of the brave and sheltered Apollonia to be her guardian, whatever she looked like under that brown drape. I was too much of a liability to fulfill the spirit of Apodemius' last instruction. I was certainly known to be no blushing virgin myself and our newly empty house provided no proper chaperone—whatever her appearance. She must understand my inclination to keep a polite distance between us.

Besides, I told myself, the lonely Tullia would benefit from Apollonia's comfort and company. Being blind, she could never be dismayed by an accidental glimpse of a disfigured sister. Nor could she be confused as I was by Apollonia's bright and provocative banter.

Only now, without warning from Justina, here she was, seven trunks, and all.

We ate and drank for some minutes in silence. I marveled at the delicacy of her manners under that clumsy veil. She deserved more than abrupt rejection but how was I to explain my decision without embarrassing us both?

'Those are all your boxes? Somehow you never struck me as a such a clothes horse, Apollonia.'

Drusilla had served us the first oranges from our southern estate, dressed with the honey of our own bees. Apollonia peeled a fruit with long, graceful fingers.

'No, Marcus Numidianus. Six of them are *your* boxes.'

'No, they—'

'Open them, Marcus, please.'

We laid down our fruit and returned to the vestibule. Each box was bound with leather straps and padlocked twice. Only the gods knew how much the girl had overpaid porters *en route* to shift these clumsy beasts all the way from Gratian's estate.

Together we matched each padlock to individual keys carried inside a purse she hid on a belt under her *stola*. We lifted the lids together, one by one. When they were all opened wide, I gazed down on a pack-rat's worth of old documents—stained or shabby bits of *taeneotic* or *emporitica* papyrus interlayered with valuable vellum packets worth a fortune to any scribe energetic enough to erase them clean.

'There it is, Marcus, all yours, Apodemius' secret files, just as he smuggled them out from under Otho's nose, week by week, in a cleaning slave's buckets.'

'Hidden for six months? Where?'

'In Gratian's library.'

'That old drunk?'

'Precisely. A bitter veteran so burned by his experience in Constantinian politics that he drinks himself into a stupor every day. No one bothers him any longer. He certainly never goes into the old library. Tribune Valentinian is away on duty with the army all the time, rebuilding the family's reputation. Neither he nor his brother, Valens, had any idea.'

'And Marina Severa?'

'Justina told her that these are the Picenus family papers, of importance to no one else. Severa believes I'm delivering them at long last to Justina's brother Cerealis.'

I glanced at one dossier or file after another. Apollonia watched me from a bench. From time to time, she pointed out something particularly interesting or sensitive. It became obvious that she was quite familiar with the contents of the old man's hoard.

Apodemius had records on all of Constantius' *consistoriani*, of course, but also on the men who were preparing this very minute to march into Shapur's desert at the head of Julian's army next summer.

There was an entire box on Eusebius—his corrupt dealings with powerful clerics and bishops in the West and his blackmailing network of once-influential eunuchs in the Eastern imperial chambers. More useful to us now was his intelligence on regions our network couldn't cover yet, not to mention assets and informants across the entire Empire unknown to me until tonight.

Only a fraction of this treasure could have fit in that safe box under his watch in the Castra. Where had the rest of it been cached? What should I do with it now? Tullia had warned I'd been under surveillance. Could a family like the Manlius clan, so recently cleansed of suspicion of rebellion, risk storing this library of secrets without risking political suicide?

—THE BURNING STAKES—

For that matter, where could this be hidden in any city without someone watching me eventually suspecting?

'Apollonia, the discovery of this might land us all with fresh charges of treason.'

'Don't you understand? Apodemius told me he saw immediately in Numidia that you were a bit of a showoff, especially for a slave.'

'I was.'

'—and very proud of your ability to memorize long passages of Homer? To recite Virgil? I tested you myself as we traveled to Sirmium. Apodemius knew you were the one man capable of sifting and editing this collection and then committing the most sensitive secrets to your memory.'

'That would take weeks! Months!'

'Yes,' Apollonia said. 'You must be left alone in peace for such a task, which is why Apodemius told me to wait until all lingering suspicion about you was allayed by time. And I've come to assist you, Marcus.'

'You know the contents of every file here?'

'Of course.'

'And once the useful secrets are selected and committed to memory?'

'Then together we burn these boxes and—'

She stopped.

'What is it, Apollonia?'

'Is he really dead, Marcus? Are you sure?'

'Yes, Apollonia, I watched him die with my own eyes. He was well prepared. He took a draught of something to bring on a painless sleep. When it was over, I rescued a buckle from his *pugio* sheath out of the ashes as I left the execution ground.'

From my belt purse, I took out the simple metal square, still charred black, and placed it between her fingers.

I braced myself for tears, a moan—any outburst of grief. Instead she said with a deep sigh: 'Then I am released.'

She reached behind her head to extract gold pins at the nape and to detach the heavy coil of hair-wrapped rope that fronted her brow like a crown.

Then she lowered her head and untied the many ribbons of her *vittae*. She unwrapped a turban and revealed the eight horizontal lines of braided hair. She undid braid after braid and loosened each plait. Soon the back of her head was enveloped by a cloud of chestnut waves. Finally, she lowered her chin and began to detach the protective brown linen that shielded her face from strangers' pity.

She lifted her face and gazed straight into my eyes.

I was staring openmouthed into the face of Apodemius—made young, beautiful, and completely unmarred—smiling up at me. In a reversal of time, his wrinkles dissolved and his halo of thin, white hair turned dark and full. Apollonia was female and lovely, but there was no mistaking the familiar line of the wide brow, the scrutiny of the intelligent eyes, the aristocratic line of the nose, and the set of a softer, yet still determined jaw.

'You were more than his ward.'

'I am his granddaughter.'

'Apodemius was your *grandfather*? Not merely your protector? Or sponsor? Or mentor?'

'My own grandfather. He confided in me as he confided in no other living being.'

I fell back on my haunches against a pillar for support. 'That is how you knew so much about me, about Kahina, the Commander, and my bad time at Mursa? And all the other secrets I'd confessed in his study?'

'Not only you, Marcus. I know the secrets of hundreds of Romans—and barbarian kings and Persian commanders, too. I know the way Constantius used the army to kill off his family, the crimes of the *consistoriani* one against the next, the insatiable appetites of Eusebius, and the frustrated loyalty of his minions, and—'

'And you listened all these years, hidden away by the Vestals?'

'I had to. Look at me, Marcus. To look on these features, this nose, these eyes, this chin, my brow, is it not to recognize the last leaf of Apodemius' family tree?'

'You're like a mirror cleansed of all his weariness and cynicism. How uncanny such an old coot could produce this lovely face.'

'I carry the last blood of our ancient family. Before the ruins of our house had cooled, he realized I was still in danger. He let it be thought throughout the Senate, the palaces, and the courts that even little Apollonia had perished, suffocated by smoke and abandoned in my burning crib by a panicked wet nurse.'

'While he devised his plan with the Vestals' help?'

'Because to threaten me was to threaten Apodemius' freedom of action. Gain control of me, and any man could tell Apodemius what to do. To kidnap me was to seize control of the *schola*—its missions, its dossiers, and its independence. Standing in the shadows with a knife at my throat, anyone could corrupt the most honorable department of the entire empire.'

'But I still don't understand. So there was a fire?'

I reached over and after a second's hesitation, stroked a flawless cheek.

She smiled, as if this novel caress pleased her. 'There was indeed a fire, a raging inferno, an act of cruelest arson that devoured our whole family but Apodemius and myself. It swallowed up my grandmother, his daughter and her husband—my father—my older brother, my widowed aunt, and her son. Only I was saved, tossed from a window in my crib blanket into the arms of an *aquarius* working his *sipho*'s water pump between the *vigiles* spreading mattresses on the street below.'

'Only you lived?'

'A *vigil*'s wife nursed me until Apodemius found me a month later. He'd assumed I was incinerated along with everyone else. He said it was the last time he ever experienced true joy.'

'No wonder Apodemius seemed the most detached, least emotional man in the world.'

'He was, Marcus. He had only the *schola* and myself. Only if I were well hidden, was he free to do his duty, to protect the truth and chase down the lies and crimes of powerful men.'

'That's why you said in the carriage that it was your duty to remain veiled. I didn't understand your choice of word.'

'It was my duty, so that he could work with an unfettered conscience.'

'And there really was no other way?'

'Nothing terrified Apodemius so much as the possibility we'd be linked by our uncanny resemblance to each other. And each year I grew more like him, not less. Eventually he grew convinced that even a false name or a distant Roman fortress couldn't hide my features from his enemies. A great Roman line had been almost burned out of history forever. Only my obliteration from society could save it.'

I sat down next to her on the bench. 'And he hid himself away as well.'

'That wasn't always his nature. But after the fire, he turned reclusive, working by night to keep his own features known to as few Romans or visiting officials as possible. Even when the arsonists had been arrested and punished, he still worried I'd be taken hostage by new political enemies whose demands he'd be unable to refuse.'

'Did he trust no one but the Vestals? Not even Constantius?'

'*Especially* not Constantius, such an insecure, mercurial ruler who let Paulus Catena torture anyone on the slightest hint of treason.'

What must it have meant for her, so fresh and sociable, to cloister herself away?

'And you were willing to do this for our service?'

'Anything for him. Anything for *his* service, as long as he breathed. But once he died, he promised, the danger would have passed. How could I be ransomed by a dead man? How could the *schola* be taken hostage when the *schola* itself was publicly extinguished?'

She tossed the long veil across the floor. 'I am manumitted, Freedman Numidianus. Apodemius' death is my liberation.'

I took in her courage, her rueful smile, and the curiously familiar expression in her eyes that might well have been beaming at me from the old man's wizened version.

'Apollonia, tell me this: why did he choose me? There are other *agentes* more highly placed, *ducenarii* and *principes officii* across the Empire. There are more astute *agentes*, or men with more *gravitas*. Surely not just for my quick memory?'

She cocked an artful eyebrow. 'You weren't the only candidate, Marcus. I know, because he trusted me as he trusted no other living soul. We discussed other men and their qualifications but you seemed the right choice. There are few things you can hide from me. I've known about you for far longer than you've known about me.'

—THE BURNING STAKES—

'Tonight, I feel I've known you for a very long time, Apollonia.'

She smelled of sweet almonds. I couldn't stare hard enough at her whimsical expression.

'In a way, you have. Sometimes I watched you striding back from the Castra toward this hearth to join your people on the hill here. But of course, you never noticed a young veiled girl in her curtained litter waiting for the *magister* in the dawn shadows under the Aqua Claudia.'

I took her by both shoulders and drew her closer to me.

'Apollonia, are you here to help me—for a long time?'

'Yes, Marcus Numidianus. I promised my grandfather I would help you preserve the service.'

'You knew he bequeathed me responsibility for you?'

'It was my own wish, Marcus Numidianus. Yet you didn't summon me. I came to understand your silence. I delivered these boxes only when I'd come to accept your wishes were otherwise. You may send me away whenever convenient.'

'And if I do not want to send you away?'

'I will stay on,' she whispered.

I gazed down at the thick brown lashes hiding her lowered eyes. 'And will you stay on to love me, Apollonia?'

'For an even longer time, Marcus. That is my promise to you.'

I grasped her to me and whispered in her ear, 'I lied to you, Apollonia. I lied to you on our carriage ride to Sirmium. I said no woman was perfect.'

'And no woman is, you fool. Oh, I can be very tiresome,' she said with a shake of her thick waves. She pulled away from my embrace.

'For one thing, Numidianus, I'm quite stubborn when I don't get my way. You see, I wanted you and no one else.'

'And I wanted you but had no idea why.'

'And for another, I have a terrible habit of quoting books to show off.'

'You've read them all, I suppose?'

'They were my only companions for many long and lonely years.'

'Then I have a library in the back of the house to show you now. Though I warn you, some of the Commander's poetry may shock a Vestal.'

She laughed and suddenly gave me a deep and daring kiss. 'Shock me? I was never inducted as a true Vestal, Marcus.'

I kissed her back. I couldn't wait to marry her. We would fill the echoing Manlius home from atrium to garden with more children.

'Well, if not shock you, then make a new bride blush.'

She ruffled my hair and laughed. 'We'll see. Don't forget, Marcus, I passed many illuminating days in a Sirmium brothel last December.'

The End

Historical Notes

Julian's complete suppression of the *agentes in rebus* was a radical move. As soon as he assumed the throne, the new emperor shifted important responsibilities, particularly for the imperial mail service and state road network, away from the Castra Peregrina to his own staff. According to one report, he left only seventeen *agentes* in place, presumably to ease the transition.

But Julian's purge lasted no longer than his truncated reign. The *schola* survived, though history doesn't detail how. Historians are increasingly giving the *agentes* their due, despite condemnations from Libanius and other contemporaries from a privileged class who suffered under the *agentes*' watchful eyes.

Emperors after Julian seemed to have found the service useful enough. History records by 430 AD no fewer than 1174 agents were registered in the Eastern Empire alone—plus more on a waiting list. By 470 AD, Emperor Leo was trying to set a limit to the *agentes* by rank, e.g. '*ducenarii* in post shall not exceed 48, *centenarii* shall not exceed 200, *biarchi* shall be limited to 250 men, the *circitores* to 300, and the *equites* to 450.'

Whether you see Apodemius as a villain through the eyes of Ammianus Marcellinus or as the father figure admired by our fictional protagonist, the *Magister* would have been proud of his *schola*'s resilience in a shrinking and divided empire.

Of course, the 'service' was hardly perfect. As noted by A. H. M. Jones, Constantius had already corrected troubling malpractice in the recruitment of his trusted corps of *agentes in rebus* in 359 AD. But all imperial departments were vulnerable to corruption. *The Cambridge Ancient History* notes that spreading various tasks and responsibilities across two or more departments was a standard precaution in Late Roman statecraft to ferret out incompetence or corruption by means of competitive supervision.

The Burning Stakes is the sixth volume in a cycle of stories that has grown more complicated as the stories unfold. Without having read the preceding novels, even the quickest reader might not fully appreciate the competing forces that came to a head in that tribunal room in Chalcedon.

For example, the true account of Barbatio's sudden downfall thanks to his wife Assyria's jealous paranoia or the strange political shifts of the *consistorium* derailed by Constantius' unexpected demise are less surprising events if one has followed the politics of the previous fifteen years.

The Burning Stakes' setting offered an opportunity to speculate on the atmosphere of compromise and revenge-taking that swept through Roman leadership circles as Julian seized the reins of control. We've tried to capture the atmosphere of confusion and fear spreading among the privileged survivors of Constantius' reign in an era of uneven communications and high-stakes betrayals.

Did the Chalcedon tribunal resemble a 'Stalinist purge' or a modern military kangaroo court? Adrian Murdoch calls Paulus Catena the 'Beria' or 'proto-Torquemada' of the Constantius era, so his painful end was sure to go unmourned. But the other Chalcedon victims are harder to dismiss in one stroke as guilty. The relatively moderate exile of Consul Taurus to Vercellae demonstrates that there were nuances and time limits in the political vindictiveness displayed.

For example, Taurus' sons not only did not suffer, but thrived: Armonius lived another thirty years, his brother Eutychianus, praetorian prefect of the East and consul in 398, was immortalized for his pro-Gothic policies in *Aegyptus sive de providentia* by Synesius. A third son, Aurelianus was praetorian prefect of the East and consul in 400 AD and even earned a golden statue erected to him after a career as the most powerful civilian official serving the court of Emperor Arcadius.

Similarly, the fate of his fellow consul was ambiguous. When *agentes* finally reported to Julian where Consul Florentius and his family were hiding out, the new emperor shrugged it off with indifference. Julian had moved on to bigger things.

During the trial itself, Julian doesn't emerge well from the picture painted even by his ardent admirer and apologist Ammianus Marcellinus. Adrian Murdoch sums up; 'It is stretching the truth to suggest, as Libanius does, that the trials show Julian as a noble defender of the people.'

—THE BURNING STAKES—

The venerable scholar Jones suggests an intriguing variation to some historians' assertion that Julian was the instigator of the trials. As one piece of evidence to the contrary, he quotes Julian's phrasing in his letter to a certain Hermogenes that directs the responsibility for Chalcedon away from himself. Second, Jones shows how inconsistencies in the verdicts and punishments suggest that the Roman army—not the new emperor—was launching a vendetta at the outset to restore its military reputation so damaged by the loss of Amida to the Persians.

Otherwise, Jones notes, it is unlikely that Apodemius and Gaudentius—both of whom Julian hated—would have been ignored among the early victims.

Yet warrants for Apodemius, Gaudentius, Eusebius, Pentadius, and Palladius came soon enough—all of them linked to the Gallus affair.

Given how many of the Chalcedon tribunal's inquiries involved people who were tainted by the downfall of Gallus, it seems hard to follow E. A. Thompson: 'It is safe to assume then that the tribunal was in no way interfered with by Julian.' Thompson also refers to Julian's 'customary veracity and candor,' but not all historians since Thompson have left Julian's veracity unchallenged. G. W. Bowerstock proves that Julian dissembled or distorted timing or events more than once to whitewash his ambitions.

So even an amateur may ask, how honest were Julian's protestations with regard to Chalcedon—in light of his disingenuous account of a reluctant rise from caesar to 'emperor' status, his suspicious time gaps in the 'spontaneous' uprising acclaiming him emperor, or his demonstrably false assertions of Christian loyalty to his cousin Constantius, all the while disguising his bitter hatred over mistreatment of his family and private pagan worship?

In short, one can make absolutely no 'safe' assumptions about Julian's role in the Chalcedon tribunal. We know *nothing* about either the communication links or possible collusion between Constantinople and the tribunal convened on the jutting Bithynian peninsula facing the Great Palace just across the mouth of the Bosporus. Even in the 4th century, suburban proximity to the capital was close enough for Chalcedon's elders to complain that Constantine's imperial building boom had stripped their town clean of construction materials.

Meanwhile, even experts of the 4th century may have tripped for a moment over Emperor Constantius II's confidence in the 'Rocking Therapy' as a sure cure for his fever. This was, according to a note from Bill Thayer's useful online site *Lacus Curtius*, 'not some vague idea, but a precise medical prescription' recommended by Ascelpiades and overviewed by the medical encyclopedist Celsus over a dozen times in *de Medicina*.

Rocking was prescribed to speed recovery for chronic maladies which were already abating; it was also for those who were entirely freed from their fever but still too weak to take exercise.

No doubt simple rocking increased blood circulation and sped the evacuation of toxins from the weakened patient. However, Celsus adds: 'There are many sorts of rocking, and they are to be regulated both by the patient's strength and by his resources, lest either a weak patient undergo overmuch depletion, or a poor man come short. The gentlest rocking is that on board ship either in harbor or in a river. More severe is that aboard ship on the high seas, or in a litter, even severer still in a carriage: but each of these can either be intensified or mitigated. Failing any of the above, the bed should be so slung as to be swayed; if not even that, at any rate a rocker should be put under its foot so that the bed may be moved from side to side by hand.'

Constantius II was by no means a studious man, so we suggest that his faith in 'rocking' came from seeing imperial or military doctors succeed with this 'cure.' Unfortunately rocking by *equitatio* did Constantius no good.

The date on which he died is disputed. We have chosen November 3 as opposed to the alternative—October 5—which appears in the manuscript of Ammianus Marcellinus' *Res Gestae*. The German classicist Otto Seeck corrected *tertium nonarum Octobrium* to *tertium nonarum Novembrium*, the equivalent of November 3. T.D. Barnes provides indirect evidence that November 3 is a better fit.

Historians may smile at Marcus' hesitation over Antoninus Drusus' suggestion that the Christian *grammaticus* Ausonius polish Leo's education in Bordeaux to prepare for public life in

—THE BURNING STAKES—

Roma. Less than a decade after this story, Emperor Valentinian I recruited Ausonius to teach his own son, Gratian, his imperial heir-apparent (the noisy two-year old in Cibalae in this book) by Marina Severa.

Meanwhile, Marina Severa faded into history while Justina rose to realize her childhood dream as Valentinian's empress and the mother of Emperor Valentinian II.

When Valentinian I took Gratian on the German campaigns of 368-9, Ausonius accompanied them. In recognition of his services, Emperor Valentinian bestowed on Ausonius the rank of *quaestor*. Gratian liked and respected his tutor, and when he himself became emperor in 375 AD he began bestowing on Ausonius and his family the highest civil honors.

Who knows if Leo might have been at his side?

Places and Glossary

a secretis—a corps of confidential imperial secretaries, entirely separate from the Prefecture, who acted as officials for judicial proceedings before the *consistorium*

acetum—disinfecting vinegar, used for sterilization by army medical officers

apodemus—mouse

adiutor, adiutores—batman or assistant

aedile, aediles—responsible for maintenance of public buildings (*aedēs*) and regulation of public festivals. They also had powers to enforce public order.

agens, agentes in rebus—imperial officers in charge of roads, postal services, customs regulations and intelligence gathering in the Late Roman Empire

Agri Decumates, (Decumates Agri)— were a region of the Roman Empire's provinces of Germania superior or Upper Germania and Raetia; covering the Black Forest, Swabian Jura, and Franconian Jura areas between the Rhine, Main, and Danube rivers; in present southwestern Germany, including present Frankfurt, Stuttgart, Freiburg in Breisgau, and Weissenburg in Bayern.

alarum—danger signal, warning, call to arms

Amida—Diyarbakır, Turkey

amphora, amphorae—storage containers, often ceramic or pottery with pointed bottoms and double handles

annona—imperial welfare handout, or tax in coin or produce

aquarius, aquarii—firemen of the *vigiles* with an accurate knowledge of water locations, and pumped water onto the fire or formed bucket brigades to bring water to the fire

arca—special box for scroll

arcanus—the word *areanus* appears once in Ammianus Marcellinus (28.3.8) and is thought to be a misspelling of *arcanus* and to match a single memorial in Roman Britain to a *miles arcanus*. According to A.M., 'This was an organization founded in early times, of which I have already said something in the history of Constans... (ed. note in lost books). Their official duty was to range backwards and forwards over long distances with information for our generals about disturbances among neighboring nations.' Little else seems to be known about this service but they certainly did exist—they were disbanded by Count Theodosius for suspected betrayal of the Empire in 367 during the Great Conspiracy in Britannia.

assessor, assessores—judicial adviser or official
Ariminum—Rimini, Italy
Athina—Athens, Greece
augur, augures—interpreters of omens
augustus, (auguste, vocative*) Augustus*—honorific for emperor
ballista—a torsion-powered missile projector/catapult developed over many centuries. By the Late Roman era the largest *ballista fulminalis* could deliver darts farther than 1,100 meters, e.g. the width of the Danube River.
barbitio depositio—first whiskers deposited in puberty ceremony
basileus—Eastern Roman Empire's Greek term for emperor
biarchus—a regimental grade between *circitor* and *centenarius*, borrowed from the cavalry by the *schola* of *agentes in rebus*, who limited themselves to six classes of the cavalry's ten, i.e. *eques, circitor, biarchus, centenarius, ducenarius,* and *princeps*.
birrus—common hooded cloak
Bononea—Boulogne-sur-Mer, France
bruma—winter haze and fog of the shortest day of the year
Burdigala—Bordeaux, France
Caesaria, Palaestina—Caesarea, Israel
calamistrum—heated curling tongs
caldarium—the hottest room in the sequence of Roman bathing; after the caldarium, customers would progress through the moderately heated tepidarium to the coolest room, the frigidarium to relax/swim.
calceus, calcei—marching boots
caliga, caligae—heavy, hobnailed, high-cuffed boot
campagi—polished, black shoes worn by Late Roman officials

candidatus—Late Roman imperial guards known by white tunics, as opposed to magisterial candidates in earlier periods
capilli Indici—Indian wigs and hairpieces
capsarius—army medical surgeon
cardo—the main north–south-oriented street in Roman cities, military camps, and colonies
Carthago—Carthage, now suburb of Tunis, Tunisia
Castra Peregrina—headquarters in Rome of the *schola*, the *agentes in rebus*, barracks on the Caelian Hill in Rome, Italy build for the *peregrini*, soldiers detached for special service in Rome from the provincial armies. The Castra later became the headquarters for the military couriers and then the Empire's secret services, the *frumentarii* until their disbanding by Emperor Diocletian. They were succeeded by a reformed service, the agentes in rebus. The ruins of a part of the *castra* and several inscriptions connected with them were found in 1905 under the Convent of the Little Company of Mary, just southeast of S. Stefano Rotondo.
castratus—eunuch
cathedra—low, wide-seated armchair
caupona—the lowest category of roadside inn/brothel, frequented by thieves and gamblers
cauterium—cauterizing iron
cena—meal
centenarius—the penultimate rank of *agentes in rebus*, before *ducenarius* (see *biarchus*)
Chalcedon—Kadıköy District, Istanbul, Turkey, an Attican Greek colony of 685 BC founded in Bithynia, Asia Minor, named after a stream called the Chalcis. Chalcedon sat directly opposite Byzantium, south of Scutari (modern Üsküdar).
chartularius—official ranked below *adiutores* to higher officials
chlamys—military cloak, semi-circular, hip to calf length
cingulum—wide belt worn by officials and officers in 4th century, sometimes strutted or jeweled
circitor, circitores—second lowest rank in *agentes in rebus*, after *eques*, (see *biarchus*)
clarissimus, clarissimi—third rank of imperial official

clepsydra, clepsydrae—water clock

codex, codices—paged books bound to a spine, as opposed to scrolls

columbaria—alcoves cut like dovecotes to hold funerary urns

comes, comites—sometimes translated as 'counts.' Though not feudal, comites wielded posts of every description, from the army to the civil service, while never surrendering their direct links and access to the emperor. They headed major secular departments after Constantine or held military appointments, higher than dux, but under a *magister peditum/magister equitum*. On a simpler level, it could mean a local figure's staff.

commendationes—letters of reference, references

comitatus—suite of officials, often comes, around the emperor

conditum—wine flavored with flowers or spices, e.g. coriander, anise, pepper, cinnamon

consistorianus, consistoriani—member of the consistorium

(sacrum) consistorium—secret imperial council of the post-Constantine or 'Dominate' period. There is a difference of opinion as to its membership. It was composed mainly of the heads of the various departments of administration, certainly of those most intimately connected with the imperial household (*dignitates palatinae*): the Minister of Finance (*comes sacrarum largitionum*), the Minister of the Privy Purse (*comes rerum privatarum*), the Quaestor (*quaestor sacri palatii*) or emperor's legal adviser, and the Master of the Offices, (*magister officiorum*.) The prefect whose seat of government was at the capital (*praefectus praetorio praesens*) was probably a member, as well as the Grand Chamberlain (*praepositus sacri cubiculi*), and some officials of the grade *spectabilis*. The members of the council were called *comites consistoriani* or *consistoriani*. It was presided over by the emperor, or in his absence by the quaestor who was obliged to give his decisions in writing; proceedings were taken down by secretaries and stenographers (*notarii*).

contubernalis, contubernales—tentmate, eight to a tent

cornicularius—chief official, sometimes ranked over *primiscrinius*

—THE BURNING STAKES—

cottidiana—index of day-by-day (quotidien) transactions of the imperial court
cucullus—hood of a cloak
Cularo—Grenoble, France
cultor deorum—pagan worshipper
curiales—town elders
curiosus, curiosi—popular insult showing contempt for agentes,
Cursus Clabularis—specially engineered roads capable of handling heavy cargo traffic
Cursus Publicus—state-managed empire-wide network of roads and comfort/layover stations
Danuvius River—Danube River
delicatus—house favorite among slaves
dispensator—household manager, custodian, majordomo
domesticus, domestici—imperial household servant
domina—lady, term of respect
dominula—very young lady, diminutive of *domina*
domus—household, family
ducenarius—the highest rank of agens before appointment as princeps attached to a top civil servant
dux—provincial governor
Dyrrhachium—Durazzo, Albania
emporitica—packing paper normally considered too rough for writing
eques, equites—lowest rank in the *agentes in rebus*, (see *biarchus*
evectiones diplomatae—evectio—a license/road warrant to use facilities of the *Cursus Publicus* network, passport for official travel use, permit to travel by public post
explorator, exploratores—army reconnaissance men
fabrica, fabricae—factories, often state weapon manufacturers
Fanum-Fortunae—Fano, Italy
fauces—narrow passage, entryway
fibula, fibulae—shoulder brooches holding tunics
flamen, flamines—pagan priests
forum, fora—open main public squares in Roman cities
fritullus—dice box
frumentarii—the agentes' predecessors as imperial information gatherers during the Republican and Principate periods

ending with their disbandment by Emperor Diocletian on charges of rampant corruption

garum—ubiquitous fish sauce used to season everything

gens gentes—clan, family, lineage

grammaticus—teacher

gratia—political connections

gravitas—importance, presence, influence

Hadrianopolis—Edirne, Turkey

harpastum, (harpustum)—game using ball about the size and solidity of a softball and involving speed, agility, and physical exertion. Little is known about the rules, but it could be violent, with players often ending up on the ground.

haruspex, haruspices—soothsayers

homo privatus—retiree, pensioner

honestiores—privileged classes of Rome, persons of status and property

Horreum Magi—Ćuprija, Serbia

ignoramus, ignorami—know-nothing

imago, imagines—ancestral portraits hanging in the atrium of a noble Roman family home; death masks or busts often labeled with details of the deceased

immunis, immunes—soldiers exempted from combat duty through performing a more specialist role

imperator—emperor

infula—vestal headdress

insigne, insignia—badges of office

insula, insulae—apartment, apartment buildings

instrumentarius—chief of archives

Korinthos—Corinth, Greece

labrum—basin

laetus, laetus—non-Roman immigrant granted landed in exchange for supplying recruits

lararium—household shrine to the *lares*

lares—household gods

latifundium—agglomeration of farming estates, often employing thousands of slave or prison laborers

—THE BURNING STAKES—

latrunculi—also *ludus latrunculorum* or *latrones*, a 'capture' board game for two players moving cones or 'dogs' around a grid or 'city,' (might resemble chess or draughts)
lectica, lecticae—litter with couch, palanquin, often curtained
libertus—freedman
Lilybaeum—Marsala, Sicily
Pachynum—Pachino, Syracuse, Sicily
Lissus—Lezhë, Albania
literatus, literati—intellectual, man of letters
litterae caelestes—formalized Late Roman court handwriting
Londinium—London, England
Lutetia—Paris, France
macellum—market stalls
magister—head of a government department or schola, or general commander
magister agentium in rebus—Master of the *Agentes in Rebus* service, reporting to the *Magister Officiorum*
magister equitum—Master of the Horse, a title revived in the Late Roman Empire, when Constantine I established it as one of the supreme military ranks
Magister Equitum in Praesenti/Praesentalis—the Master of Horse attending the emperor
magister memoriae—master of the rolls, reporting to the *magister officiorum*
magister militum—Master of the Infantry, previously *magister peditum* under Constantine I, eventually amalgamated with *magister equitum* in the Late Roman Empire
magister officiorum—a senior imperial officer (in charge of the palatine secretariat,) created under Constantine (306-337) to limit the power of the praetorian prefect, until then the emperor's chief administrative aide.
magistriani—magistrates
manceps, mancipes—managers and landlords of state-franchised layover or stopover stations on the Cursus Publicus
mansio, mansiones—state-franchised stopovers on the Cursus Publicus
marginalia—commentary written in margin of manuscript
Margus River—the Velika (Great) Morava River

Mauretania Tingitana—Roman province at the northwestern tip of North Africa, approximately the northern part of present-day Moroccan and Spanish possessions, Ceuta and Melilla

mater—mother

mausoleum, mausolea—tombs

medicus—army doctor

Mediolanum—Milan, Italy

memoria—memorial plaques

meritum—service

merum—crude undiluted wine

mensor, mensores—army surveyors

Mopsucrenae, (Mobsucrene)—small town twelve miles outside Tarsus in modern Cilicia, Turkey

Mount Dinara—Dinaric Alps or Dinarides, a mountain chain spanning areas of modern Albania, Bosnia and Herzegovina, Croatia, Italy, Kosovo, Montenegro, and Serbia

mulsum—an aperitif of wine mixed with honey

mutatio, mutationes—layover stations

Naissus—Niš, Serbia

Neapolis—Naples, Italy

Nomentum—Mentana, Italy

notarius, notarii—notary, high official often used in Late Roman Empire to investigate affairs or execute orders on behalf of court or emperor

novendiales—the nine days of official mourning

nummus—Late Roman low-value silver-clad coin, continually debased from the monetary reforms of Diocletian

occidum—West

optio tribuni—'chosen man of the tribune,' i.e. assistant to a tribune

orbiculus, orbiculi—large embroidered ovals, rounds, or rectangles appliqued to an official's tunic

ostiarius—gatekeeper, porter, doorman

paenula, paenulae—long, hooded cloak for men associated with guards; for women, a rectangular shawl or longer cloak *palla/paenula,(ae)*—long, hooded circular cloak that became associated with praetorians and other guards over the centuries, for woman, a rectangular shawl or longer cloak

Patavius—Padua, Italy

the Parcae—the Fates

Parma—Parma, Italy

pars urbana—genteel gardens surrounding a villa, as opposed to the *pars rusticana* for cultivating and pasturage

paterfamilias—patriarch of the *familia*, the entire household including slaves

petanus—non-combat riding helmet

pileus—brimless flat-topped felt or fur hat of the Late Roman era worn by officers and civilians alike

Placentia—Piacenza, Italy

popina—inn offering food and prostitutes

posca—a refreshing herb-flavored mix of sour wine, or water with vinegar concentrate added by travelers to make a refreshing drink

Posonium—Bratislava, Slovakia

potentia—political clout

potestates excelsae—well-placed officials, 'movers and shakers'

praefectus—prefect

praepositus sacri cubiculi—Lord Chamberlain of the Bedchamber, the most senior chamberlain of the Empire, managing the sovereign's private chambers and rest of staff

prima mensa—main course after appetizers or *gustatio*

primiscrinius—second-highest ranking official for judicial courts responsible for, among other things, timekeeping of judicial procedures

princeps—chief

princeps officii—secretary general drawn from the agentes in rebus, serving during this era as watchdog over important civilian officers in an administration agency, such as a praetorian or urban prefecture or pro-consulate

principatus—first-ranked

proskynesis—full-length prostration to 'worship the purple' introduced from the Persian custom by Diocletian and stressed in post-Constantine courts as recognizing the Christian emperor as Christ's vice-regent on earth

protector domesticus, protectores domestici—an elite guard unit of the Late Roman army, who served as bodyguards and staff officers to the emperor
proximus, proximi—courtier allowed close contact with the emperor
pugio—standard-issue Late Roman army dagger
puls—lentils
quaestor sacri palatii—leading imperial legal expert
quaestor, quaestores—financial, auditing, or legal counselor
rescript—written appeals to the emperor on which he appended his decision below the petition with his signature and returned to the appellant
retiarius—gladiator armed with trident and net
rex—king
rhetor—teacher of rhetoric
riparienses—*limitanei* troops guarding riverbank borders, from the Latin *ripa* for riverside
Roma—Rome, Italy
Romanitas—Roman culture, the qualities of being Roman
sacra scrinia—imperial secretariats
sacrum consistorium—the emperor's advisory cabinet or secret imperial council of the post-Constantine or 'Dominate' period. There is a difference of opinion as to its membership. It was composed mainly of the heads of the various departments of administration, certainly those most intimately connected with the imperial household
sagum, saga—short, riding cloak
Salona—Salon, near Solin, Croatia
sarcophagus, sarcophagi—sarcophagus (meaning 'flesh-eater' as made of corrosive limestone)
Saturnalia—seven-day pagan holiday, marking the winter solstice
Savus River—Sava River, Croatia
schola—Late Roman government department
scholares—imperial guards who replaced the disbanded praetorians of earlier Rome
scriba librarius—scribe assigned the work of a junior copyist (*librarius*)
scrinium, scrinia—four bureaus of the Palatine Secretariat

—THE BURNING STAKES—

Scrinium Epistularum—secretariat manned by *epistulares*, correspondence with foreign potentates and with the provincial administration and the cities

Scrinium Memoriae—secretariat handling letters, appointments, and imperial decisions called *annotationes*, because they were notes made by the emperor on documents presented to him and also handled replies to petitions to the emperor.

Scrinium Libellorum— the third dealt with appeals from lower courts and petitions from those involved in them

scutarius, scutarii—well-equipped light infantry targeteers armed with swords, shields and heavy javelins

segmenta—embroidered panels, embroidered elements, or appliques to tunic or cloak

sella, sellae—sedan chair

Sequana River—the Seine River

Seni Crines—elaborate hairstyle and headdress of the Vestal Virgin sisterhood

sigillaria—Saturnalia trinkets and figurines, also the last day of Saturnalia festivities

sigillarius—*sigillaria* vendor

silentiarius, silentiarii—courtiers assigned the job of keeping silence and order within the palaces

Singidunum—Belgrade, Serbia

sipho—horsedrawn firefighting water engine equipped with pump and water reservoir

Sirmium—Sremska-Mitrovica, Serbia

Siscia—Sisak, Croatia

solidus, solidi—4.5 gram gold coin issued by Constantine to replace the *aureus*

spatha, spathae—double-bladed sword in Late Rome replacing the shorter *gladius*, used as Roman side-arm

spectabilis, spectabilii—officials/notables ranked in imperial hierarchy

spongia—Roman substitute for toilet paper, sponge on a stick

stabulum—stable

stilus, stili—pointed instrument for writing on wax-covered tablets

stola—women's long over-tunic

strigil, strigiles—body scraper for use at baths
suffibulum—square, draped head cloth forming veil
suffragium—political patronage
susurna—rough peasant's or student's blanket
taberna, tabernae—tavern, restaurant
taeneotic—third grade papyrus/paper sold by weight
tempora—the times (we live in); Numidianus is thinking of Cicero's oration against Cataline, O tempora, o mores!)
tesserae—mosaic tiles or dice
Tiberis—Tiber River
tiro, tirones—recruit, novice
titulus—title
togati—clients or hangers-on
Treverorum—Trier, Germany
tribunus—tribune
tribunus stabili—tribune in charge of the stables
triclinium—dining room
Triptolemus—The Homeric Hymn mentions Triptolemus as one of one of the original priests of Demeter, the first to learn the secret rites and mysteries of the Eleusinian Mysteries Porphyry (On Abstinence IV.22) ascribes to Triptolemus three commandments for a simple, pious life: 'Honor your parents', 'Honor the gods with fruits' (including grain) and 'Spare the animals.' Triptolemus is depicted as a young man with a branch or diadem in his hair, sitting on his winged chariot adorned with serpents.
tutela impuberum—guardianship over a legal minor
tutela mulierum—guardianship over a free woman
tutela testamentaria—guardianship established by deceased in a will
vitulinum—vellum, expensive writing material from animal skin
Vercellae—Vercelli, Italy
veritas—truth
Vienna, Gallia—Vienne, France
vigiles—firemen (In addition to extinguishing fires, the Vigiles were the night watch of Rome. Their duties included apprehending thieves and robbers and capturing runaway slaves. The task of guarding the baths was added as a duty of the Vigiles during the reign of Alexander Severus when

the baths remained open during the night. They dealt with petty crimes and looked for disturbances of the peace while they patrolled the streets. Sedition, riots and violent crimes were handled by the *Cohortes urbanae* and (to a lesser extent) the Praetorian Guard until their disbandment, though Vigiles could provide a supporting role in these situations. The Vigiles were considered a para-military unit and their organization into cohorts and centuries reflects this.)

vittae—ribbons hanging from braided hair in the Vestal's *Seni Crenes* hairstyle

volo, voluntarius—slave earning manumission by military service

volumina—volumes, scrolls

weregild—"man price", a value placed on every being and piece of property in the Frankish tribal custom. If property was stolen, or someone was injured or killed, the guilty person would have to pay a *weregild* as restitution to the victim's family or to the owner of the property

Acknowledgments

A special thanks to the site, *Lacus Curtius,* and Site Master Bill Thayer for translation and footnotes to the history by Ammianus Marcellinus

Ammianus Marcellinus, *The Later Roman Empire (AD 354-378)*, Penguin Classics, Penguin Books, London 2014

Berger, Adolf, *Encyclopedic Dictionary of Roman Law (Middlebury Bicentennial Series in Environmental Studies)*, The Lawbook Exchange reprint, American Philosophical Society, Philadelphia, Pennsylvania, 1953

Bowerstock, G.W., *Julian the Apostate*, Harvard University Press, Cambridge, Massachusetts, 1978

Bowerstock, G.W., Peter Brown, Oleg Grabar, ed. *Late Antiquity, A Guide to the Postclassical World*, The Belknap Press of Harvard University, Cambridge, 1999

Browning, Robert, *The Emperor Julian*, University of California Press, 1978

Cameron, Averil, *The Later Roman Empire*, Fontana History of the Ancient World, Fontana Press, London, 1993

Carcopino, Jerome, *Daily Life in Ancient Rome*, Folio Society, London, 2004

Faas, Patrick, *Around the Roman Table*, Macmillan, London 1994

Greenwood, Thomas, *The History of the Germans, Book 1, Barbaric Period*, Longman, Rees, Orme and Co., London, 1836

Heather, Peter, *The Fall of the Roman Empire*, Macmillan, London, 2005

Heather, Peter, 'Senators and Senates,' *Cambridge Ancient History*, Vol. 13, Cambridge University Press, Cambridge, England

Hunt, David, 'Julian,' *Cambridge Ancient History*, Vol. 13, Cambridge University Press, Cambridge, UK

Kelly, Christopher, *Ruling the Later Roman Empire*, Harvard University Press, Cambridge, Massachusetts, 2009

Jones, A. H. M., *The Later Roman Empire, 284-602*, Vol. 1, John Hopkins University Press, Baltimore, Maryland, 1986

Julian, (Flavius Claudius Iulianus Augustus,) *The Works of the Emperor Julian*, Loeb Classical Library, Harvard University Press, Massachusetts, 1993

Lenski, Noel, *Failure of Empire: Valens and the Roman State in the Fourth Century AD, (Transformation of the Classical Heritage)* University of California Press, 2014

Murdoch, Adrian, *The Last Pagan, Julian the Apostate and the Death of the Ancient World*, Sutton Publishing Ltd., UK, 2003

Nixon C. E. V., Barbara Saylor Rodgers, *In Praise of Later Roman Emperors, The Panegyric Latini,* University of California Press, Oakland, Calif., 1995

Potter, David, *The Roman Empire at Bay AD 180-395*, Routledge History of the Ancient World, Routledge, London, 2014

Salzman, Michele Renee, *The Making of a Christian Aristocracy: Social and Religious Change in the Western Roman Empire*, Harvard University Press, Cambridge, Massachusetts, 2009

Socrates Scholasticus, *Book III*, transl. A.C. Zenos, *Nicene and Post-Nicene Fathers*, Second Series, Vol. 2., ed. Philip Schaff and Henry Wace, Christian Literature Publishing Co., Buffalo, NY 1890, revised and edited, Kevin Knight, New Advent online edition

Stambaugh, John E., *The Ancient Roman City*, John Hopkins University Press, Baltimore and London, 1988

Sumner, Graham, *Roman Military Clothing AD 200-400*, Osprey Publishing, Oxford, 2003

Thompson, E. A. *The Historical Work of Ammianus Marcellinus*, University Press, Cambridge, England, 1947

Reedy, Larry, *Justice at Chalcedon: A Defense of Julian's Political Tribunal,* academia.edu

Veyne, Paul, ed. *A History of Private Life, Vol. 1, From Pagan Rome to Byzantium*, transl. Arthur Goldhammer, The Belknap Press, Harvard University, Cambridge, Massachusetts, 1987

Watts, Edward J. Watts, *The Final Pagan Generation*, University of California Press, Oakland, California, 2015

Zozimus, *New History, Book 3*, Green and Chaplin London, 1814

Olszaniec, Szymon, *Prosopographical Studies on the Court Elite in the Roman Empire (4th century AD)*, Jacek Wełniak, Małgorzata Stachowska-Wełniak, transl., Nicolaus Copernicus University Press, Torun, Poland, 2013

About the Author

Q. V. Hunter's interest in classical history began with four years of high school Latin followed by university courses in ancient religions. A fascination with Late Antiquity deepened when Hunter moved to a two-hundred-year-old farmhouse near an ancient Roman colony. The farmhouse is easily reached by modern road, but also by a Roman road running more directly down to the *Colonia Equestris Noviodunum.*

Noviodunum was founded around 50 BCE as a retirement community for Julius Caesar's cavalry veterans. It's listed as the *civitas Equestrium id est Noviodunus* in the *Notitia Galliarum,* (the fourth-century directory listing all seventeen provinces of Roman Gaul.)

Noviodunum became Rome's most important colony along Lake Leman—with a forum, baths, basilica and amphitheater. Potable water came via an aqueduct running all the way from present-day Divonne, France. Noviodunum belonged to a network of settlements radiating out from Lugdunum (Lyon, France) around the Rhône Valley. Roman colonists were encouraged to supervise the Celtic Helvetii who had been transported to the area against their will after their defeat at the Battle of Bibracte in 58 BC.

Much of Roman Noviodunum was razed during Alemanni invasions in 259-260 AD, well before the period of our story, but it flourishes again today as the Swiss town of Nyon.

Hunter is married to a self-proclaimed '*Ur*-Swiss,' a descendant of those very Alemanni barbarians who settled farther north of Nyon in the Alpine lake region that gave birth to the three founding cantons of the Confederation Helvetica, i.e. Switzerland, in 1291 AD.

They have three adult children, all of whom managed to study Latin and Greek in high school before the Swiss cantonal authorities cut Classics from the state curriculum.

—Q. V. HUNTER—

Printed in Poland
by Amazon Fulfillment
Poland Sp. z o.o., Wrocław